A HISTORY OF JEWISH LITERATURE
VOLUME IX

Israel Zinberg's *History of Jewish Literature*

Vol. I	*Part One:*	The Arabic-Spanish Period
Vol. II	*Part Two:*	French and German Jewry in the Early Middle Ages
	Part Three:	The Jewish Community of Medieval Italy
Vol. III	*Part Four:*	The Struggle of Mysticism and Tradition Against Philosophical Rationalism
Vol. IV	*Part Five:*	Italian Jewry in the Renaissance Era
Vol. V	*Part Six:*	The Jewish Center of Culture in the Ottoman Empire
Vol. VI	*Part Seven:*	The German-Polish Cultural Center
Vol. VII	*Part Eight:*	Old Yiddish Literature from Its Origins to the Haskalah Period
Vol. VIII	*Part Nine:*	The Berlin Haskalah
Vol. IX	*Part Ten:*	Hasidism and Enlightenment (1780–1820)
Vol. X	*Part Eleven:*	The Science of Judaism and Galician Haskalah
Vol. XI	*Part Twelve:*	The Haskalah Movement in Russia
Vol. XII	*Part Thirteen:*	Haskalah at Its Zenith (published posthumously, 1966)

An Analytic Index to the *History of Jewish Literature* will appear in Volume XII.

Israel Zinberg

A HISTORY OF JEWISH LITERATURE

TRANSLATED AND EDITED BY BERNARD MARTIN

Hasidism and Enlightenment (1780-1820)

HEBREW UNION COLLEGE PRESS
CINCINNATI, OHIO

KTAV PUBLISHING HOUSE, INC.
NEW YORK, NEW YORK
1976

The full translation into English of Israel Zinberg's HISTORY OF JEWISH LITERATURE, comprising twelve volumes, is being brought to publication by the generous and continuing support of the Memorial Foundation for Jewish Culture.

Library of Congress Cataloging in Publication Data

Zinberg, Israel, 1873–1938.
Hasidism and enlightenment (1780–1820)

(His A history of Jewish literature; v. 9)
Translation of Ḥasides un oyfklerung, which was published as v. i of the author's Di geshikhte fun der literatur bay Yidn.
Bibliography: p.
Includes index.
1. Hasidism—History. 2. Haskalah—History. I. Title.
PJ5008.Z5313 vol. 9 [BM198] 809'.889'24s [839'.09'09]
ISBN 0–87068–476–0 76–8928

Printed in the United States of America.

Contents

A Note on Israel Zinberg / xi

Foreword / xiii

Acknowledgments / xv

Transliteration of Hebrew Terms / xvii

Transliteration of Yiddish Terms / xix

Abbreviations / xxi

PART TEN: HASIDISM AND ENLIGHTENMENT (1780–1820)

Chapter One: **JACOB FRANK AND THE FRANKIST MOVEMENT** / 3

The after-pangs of the Shabbetai Tzevi messianic movement—The sectarians in Podolia—The rabbis and their ban—Jacob Frank as a person—Frank among the Sabbatians in Salonika—The incarnate *Malka Kaddisha* (Holy King) and the reincarnation of Shabbetai Tzevi—The Frankists and their conduct—Jehudah Jeiteles and his *Siḥah*—Reminiscences of the Frankists in Offenbach by Moses Porges—Jacob Frank's two Hebrew proclamations—The philosophy of the Frankists—Jacob Frank's legends and tales—The predetermined downfall.

Chapter Two: **ISRAEL BAAL SHEM TOV** / 27

Rabbi Israel Baal Shem Tov—His childhood—His solitude—The orphan becomes an assistant to a teacher of small children—His love for melodies and songs—The assistant becomes an under-sexton in a small synagogue—His eagerness for Kabbalah—The under-sexton becomes familiar with the writings

of the Kabbalist Rabbi Adam—His friendship with Rabbi Adam's son—The young Kabbalist is married and soon becomes a widower—Israel's years of wandering—His marriage to the sister of the rabbi of Brody, Rabbi Abraham Gershon of Kutow—The rabbi and the ignoramus—Israel's solitude in the Carpathian mountains—The crisis in the world outlook of the young Kabbalist—Israel's ways of earning a livelihood—The tavern-keeper and village teacher becomes a *baal shem*—The Baal Shem Tov's revelation—The Baal Shem Tov's world outlook—"There is no place void of Him"—The Baal Shem Tov's optimism—The influence of Naḥmanides and Rabbi Isaac Luria—The Baal Shem Tov's opposition to ascetism—The meaning of prayer; the idea that one can also pray "through common talk"—On sweet and bitter medicines—God can be served only with joy—The Baal Shem Tov and the scholars—The individual and the *tzaddik* in the Baal Shem Tov's system—The Baal Shem Tov's letter about "ascent of souls"—The Baal Shem Tov and his "fellowship."

Chapter Three: THE DISCIPLES OF THE BAAL SHEM TOV / 63

The Baal Shem Tov's disciples—His successor Rabbi Dov Baer, the Maggid of Mezhirech—From Medzhibozh to Mezhirech—The sources of the Maggid's teachings—*Likkutim Yekarim, Likkutei Amarim, Or Torah,* and *Or Ha-Meir*—Pantheistic conceptions in the philosophy of the founders of the Hasidic movement—The doctrine of *tzimtzum* (contraction or withdrawal) and the purpose of *maaseh bereshit* (the work of creation)—Love and *tzimtzum* as a "complete unity"—The mission of the people of Israel—The *tzaddik* in the role of the High Priest on Yom Kippur—The *tzaddik* and the *adam be-fo'al* (realized man)—Theroetical tzaddikism—The first battle against the Hasidim; the social foundations of this struggle—The excommunication booklet, *Zemir Aritzim Ve-Ḥorvot Tzurim*—Jacob Joseph Ha-Kohen, the founder of Hasidic literature; his battle against the rabbis—The significance of his *Toledot Yaakov Yosef.*

Chapter Four: TZADDIKISM AND ḤABAD / 93

From theoretical tzaddikism to practical tzaddikism—Elimelech of Lyzhansk and his *No'am Elimelech*—The manifesto of practical tzaddikism—"The *tzaddik* decrees and God fulfills"—

Two ways of Hasidism—The Rabbi of Lyady, Shneur Zalman —In the heat of controversy—Shneur Zalman's hatred for Napoleon—His death—The significance of *Tanya*—The problem of *tzimtzum* in Shneur Zalman's explication—*Or Mitlabesh* and *Or Makkif*—God as both immanent and transcendent—Shneur Zalman's extreme idealism—The purpose of the "work of creation"—"The world is created for the sake of Israel"—The three garments: thought, word, and act—The significance of study of Torah and observance of the *mitzvot*—The doctrine of the three categories: *Hochmah, Binah* and *Da'at* (HaBaD)— Two kinds of love and fear—*Ahavat Olam* (everlasting love) and *Ahavah Rabbah* (great love)—Two states in man's heart—The highest degree of love is "beyond the state of knowledge and understanding"—The Kabbalist overcomes the scholar— *Tanya* on the role of the *tzaddik*—Shneur Zalman on the secular sciences.

Chapter Five: **LOVERS OF ISRAEL: LEVI YITZHAK OF BERDICHEV AND NAHMAN OF BRATZLAV** /

The standard-bearers of "love for Israel"—Mosheh Leib of Sasov—Ze'ev Wolf of Zbarazh, Menahem Mendel of Kosov, and Meir of Peremyshlyany—Levi Yitzhak, the rabbi of Berdichev, and his *Kedushat Levi*—The "eyes of God" as man's creation—Love as the primary attribute of God and the cornerstone of the world—Love of Israel and love of the Creator—Everything in the world is filled with God's love —The cosmic role of the Jewish people—The *tzaddik* must always speak favorably of Jews—Redemption for the whole world—Liberation from fear of the seven departments of hell—The Baal Shem Tov's great-grandson Rabbi Nahman of Bratzlav—Rabbi Nahman's career—His philosophy— Questions to which there is no answer—The world is created for the sake of mercy and requires mercy—Two kinds of heretics—Rabbi Nahman's struggle against the rationalists—Simplicity and sincerity without subtleties; the "wisdom of holiness"—The great state of joy—The melody of the world—The supreme state of silence—The melody of "Rosh Amanah"—The role of the *tzaddik;* the *tzaddik* in the state of Moses the Messiah—The tales of Rabbi Nahman of Bratzlav.

Chapter Nine: ANTI-HASIDIC WORKS; THE STRUGGLE BETWEEN THE REFORMERS AND THE ORTHODOX / 233

The Mitnagdim and Hasidim combine against the new enemy —Israel Zamosc opposes the Hasidim—The tract *Maaseh Ta'-tu'im*—Jacob Calmanson against the "dangerous" sect—Mendel Levin's anti-Hasidic work *Der Ershter Khosid* and *Maḥkimat Peti*—The anti-Hasidic manuscript *Über das Wesen der Sekte Chassidim*—Joseph Perl as battler for culture—His satire *Megalleh Temirin*—Religious reform in Germany—The role of Israel Jacobson—The struggle of the Orthodox against the Reform party—*Nogah Ha-Tzedek* and the "legitimacy-verdicts"—Moses Kunitz and Aaron Chorin—Chorin's *Emek Ha-Shaveh* and *Kinat Ha-Emet*—Eliezer Liebermann and his *Or Nogah*—The significance of Liebermann's work—Naḥman Berlin's counter-argument—The *bet din* of Hamburg and *Eleh Divrei Ha-Berit*—The verdicts of the orthodox rabbis—David Caro and his *Berit Emet*—The rabbis of former days and of the present—Meir Bresselau's tract *Ḥerev Nokemet*—*Lahat Ha-Ḥerev Ha-Mithappechet*—Conclusion.

Bibliographical Notes / 265

Glossary of Hebrew and Other Terms / 283

Index / 291

A Note on Israel Zinberg

DR. ISRAEL ZINBERG is widely regarded as one of the foremost historians of Jewish literature. Born in Russia in 1873 and educated at various universities in Germany and Switzerland, he devoted more than twenty years to the writing, in Yiddish, of his monumental *Di Geshikhte fun der Literatur bay Yidn* (History of Jewish Literature). This work, published in eight volumes in Vilna, 1929–1937, is a comprehensive and authoritative study of Jewish literary creativity in Europe from its beginnings in tenth-century Spain to the end of the Haskalah period in nineteenth-century Russia. Based on a meticulous study of all the relevant primary source material and provided with full documentation, Zinberg's history is a notable exemplar of the tradition of modern Jewish scholarship known as *die Wissenschaft des Judentums* (the Science of Judaism).

In addition to his *magnum opus*, Zinberg, who earned his living as a chemical engineer, wrote numerous other valuable monographs and articles on Jewish history and literature in Russian, Hebrew, and Yiddish. In 1938, during the Stalinist purges, he was arrested by the Soviet police and sentenced to exile in Siberia. He died in a concentration camp hospital in Vladivostok in that same year.

The reader who wishes a fuller introduction is invited to consult the Translator's Introduction to Volume I of Zinberg's *History of Jewish Literature.*

Foreword

In 1972 the Case Western Reserve University Press began publishing an English translation of Israel Zinberg's *History of Jewish Literature.* Zinberg, an engineer by profession, was a scholar by choice and inclination. In thirty years of intensive study in the great Jewish libraries of St. Petersburg (later Leningrad), he produced eight volumes in Yiddish portraying the course of literary creativity among the Jews beginning with the Golden Age of Spanish Jewry and continuing to the end of the last century. It was not until many years after Zinberg's death that a Hebrew translation was prepared and published in the State of Israel.

There has been no work of similar scope and magnitude in the English language, despite the fact that the Jewish reading public in Britain, South Africa, Canada, and the United States constitutes about half of the Jews in the world. Now, however, the Zinberg volumes have been beautifully translated into English by Dr. Bernard Martin, Abba Hillel Silver Professor of Jewish Studies and Chairman of the Department of Religion at Case Western Reserve University in Cleveland, Ohio. All the English-speaking lands are indebted to Professor Martin for his endeavor to make accessible a literary history such as Zinberg's, a history which depicts the intellectual strivings of the Jews, their aspirations, yearnings, and spiritual search in the medieval and modern worlds, in both of which they have played a not undistinguished role.

Special gratitude is due to the Press of Case Western Reserve University which inaugurated the challenging task of publishing this handsome and very important series of books. Each volume is an aesthetic as well as intellectual delight. The Case Western Reserve Press was aided in publication by a generous grant from the Memorial Foundation for Jewish Culture. The grant is, indeed, a memorial to the martyred Zinberg, who was arrested by the Soviet police in 1938 and deported to Siberia, where he died. We, for our part, are pleased with this opportunity to express our gratitude to the Memorial Foundation for the support which made possible the publication of the first three volumes.

Unfortunately, the economic difficulties from which many universities are now suffering has led to the dissolution of the Case Western Reserve Press and made it impossible for it to continue with the remaining nine volumes. That is why the Hebrew Union College—Jewish Institute of Religion, realizing the importance and cultural implications of this work, is cooperating with the Ktav Publishing House, Incorporated, in the publication of the remaining volumes.

The completion of this series will make available to the English-speaking world a magnificent account of the literary and cultural treasures created by the Jewish people during their millennial history.

Hebrew Union College—
Jewish Institute of Religion
Cincinnati, Ohio
January 1976

Alfred Gottschalk
President

Acknowledgments

The generous support of the Memorial Foundation for Jewish Culture, New York City, of the Morris and Bertha Treuhaft Memorial Fund, the Leonard, Faye, and Albert B. Ratner Philanthropic Fund, and Mr. and Mrs. John K. Powers, all of Cleveland, is gratefully acknowledged by publisher and translator alike. Without this generosity it would not have been possible for Israel Zinberg's monumental work to reach the new audience that it is hoped a translation into English will afford. The editor and translator wishes to express his appreciation to his friend Dr. Arthur J. Lelyveld, Rabbi of the Fairmount Temple of Cleveland and President (1966–1972) of the American Jewish Congress, for his aid in securing a grant from the Memorial Foundation for Jewish Culture for the publication of this work.

The translator also wishes to express his deep appreciation to Dr. Nathan Susskind, formerly Professor of German at the College of the City of New York and Visiting Professor of Yiddish at Yeshiva University, for his invaluable help in clarifying the meaning of many terms and concepts in Zinberg's Yiddish and Hebrew text. Responsibility for any errors of translation is, of course, the translator's.

It should be noted that Yiddish books with Hebrew titles are usually rendered according to the modern Sephardic pronunciation of Hebrew.

A gift to my loyal friend
and life-companion—my wife.

—Israel Zinberg

Transliteration of Hebrew Terms

א is not transliterated	ו = v (where not a vowel)	ל = l	פ = f
בּ = b	ז = z	מ = m	צ = tz
ב = v	ח = ḥ	נ = n	ק = k
גּ ,ג = g	ט = t	ס = s	ר = r
דּ ,ד = d	י = y	ע is not transliterated	שׁ = sh
ה = h	כּ = k	פּ = p	שׂ = s
	כ = ch		תּ ,ת = t

◌ָ = a	◌ֶ = e
◌ַ = a	◌ִ = i
◌ֹ ,וֹ = o	◌ֵ = ei
◌ֻ ,וּ = u	◌ֱ = e
short ◌ָ = o	◌ֳ = o
◌ֵי = ei	◌ֲ = a

vocal *sheva* = e

silent *sheva* is not transliterated

Transliteration of Yiddish Terms

א	not transliterated	יי	ey
אַ	a	ײַ	ay
אָ	o	כּ	k
ב	b	כ,ך	kh
בֿ	v	ל	l
ג	g	מ,ם	m
ד	d	נ,ן	n
ה	h	ס	s
ו,וּ	u	ע	e
וו	v	פּ	p
וי	oy	פֿ,ף	f
ז	z	צ,ץ	ts
זש	zh	ק	k
ח	kh	ר	r
ט	t	שׁ	sh
טש	tsh. ch	שׂ	s
י	(consonant) y	תּ	t
י	(vowel) i	ת	s

Abbreviations

JQR	*Jewish Quarterly Review*
JQR, n.s.	*Jewish Quarterly Review*, new series
MGWJ	*Monatsschrift für die Geschichte und Wissenschaft des Judentums*
PAAJR	*Proceedings of the American Academy for Jewish Research*
REJ	*Revue des Études Juives*
ZHB	*Zeitschrift für hebräische Bibliographie*

This volume is dedicated
to
Helen Regenstein
a woman of culture
devoted to the pursuit of beauty and learning

HASIDISM AND ENLIGHTENMENT
(1780–1820)

CHAPTER ONE

Jacob Frank and the Frankist Movement

The after-pangs of the Shabbetai Tzevi messianic movement—The sectarians in Podolia—The rabbis and their ban—Jacob Frank as a person—Frank among the Sabbatians in Salonika—The incarnate *Malka Kaddisha* (Holy King) and the reincarnation of Shabbetai Tzevi —The Frankists and their conduct—Jehudah Jeiteles and his *Siḥah*—Reminiscences of the Frankists in Offenbach by Moses Porges—Jacob Frank's two Hebrew proclamations—The philosophy of the Frankists—Jacob Frank's legends and tales—The predetermined downfall.

IN THE sixth volume of our work we noted that the persecutions of 1648, and the frightful confusions and wars which ensued in the Polish territories, brought economic and moral ruin to their Jewish settlement for generations. This ruin became even greater in the eighteenth century with the decline and collapse of the entire country.

Even in the seventeenth century, after the great catastrophe, when wild bands of Cossacks destroyed hundreds of communities on their bloody march, one idea became ever sharper and more insistent in the consciousness of the people frozen with dread: It is not possible to go on living this way! Something must come and make an end to the unbearable sufferings! The great misfortunes that have taken place are surely the "pangs of the Messiah" which announce the approaching redemption!

This elemental thought dominated the consciousness of the people and injected the salve of hope into grieved hearts.

Hence, one can understand quite well the colossal jubilation which the triumphant proclamation of the mystic of Smyrna, "I, your Messiah, Shabbetai Tzevi!," evoked in the Polish communities.[1] But the glorious hope was not fulfilled and the "advent of the Messiah" ended tragically. The awaited redeemer was imprisoned by the sultan and converted to Islam. The powerful national-political movement which this remarkable dreamer had called forth could not, however, be entirely destroyed; it was too intimately associated with the demands and hopes of the people. The mighty movement merely disintegrated into numerous narrow and hidden streams.

At various points in Poland appeared enthusiastic mystics (such as Jehudah Ḥasid, Nehemiah Ḥayon, Ḥayyim Malach, and many others), who summoned and admonished the people to fast and repent, for the redemption *will* and *must* soon come. The situation of the Jewish masses became ever more intolerable. Militant Catholic clericalism intensified its persecutions. Blood libels, or ritual murder charges, increased every year, and with them the stakes on which martyrs were tortured to death, as well as cruel expulsions. From within, in the community itself, there was exploitation and wickedness on the part of the "important figures" at the top, the men of power and leaders of the community council *(kahal).*[2] The oppressed masses were powerless to struggle not only against the external enemy but even against their oppressors in the *kahal*, for the latter always found support in their battle against the "multitude" among the rulers and wielders of power.

Thus, Jews sought consolation in their distress and unguent for their wounds, attempting to alleviate their hurt and strengthen their flickering hopes. It was clear that men with restless souls and believing, longing hearts could not be satisfied by arid *pilpul* with all its subtleties and clever, dialectical notions. In the atmosphere of overly pointed *pilpul*, empty pedantry, and congealed routine, these men yearned for the living source of fervent belief and religious sentiment. They sought this source on bypaths which not infrequently led them astray into narrow labyrinths filled with stumbling blocks and poisonous miasma. We have observed[3] that among the mystics and devotees of the Shabbetai Tzevi sect, along with rigorous ascetism and frequent fasting and mortification of the flesh, an

1. See our *History*, Vol. VI, p. 157.
2. See our *History*, Vol. VI, pp. 217ff.
3. *Ibid.*, 169ff.

antithetical tendency became ever more clearly noticeable—and this, in fact, under the influence of Shabbetai Tzevi's ideas—a tendency to liberate oneself from the rabbinic severities and prohibitions in the realm of ritual and ethics.

These two opposing currents, ascetic rigor and moral profligacy, were not infrequently braided together into one confused skein. Ḥayyim Malach, Jehudah Ḥasid's collaborator, after returning from Turkey to Poland, began, as an ardent adherent of Shabbetai Tzevi's doctrine, energetically to propagate the idea that, to be hallowed and triumph completely over the *kelipot* or "husks," one must first go through the forty-nine gates of uncleanness, for evil is—after all—the source of good. The highest and truest levels of purity can only be obtained by the soul that has descended into the abysses of filth and tasted the venomous liquid of sin.

Thus, in Poland, mainly in Galicia and Podolia, which were close to Turkey and the chief locus of the Sabbatian sect, Salonika, whole groups of sectarians developed. The people quickly crowned them with the title "Shabsay-Tzvinikes" or, in shortened form, "Shebsen." Pathological-mystical fantasy, messianic hopes and dark superstition were interwoven among these sectarians with a vague protest against the heavy yoke of the *Shulḥan Aruch* and with a semi-instinctive thirst for revival and liberation. In this stifling, unhealthy atmosphere, searching but crippled thought became impotently entangled in a labyrinth of contradictions and lost all clear notions of good and evil, of permitted and forbidden. Of course, one must deal very cautiously with the information provided by such grim opponents of everything bearing the least hint of Sabbatian "heresy" as the fanatical Jacob Emden. Nevertheless, it is indubitable that the mystical sectarians of Ḥayyim Malach's school would frequently permit themselves deeds that were inconsistent not only with the rabbinic codes but also with the principles of European ethics.[4]

The rabbis perceived serious danger in the "heretical" ideas disseminated by the covert "Shabsay-Tzvinikes" and decided to adopt the harshest measures against them. They believed that with the punitive instrument of excommunication they would succeed in destroying the poisonous seeds that Shabbetai Tzevi and his collaborators had sown. We have noted[5] that, with their excommunications and persecutions, they

4. See our *History*, Vol. VI, pp. 169ff.
5. *Ibid.*, Book Two, Chapter Three.

managed to crush the lovely, romantic flower that appeared in the ghetto—the dreaming poet Moses Ḥayyim Luzzatto. In point of fact, these "shepherds of Israel" had no weapons other than excommunications and persecutions available to them. The leaders of the generation well understood that "it was not peaceful in the tents of Jacob." They realized into what perilous and slippery paths the messianic-mystical strivings were leading men astray, but they were powerless to struggle against the impending danger with the weapon of persuasion, with the enthusiastic sentiment of the inspiring word.

It is clear that among the disciples and followers of Jehudah Ḥasid, Ḥayyim Malach and the like, there were not only adventurers of such altogether low moral character as Nehemiah Ḥayon but also profoundly moral "seekers" whose sensitive conscience could give them no rest. On the confused mystical-theosophical ways, veiled in mystery, their longing souls sought a solution to the grievous enigma of life, hoped to find a definitive answer to the painful problem of the reign of evil in the world and the unredressed suffering of the chosen people, the bearer of the holy covenant.

What could be given these restless, searching souls by the rigid supervisors of *Shulḥan Aruch* rabbinism who squandered all their spiritual powers on fruitless, arid *pilpul* and whose entire power of creation was exhausted in collecting mountains of ever new notes and subtleties to the codifiers and religious codices of earlier generations? Even against one of their own foremost leaders and representatives, the brilliant Jonathan Eybeschütz, whom they suspected of Sabbatian heresy, they had no weapon other than excommunication and persecution. Indeed, it was as a result of this "battle of amulets" that the institution of the rabbinate disclosed to the entire Jewish world all its corruption and rigidity.

At the very time when, in the communities of Germany and Bohemia, the obdurate controversy centering around the amulets of the *rosh yeshivah* of Prague who was suspected of covert Sabbatian heresy was being carried on, there erupted in the southern provinces of Poland, chiefly in Podolia, an even more bitter struggle against a newly created Sabbatian sect led by the notorious Jacob Frank.

We have noted the close economic and ideological ties which existed at that time between Podolia and the Turkish centers. For twenty-seven years (1672–1699) Podolia was under Turkish rule. Even after it returned to Poland, the populace of Kamenetz, which was almost at the Turkish border, barely two miles from Chotin, represented a "mixed multitude" of various provinces and different religions. Kamenetz had the closest connections with Salonika. Many Turkish Jews would come to its fairs, as well as to the fairs in Satanow, Husyatin, and other towns.

With the center of the *Vaad Ha-Medinah* (Council of State), Lemberg, and its rabbis and scholars, the Jews of Podolia tried to have as little to do as possible, so that their share in the heavy taxes might be all the smaller. The *Vaad Ha-Medinah* was naturally very displeased with this state of affairs and fought against these separatist tendencies.[6] This, however, was of no avail, and in 1715 Podolia withdrew completely from the *Vaad Ha-Medinah* in Lemberg and became a *medinah* or state in itself. The then still relatively sparse Jewish population in Podolia was scattered among very small communities, isolated from significant centers of culture. The populace was ignorant and had little fondness for study of Torah. For this reason Podolia was an extremely favorable area for the activity of all kinds of Shabbetai Tzevi propagandists, mystics, and miracle workers.

In 1722 a conference of rabbis delegated by various communities took place in Yaroslav and there, with blasts of the *shofar* and snuffed-out black candles, the followers of Shabbetai Tzevi's doctrine who had been exposed in Podolia were banned, with the decree of excommunication circulated to all the Podolian communities. "We order that our decree of excommunication," declared the verdict,

> shall be proclaimed in all the synagogues in the entire land of Podolia . . . And the heads, officers, potentates and chiefs of the land give authority and a rod and lash to the heads of districts and the heads of communities that they may persecute these people and punish them with disgrace and fines and imprisonment, even with the laws

6. It is interesting that this struggle even found an echo in Hasidic wonder-tales about the Baal Shem Tov. One of these tales relates that when the young Israel ben Eliezer was a teacher in a village near Lemberg he had occasion to lead the prayers on the Sabbath. His conduct of the service so pleased the Jews of the village that they begged him to be their prayer-leader on the Days of Awe so that they would not have to travel to the city for these days. The Baal Shem Tov agreed, and the villagers made a prayer quorum for themselves on the High Holy Days. This, however, greatly irked the leaders of the Lemberg community, and in the story the reason for this attitude is at once explained: "Because the *kahal*, or community council, had sustenance from the villagers." It is also related at length how stubbornly the community council fought against the villagers. The latter, in fact, were punished for their "impudence;" all of them had to go barefoot dressed in the *kittel*, or robe worn on Yom Kippur, from the gate of the city to the rabbi's house (*Sippurim Neḥmadim*, 4–5).

of the nations. And these people shall be separated all their days. Even when misfortune shall befall them, they shall not be given aid but be isolated from the community of the exile.[7]

Apparently these harsh measures were of little avail, for three years later the rabbis deemed it necessary to issue forth once more against the Sabbatians of Podolia with the old weapon of excommunication. One of them was a certain Jehudah Leib of the little town of Korolowka, a scholarly Jew but an ardent devotee of Sabbatian ideas. Because of this he was persecuted and had to move to Wallachia.[8] Around 1726 a son was born to him. This son, who later played such a sad role in the history of Jewish sectarians, was named Jacob. Endowed with great physical strength, an ardent, ebullient temperament, and a heated imagination, the young Jacob ben Leib found the melancholy Jewish milieu overly restrictive. For the arid Talmudic studies which he pursued at school in Chernowitz he manifested no liking whatever. He would run about for entire days with a company of youths over whom he was "Ottoman." The boys used to carry on "wars" or play "robbers."[9]

After his parents moved to Bucharest they found employment for him as an assistant to a Jewish merchant named Mordecai Margolis who traded with Turkey. The merchant took his young assistant along on his journeys to Salonika, Constantinople, and Smyrna. There Jacob ben Leib, who was given the surname Frank by the Turkish Jews, became acquainted with the Turkish Sabbatians (the Dönmeh). The Sephardic *ḥacham* Issachar familiarized the young Frank in Smyrna with the mysteries of the *Kabbalah* and the ideas of the Sabbatians.[10]

A particularly strong impression was made on Frank by two theses that were extremely popular among the sectarians in Salonika. The first of these was that Shabbetai Tzevi was the bodily garment, the human form, of the *Malka Kaddisha* (Holy King), who is the *Ze'er Anpin* (Small Face)—the offspring of the first two *partzofim*, "configurations" or "faces," the *Abba* or "father," the primordial source of the active-masculine, and the *Imma*, the "mother" and foundation of the passive-feminine. After Shabbetai Tzevi's death the belief took hold in certain

7. See Litinski, *Korot Podolye Ve-Kadmoniyyut Ha-Yehudim*, p. 64.

8. A. Kraushaar, *Frank Ve-Adato*, II, 11.

9. Kraushaar, *Frank Ve-Adato*, I, 51.

10. Two other Kabbalists, Mordecai and Naḥman, also had a certain influence on Frank.

Sabbatian circles that, just as Moses had spent forty days in the heavens and then returned to earth, so the Messiah Shabbetai Tzevi would come back forty years after his death to complete the redemption. The second idea that made a profound impression on Frank was the firmly held Sabbatian belief, intimately associated with the teaching of Rabbi Isaac Luria on the mystery of transmigration of souls, that the *Malka Kaddisha* finds its human embodiment in various generations. The soul of the Messiah is transmigrated and obtains a new garment, and the Messiah, in order to be hallowed and triumph completely over the *kelipot* or "husks" and bring full redemption, must first go through the forty-nine gates of uncleanness, for evil is—after all—the foundation of good.

Frank's turbulent capacities, his sparkling imagination, stormy temperament, and drive for power and domination found an ideological support, a goal-defined justification. Most historians and students of culture portray Jacob Frank as an adventurer, a terrible swindler and debauched pursuer of sexual license. This is certainly correct; nevertheless, the total nature of his personality is not exhausted thereby.[11]

Frank was a contemporary of Casanova; indeed, there is something of an affinity between him and the brilliant Italian adventurer. This affinity is perceptible not only in his licentiousness but generally in his unquenchable thirst for pleasure and his drive for spaciousness, beauty, and physical power. He was destined, however, to live under circumstances very different from those of his Italian contemporary. With his eagerness for life and joy, Jacob Frank was disgusted by the oppressiveness of the Jewish condition, by the crooked backs and pale, frightened faces, by *Shulḥan Aruch* rabbinism with its thousands of "fences" and restraints and its timorous stamping of the earthly and physical with the shameful brand of sin. He wished to make an end to all this. He, the incarnation of Shabbetai Tzevi, the embodied *Malka Kaddisha*, the S-S (acronym of *Santo Señor*),[12] would be the redeemer of the people; he would straighten crooked backs and give strength to the flabby. The "sinful" would become hallowed and revered.

It is not our aim to present a history of the Frankist movement.[13] We shall dwell merely on the world of ideas of the

11. The first attempt to give a more objective and exhaustive portrait of Frank's personality was made by Joseph Kleinmann in his extremely interesting work in *Yevreyski Almanakh*, 1923, 195–227.

12. See Jacob Emden, *Sefer Shimmush*, folios 3a, 7b.

13. For a discussion of the movement, see Jacob Emden, *Sefer Shimmush;* A. Kraushaar,

Frankists, on their searchings and gropings. When, in the middle of the 1750's, Frank returned from his journey to the East and began to propagandize in Podolia, he attracted not only people from the common multitude but also scholars and rabbis, e.g., Wolf ben Shalom, Elisha Shor with his two sons and his daughter Eve who knew the entire *Zohar* by heart, the rabbi of Busk, Rabbi Naḥman, and the rabbi of Glinyany. Even later, after Frank and his entire camp converted to Catholicism, burned the Talmud at the stake, and issued forth together with the Catholic clergy against their erstwhile brethren with the outrageous blood libel, there were among the Frankists many scholars, such as Leib Melamed of Brody,[14] and pure truthseekers of the highest moral quality. Even the typical "enlightener" of Herz Homberg's type, Peter Beer (born in 1758), is compelled to admit that among the Frankists were men "of the finest moral character" and of great scholarship.[15]

An extremely interesting picture of the Frankists in Prague after Frank's death is given by the well-known contributor to *Bikkurei Ha-Ittim*, Jehudah Jeiteles, in his *Siḥah Bein Shenat 5560 U-Vein Shenat 5561*.[16] Jeiteles was a convinced *maskil* and ardent devotee of "man's sound common sense" (*ibid.*, 19), and, as such, a determined opponent of the Frankist movement. He was not, however, a fanatic and believed that one must fight against harmful ideas, not against persons.[17] He therefore concludes his anti-Frankist brochure with a heartfelt wish that the confused sectarians may obtain enlightened eyes and realize that they have stumbled in great darkness (*ibid.*, 35–36).

"I must speak the truth and cannot deny," says Jehudah Jeiteles, "that they [the sectarians] are not ignorant men. They are not void of Torah and are familiar with *aggadot* and *midrashim*. The men are eager for knowledge and the women are of Lapidoth[18] quality and by no means weak-headed."[19] It is true, he says further, that they are people of wisdom and knowledge.

Frank i frankiści polscy (we have utilized Sokolow's Hebrew translation); H. Graetz, *Frank und die Frankisten* (1868); M. Balaban, "Le-Toledot Ha-Tenuah Ha-Frankit," *He-Atid*, V; M. Wischnitzer in the first volume of "History of the Jewish People" (Russian), pp. 458–486; A.J. Brawer, "Mekor Ivri Ḥadash Le-Toledot Frank Ve-Adato," *Ha-Shiloaḥ*, XXXIII, 1917, XXXVIII, 1921.

14. See David Kahana in *Ha-Shiloaḥ*, VII, pp. 569–570; S. Dubnow, *ibid.*, pp. 318–330.

15. *Geschichte, Lehren und Meinungen*, II, p. 257.

16. Printed in Prague in 1800, it is now extremely rare.

17. *Ibid.*, 28: "And on this Beruriah, the wife of Rabbi Meir, said: Let sins cease from the earth, not the sinners."

18. A reference to the biblical Deborah who was the wife of Lapidoth.

19. Jehudah Jeiteles, *Siḥah*, 9.

They study the *Zohar* and devote much attention to the writings of Rabbi Isaac Luria. The sectarians, both men and women,[20] occupy themselves chiefly with the Kabbalah. It is an ordinance among them that each day they immerse themselves for an hour or two in the mysteries of the Kabbalah. The everyday conversation of these women is not at all like the chatter of other women. The spirit of the *Zohar* rests on them, and numerous expressions of Kabbalist books are constantly on their lips.[21] There are even among them prophetesses who proclaim the tidings of the advent of the Messiah. They give signs and predict events that are to happen and disclose profound mysteries in the books of Kabbalah.[22] Among the Frankists, Jeiteles admits, there is even a man of European education with extensive philosophical knowledge; he also allowed himself to be led astray by mystical fantasies and clothes Kant's philosophical ideas in the garments of the *Zohar* and the Kabbalah of Rabbi Isaac Luria (*ibid.*, 13).

From other sources, too, it is known that among the Frankists of Prague there were scholarly Jews and highly prominent residents, e.g., Noah Kossovitz, the energetic Frankist propagandist Jonas Wehle with his three well-educated and cultured sons, and Gabriel Porges, who was a son-in-law of the rabbi of Prague and not only a learned Jew but also a man with a measure of knowledge in the "Christian sciences."[23] Indeed, it

20. That among the Frankists women occupied themselves with Kabbalah equally with men is stressed by the rabbi and preacher of Prague, Eliezer Fleckeles in his *Ahavat David* (1800): "Children and women came to hear the Kabbalah of the impostor Jacob and occupy themselves together with *maaseh merkavah* (the lore of the Chariot-Throne) in order to add insult to injury. Young men and virgins, old men and youths, inquire into and explore the writings of Rabbi Isaac Luria in secret . . . More and more do they carry on this work of madness together—men and women, youths and children . . . All defile themselves with the plagues, all obligate themselves to pilgrimages to the city where he was buried—the young man, the virgin, the old man, the venerable elder" (*ibid.*, 25).

21. *Ibid.*, 11–12: "Surely they are men of wisdom and sagacity. They know that they are to study the book of the *Zohar* and stretch forth their hands to the writings of Rabbi Isaac Luria, and all their occupation is with the books of the Kabbalah. Equally for males and females it is an ordinance every day to study secret matters an hour or two. And the everyday conversation of these women is not like the ordinary conversation of other women, for the spirit of the *Zohar* and the Kabbalah rests upon them, and the words of the Kabbalah are common in their mouths—words like *sefirot, sitra aḥara, duchrei ve-nukra, Shechinta Ila'ah Vetata'ah,* and the like.

22. *Ibid.*, 24: "And there is another sickening and great evil against this sect—that they have women who prophesy and foretell the advent of the time of the Messiah according to their dreams and the visions which they see; they tell signs of things that are to come later, reveal deep mysteries in the books of Kabbalah."

23. See N.M. Gelber, *YIVO Historishe Shriftn*, 255.

was his son, Moses Porges (later Von Portheim) who left some rather interesting reminiscences of the Frankist court at Offenbach at the turn of the century (1799–1800) when the "lady" *(gevirah)*, Jacob Frank's daughter Eve, presided over the Frankists.[24]

Moses Porges relates that when he was fourteen years old his father called him into his room and, in a solemn manner, posed the question: Did he believe the Torah, just as it was given to us in revealed form, contains everything we need to know for the salvation of our soul and for human bliss in this world and in the world to come? Then the father emotively explained that, along with the Torah, there is also the holy book, the *Zohar*, which reveals the mysteries to which the Torah only alludes and which tells us how to attain perfection. There are now many "noble persons" who devote themselves to the new Torah; their goal is *liberation from spiritual and political oppression.*[25] God, as in previous times, has also been revealed of late.[26]

In order that his son might "become aware of all this," Gabriel Porges handed the fourteen-year-old Moses over to one "of our fellowship," Noah Kossovitz, that the latter might teach him the secret doctrine. Kossovitz told him a great deal about Jacob Frank—how he "was revealed as the Messiah, gathered around himself many Jewish scholars who believed in him . . . He obtained numerous disciples; his prophecies and his promise to bring spiritual and bodily redemption, eternal life, literally forged these followers to him."[27] Frank and his family converted to Catholicism, together with a large part of his followers, "in order to liberate the *Shechinah* which Rome had taken captive."[28]

When Moses Porges later came to the "holy camp" at Offenbach, one of the "believers" immediately explained to him on his arrival:

My son, the *Shechinah* is in distress, the *Shechinah* is in exile! Edom and Ishmael hold her captive, and her children must redeem her and must, for this reason, experience afflictions along with her. As soon as the three *sefirot* become united in the proper manner as a tri-unity,

24. Porges' memoirs were first published in the *YIVO Historishe Shriftn*, I, 1929, pp. 265–288.
25. Italicized by me—I.Z.
26. *YIVO Historishe Shriftn*, I, 1929, p. 266.
27. Porges, in *Historishe Shriftn*, I, 1929, p. 267.
28. *Ibid.*

a triple thread, the redemption will come. Two of them have already appeared in the form of men. We must await the third. Happy is he who has been chosen to be united with *Tiferet*, for from him the redeemer of the world will be born. Carry on your service and stand on guard, so that you may have the privilege of becoming the chosen one.[29]

The "two" who "have already appeared" are Shabbetai Tzevi and Jacob Frank. The expression "to be united with *Tiferet*" is certainly an allusion to the mystical idea, extremely popular among Shabbetai Tzevi's associates, that the Messiah, Shabbetai Tzevi, is the incarnate six-edged *sefirah* called *Tiferet*, the human form of the third letter in the Ineffable Name, *Vav*, the letter which, according to Rabbi Isaac Luria's mystical system, is the symbol of the *Ze'er Anpin*.[30]

In general it is quite difficult to give a clear notion of the philosophy or world-view of the Frankists. Their founder left behind a very slight literary legacy—only two proclamations which he published in Hebrew in 1767 and 1768. His associates, however, in the course of many years wrote down Frank's sermons, tales, parables, and sayings. Frank gave his sermons in a unique jargon—a mixture of Ladino, German, Yiddish, and Polish. His associates wrote them down in Polish and in part also in Hebrew. Only the Polish have been preserved in manuscript, and the most important of these are *Ksiega słów Panskich* (a collection of maxims, anecdotes, parables, and conversations which Frank's secretary wrote down) and *Kronika Panska* (reminiscences and tales of Frank's life).[31] These two manuscripts were utilized in part by Kraushaar in his abovementioned work. Unfortunately, however, this scholar had a very limited understanding of Jewish mysticism and the world of ideas of the *Zohar* and Rabbi Isaac Luria; hence, it was difficult for him to give a clear notion of the most important content of the manuscripts he employed.

In addition, one must take into consideration that Frank and his followers expressed their views mainly only in hints and allusions, out of fear of the Catholic clergy, who always regarded the Frankists with suspicion and did not believe that they had converted to Christianity wholeheartedly. And, indeed, it is beyond doubt that conversion, for the Frankists, was

29. *Ibid.*, p. 273.
30. See our *History*, Vol. V, p. 166, Note 22.
31. Only two manuscripts have been preserved: (1) *Ksiega Proroctw* (the Book of Prophesies), and (2) *Ksiega Słów Panskich* (the Book of Visions).

a compulsory act, which they carried through only because they had no other recourse. The situation in which Frank and his associates found themselves after the Jewish populace of the little town of Lantzkorona attacked them on a winter's night in 1756, when in a secluded house with closed shutters they conducted their mysteries with dancing, singing, and ecstatic, erotic "prayers," is well known. They were beaten murderously and the indignation of the Jews was so intense that they wished to burn the "heretics."

After the Council of the Land of Podolia collected all the accusatory material against the sectarians who participated in the mysteries of that night,[32] it, together with the Council of the Land of Russia, as well as numerous rabbis from the largest Polish communities, issued at Brody the "great excommunication" against the Frankists. These "sinners in Israel" were excluded from the Jewish congregation; their wives and daughters were declared whores and their children bastards, and it was decreed that they may not be received in the Jewish community to the tenth generation. No intercourse whatsoever was permitted with them; their bread was declared "bread of the Samaritans," their sacrifices were "sacrifices of the dead," and their vessels were an "abomination" which no Jew may touch.

The decree of excommunication was published under the title "Ḥerev Pifiyot" (A Doubled-Edged Sword)[33] and was circulated to all the Jewish communities and proclaimed with the sound of the ram's horn and snuffed-out candles. Hatred of the sectarians was so intense that in one attack on the Frankists the aged Elisha Shor perished, and on another occasion Leib Krisa almost died in the same way. Beaten and bruised, he escaped barely alive from the hands of the enraged mob. The Frankists had no alternative. Excluded from the Jewish community, they had to turn to Christian society. The Catholic clergy, led by the bishop of Kamenetz, Dembowski, wished, above all, to exploit the sectarians as an instrument to intensify persecutions of Jews and Judaism and, incidentally, to obtain new souls, "lost sheep," for the Christian church. Under strong pressure from both sides, the sectarians had no way out, burned their bridges

32. According to this accusatory material (published in Emden's *Sefer Shimmush*, 5–6), some of the women who participated in the mysteries gave themselves sexually, with the consent of their husbands, to other "comrades" as a religious duty, because they believed that thereby they "combined" a divine "name" and brought about a unification between the Holy One Blessed be He and the *Shechinah*.

33. Reprinted in Joseph Kohen-Zedek's *Otzar Ḥochmah*, I, 22–29.

behind them, and not only issued forth as bitter enemies of the Talmud, which they hurled into the fire with their own hands, but even charged their former brethren with the blood libel.[34]

At the same time, they took all possible steps to separate themselves from the Christian world. To be sure, the Frankists informed the Catholic priests that they also believed in the trinitarian God, but this was the God of the three *sefirot* of the *Zohar*, not of the Catholic Church. With great obduracy they resisted adopting the Christian faith, and when they were coerced by the Catholic clergy into conversion, they did this in fact only ostensibly. One must cast off the *kelipah* or "husk," Jacob Frank then explained, in order to save the "kernel" of the faith. "Guard yourselves," he warned his disciples, "from the cross; it points with its corners to four different directions, and so one can easily be led astray."[35]

To be sure, the sectarians and their followers in the first "manifesto"[36] which they submitted to Dembowski on August 4, 1756, declared that Jerusalem will no longer be rebuilt and the Messiah will not come, for the Messiah is the God who has assumed human form.[37] By this Messiah, however, they meant not Jesus but Shabbetai Tzevi and his incarnation, Jacob Frank. Even after the Frankists adopted Catholicism, they had no desire whatever to mingle with the Christian populace. In the Catholic Church itself they sang their special hymns and prayers, "Yigaleh" and "Berechyah."[38] They also specified conditions, requesting that they be permitted to have beards and ear-locks, to celebrate both Sabbath and Sunday, to study the *Zohar*, to occupy themselves with the Kabbalah, not to eat pork, to wear the Jewish costume, and not to intermarry with the neighboring populace.[39]

Jacob Frank submitted a petition to the Polish king, requesting that the sectarians be given a certain territory near the Turkish border which belonged to the crown, so that they might live apart and continue their propaganda.[40] Later also,

34. For a discussion of this charge on the part of the Frankists and on the disputation with the rabbis, see Brawer's work, cited above, in *Ha-Shiloaḥ*, XXXVIII, pp. 16–22, 231–238, 349–354, 441–450.

35. *Frank Ve-Adato*, 278.

36. The Hebrew text is printed *in toto* in Jacob Emden's *Sefer Shimmush*, Part III *(Shevet Le-Gav Kesilim)*.

37. *Ibid.*, folio 62.

38. The text of the last prayer is printed in *Sefer Shimmush*, 4.

39. *Frank Ve-Adato*, 34, II, 12; Ber of Bolechow's *Imrei Binah* (in *Ha-Shiloaḥ*, XXXIII, pp. 444–445).

40. *Frank Ve-Adato*, 152; *Sefer Shimmush*, 82.

when Frank's daughter was the Austrian emperor's paramour, the Frankists again hoped that they would obtain a separate territory where they could conduct their religious mysteries freely and without hindrance.[41] Even in their conversations with the Catholic clergy, the Frankists indicated that they had converted in order to save Christian souls. This is certainly associated with the teaching of Rabbi Isaac Luria about the special "mission" of the Jewish people, which is "scattered and sown" among the nations of the world because thereby all the souls of the other peoples in which the "holy sparks" are found obtain *tikkun*, or correction; thanks to their proximity to the Jewish people, these souls are liberated, under its influence, from the impure *kelipah*, or "husk," and unite with the *Shechinah*.[42]

Jacob Frank, whom the Jews persecuted as a terrible betrayer and seducer, does, indeed, speak with great indignation of the Jews. "There is no other people in the world that follows such corrupted ways as the Jews . . . They are like snakes and scorpions: there is no peace or brotherliness between them, only jealousy, hatred, and controversy."[43] Nevertheless, he also declares to his associates:

> I tell you that even if all the kings of the nations were to come to me, this would be of no value for me. My whole intention and desire is that *the Jews should come to me.* And the Jews *will* come to me in great hosts, each host under a special flag. Each flag will have its own color; only the black and blue flags will go at the end. Utterly new things will be revealed on these flags, and all the world will come to me and relate what they have seen on them. You are destined to go with my flag, for *we will go with the flag to a definite goal.*

"What has been done until now," declares Frank, "was all done in order to maintain the Jewish people and that the name of Israel might not be destroyed. But neither commandments nor prayers are any longer required. It is necessary now only to follow the order and to proceed until we finally reach the destined, hidden goal."[44] In what did this hidden goal consist? We have already noted that the Frankist literature is a very meager one. Nevertheless, some interesting details of Frank's doctrine have been preserved, and from them it is possible to give a more or less clear answer to this question.

41. See Kleinmann, *op. cit.*, p. 219.
42. See our *History*, Vol. V, p. 75.
43. *Frank Ve-Adato*, 35.
44. *Ibid.*, 122.

It is known that the Catholic clergy suspected Frank of not adopting the Christian faith with complete sincerity and that he was therefore detained for years in the fortress of Czestochowa. Among the Frankists this fortress was then called *Tarei De-Romi* (the gates of Rome), an allusion to the well-known Talmudic legend that the Messiah, before his disclosure, will sit before the gates of Rome "among sick men and beggars covered with boils."[45] There, in the *Tarei De-Romi* a unique sectarian faith entitled "the religion of Edom" was created. Under the *kelipah*, the garment of Christian terminology, a special, purely Kabbalist "content" is hidden.

In 1767 Jacob Frank addressed a proclamation to the community of Brody, written in a unique Hebrew, Zoharic style:

Hear me out, you with your stopped-up hearts who are far removed from righteousness and stray on crooked ways! Who of you is sufficiently God-fearing to receive the voice calling in the wilderness of the peoples? Woe to you when the great lion will awaken and remember the hind.[46] It is written: "Surely the Lord God will do nothing, except He reveal His secret" (Amos 3:7). If you are indeed children of God, how is it that you do not know what will occur at the end of these days, in the present times? The beginning has already taken place, and what will further come *I* proclaim to you. I already foresee the end, that you must mourn and weep for the inhabitants of Cracow and its environs. Gird your loins with sackcloth, mourn and lament on all the streets, because, for their great sins, a fire has broken out which will consume the entire city. Some will fall by the sword, some through hunger, some through the plague, and some through captivity. Their corpses will roll about like manure on the ground, and dogs will lick their blood. God's storm has broken out with wrath, rages over the head of the wicked, and will burn everything to the depths of the abysses of hell. And he who will escape from the sword will be caught in a snare. Therefore you must weep and lament for them, and they must also mourn for the inhabitants of your community and its environs. For a people comes, a people of the children of Edom hastens; a voice concerning great distress, when a king will rise against a king, is heard. Men will be purified and refined. The wicked will remain in their malevolence and will not understand, but all the understanding will realize that anyone who has a spark of the seed of Abraham, Isaac, and Jacob must accept the "holy religion of Edom." And whoever accepts this religion with love

45. *Sanhedrin*, 97. The mystic Solomon Molcho also took strong account of this legend (see our *History*, Vol. V, pp. 32ff).

46. The expressions *ayyala* and *ayyalta*, meaning a "hind" are employed quite frequently in the *Zohar* as a mystical symbol.

will be saved from all the afflictions and be privileged to enjoy all the consolations that are described by Isaiah and the other prophets. Sealed and signed, Jacob Joseph Frank.

The next year, 1768, a great Jewish community was in fact destroyed. A "people of the children of Edom," Gonta and his Haidamacks, slaughtered the community of Uman, and Jacob Frank then addressed another proclamation[47] to all the Jewish communities from his prison at Czestochowa. In prophetic style he reproves the stubborn people that "remains in darkness and does not heed his warning words." Let them now know that a dark time is coming upon them; a terrible affliction awaits them in all the lands they inhabit.

Woe, woe for this time that will soon come upon you, upon your wives and your children. Those who will be in houses will perish in these houses, and there will be no one to bring them to burial—so numerous will the dead be. And one who finds himself in the open field will be pursued by death in the field, and dogs will drag his corpse around . . . I tell you that it cannot be otherwise; everything must be fulfilled that is written in the Torah of Moses to the effect that all [Jews] will pass over to the holy religion of Edom, just as it is written in the Torah that Jacob assured Esau: "Let my Lord, I pray thee, pass over before his servant . . . until I come unto my Lord to Seir" (Genesis 33:14). And Moses our master in fact sent messengers to the king of Edom (Numbers 20:14). Whoever stems from the seed of Abraham, Isaac, and Jacob must pass over to the holy religion of Edom . . . And when the light will appear below, the great war will break out, everything will fall apart. Powerful kingdoms will also be broken. And I proclaim to you that the *weaker will defeat the stronger* [italics mine—I.Z.], and if men understood this, they would know what will happen to them at the end.[48]

In what did this "holy religion of Edom" actually consist? And who is the "weaker" who will overcome the "stronger?" It is clear that by the "religion of Edom" Frank does not mean Christianity but his own mystical-symbolic doctrine, which he endeavored to disseminate in many larger and smaller Jewish centers through his emissaries.[49] It is also beyond doubt that Jacob Frank, a Jew by birth and an erstwhile Moslem, regarded

47. First published by Wischnitzer, *op. cit.*
48. *Ibid.*, Brawer did not know that both of Frank's letters were already published. Hence, he reprinted them in his work cited above (*Ha-Shiloaḥ*, XXXVIII, pp. 453–455).
49. As a result of this propaganda, the number of the Frankists reached approximately fifteen thousand.

Christianity with no lesser animosity and perhaps with even greater contempt than he did the Talmud. It was not Christianity that impressed him but the Christian world—and this world not with its cultural achievements, of which he had a very limited notion, but with its external brilliance and splendor.

Frank was impressed by the lusty, boisterous life of the Christian nobility, with its sword-play and horsemanship, its dancing and singing, its laughing young women and foaming wine. And he, the gigantic, powerful man with ardent temperament and boiling blood, was disgusted by the pious, melancholy Jewish ghetto, by the bent Jewish back with its humility and weakness. "You always say in your prayers, 'As a father hath compassion upon his children, so the Lord hath compassion upon us.' Where is this compassion?" "Know," Frank preached to his disciples,

> that God rests only on those who are crowned either with knightliness, or with wealth or wisdom. But what do we have? There is no knightliness, no wisdom, no wealth among us. You yourselves see how our backs are bowed to the ground. I do not look to the heavens and hope that salvation will come thence. I wish only to see what God will make to pass here in *this* world, on our earth.

"Man is born for happiness." This slogan of the *Aufklärer*, or enlighteners, of the second half of the eighteenth century had already been felt by this mystical adventurer in all his bones. True happiness is not in the world to come, in the celestial palaces of paradise, but here on earth. Earthly pleasures, the beauty of women, luxury and splendor, everything inspirited with the fiery breath of the intoxicating elixirs of the earth, everything that the rabbis with their books have stamped with the shameful brand of sin—these are true happiness, the greatest human joy. Not to free men *from* sin, but to free sin itself, to recognize its true value, is of the essence. That which obscurely and unconsciously flickered in the heart of the suffering community—the feeling that it is no longer possible to live this way, that there must be liberation from the intolerable burden—was openly and clearly enunciated by the life-loving mystic of Podolia.

Frank expressed himself with emotion and veiled his ideas and demands in poetic, imaginative, Oriental tales and parables. "I do not wish to teach you with laws and commandments," he declares to his disciples, "but with tales and parables."[50] And the stories are told in Oriental fashion, with Oriental fantasy and splendor. Hence, it is not surprising that these sermons made an enormous impression on mystically-minded men of feeling. Jehudah Jeiteles tells of numerous family tragedies—how men would abandon their children and families and join Frank's "camp."[51] Even after his death, entire families, including wives and children, would make pilgrimages to Offenbach to visit Frank's grave and pray with great reverence in the room where the messiah they had deified spent the last moments of his life.[52] The verse of the mystical poet Solomon Alkabetz always resounded in Frank's ears: "Arise, leave your ruins; long enough have you dwelt in the valley of weeping."[53] But he refused to draw the poet's conclusion; not to Zion did he call his disciples and followers, not to Jerusalem and the Temple with its priests and sacrifices, but into the wide, free world with its earthly joys and boisterous clamor.

J. Kleinmann is quite right when he notes that, in this respect, Frank must be considered a forerunner of the *Aufklärer.*[54] "It is explicitly written," Frank preached to his camp,

> "You shall live by your sword." Why then do you not live by the sword? I tell you that, as long as you are not compelled to gird on the

50. *Frank Ve-Adato,* 33.
51. Jeiteles, *op. cit.,* 26.
52. These pilgrimages took on such an extensive character that the then well-known preacher of Prague, Rabbi Eliezer Fleckeles, found it necessary to attack in the sharpest fashion the pilgrimaging to Offenbach and the whole Frankist movement in special sermons which he later published in his *Ahavat David.* Ironically he asks his hearers: "What actually have you to do there, in this little town [Offenbach], among men who are neither Jews nor Christians nor Egyptians nor Turks nor Italians? If you wish to study natural sciences, philosophy, ethics there, are there not in the land of our emperor, or in other lands, enough expert professors in all branches of science? If you desire to become familiar with Christian doctrine, are there lacking Christian theologians in every city and every province? If you yearn for the wisdom of Kabbalah, is there a shortage here of honest, pious men who occupy themselves with speculation and are competent in this wisdom? If you wish to learn God's Torah, *Gemara* and codes, then, praise God, we have among us enough renowned scholars, great men of learning who teach Torah to many." Further on Fleckeles asks with irony, having in mind the military mystery along with the war exercises which Frank introduced into his capital: "Perhaps you wish to learn military tactics. Do you not have enough warriors and strategists among the kings and rulers in the land? . . . Another thing I would ask of you: Why do not only men, but women and children as well, run there? . . . These childish fools who relate joyously that their Messiah who is anointed with the fat of swine will soon be resurrected . . ." (*Ahavat David,* 25–26).
53. See our *History,* Vol. V,p. 53.
54. Kleinmann, *op. cit.,* pp. 223–224.

sword, you cannot be redeemed. The resurrection of the dead will also take place only with the aid of the sword. Women, too, must bear a sword, and when Jews will accept the religion of Edom, even six-year old children will engage in military tactics.

In this connection Frank tells the story of a child, a prince, who was exiled abroad and no one knew whence he came. He was given all kinds of toys but refused to touch them. As soon as he saw a sword, however, he happily buckled it around his loins. Then it was understood that this child was a prince, of the seed of kings. The parable also applies to you: If you are really of the seed of the royal house of David, you would not have to do with your books and all kinds of statutes and laws, but would demand weapons.

Frank relates a fairy tale of a hidden island in the ocean.

At the shore of this island stands a great ship filled with weapons. On the island live pious and God-fearing Kabbalist Jews. Every month these go in little boats to the great ship and inquire whether the time has come to declare war against all four corners of the earth. On this island is a tremendous mountain, and no man can climb it. On the mountain is a golden rod. A man from abroad will come and rap on the ship. Then the hour will arrive *to begin the war.*[55]

"I charge you," says Frank to his disciple Andreas Dembowski, "to learn to shoot, to hold a spear in your hand, and to fight a duel."[56] "What has been, has been," he preaches to his "camp." "Now a very different time has come. We shall no longer occupy ourselves with what concerned us formerly; we shall only study military tactics."[57]

Transvaluation of values! Everything must be revaluated and, for this, the old must first be rooted out and forgotten. The ancient rabbinic books must be cleared away, all memories of laws and precepts must be erased from the heart. "You must trample on all the laws that have been in effect until now," Frank teaches his disciples. "Listen to what I tell you. If the least memory of the old studies remain among any of you, he and all around him will perish. For the place to which we are proceeding cannot endure any laws and statutes, for these bear death in themselves and we go toward life." "Do not turn your faces," Frank admonishes, "to the past, to what is gone!" "All

55. *Frank Ve-Adato*, 118.
56. *Ibid.*, 285.
57. *Ibid.*

the beliefs, all the laws, all the books which have been up until now, and also all those who study these books—are dead and withered." "I have come to you in Poland to nullify all the beliefs and all the customs, for *I desire to bring life to the world.*" "Everyone of you must have the heart of a lion, so that he will not be afraid of anyone and not know what trembling means." "I will make courageous knights out of Jews."

Frank himself became a knight, purchased a castle from an impoverished nobleman, assumed the title of "baron," and surrounded himself with military guards from his young disciples who wore the uniform of hussars and lancers and daily performed military exercises. He dreamed of having his own legions that would win territory for him by the sword. He hoped that this would easily be obtained when a world war broke out. "When dogs fight," Frank told his disciples,

> a man can come and strike them with a staff and they will not even notice it but go on biting each other. When bloodshed will occur in the world, we shall manage in the tumult to obtain what we strive for. Murky waters are good for catching fish. When the world is filled with bloodshed and warfare, we will succeed in capturing what belongs to us.

"Everywhere we go, we must cast off our old customs, our old clothing and language, and speak the language that the surrounding populace speaks." "I wish to erase your names, and your children also will not bear your names. New names will you and your children receive."

It would be erroneous, however, to believe that Frank preached complete assimilation, that Jews should be absorbed by the peoples among whom they live. His instincts, his longing for the joys of life, and his feeling of contempt for the melancholy, arid, and respectable *Shulḥan Aruch* rabbinism certainly drove him out of the tents of Jacob into the tents of Esau. "I tell you," Frank declared to his disciples, "my God is also in Esau, in the power and wealth of Esau. I tell you that among Jews there is nothing, and among the other peoples there is so much wealth." He wished to put an end to the ethic of Judaism, to root out the ancient Jewish books so that no recollection of them remained, to erase from memory the traditional world-view of Judaism.

Frank, who in his stormy life violated the Seventh Commandment no less than his contemporary Casanova, attempted to place the ideal of woman on the highest pedestal.

I tell you that the Jews are in such great distress because they wait for the coming of the redeemer but not for the *virgin.* Consider the other peoples, how they sit peacefully in their places. This is because they rely on their virgin, who is the reflection of *our virgin* . . . Now, go to her, fall at her feet, kiss the dust of her steps, and when she asks you, "What do you wish?," tell her, "Hitherto we have served God; now we beseech *you* to show us the way . . ." And whoever will be privileged to see her in all her beauty *will attain the life of the world to come,* for she herself is the life of the world to come!

Frank wished to eradicate the old Jewish books, the old world-outlook. But the only bit of knowledge that he himself had obtained was in the ancient Jewish book called the *Zohar,* and the mystical doctrine of this remarkable work ruled without restraint over his ardent imagination. It was not merely out of trickery, to defraud the people, that he declared himself the incarnation of Shabbetai Tzevi. He actually felt himself in close affinity with the mystic of Smyrna, and wished to fulfill his mission—but through different means and in different ways. "Shabbetai Tzevi," Frank declared to his disciples, "did not attain the supreme level of perfection because he did not taste the loveliest pleasure in the world—the sweetness of dominion and power."[58]

Frank wished to drink from this intoxicating cup. He demanded of his disciples servile subjection, blind apotheosis of himself. He played the knight, the baron, rode around in splendid carriages, led an extravagant life, but always wore a red cloak, for the mystical power of the Biblical verse, "Who is this that cometh from Edom with dyed garments . . . ?" (Isaiah 63:1), ruled over him.

"I have come," Frank preached to his associates, "to destroy everything, and everything that will then be built up will have an everlasting existence." "And as I have been diligent in destroying and crushing, so will I be diligent in building and planting." He wished to be not merely a destroyer but a builder. "Have we taken on this faith [Catholicism] so that we might sit like the dead? We must let the nations of the world hear something. And you will see how astonished they will all be, how they will all gape. Have I not told you that I am like the burning bush that is not consumed?"

We have noted that among Frank's disciples there were also rabbis and scholars. These he addresses with a certain irony.

58. *Ibid.,* 59.

I was in your eyes a common man, a vulgar man, who knows no Torah, who has no knowledge in writing and speaking . . . And because I was an ignoramus in your sight, you thought that through me the whole Torah would fall. You must know that if you had needed wise men, scholars and book-men would have been sent to you . . . But I tell you that, even though you have studied much Torah, you have distorted God's living word with your tortuous interpretations. The Torah is indeed full of truth, but you have not understood a single word of it.[59]

And Frank proceeds to relate a tale about a pearl. A man once obtained a marvelous pearl and travelled around with it from city to city, everywhere seeking the artful jeweler who might be able to pierce it. But no master jeweler was willing to undertake the task because he was afraid of spoiling the priceless pearl. In one city the man came with his pearl to a master jeweler and did not find him at home. Only the master's assistant, a common worker, was there. The owner showed him the pearl, told him nothing of its great value, and the workman pierced the pearl without any fear. The owner paid him very handsomely and went away filled with joy. "The same thing is true of me. Many wise men wished to pierce but could not, because they were afraid; but *I have been chosen to carry through the great 'correction' (tikkun), to diminish the 'husk' (kelipah)*, because I am a common man and I will bore through and do everything as is proper."[60] *"For my thoughts are not like yours; I go a new way which no man has trodden before me."*[61] "You know," he further says, "that the physician comes to heal not the well but the sick. I also have come to heal sick men—those whose faith was shaken by doubt and who remained almost as if without a God. I have come to you with the good tidings that there is a true God in the world, and I will reveal Him to you."[62] And he further related to them a parable.

Every man has with him two guardians, one revealed, whom everyone can see, and the other a hidden one. These accompany the man wherever he goes. The first guardian discloses himself before the whole world; all perceive his beauty and praise and marvel at him. But how much more beautiful is the other, the concealed one! And I lead you so that you may see the concealed.[63]

59. *Ibid.*, 33, 265.
60. *Ibid.*, 120.
61. *Ibid.*, 264.
62. *Ibid.*, 265.
63. *Ibid.*

"The Jews," says Frank, "are tremendously degraded and despised by all peoples. They fall ever lower, and when they attain the last abyss, then the ascent, the rise and incessant climb to the heights, will begin. And this is the ladder the patriarch Joseph saw in a dream, the ladder on which angels were ascending and descending."

"We must descend to the last abyss"—this is the slogan that Frank set forth. "He lifteth up the needy out of the dunghill" (Psalms 113:7). One must not fear dirt and filth, if he wishes to be raised and redeemed. Frank, who rejected the old Jewish ethic, declared that all means are permitted to attain the desired goal. And he relates in this connection, as is his manner, a tale. Once a king besieged a certain fortress, but it was impossible to conquer it. So the king issued an order to the effect that whoever managed to penetrate the fortress would be given half his kingdom, as well as his daughter to wife. Then someone who had thoroughly explored the environs of the city came to the king and told him that, if he provided him with a certain number of warriors to help, he would capture the fortress at night. The king agreed. In the dark of night the man then descended with his soldiers into the canal out of which all the sewage of the city flowed, and through this nauseating passage of filth and stench he invaded the fortress, conquered the city, and obtained the princess for his wife.

The lesson inherent in this tale dominates Frank's philosophy and his propaganda program. We find this very clearly expressed also in the proclamation[64] that his followers issued in 1800, several years after his death. There it is pointed out, relying on a statement in the *Zohar*, that "precisely from the most shameful place will redemption come and from the darkest point will light appear." "When I converted," Frank reminded his associates, "I said to you: 'From now on—the burden of silence. Place a lock upon your lips.' "

Esau, Edom, the Catholic Church—these, according to Frank's explanation, are merely "cities of refuge," "dunghills," "the most shameful place" from which Jacob's children will be exalted and "all will be subject to them." "If Jacob in his day had conquered Esau, then the time of Esau's kingdom would now come. For this reason, indeed, did Jacob then say, 'Let my lord pass over before his servant,' but now comes the time of Jacob's dominion, and it will last forever!" "Abraham dug and sought the spring, Jacob dug and sought the spring, all dug and

64. Published by Wischnitzer in the work cited.

strove toward a definite goal. I also dug, because I wished that you should be *masters over the whole world.*" "I desire to give each of you individually a crown." This is the meaning of the words with which Frank concluded his proclamation of 1767, saying that the weaker would vanquish the stronger.

Jehudah Halevi, Joseph Ibn Yaḥya (the author of *Torah Or*),[65] the Maharal of Prague, and others endeavored, each in his own way, to give a historical-psychological explanation why the Jews are the chosen people—"My son, My firstborn, Israel." They perceived Israel's chosenness in its great moral power which enables it to become the "light of the nations," the illumination and guide of all peoples. Jacob Frank, who appeared in the middle of the eighteenth century, in the deepest twilight period of Jewish history, in the atmosphere of sad disillusionment and utter demoralization that dominated the moribund land of Poland, dared, while remaining faithful to the idea of chosenness, to reject all ethical values and all traditions of past generations, to set forth as the supreme ideal the sword, and to proclaim as the highest slogan: Everything is permitted; all means, not excluding the filthiest and most shameful, are justified, if they lead to the desired goal!

It is clear that Frankism from its beginning was condemned to failure and ruin. Frank assured his disciples that "as many hairs as he had on his head, so many Jews would pass over to him."[66] But he was mistaken. Cut off from its own living roots and filled with the profoundest inconsistencies and antitheses, Frankism roamed for several decades over the hidden corners of the ghetto like a phantom until it finally disappeared without a trace.

At the same time, in the same environment, and indeed under the same circumstances which called forth Frankism, another movement was born—a related and yet fundamentally different one. Completely different also were its fate and role in the history of Jewish culture. Its founder was born in the very region where Jacob Frank first saw the light of the world. He was called Israel Baal Shem Tov.

65. See our *History*, Vol. IV, pp. 56–59.
66. *Frank Ve-Adato*, 64.

CHAPTER TWO

Israel Baal Shem Tov

Rabbi Israel Baal Shem Tov—His childhood—His solitude—The orphan becomes an assistant to a teacher of small children—His love for melodies and songs—The assistant becomes an under-sexton in a small synagogue—His eagerness for Kabbalah—The under-sexton becomes familiar with the writings of the Kabbalist Rabbi Adam—His friendship with Rabbi Adam's son—The young Kabbalist is married and soon becomes a widower—Israel's years of wandering—His marriage to the sister of the rabbi of Brody, Rabbi Abraham Gershon of Kutow—The rabbi and the ignoramus—Israel's solitude in the Carpathian mountains—The crisis in the world outlook of the young Kabbalist—Israel's ways of earning a livelihood—The tavern-keeper and village teacher becomes a *baal shem*—The Baal Shem Tov's revelation—The Baal Shem Tov's world outlook—"There is no place void of Him"—The Baal Shem Tov's optimism—The influence of Naḥmanides and Rabbi Isaac Luria—The Baal Shem Tov's opposition to ascetism—The meaning of prayer; the idea that one can also pray "through common talk"—On sweet and bitter medicines—God can be served only with joy—The Baal Shem Tov and the scholars—The individual and the *tzaddik* in the Baal Shem Tov's system—The Baal Shem Tov's letter about "ascent of souls"—The Baal Shem Tov and his "fellowship"

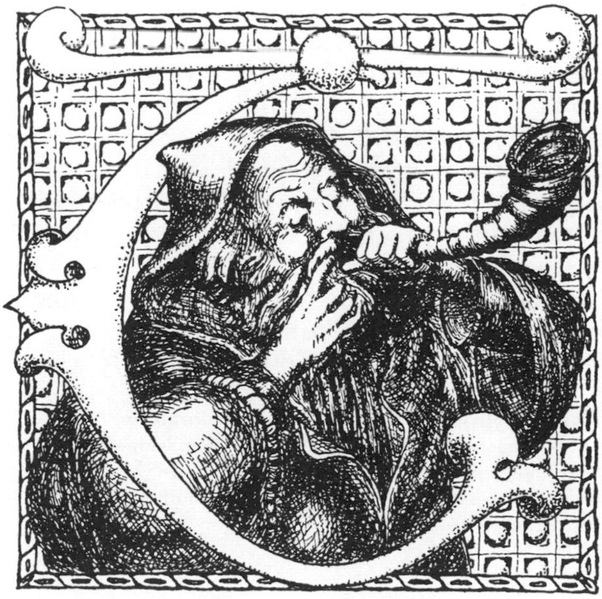

HE HISTORICAL form of the founder of Hasidism appears to us through a haze—a haze of marvelous tales with which popular legendry crowned the head of its beloved hero. A heavy veil, woven in the imagination of his contemporaries and of later generations, conceals from our eyes the true form of the Baal Shem Tov, so that at times it seems to us that he never existed as a living person, that his is only a fabricated name which was linked to the religious movement that shook the Jewish world." With these lines the historian Dubnow begins his history of Hasidism. On the threshold of a new era, in the second half of the eighteenth century, in the "generation of science and enlightenment," when sound common sense was declared the only reliable authority on man's entangled paths, the great miracle took place: a human life, the life of a simple Jew, was transformed into an imaginative legend, an *aggadah* of ancient times.[1] So enormous was the impression made on his milieu by this itinerant village teacher and exorcist. And through this fantastic, often naively superstitious specter clearly shines a real form, remarkably beautiful in its harmonious integrity and glorious simplicity.

Israel Baal Shem Tov was born around 1699 in the little Podolian town of Okup near the Turkish border. The breadwinner of his family apparently was not his father Eliezer but his mother Sarah, who was a midwife. The boy was therefore called "Israel, the midwife's child."[2] At a very early age young Israel lost his father. Before he expired, the dying Eliezer said to his only son: "My beloved child, remember as long as you live that God is ever with you, and therefore you must not be afraid of anything." Soon afterward his mother also died and the young orphan was handed over to strangers. The community council, or *kahal*, made provision for the orphan to study in the *ḥeder*, or elementary school, but the dark, old-fashioned *ḥeder* cast a pall on the dreaming boy with his rich imagination. "His way," relates *Shivḥei Ha-Besht*, "was to study for some days and then run away from the *ḥeder.*"

We noted that Jacob Frank was not a diligent student either. But Frank, in running away from the *ḥeder*, would gather around him a band of wild youths, to play "robbers" with them and terrorize the people with their wild forays.[3] When the orphan Israel ben Eliezer who had run away was sought, however, he would be found sitting alone in the forest. He was then

1. The biography of the Baal Shem Tov *(Shivḥei Ha-Besht)*, adorned with legends and fantastic details, was published in 1815 in Kapust by Dov Baer bar Samuel Shoḥat whose father-in-law Alexander Shoḥat was the Baal Shem Tov's scribe. In the same year *Shivḥei Ha-Besht* was published with extensive changes of text in another edition in Berdichev, and also in a re-working into Yiddish.

2. See *Shivḥei Ha-Besht*, 25.

3. *Frank Ve-Adato.*

brought back to the teacher, but in a little while would again flee to the forest to be alone. The forest, veiled in mystery, was apparently more congenial to the dreaming boy than the narrow, darkened *ḥeder* and the school studies with their overly subtle *pilpul.* The leaders of the community finally despaired of the orphan; it was obvious that he would not be a scholar, and so they left him alone.

Young Israel had to begin thinking of earning a living and soon became an assistant to a teacher of small children. He used to perform the tasks assigned to him with great alacrity—leading or carrying the little children on his back to school and to the house of study. "When he led the children," relates *Shivḥei Ha-Besht,* "he would sing with them in a sweet voice." The Baal Shem Tov's biographers note with special frequency his great love for song and music. He listened very fondly even to the songs the gentiles would sing in the taverns. His associates used to relate that, from the melody of each musical instrument, he would at once know the entire career of the player.[4]

Soon the young assistant was transformed into an under-sexton in a little synagogue. There also Israel ben Eliezer displayed his love for solitude. In the daytime, while the students sat in the synagogue and studied, the young under-sexton would sleep, and late at night, when all others were sleeping, he was awake and quietly—so that no one would know of it—carried on his "perfect work," praying or looking into his beloved books. His favorite volumes were *Ein Yaakov* and the *Zohar.* He was also extremely devoted to Rabbi Isaac Luria's Kabbalah. The works of Ḥayyim Vital, which set forth Luria's doctrine, were not yet printed at that time; they merely circulated in various copies.

Shivḥei Ha-Besht relates the most fantastic legends about how the young Israel ben Eliezer penetrated into the profound mysteries of Luria's "practical Kabbalah," but it is not difficult to extract from this mass of legends the kernel of truth. To the little town where the young Israel grew up, the son of a certain Kabbalist named Rabbi Adam came to live as the son-in-law of one of the residents. This young man brought with him whole packs of writings which he had inherited from his father. The young under-sexton became friends with him, and the two would seclude themselves in a room outside the town and immerse themselves in the mysteries of the theoretical and practical Kabbalah. They would also fast and engage in fre-

4. Abraham Kahana, *Rabbi Yisrael Baal Shem Tov,* 1900, p. 14.

quent ablutions in order to be worthy of occupying themselves with the experience of the Kabbalists and the wonder-workers.

When Israel reached the age of fifteen, the townspeople considered it their duty to marry off the orphan who so diligently occupied himself with Torah and prayer. Israel's wife, however, soon died. Within a short time he also lost his comrade, who was terribly emaciated from frequent fasting. The young widower then left his birthplace and set out for eastern Galicia. For a time he was a village teacher and had occasion to become familiar with the grievous situation of the villagers that is portrayed in such sombre colors by Solomon Maimon in his *Lebensgeschichte.* Later he settled as a teacher in a community not far from Brody.

The young teacher was very popular among the people by reason of his integrity, kindliness, tenderness, and sense of fairness. When a controversy arose between men of the community, he would frequently serve as mediator. In such an arbitration between two parties, Israel ben Eliezer once had occasion to meet Ephraim of Kutow, the father of the then well-known rabbi of Brody, Rabbi Abraham Gershon. The young teacher greatly pleased Ephraim. Learning that he was a widower, the old man proposed that he marry his daughter Hannah, who was a divorcee. The match was arranged and the articles of engagement were promptly drawn up. Ephraim, however, soon died and his son, the rabbi and scholar, to his amazement found among his father's papers written articles of engagement, from which he learned for the first time that his sister was engaged to a certain Israel ben Eliezer. Soon the prospective bridegroom presented himself. Legend relates that he appeared in rough clothes, "like one of the worthless fellows," in a short coat with a broad belt, and entered the room of the rabbi of Brody and spoke crudely and harshly, like a boor. He showed him the engagement document and demanded, "Give me my wife!"

There is no doubt that there is an element of truth in this legend, for in the later attitude of the Baal Shem Tov (before his "revelation") toward his brother-in-law the rabbi, a certain hidden irony toward the proud scholar and dialectician, with his contempt for the ignorant and common Jew, is discernible. Rabbi Gershon of Kutow was stricken with fear. He went at once to his sister to tell her the whole story and asked if she would consent to marry such an ignoramus. She replied that she was obliged to fulfill the will of their deceased father. The great rabbi, however, was not pleased at the prospect of having such a boorish brother-in-law near himself; immediately after the wedding, he proposed to his sister that she and her husband leave Brody, and he gave her a horse and wagon as indemnity. The couple settled near a town between Kutow and Kasov deep in the Carpathian mountains. As had the young Isaac Luria in his day on the banks of the Nile, so the Baal Shem Tov spent a long time in solitude amidst the high Carpathian mountains overgrown with thick forests. Twice a week his wife would come to him with her horse and wagon. He would dig lime in the mountains, fill up a wagon-load, and his mate would take the lime and sell it in the nearby town. So the couple managed barely to keep body and soul together.

During the first period of his isolation the Baal Shem Tov, legend relates, conducted himself like the Kabbalists and solitaries of the severely ascetic type. Solomon Maimon vividly portrays such ascetic Kabbalists in his *Lebensgeschichte.* He tells us of a certain Rabbi Simeon Lubitcher who devoted his whole life to purifying his soul through the most rigorous penitence. After *teshuvat ha-kanah* he proceeded to *teshuvat ha-mishkal,* i.e., to weighing each sin and afflicting his body to an extent corresponding to the weight of the transgression in question. But when he calculated his sins, he discovered that their number was too large for him to be able to make amends for them through *teshuvat ha-mishkal.* He thereupon decided to gain expiation for his sins in a simple way—to refrain from food until his soul expired. And so he did; some time later he was found dead near a village, lying with the *Zohar* in his hand.[5]

In the first period of his solitariness, the Baal Shem Tov would also engage in intermittent fasting and eat only a bit of bread between one fast and another. During the time the young Kabbalist spent in solitude amidst the Carpathian mountains with their majestic splendor, a definite change in his whole world-outlook apparently took place. The words of his dying father, "Remember as long as you live that God is ever with you, and therefore you must not be afraid of anything," which had made such an enormous impression on the sensitive child, now obtained for the Kabbalist in the lap of divinely beautiful nature a new meaning of much broader and deeper scope.

Surrounded by the mighty mountains with their peaks perpetually covered with snow and shimmering with a thousand colors in the dazzling rays of the sun, listening to the sounds

5. Maimon, *Lebensgeschichte,* p. 132.

of the forests and the whispering of the mountain streams and the springs modestly hidden in thick grasses and green growths, the ascetic of Podolia saw the unveiling of the profound mystery hidden in the words, "The whole earth is full of His glory" and "There is no place void of Him." There is a certain symbolic truth in the legend that in the Carpathian mountains the Baal Shem Tov learned to understand the language of the birds and plants.[6] Not through speculative thought but with his whole being, with the palpitation of his ardent, sensitive heart, he grasped that everything in the world is an incarnate revelation of God, everything bears the seal and reflection of God, who is pure kindness and graciousness. He perceived that God can be served not only with study of Torah, mortification of the flesh, and *teshuvat ha-mishkal*, that these are not the sole ways leading to God and knowledge of Him.

Thus the Baal Shem Tov spent several years isolated from people. Apparently his wife, and perhaps he himself also, became tired of living in such dire poverty, and so they returned to Brody. The brother-in-law, Rabbi Abraham Gershon of Kutow, in order to keep "the defective one" as far away from himself as possible, leased for him a tavern in a village not far from Kutow. As was the custom in those times, the tavern also served as an inn for travelers. The breadwinner was the Baal Shem Tov's wife Hannah; it was she who concerned herself with their livelihood, and he only helped her at times. In his free time the Baal Shem Tov would sit in a small isolated cabin on the bank of the river Prut and study the "mysteries of the Torah." This episode in his life is reported in two versions in *Shivḥei Ha-Besht*, one in the name of the Baal Shem Tov's secretary, Alexander Shoḥat, and the other in the name of Rabbi Shneur Zalman.

According to the first version, the Baal Shem Tov, while living in the village near Kutow, spent his days in fasting and would eat only once a week. Shneur Zalman's more credible version says nothing of the Baal Shem Tov's fasting but merely notes that he derived an adequate living from the tavern: "And God sent blessing and prosperity on the work of his hands, and they received travelers, giving them food and drink in great honor." Some time later, however, the tavern was leased away from the Baal Shem Tov, and he had once again to take up his erstwhile occupation—teaching. For a while he traveled

6. See the preface to the Berdichev edition of *Maggid Devarav Le-Yaakov; Seder Ha-Dorot Ha-Ḥadash*, 3.

through villages and taught Torah to the children of the villagers. He also opened a *ḥeder*, or elementary school, in the town of Tluste, but apparently he had a scant livelihood from teaching, and *Shivḥei Ha-Besht* relates that at that time he used to go around "dressed in a coat of cheap cloth and his toes would stick out through the holes of his shoes, for he was extremely poor." Gradually, however, the Baal Shem Tov obtained another source of income, in addition to teaching; he also became a *baal shem*.

In that era of barbaric superstition, when the whole atmosphere of the ghetto was filled to overflowing with all kinds of destroying spirits, evil ones, warlocks and *dybbukim*, the *baal shem* played an important role in Jewish life, especially in the life of village Jews. The latter would rarely apply for medical help to a doctor but go rather to an exorcisor and *baal shem*. The *baal shem* treated all diseases through various kinds of formulas, exorcisms, and amulets. He would manifest his power chiefly in driving out *dybbukim*, or removing "evil ones" and destroying spirits from Jewish homes.[7]

Israel Baal Shem Tov, when still quite young, had opportunity to become familiar with many formulas written down in the writings of the Kabbalist and miracle-worker Rabbi Adam. It is highly probable that in the years he spent in the Carpathian mountains he learned about the curative power of various grasses and herbs. During his period of teaching in the villages he would often treat sick villagers with all sorts of formulas, incantations, and amulets. A man with such a firm belief in God's graciousness and that God was always with him could certainly have a hypnotic effect on hysterical persons and those afflicted with nervous diseases. Thus the tavern-keeper and teacher was gradually "revealed" as a *baal shem* and miracle-worker, capable of driving out *dybbukim*.

Israel's reputation grew ever greater. He was invited to various cities and towns. Eventually he became so renowned that he no longer had to travel around; people came from all corners of the Ukraine to the town where he lived, first Tluste and later Medzhibozh, where he moved around 1740 and remained for the rest of his life.[8] If people could not come to him, they applied to him in letters. He was requested to give advice and was petitioned for amulets as healing agents. His clientele be-

7. See our *History*, Vol. VI, pp. 162ff.
8. The Baal Shem Tov died on Shavuot, 1760.

came so large that he had to employ a full-time scribe, and in his later years even two scribes.

To distinguish him from every other *baal shem*,[9] Israel was no longer called simply Baal Shem but Baal Shem Tov (the good *baal shem*), for now it was not merely those who were physically or mentally ill who came to him for help but also questing spirits who found no satisfaction in the old ways, in the old religious outlook. They did not seek remedies or miracles from him but the living source of knowledge of God, the right way of serving God. To him, the "common man" whom the scholar Rabbi Abraham Gershon considered it a slight to have in his presence, renowned scholars and rabbis traveled, becoming his ardent disciples. Rabbi Abraham Gershon himself also "repented" and at last acknowledged his brother-in-law's greatness.

By what were all these men so carried away? How did this common *baal shem* and writer of amulets become the legendary hero of *Shivḥei Ha-Besht*, the founder and teacher of a mighty popular movement?

Like Rabbi Isaac Luria in his day, the Baal Shem Tov did not write down his doctrine. Only one letter[10] of his, written to his brother-in-law Rabbi Abraham Gershon, has come down to us. This letter is quite important for the Baal Shem Tov's world-view, but it can serve in only very slight measure as material for a reconstruction of the system and doctrine of the founder of Hasidism. Of the Baal Shem Tov, the historian of the Hasidic movement, S. Dubnow, writes:

He possessed a peculiar capacity; he taught through conversations with individuals, through sayings and maxims, like the ancient

9. *Shivḥei Ha-Besht* relates that at first, when the Baal Shem Tov settled in Medzhibozh, he was not particularly respected by the local scholars and important people, such as Rabbi Ze'ev Kitzes and Rabbi David Furkes "because of the name by which he was called, for this name is not appropriate to a *tzaddik*" (p. 27). The same thing is also told of the Kabbalist Israel, the author of *Tiferet Yisrael*. Israel also at first reproached the Baal Shem Tov: "I would like you if you were not a *baal shem*" (*Maasiyyot U-Ma'amarim Yekarim*, 11–12). There also is a story about another scholar who came to the Baal Shem Tov with the complaint: "Why do they call you a *baal shem*, for this name is not proper for a great man?"

10. Printed at the end of Jacob Joseph's *Ben Porat Yosef*; see also the beginning of *Keter Shem Tov*. In modern times there has even appeared (Jerusalem, 1924) a collection of letters and documents, *Ginzei Nistarot*, in which the Baal Shem Tov's few letters are also published. However, the suspicion is very strong that these letters, like most of the letters in this collection, are fraudulent (see Dubnow's article in *Kiryat Sefer*, II, 290).

founders of religions. In his talks with others the holy spirit rested on him, and his thoughts would clothe themselves in the form of parables, brief proverbs, and interpretations of verses of the Torah. His listeners were enchanted by their originality, by the depth of their religious sentiment, and by the fundamental idea that unites all the sayings into one definite system.

Shivḥei Ha-Besht, as well as the opponent of Hasidism, the *maggid* David of Makow, relate that the Baal Shem Tov loved to go about the streets and marketplaces with cane in hand and pipe in mouth and tell anecdotes and parables to simple village Jews and women. His conversations and sayings were preserved in the memory of his disciples, and while he was still alive some of them attempted to write down his doctrine. Apparently, however, the hands that undertook this were incompetent. One of the Baal Shem Tov's admirers, *Shivḥei Ha-Besht* relates (page 286), wrote down the teaching that he used to hear from his master's mouth. Once the Baal Shem Tov saw that a demon was walking around with a book in his hand and he asked him: "What sort of book are you carrying?" He answered: "This is *your* book." The Baal Shem Tov at once realized that someone was writing down his doctrine. He then gathered all his associates and asked: "Which of you is writing down my Torah?" One of them confessed and brought his writings to the Baal Shem Tov. The latter read through them and said: "There is not here a single word that I have really spoken."

Only about twenty years after the Baal Shem Tov's death did one of his major disciples, the rabbi of Polonnoye, Jacob Joseph Ha-Kohen, publish three books in which he introduces into his long sermons on the Torah and on the Talmudic Aggadah hundreds of the Baal Shem Tov's brief sayings and parables which he himself heard from his master's mouth or in the name of the master from his colleagues.[11] These quotations are accompanied by the stereotyped formula, "I heard from my master" or "I heard in the name of my master." All these sayings and proverbs, as well as the Baal Shem Tov's sayings quoted in the two books *Maggid Devarav Le-Yaakov* (1784) and *Likkutei Amarim* (1792) which his disciples and the Maggid of Mezhirech

11. The author of *Toledot Yaakov Yosef* in places indicates that he does not report the whole teaching of his master. He writes, for example: "I received from my teacher orally, and it is impossible to explain in a book" (*Toledot,* "Parashat Naso"), or "The glory of the Lord is the hiding of a thing." Another time he notes, "I heard from my teacher and at the same time forgot" (*ibid.,* "Parashat Kedoshim").

published were soon collected in special editions: *Keter Shem Tov* by Aaron Ha-Kohen of Apt (Part One, 1784; Part Two, 1792) and *Tzava'at Ha-Rivash* (collected by Isaiah, the rabbi of Yanov, 1792). To all these collections the view that the renowned leader of *Ḥabad* Hasidism, Rabbi Shneur Zalman, expressed in regard to *Tzava'at Ha-Rivash* is generally more or less applicable: "In truth, this is not at all Rabbi Israel Baal Shem Tov's testament, but only a collection of his pure words that his disciples, one after the other, assembled. They did not know how properly to adapt the language, but their content is the real truth."[12]

On the basis of these collections, and of several other books composed by men close to the Baal Shem Tov and the Maggid of Mezhirech, such as *Degel Maḥaneh Efrayim* (the author of which was the Baal Shem Tov's grandson, Moses Ḥayyim Ephraim of Sudylkow), *Or Ha-Meir* by Rabbi Velvel of Zhitomir, *Yismaḥ Lev* by Rabbi Naḥum of Chernobyl, and *Kedushat Levi* by Rabbi Levi Yitzḥak of Berdichev, one can obtain a more or less accurate notion of the Baal Shem Tov's worldview and religious system. It is even highly probable that certain maxims and aphorisms were inscribed in the memory of his disciples verbatim in the master's style, e.g., the statement quoted in *Toledot Yaakov Yosef*:[13] "It is always said that truth wanders over the whole world; this means, it is chased from one place to another."

The Baal Shem Tov's entire system is based on the fundamental principle so clearly enunciated in the *Zohar*—the total merging of divinity with the cosmos, of the divine world with the human world, of the heavenly with the earthly. "Let man," the Baal Shem Tov teaches,

> know this principle: that in the hour of Torah and prayer there is no barrier whatever between a man and his God, even if at that moment various "strange thoughts" enter his mind, for these strange thoughts, too, are only garments and veils under which the Holy One Blessed Be He hides Himself. And as soon as a man realizes that divinity is concealed under them, they are no longer a concealment.[14]

Divinity, the founder of Hasidism declares, does indeed hide itself behind many barriers, but men of understanding know that all the barriers and iron walls, all the garments and concealments, are also of God's essence.

12. "Iggeret Ha-Kodesh," supplement to *Sefer Tanya*, folio 20b (we quote according to the Shklov edition, 1814).
13. *Ibid.*, "Parashat Bo."
14. *Ibid.*, "Parashat Bereshit."

In this connection Israel relates, as is his manner, a parable. There was once a king, a very wise man, who through optical illusion and deception set up great walls, towers, and gates, and issued a decree that whoever wishes may come to him through the gates. But, along with this, he commanded that at every gate treasures from his storehouses be placed. And so it came about that no one arrived at the king himself, for each person, as soon as he saw the treasures at the gates, filled his pockets with them and at once went home. But then the son of the king came and strained all his powers that he might reach his beloved father. And he realized that there was no barrier whatever separating him from his father, for everything is no more than illusion.[15] The explanation of the parable follows immediately: The Holy One Blessed Be He hides Himself with numerous garments and barriers, but everything is, after all, created out of His own essence, and no barrier separates man from God, and there is not a single place that is void of God or where He is not. The world is from God and in God. "Let man know that in every motion, the Lord of the universe is present, and where man is, there also is God."[16]

We have noted[17] that in the *Zohar* the sharpest antitheses—the infinite and the limited, the universal, hidden, incomprehensible "No" and the concrete "Yes"—are merged in dialectical fashion. The Baal Shem Tov goes even further and draws logical inferences. "The whole earth is full of his glory": even the place of sin and the pleasure felt at the moment of its commission derive from where the heavenly pleasure *(taanug ha-elyon)* is found. The *Shechinah*, Israel ben Eliezer further says, extends from across the highest heavens to the depth of the lowest levels, and in this lies the mystery of the words, "And Thou preservest (or: givest life to) all of them" (Nehemiah 9:6). Everywhere, throughout the space of the world, which *Kav Ha-Yashar* and *Shevet Musar* filled to overflowing with destroying demons, the Baal Shem Tov perceived only God's glory and splendor, His infinite grace and love. Even if a man commits a transgression, the *Shechinah* is incorporated therein, for without it a person cannot move his least limb. It is his life-spirit and alone gives him power and vitality.[18]

The *Shechinah* embraces in itself all worlds and creations: minerals, vegetables, animals, and humans, and all the creatures of the world, both good and evil. The true unity is the

15. *Keter Shem Tov*, 7 (we quote according to the Lemberg edition of 1858).
16. *Ibid.*: "And in a place where a man is, the glory of God Blessed be He is found."
17. See our *History*, Vol. III, pp. 48ff.
18. *Degel Mahaneh Efrayim*, "Tetze."

Shechinah alone. But how, then, can it include or bear in its unity such total opposites as good and evil? This contradiction is explicable very simply by the fact that men live in error. The opposites are, in fact, not absolute. Under the covering husk or *kelipah* of the evil are hidden the good and the pure. "The absolutely evil does not exist; evil is merely a footstool for the good." Only thanks to the evil does the good obtain its real substance, its proper value. Darkness and light also are not two separate worlds, for "the excess of light is drawn from the darkness." The one is associated with the other, as it is said in the scriptural verse: "And it was evening and it was morning, *one* day." From light and darkness came a total unity.[19]

"Everything in the world," the Baal Shem Tov concludes, "is completely good." He, the son of an orphaned generation, who grew up in the stifling atmosphere of decay, of social collapse and bloody persecutions and oppressions, remained an unshakeable optimist throughout his entire life. This unlettered dreamer and mystic of Podolia was convinced, no less than the *Aufklärer* of European culture, that "man is born for happiness."

It is by no means accidental that the Baal Shem Tov quite frequently mentions Naḥmanides in his conversations. We have seen[20] how, for Naḥmanides, the miraculous was the *most ordinary*. For him the whole world was one great miracle, a marvelous revelation of God's limitless power. Permeated with a firm belief in the Creator's compassion and in the infinite glory of His works, the medieval rabbi regarded in amazement, with the enchanted eyes of a simple child, the world about him in which everything is so wondrously beautiful, everything bears the stamp of God's grace and indescribable wisdom. The Baal Shem Tov looks at the world with similar eyes. "Woe to us," he exclaims; "the world is full of radiant glory and the most marvelous mysteries, and man's little hand is raised before the eyes and conceals all the brilliant lights!"[21]

With fine irony Israel tells a parable about a deaf man. A musician once stood on the street with his instrument and played a melody to himself. The playing was so sweet and melodious that men stopped, enchanted by the lovely music. Gradually they began to dance to its beat, and the move-

19. *Toledot*, "Bereshit"; *ibid.*, "Lech Lecha"; *ibid.*, "Mishpatim"; *Keter Shem Tov*, folio 4b; *ibid.*, II, 19.
20. See our *History*, Vol. III, p. 22.
21. *Likkutei Moharan*, Part One, No. 133.

ments of their bodies were adapted to its rhythm. The dance became ever stormier, and the enchantment of the people grew ever greater. Just then a deaf man passed by and gaped in astonishment. Here was someone standing and moving his hand, and all around him were people dancing like madmen with great enchantment. He could not understand what sort of rejoicing there was here. But if he had realized that men were dancing because of the sweetness of the music, he would have joined them in their dance.[22] And Israel ben Eliezer, the village teacher of Podolia, heard and marvelled at the wondrous melody resounding in the infinite space of the cosmos.

In his previously mentioned letter to Rabbi Abraham Gershon of Kutow, the Baal Shem Tov refers to his teacher but does not call him by name. His disciple Jacob Joseph, the author of *Toledot Yaakov Yosef,* however, reports that the Baal Shem Tov's teacher was the prophet Ahijah the Shilonite of King Solomon's times, who would come to him in his dreams to reveal profound mystical secrets. In the Baal Shem Tov's doctrine, however, we find the powerful influence not of the virtually unknown prophet of ancient Biblical days but of the mystic of sixteenth-century Safed, Rabbi Isaac Luria. Luria was the man with open ears who perceived in every sound and movement, in the start of a wave, in the trembling of a leaf, in the quiet whispering of reeds on the shore, even in the silent, rigid rocks—everywhere—the mighty breath of immortal life. Everywhere he felt living souls pleading for *tikkun* or "correction," begging to be freed from captivity, to be redeemed from the terrible sorcery and choking bands in which dead and formless matter holds them imprisoned.[23]

This was also the Baal Shem Tov's credo. Everything is the revelation of God. The links in the endless chain of phenomena are merely various colorful garments of the sole divinity. "In everything," Israel taught, "there are whole worlds of divine souls." God is in all that exists. With every object that man uses and enjoys, he "corrects" or "repairs" the divine "sparks" in that object, for without the spark of spirituality nothing could have any being. Man must have great love for everything he touches and uses, for in it holy sparks are hidden.[24] The Baal Shem Tov portrays in poetic fashion how every spark in a

22. *Degel Maḥaneh Efrayim,* "Parashat Yitro."
23. See our *History,* Vol. V, p. 64.
24. *Tzava'at Ha-Rivash,* 9.

plant or a mineral is like a creature locked up in a prison that cannot move hand or foot but lies twisted with its head between its knees. And whoever is in a position, with his good thought, to raise the spark of the mineral or plant to the level of *ḥai medabber*, a living thing that speaks, thereby brings the spark from slavery to freedom. No greater "redemption of captives" than this is conceivable.[25] The medieval *Perek Shirah*,[26] in which every creature chants its song of praise to the sole Creator, is full of profound significance for the Baal Shem Tov. Even the worm, he declares, serves the Creator with all its power and understanding.[27]

Nevertheless, there is a vast difference between the world of ideas of the founder of Hasidism and Rabbi Isaac Luria. One of the first historians of Hasidism, Mendel Bodek, the author of *Seder Ha-Dorot Ha-Ḥadash*, already noted: Our teacher, the Baal Shem Tov, followed Rabbi Isaac Luria in disclosing divinity in this low, earthly world, in each individual thing. What Rabbi Isaac Luria, may his memory be for blessing, revealed was in regard to the celestial worlds and the upper luminaries, and not every mind can grasp what transpires in the exalted heights. The Baal Shem Tov revealed divinity here on earth, especially in the lowliest person, in whom there is not a single limb or force that is not a garment for the divine power concealed in it. In earlier generations rabbis and great scholars occupied themselves with God's Torah, but the poor folk who were engrossed in the concerns of earning a living did not understand the Torah and derived no benefit from it. They walked in darkness because they could not study the Torah and penetrate into its chambers. Then the Master of the universe, in His vast grace, sent down to us an angel from heaven, the Baal Shem Tov of blessed memory, who illuminated the way of piety *(ḥasidut)* in the world, the way in which man should go even when he is deeply absorbed in his worries and concerns.[28]

But it is not only in this that the paths of Rabbi Isaac Luria and the Baal Shem Tov diverge. We have observed[29] that Luria's ear perccived in the sound of the Nile's waves a sorrowful epic concerning a fearful number of worlds that perish in the

25. *Keter Shem Tov*, pp. 22, 25.

26. Mendele Mocher Seforim reworked *Perek Shirah* into Yiddish (1875).

27. *Tzava'at Ha-Rivash*, 2.

28. Mendel Bodek, *Seder Ha-Dorot Ha-Ḥadash*, 3–4 (we quote following the Lemberg edition of 1865). See also *Divrei Tzaddikim*, 45 (Lublin edition, 1899).

29. See our *History*, Vol. V, pp. 63ff.

net of evil. Our world is also in deathly peril, for from all sides the magical powers of sin and evil stream toward it. The dangerous circle of sorcery must be broken at once; the captive spirit must be liberated from the material "husks" that imprison it on all sides. And Luria, the solitary ascetic on the banks of the Nile, felt that he must accomplish this; he must be the liberator. He must battle against the *sitra aḥara* (other side) with incantations and magical "names." Through mortification of the flesh and fasting, he must atone for the sins of the world, bring near the "end," the glorious day of the advent of the Messiah.

Quite different was the Baal Shem Tov. He wished to rend the web of leaden melancholy hanging over the Jewish quarter, to dispel the dark spirits of fear and dread that dominated the outlook of *Kav Ha-Yashar* and *Shevet Musar*. As guiding star and pointer of the way in the issue of *olam ha-zeh* (this world), the Baal Shem Tov took not Rabbi Isaac Luria but Naḥmanides. He did not wish to follow the path of ascetism or to regard the "sinful" *olam ha-zeh*, the present world, with contempt and scorn. For him, as for Naḥmanides, all revelations of the neighboring and near, the earthly, were precious and beloved, for in the earthly world also, in every palpitation and quiver of life, Israel ben Eliezer saw, as had the mystic of Gerona in his day, the hidden, unfathomable mystery of divine wisdom.[30]

Characteristic in this respect is the Baal Shem Tov's teaching on the role of prayer in human life. We have noted a number of times the enthusiasm with which the Jewish mystics emphasized the immense significance of prayer. Already in the *Zohar* the *sod ha-tefillah* (mystery of prayer) occupies an especially honored place. Every word of a prayer, in the view of the *Zohar*, lives a separate life, is replete with profound significance, purifies and raises the soul to the source of light and beauty. Israel ben Eliezer also perceives in prayer the deepest mystery. "Prayer is union with the *Shechinah*";[31] "Prayer, which is a limb of the *Shechinah*";[32] "Prayer, which is the *Shechinah*."[33] The goal of the prayer that pours out of the depths of the heart is to be united with the light of the *Ein Sof*, or Infinite. Man has no conception of the fact that, with his prayer, he brings an influence to bear on all the worlds, and

30. See our *History*, Vol. III, pp. 22ff.
31. *Tzava'at Ha-Rivash*, 5.
32. *Toledot Yaakov Yosef*, "Va-Yikra."
33. *Ibid.*, "Va-Yetze."

that even the angels are sustained by it.[34] He must realize that abundance streams constantly from the "divine source on high," for the essence of the divine source is to bestow its goodness and grace in full measure on all its creatures. The recipient, however, must be suited to receive the divine abundance. When a man prays he becomes the proper *tzinor* or channel for the divine source, and God's abundance streams, through him, upon him and upon the whole world.[35]

A man, the Baal Shem Tov admonishes, must not aim at any personal, material benefits in his prayer, for by introducing profane, physical requirements into spirituality he erects a barrier between himself and the *Shechinah.*[36] In this connection the founder of Hasidism tells a parable in the form of a commentary on the verse, "A prayer of the poor when he fainteth and poureth out his plaint before God" (Psalms 102:1). Once a king, on a day of great joy, issued a decree that every one of the inhabitants of his land might come to him with his wish and each person's desire would at once be fulfilled. One man requested power and glory, another wealth; the wish of each was granted. But there was a certain sage there who said that his only desire was that he might speak personally with the king three times a day. This greatly pleased the king—that the man regarded a personal interview with himself as more precious than wealth, power, and glory. So he commanded that his royal palace be opened to this man, and that he might speak with the king whenever he wished. And thereby all the royal treasures, all the riches of the world, were accessible to him.[37]

Prayer must be done with *kavvanah* (concentration and intention) and *devekut* (cleaving to God), with joy and with feeling.[38] One must take no account of whether those who witness prayer mock it.

When a man is drowning in a river, he makes all kinds of motions to wrest himself out of the waters that are flooding him, and those who observe this will certainly not laugh at him because of his motions. So also there is nothing to ridicule in a man who makes movements in praying, for he is saving himself from the stormy waters—which are the *kelipot* or "husks" and the alien thoughts that come to lead him away from his *kavvanah* at the hour of prayer (*Likkutei Amarim*, 14b).

34. *Keter Shem Tov*, 16.
35. *Ibid.*, 24.
36. *Tzava'at Ha-Rivash*, 4.
37. *Toledot Yaakov Yosef*, "Parashat Vayiggash."
38. *Tzava'at Ha-Rivash*, 15.

Shivhei Ha-Besht relates that the founder of Hasidism once entered into such ecstasy in praying that the grain-filled kegs that stood in the room began to dance with him.

The Baal Shem Tov, however, also tells of another kind of prayer. At times, he declares, a man prays before God and makes no motion whatever, and an outsider looking on might think that this person is utterly without *devekut*, or cleaving to God; nevertheless, this is the supreme level. Here the man's very soul is praying! This is an inward prayer that draws with the greatest love to God the Creator; it is the supreme level of cleaving to God, without any semblance of corporeality.[39] As in wood that is burning, the Baal Shem Tov elsewhere explains, only the flame rises to the heavens but the heavy parts remain in the form of ashes, cold and gray, so also in the hour of prayer only the fervor and *devekut* of a man rise but his words are poured out like ashes.

Yet Israel ben Eliezer a number of times insists that prayer is not the only path to man's union with his Creator. One can unite with God in various ways with the aid of the word. "There are unifications in the word of Torah and prayer, but also in the words that a man speaks with another in the marketplace." One can unite with God even through the simplest acts. "At times one prays even by speaking corporeal words with his friends."[40] Not only through "holy speech" but also through "common speech," through plain, everyday words that one exchanges with his comrade in the street, can he raise himself to the exalted divine levels.[41] Everything that you are able to do, the Baal Shem Tov teaches, you must fulfill, but you must purify the material, corporeal acts through thought and unite them with the Creator.[42] For, he goes on to say, man is a ladder that stands with its lowest rungs on the earth and is appointed "to do earthly, corporeal things," but its top reaches to the heavens. The head, through the power of thought, can elevate simple physical things to the high heavens.[43]

We have seen[44] how strictly "the soul of the Mishnah" admonished her beloved son Rabbi Joseph Karo not to interrupt his study of Torah even for a moment, since whole worlds are thereby destroyed. The Baal Shem Tov sets forth a completely different thesis. A man, after all, has very frequent occasion to

39. *Ibid.*, 8–9; *Keter Shem Tov*, 26.
40. *Toledot*, 29.
41. *Keter Shem Tov*, II, 23.
42. *Toledot*, "Parashat Vayyere"; *ibid.*, "Va-Yeshev"; *ibid.*, "Be-Har."
43. *Ibid.*, "Parashat Va-Yetze."
44. See our *History*, Vol. V, p. 35.

speak with other men and thereby ceases studying, or he finds himself on a journey and cannot study Torah or pray. Let him have no anxiety about this, for "God desires that man serve Him in all ways"—sometimes in one way and sometimes in another,[45] sometimes through studying and sometimes through common things, "even through eating and drinking and other corporeal matters." Man must only remember, and through his acting and thinking unite everything that exists in the world with God's name, for there is nothing in the world that is outside Him and outside His unity. In short, man must always bear in mind the "mystery of God's unity," that "He and they together are one," and that every "corporeal deed" that he does must be united through the power of thought with "the Holy One and his *Shechinah.*"

In this connection the Baal Shem Tov tells a parable of a prince whose father sent him away to a distant village so that the son might later yearn greatly to return to the king's palace. The son, however, became ignorant and crude in the village environment. He imitated the peasants around him both in dress and conduct and completely forgot the splendor of the royal palace. Sometime later the king dispatched his officers to bring the son back to him, but the son refused to return. The king repeatedly sent officers, one greater than the other, to fetch the son, but none of these could prevail upon the prince to leave the village and return to the palace. However, there was one clever officer who took off his rich garments and put on poor village clothing. He came to the prince and spoke to him in crude, peasant language, and he was pleasing to the prince who saw in him his like. Thus, descending to a common level, the officer managed to bring the prince back to the royal palace.[46]

The Baal Shem Tov decisively rejected the way of asceticism. There are, he says, two kinds of doctors. Some heal with bitter medicines, but others—and these are the better ones—heal with medicines that are "sweeter than honey."[47] The founder of the Hasidic movement himself believed that one ought to cure with sweet medicines. "Mortifications of the flesh induce sorrow," he declares. "There is no need to mortify oneself." It is the evil inclination that incites a man to be sad.[48] Through fasting, mortification, and constant study, a man falls

45. *Tzava'at Ha-Rivash*, 1; *Likkutei Yekarim*, 15a.
46. *Toledot*, "Parashat Emor."
47. *Toledot*, supplement at the end.
48. *Likkutei Yekarim*, folio 1b.

into sadness and judges harshly all other men who do not act as he does and "forget the life of eternity." This is healing through bitter medicine. "The principal thing is to remove sadness and cling to joy," he frequently reiterates. "When the body is weakened, the soul is also weakened; hence, a man should take great care of the health of his body."[49]

The founder of Hasidism constantly reminds his disciples that eating and drinking are also a service of God, and that "bodily pleasure" can be raised to the level of "divine pleasure."[50] The fact that matter (the human body) is satisfied through eating and drinking also gives man the possibility of enjoying spiritual bliss. Thus the material or "husk" becomes a footstool for the holy, and the physical is raised to the level of the spiritual. "Everything is good, and there is no distinction between matter and spirit."[51] If, says Israel, a man fasts from one Sabbath to the next, but even the thought that he is doing a great thing by fasting crosses his mind, he immediately falls into the *sitra aḥara* (other side).[52]

In the time of the Baal Shem Tov, a legend relates, there was a man who practiced mortification and was always running to the *mikveh* (ritual bath) so that he might obtain the level of the holy spirit. Israel said of him, "In the other world they laugh at this man."[53] The Talmudic statement, "Many have acted like Rabbi Simeon ben Yoḥai and did not succeed" is thus explained: Because they desired to obtain the level of Rabbi Simeon ben Yoḥai through mortification and fasting, they did not succeed in doing so. But Rabbi Simeon ben Yoḥai also, the Baal Shem Tov notes, upon coming forth with his son from the cave where the two of them had been hidden for so many years and seeing that men "forsake eternal life and concern themselves with the ephemeral life of the present," was extremely angry and cursed the world, for he believed that it can be cured only with "bitter medicine," i.e., that God can be served only with Torah, prayer, fasting, weeping, and the like. Thereupon a *bat kol* (voice from heaven) called out: "You wish to destroy the world; return to your cave!" So Rabbi Simeon and his son remained there for another twelve months, and only then did they learn the right way—that one must heal with "sweet

49. *Keter Shem Tov*, 26; *Tzava'at Ha-Rivash*, 9; *Likkutei Yekarim*, 16: "When his body is sick, his soul is also weak."

50. *Keter Shem Tov*, II, 6; *Toledot*, "Parashat Va'era."

51. *Toledot*, "Parashat Bo."

52. *Keter Shem Tov*, 25.

53. *Or Ha-Meir*, "Parashat Vayyere."

medicines," that is, the way of compassion which teaches that God can be served "through all human acts and deeds."[54]

It is written: "Hearing a woman's voice is indecency." But when the voice of a woman helps "to drive away sadness," it is raised from its low level. In the letter sent by the Baal Shem Tov to his disciple, the rabbi of Polonnoye, Rabbi Jacob Joseph Ha-Kohen, which has been preserved, he declares that he read with strong indignation his disciple's statement that he must carry on a regimen of fasting. He implores Jacob Joseph not to bring himself into such danger, for this is "a work of melancholy and sadness" and the *Shechinah* rests not in sadness but only in the joy of the *mitzvah*, or divine commandment.[55] Israel was once asked: "What is the essence of service?" To this he replied: "I have come to show another way, to let man know that he must take upon himself three things—love of God, love of Israel, and love of Torah—and there is no need of mortifications."[56]

It happens quite frequently, Israel ben Eliezer teaches, that precisely such ordinary things as eating and drinking or business discussions, which lead one to neglect of Torah, refresh the soul so strongly that it thereby becomes suited to attain the supreme level of *devekut*, or cleaving to God.[57] Let man therefore not fall in his own estimation "if he chance to incur some neglect of the Torah." *Shivḥei Ha-Besht* relates that when Israel was once shown an amulet that a pious Kabbalist had written "while he was still engaged in ablutions and fasting," he smilingly remarked: "I will write such an amulet immediately after eating, sitting on my bed."[58]

The Baal Shem Tov had the courage to declare to his generation, which was raised in the oppressive, melancholy atmosphere of *Kav Ha-Yashar* and *Naḥalat Tzevi*, that when sadness overcomes a man "he should consider himself in the category of the wicked," and that he must rather eat and drink and enjoy himself.[59] As is his manner, Israel tells a parable of a prince who lived among ignorant villagers. When the prince received a loving letter from his father the king, he was beside himself with joy but was ashamed to display his great happiness to those about him. So he assembled the villagers and treated

54. *Toledot*, "Parashat Va-Yetze"; *ibid.*, supplement at the end.
55. Horodetzky, *Ha-Ḥasidut Veha-Ḥasidim*, I, 38.
56. *Ibid.*
57. *Keter Shem Tov*, 5.
58. *Shivḥei Ha-Besht*, 31.
59. *Keter Shem Tov*, II, 2.

them to wine. Thus, they rejoiced in their way, and he, the son of the king, rejoiced "in the joy of his father."[60]

The founder of Hasidism was a man who practiced what he preached. He used to cheer his associates with wine, and they would dance happily around their master. *Shivḥei Ha-Besht* tells of one such joyous dance in his home. Once on Simḥat Torah the Baal Shem Tov's choice comrades became extremely merry and danced and drank much wine from his cellar. His wife realized that the Hasidim would not leave any wine for *kiddush* and *havdalah*, and so she went to her husband and requested that they stop drinking and dancing; otherwise, he would be without wine for *kiddush* and *havdalah*. The Baal Shem Tov said smilingly: "You are right; tell them to stop and go home." She opened the door of the room where the Hasidim were dancing in a circle, and the dance was so enthusiastic that she actually saw a ring of fire drawn around them. At once she herself took vessels, went to the cellar, and brought them as much wine as they wished. Afterwards the Baal Shem Tov asked her: "Did you tell them to go home?" "You should have told them yourself," the righteous woman replied.[61]

When someone, Israel notes, tells another simple stories but thereby dispels his sadness, this is the greatest union with God,[62] for God can be served only with joy. "Let a man always be joyous." "Let him remove himself from sadness and let his heart rejoice in the Lord." "A man should always be in joy and believe with perfect faith that the *Shechinah* is with him."[63] The Baal Shem Tov does not tire of repeating this idea, and he several times quotes the Midrash about the two common jesters for whom the *olam ha-ba* (world-to-come) is prepared, because "they drove away man's sadness through their cheerful words" and thereby raised him to *devekut*.[64] The way of asceticism, the founder of Hasidism believes, is a dangerous way which very frequently removes a man from true service of the Creator. It is the evil inclination that incites a man thereto and casts upon him the fear that he has not fulfilled his religious obligations; thereby he falls into sadness (*Likkutei Yekarim*, 1). And sadness is a great hindrance to service of the Creator.

Even if a man has committed a transgression, "let him not

60. *Ibid.*, II, 25.
61. *Shivḥei Ha-Besht*, 13.
62. *Keter Shem Tov*, 11.
63. *Tzava'at Ha-Rivash*, 12.
64. *Keter Shem Tov*, 5; *Toledot*, "Parashat Va-Yetze."

increase sadness." Since he regrets it with his whole heart, "he will return to rejoice in the Creator."[65] Be not overly pious or too strict in observance, the Baal Shem Tov repeatedly admonishes. If a man fulfills only one commandment but does so with *kavvanah* and great love and cleaving to God, it is as if he fulfilled all the commandments of the Torah.[66] *Shivḥei Ha-Besht* relates numerous tales of the Baal Shem Tov's leniency in ritual questions—how, for instance, when a slaughterer killed an animal and declared it ritually unfit, the master, who had himself once engaged in ritual slaughtering, quietly requested that a piece of the meat be cut off and broiled for him.[67]

Trust, not fear—the founder of Hasidism teaches—should be the guide of man. "Where there is fear there can be no joy."[68] It is the palpitation of joy that leads to genuine reverence for God. One who lives with trust and firmly believes in the grace of God abides in the *sefirah* called *Ḥesed* (Lovingkindness). But a person who is always fearful of God's punishment thereby unites with the *sefirah* of strict judgment, and this itself may bring him—God forbid—to evil.[69] Hence the Baal Shem Tov strongly deplores the preachers who, like the author of *Kav Ha-Yashar*, terrify the people with anxiety-engendering punishments.

Once, relates *Shivḥei Ha-Besht*, when Israel spent the Sabbath in Nemirov, a preacher in the synagogue there vehemently berated the people and ranted that Jews do not fulfill all the commandments and precepts properly. This greatly angered the Baal Shem Tov, who declared that the preacher was "a slanderer of Israel." This was told the preacher who, the next day, came to the Baal Shem Tov, introduced himself, and asked why he was angry with him. The Baal Shem Tov at once sprang from his seat, tears in his eyes, and said:

> You speak evil of Jews. Know that when a simple Jew goes about all day in the marketplace and at twilight suddenly remembers and says, "Woe is me, I may have passed the time for reciting the afternoon prayer," and rushes into a house, quickly recites the prayer, and does not even know what he is saying, all the seraphim and angels in the heavenly household tremble at this prayer.[70]

65. *Tzava'at Ha-Rivash*, 4.
66. *Toledot*, "Parashat Yitro"; *Keter Shem Tov*, 13.
67. *Shivḥei Ha-Besht*, 26; see also *ibid.*, 31, the story about *tzitzit*, or fringes on the corners of one's garment.
68. *Toledot*, "Parashat Be-Ḥukkotai."
69. *Keter Shem Tov*, 26.
70. *Ibid.*, 29.

The founder of Hasidism, however, was indignant not only at the harsh preachers but also at the students and scholars, and he battled against them with the keenest of weapons—sarcasm, arrows sharply pointed with fine humor. "The evil inclination," he says smilingly, "comes to a scholar disguised in the form of the good inclination which ostensibly wishes to fulfill a commandment."[71] The evil inclination, he further asserts,[72] does not attempt to persuade a man not to study Torah, because it knows that the man will not listen to him, for if he does not study he will gain no esteem among those around him; he will not be considered a scholar. What, then, does the evil inclination do? It convinces the man that he should not study such works as might lead him to reverence for God—for instance, a book of *musar*, or the *Shulḥan Aruch*, so that he might be clear about a law; instead, it induces him to occupy himself constantly only with the *Gemara* and the commentaries. Once, his associates relate, the Baal Shem Tov looked at a certain scholar sitting in deep thought and studying, and he said of him: See, this man is so engrossed in his Torah that he has even forgotten whether there is a God in the world.[73]

We have referred to the covert irony with which Israel regarded his brother-in-law, the great scholar and rabbi, Abraham Gershon of Kutow, before his "revelation." Rabbi Gershon, greatly angered by his brother-in-law's manner of putting on his phylacteries, once asked him: Whence did you take this law? The latter calmly answered: I saw it in the "Sifrei Taytz," i.e., in the Judeo-German, or Yiddish, books.[74] It suffices to recall how the majority of scholars and rabbis in earlier generations regarded these "Sifrei Taytz" when it was a matter of interpreting or deciding laws[75] to understand the caustic irony of the Baal Shem Tov's reply.

With bitter sarcasm the founder of Hasidism speaks of the scholars for whom the chief thing is arid learning, the keenness of *pilpul*, without the moral substance and the drive for truth that exalt and purify the soul. To him the congealed form, the mechanical fulfillment of the commandment without fervent sentiment, was utterly repugnant. He, the simple writer of amulets, has nothing but contempt for those who "in truth

71. *Toledot*, "Parashat Ki Tissa."
72. *Tzava'at Ha-Rivash.*
73. Abraham Kahana, *Rabbi Yisrael Baal Shem Tov*, 95.
74. *Shivḥei Ha-Besht*, 5.
75. See our *History*, Vol. VII, pp. 216ff.

study only the precept learned of men that they might seem wise," that they might be considered scholars and accorded great honor. It is to these that the Biblical phrase "wise in their own eyes" refers.[76] The true Torah is only that which leads a man to union with Him who is hidden in it. Without *kavvanah* and *devekut,* without devotion and cleaving, says the Baal Shem Tov, neither study nor prayer has any value; they are blasphemy.

There are, Israel declares, two kinds of persons. The first is completely wicked; he knows that there is a God but deliberately decides to rebel against Him. The second, however, has his eyes blinded by the evil inclination; he is, in his own estimation, totally righteous, and is also so regarded by his fellows. In truth, however, even though he studies constantly, prays, and mortifies his body, it is all in vain. It has no actuality or substance, for there is in it no cleaving to the Creator. This man lacks the perfect faith constantly to unite his thought with God and does not know in what real service consists—how one ought to study Torah, pray, and fulfill a commandment for the sake of God. And the difference between these two is this: in the case of the wicked man, it is still possible that he may find the right path, when the feeling of penitence awakens in him and he returns to God with his whole heart; but for the second, there is no "correction," because his eyes are closed to the Creator's greatness and he considers himself righteous. How, then, can he possibly repent?[77]

On the other hand, the Baal Shem Tov regarded with a certain respect those who sought God but stumbled and became entangled in false paths. Of Shabbetai Tzevi he said that there was a "holy spark" in him, and when the Frankists, who were harshly persecuted by the rabbis, issued denunciations and slanders and brought it about that the Talmud was burned at Kamenetz-Podolsk, he poured out his wrath not on the sectarians but on the rabbis. "It is those who devise lies and falsehoods," he argued, "that have brought things to this pass."[78] When the Frankists finally had no other way out than to convert to Catholicism, the Baal Shem Tov said: "The *Shechinah* mourns and declares that as long as the limb is connected to the body, there is still hope that it may be healed. But if one cuts off the limb, it is lost forever. And every member

76. *Keter Shem Tov,* 27.

77. *Tzava'at Ha-Rivash,* 15; *Likkutei Yekarim,* folio 16a.

78. *Shivḥei Ha-Besht,* 9.

of the people of Israel is still a limb of the *Shechinah.*"[79]

Typical is the story related in various sources[80] that the founder of Hasidism once came to a community where a session of the *Vaad Arba Ha-Aratzot* (Council of Four Lands) was taking place. At this session the question was raised how the Baal Shem Tov, who is not a scholar and yet is considered a miracle-worker by many persons who assert that the holy spirit rests upon him, is to be regarded. Israel was summoned, and when he arrived, the *parnass* or president of the Council, Rabbi Abraham Abba, addressed him with the following words: "By the manner of your conduct, it appears that the holy spirit rests upon you, but others say that you are an ignoramus. Let us, then, hear from your own mouth whether you know anything about Jewish law." And because it was Rosh Ḥodesh (the first day of the new month) just then, the Baal Shem Tov was asked what one should do if he forgets, in praying on Rosh Ḥodesh, to recite the prayer "Yaaleh Ve-Yavo"—a question about which there are mountains of *pilpul* and subtle theories in the rabbinic literature. The Baal Shem Tov answered the *parnass* with great simplicity: "Neither you nor I need this law, for you will forget again (because for the scholar the chief thing is the *pilpul* regarding the law, and the prayer itself is recited in a purely mechanical way, with divided attention), and I will not in any case forget."

Elsewhere the Baal Shem Tov relates a story about a simple stocking-maker who used to stand all day at the hard work from which he derived a living. He would slip quickly into the synagogue; if there was a *minyan*, or quorum, there, he prayed with the congregation; if not, he prayed at home. Even of the Psalms he recited only those he knew by heart. Yet when the Baal Shem Tov saw him, he trembled, for he realized through

79. *Ibid.*, 10. Some scholars, e.g., Heinrich Graetz in his *Frank und die Frankisten*, David Kahana in his *Toledot Ha-Mekubbalim*, Abraham Kahana in his *Rabbi Yisrael Baal Shem Tov*, and others, report as a firmly established fact that the Baal Shem Tov also participated in the disputation at Lemberg with the Frankists, along with the representatives of the rabbis led by the rabbi of Lemberg, Rabbi Ḥayyim Rapoport. More recent investigations, however, have established that this is nothing more than a legend. In the memoirs of Dov Ber Birkenthal of Bolechow, who himself had a part in the disputation, the Baal Shem Tov's name is not mentioned at all. Especially important is Meir Balaban's thorough study *Studien zur Geschichte der frankistischen Bewegung* (published in the collection in memory of S. Poznanski, 1927), in which it is demonstrated that the Baal Shem Tov's participation in the disputation is not mentioned in any of the Polish sources that describe the debate between the rabbis and the Frankists.

80. *Shivḥei Ha-Besht*, 35; Israel Loebl, *Sefer Vikkuaḥ*, 9 (1789).

the holy spirit that by the merit of this common man "who derived his living from the labor of his hands in purity" the whole community was sustained.[81] Israel himself, a legend relates, was given to understand that the fact that he was privileged to ascend to high levels and that "exalted matters" were revealed to him was not because he had studied many tractates of the Talmud and numerous rabbinic codes, but because of his praying with great *kavvanah.*[82]

Shivḥei Ha-Besht recounts that a rabbinic scholar once stopped for the night at the inn which the future founder of Hasidism was then keeping.[83] During the night the rabbi suddenly awoke and saw a fire burning under the oven. He thought the wood placed there to dry had caught fire and immediately sprang up from his bed to extinguish the flames. When he approached the oven, he saw Israel sitting there and around him shone a light full of radiance and splendor. The rabbi fell into a faint and had to be revived. In the morning he asked the Baal Shem Tov, who at that time had not yet "revealed" himself, what this meant. The latter replied, "I was only reciting Psalms; perhaps I was united with God at that moment."

Did the Baal Shem Tov himself—not merely his disciples—believe that the holy spirit rested upon him and that he could perform miracles because his will was regarded in the supernal worlds? Here we touch upon the most interesting as well as the crucial point in his outlook.

The battlers for Haskalah, or enlightenment, greatly oversimplified the question of the nature of the founder of the Hasidic movement. They concluded that here was an ignorant swindler who wished to mislead the common people. The arid scholars, the Mitnagdim, represented the Baal Shem Tov as a plain ignoramus, and in the heat of religious disputation even declared him a "drunken and mad prophet."[84] A modern historian of culture, no matter what his philosophy may be, realizes quite well how naive and crude such a characterization of the Baal Shem Tov's personality is. We emphasize the word "personality," because the Baal Shem Tov was, above all, an important, profound personality who considered the phenomena of the universe from the standpoint of a world-consciousness, a personality who felt himself co-responsible

81. *Shivḥei Ha-Besht*, 18.
82. *Keter Shem Tov*, 23; *Tzava'at Ha-Rivash*, 3.
83. *Shivḥei Ha-Besht*, 8.
84. See Dubnow, *Geshikhte Fun Khassidism*, I, 101.

for the fate of the whole world and had the unshakeable faith that, on the basis of this responsibility, he could give "correction" *(tikkun)* to the most tragic problems of the world.

The Baal Shem Tov's philosophy is, of course, a purely idealistic one. Instead of the proclamation of the Gospel, "In the beginning was the word," he set forth the basic thesis: "In the beginning was the thought, the idea." "The beginning of everything is thought."[85] "The thought is called the father of the word, and the word is the son." "The thought is wisdom, and the word is its offspring."[86] The thought, says the Baal Shem Tov, is called "Nothing" *(Ayin)*[87] because it is without limit, like Nothing. But when it is embodied in the word, it is limited and called 'I' *(Ani)*—the same substance, the same letters [in Hebrew *Ayin* and *Ani* contain the same letters], but of an altogether different scope and compass.[88] Only man has need of the word. "The word is the vitality, the life-spirit of man."[89] "Language, or speech, is the pen of the heart."[90] But there, on high, Israel declares, is the world of thought, the world of pure ideas, where "there is no speech and there are no words."[91]

When a man finds himself in *devekut* with the *Shechinah* and gives thought to the upper worlds, then he is at once *in* the upper worlds. *For whatever a man thinks of, there he is,* and if he were not in the upper world, he would not think of it.[92] Everything that is thought exists, because—everything that exists is thought. It is not superfluous in this connection to note that the *Zohar* already expressed quite clearly the thought which later occupied such a prominent and honored place in German Idealist philosophy—the idea of the complete identity of thinking and being, of the ideal and the real.[93] It must be noted particularly that in the Baal Shem Tov's mystical philosophy a central role is played not only by *devekut* (cleaving, burning ecstasy), but also by *thought,* the exalted idea.

It is characteristic that the Baal Shem Tov, who teaches that

85. *Keter Shem Tov,* 24.
86. *Likkutei Yekarim,* folio 4a.
87. On the significance of *Ayin,* see our *History,* Vol. III, pp. 13ff., 43ff.
88. *Toledot,* "Parashat Vayyeshev."
89. *Tzava'at Ha-Rivash,* 8.
90. *Keter Shem Tov,* II, 6.
91. *Ibid.,* "Parashat Tzav."
92. *Tzeva'at Ha-Rivash,* 67 (1793); *Toledot,* "Parashat Ḥayyei Sarah"; *Likkutei Yekarim,* 1: "When a man thinks in the upper world, he is in the upper worlds. For anywhere that a man thinks, there he is, and if he were not in that world, he would not think of it at all."
93. See our *History,* Vol. III, p. 46.

the essence of life is faith and trust,[94] deems it necessary to note that there are two levels of faith or belief. One person believes in God because he has received his faith through the tradition of the fathers, and another has come to his faith through the way of personal quest. The difference between them consists in the fact that the first has the advantage that he cannot be shaken or dissuaded from his faith, even if one should attempt to refute it through argumentation, because his faith is strong through the tradition of the fathers. But he has the disadvantage that his faith is "only a commandment of men, learned without reason or sense." On the other hand, the second person has the advantage that he has arrived at his faith in God the Creator through great searching; hence, his faith is strong and suffused with total love. But he has the disadvantage that he can be dissuaded as soon as one adduces, through speculation, arguments that contradict his faith. Hence, the supreme degree of faith belongs to him who has both qualities—the person who bases himself on the tradition of the fathers and has also become persuaded, through his own quest, that his faith is right and good. For this reason, the Baal Shem Tov adds, we say: "Our God and God of our fathers"—"Our God," whom we have searched out through our own investigation, and the "God of our fathers," whom we have received through tradition from our ancestors.[95]

To make clear how the founder of Hasidism regarded himself, one must first consider the immense role of the human personality in his system. We know that, in the view of the *Zohar*, man is divinity incarnate, the revelation of the absolute in limited, concrete forms, and that without the active will of the human personality, God's blessing cannot prevail.[96] This thought is also the cornerstone of the Baal Shem Tov's system. We have noted that he perceives divinity in relation to the world and nature not as transcendent but as immanent, i.e., not *beyond* or *over* the world but *within* the world itself. God is never outside the universe, separated from it by barriers and distances, for "in everything there are whole worlds of divine souls." These divine souls, however, are in captivity, imprisoned as separate sparks in the rigid, congealed *kelipah* or

94. If one wishes to punish someone, says the Baal Shem Tov, he takes away that person's trust and confidence: "And when they wish to exact punishment from one who is worthy of being punished, then they take away from him the level of trust" (*Toledot*, "Parashat Mishpatim").

95. *Keter Shem Tov*, 23.

96. See our *History*, Vol. III, p. 48.

"husk" of matter,[97] and the liberation of these captive sparks is effected by man. A spring, a stone, a plant, every creature in nature, every condition and event in the world, is redeemed through man's eye and ear, is transferred from non-being into being and becoming through man's consciousness and thought.

Man is therefore a partner in *maaseh bereshit*, the endless process of creating and becoming. The world is influenced not only by the will of the divine but also by the will and striving of man, who is the reflection of God on earth and is created in the image of God, just as it is written in the Psalms: "And Thou hast made him but little lower than the angels [literally, "than God"]." The Baal Shem Tov, who grew up in an environment in which Jews suffered disabilities and enslavement, cruel persecutions and bloody slanders, had an unshakeable belief in man's divine rights. "Man is the chief dwelling place of God," he declares.[98] It is written, "Know what is above you;" the meaning of this, he explains, is: Know that all that is above you, all that is on high, is *of* you. Between divinity and man, he affirms, there is a constant mutual influence and interaction. "Man looks at the Creator, and the Creator looks at him."[99] "The Lord is Thy shade;" this Biblical statement, Israel teaches, means that just as a man's shadow does everything he does, so also the Creator of the universe does, as it were, everything that a man does.[100] "When an ordinary mortal raises himself with his thoughts to the upper worlds, the angels tremble and gape in astonishment."[101]

Given such a standpoint, the conclusion is very logical that man can come so close to God that he feels himself like a partner in the work of creation, involved in everything that is constantly being brought into existence. Man is also able, through the highest and deepest in himself, to recognize divinity itself, to grasp the nature of the supreme power that he feels in himself, to marvel at the infinite light in its glory and splendor—the light of which he himself is a spark. The Baal Shem Tov was firmly persuaded that man is suited at certain moments of spiritual ecstasy to weave himself into the divine eternity. Because God is the all-embracing, the all-inclu-

97. See above, pp. 40–41.
98. *Keter Shem Tov*, II, 28.
99. *Tzava'at Ha-Rivash*, 12.
100. This is several times quoted in *Kedushat Levi;* "Parashat Be-Shallaḥ" (twice), "Derush Le-Furim," "Parashat Metzora," "Parashat Naso."
101. *Keter Shem Tov*, II, 28.

sive, it is impossible that He be *outside* man, that He be an entity which cannot be recognized and experienced by man. There must be a sympathy from below to above and vice versa, a reciprocal interaction of man and God.

Not without reason does Israel ben Eliezer frequently introduce the parable which teaches that man is like a ladder whose lowest rungs are on the earth and whose top reaches to the heavens. The top, the pride and crown of mankind, is the *tzaddik*, the saint or perfectly righteous man. We know what an honored place the *tzaddik* holds in the philosophy of the *Zohar.*[102] *Tzaddik yesod olam*, "the *tzaddik* is the foundation of the world," and his level cannot be attained even by the angels. The Kabbalist Meir Ibn Gabbai also asserts that "the *tzaddik* rules over all creatures."[103] The Baal Shem Tov, too, believes that "the *tzaddikim* are the emissaries or agents of the Matronita (or *Shechinah*)."[104] The *tzaddik*, he says, is like a tree planted in fertile soil. Just as the tree takes up all the nourishing elements of the earth and produces the loveliest fruits, so the *tzaddik* acts in this world; he collects all the "sparks" scattered in the world and raises them to the Creator.[105]

It is written, *tzaddik be-emunato yiḥyeh*, "the righteous shall live by his faith,"[106] for faith is *devekut*, union with God.[107] With their powerful faith, the *tzaddikim* transform God's attribute of Judgment into the attribute of Mercy,[108] sweeten judgment "with the root of mercy and lovingkindness."[109] The Baal Shem Tov explains this notion through the Talmudic legend about Naḥum Ish Gimzo who saw only good in every event and believed that everything was for the best. Naḥum, he declares, was firm in his faith and trust that God's will is only for good, that it cannot be imagined otherwise. For God's will leads everything to its ordained purpose—to the world as it ought to be. And because Naḥum was completely permeated with this belief, "so indeed it was;" everything turned out, in fact, for the good. In this, the Baal Shem Tov explains, he saw

102. See our *History*, Vol. III, 50.
103. *Ibid.*, Vol. V, p. 48.
104. *Toledot*, "Parashat Vayyiggash;" *Keter Shem Tov*, 7.
105. *Keter Shem Tov*, 2, 4.
106. In another place the Baal Shem Tov paraphrases this statement as follows: " 'The righteous shall live by his faith'—this means the righteous gives life to everyone with his firm belief."
107. *Toledot*, "Parashat Va-Yishlaḥ."
108. *Ibid.*, "Parashat Noaḥ."
109. *Ibid.*

no miracle; because he based himself so firmly on his faith and trust, it was so.[110]

There are, Israel declares, two degrees or levels of men. One conducts his affairs according to the order that governs nature, i.e., the powers of nature that are in the category of *Elohim*, which, in *gematria*, is equivalent to *ha-teva* (nature).[111] But there are also men of a higher degree. Through their cleaving to God, these rise above the "husks" of matter and conduct themselves according to an order that transcends nature, according to the divine laws of *Adonai*,[112] the Creator and Ruler of the world—laws which nullify the *gezerot Elohim*, the strict rules of nature. There, in the higher levels, the "sparks" are liberated through the power of thought from the "husks" that rule matter, and the "attribute of Justice" is raised to the "attribute of Mercy."[113] On the wings of exalted thought, through union with God, man first grasps that that in which he, with his shortsighted eyes, perceived only strict judgment, is in truth the attribute of Mercy, the grace of the divine wisdom.

However, it should not surprise men, the Baal Shem Tov notes, that even the *tzaddik* sometimes finds himself at rather low levels. This happens for two reasons. First, even the *tzaddik* cannot exert his spiritual powers strongly enough to remain always at exalted levels. At times, therefore, he allows himself to go down for a while to refresh his powers, in order afterwards to rise with new force to the divine heights. But there is also another reason. For the *tzaddik* to be able completely to fulfill his mission of lifting men from the lower levels to the higher, he must himself go down below, there unite with the sparks held captive in matter, liberate them, and raise them to the upper worlds. Associated with this, explains the Baal Shem Tov, is also the mystery that the sacred Torah at times employs the garment of stories from common, weekday life.

Here an important point to which the investigators of Hasidism have unfortunately given scant attention to the present time must be noted. The Baal Shem Tov, indeed, states that every individual "must unite with the *tzaddik* of the generation," but in this connection he deems it necessary to stress that it is not only the common multitude that requires the *tzaddik*

110. *Ibid.*, "Parashat Va-Yeḥi."

111. The letters of *Elohim* and *ha-teva* amount to the same number—86.

112. The Baal Shem Tov, however, stresses that even the Ineffable Name exists only for men, but in truth God Blessed be He "is higher than all names" (see *Or Ha-Meir*, "Parashat Shofetim").

113. *Toledot*, "Parashat Mishpatim."

but also the *tzaddik* who requires men of lower degree. These complement each other, and "one becomes the garment and footstool for the other."[114]

We have observed that Israel explains in dialectical fashion that even evil is the "footstool," the foundation, of good, for the concept of good first obtains its real substance and content through its antithesis—evil. The *tzaddik* and the multitude, he repeatedly declares, are like body and soul, like male and female; one must work upon the other.[115] The multitude and the *tzaddik* are like the six days of creation and the Sabbath day. The profane workdays are intimately associated with the Sabbath, for the Sabbath first obtains its real value when it bases itself on the days of the week, and the weekdays are hallowed and draw sustenance from the holy Sabbath day. "One cannot do without the other."[116]

It is written, "A perpetual fire shall burn upon the altar;" this means, explains the Baal Shem Tov, that the common man must work with his "sparks" so that the fire on the altar, which the *tzaddikim* of the generation maintain, be not extinguished.[117] The level of the *tzaddik* is dependent on the level of his generation; as is the generation, so are its *tzaddikim*. In a beaten down body the soul is also beaten down.[118] Hence, the common people must struggle together with the *tzaddik* and not depend on him solely. "Do not rely on the *tzaddik* alone" —this admonition is frequently repeated by the Baal Shem Tov. Man must always remember the principle, "If I am not for myself, who will be for me?" If he himself does not strive with his own powers to lift himself from the narrow boundaries of the ego to the universal spaces of the *Ayin* (Nothing),[119] no one will be able to help him.[120]

On the Days of Awe, Israel notes, the people do not rely on the *ḥazzan*, or precentor, alone, but each person individually prays to God.[121] And he tells a parable to illustrate the point.

114. *Ibid.*

115. *Toledot*, "Parashat Shemot": "The multitudes of the people are called the body, but faithful, pious Jews are the soul; they are to influence each other, like male and female."

116. *Toledot*, "Parashat Va-Yakhel."

117. *Ibid.*, "Parashat Va'era."

118. *Ibid.*, "Parashat Kedoshim."

119. See above, p. 53.

120. *Toledot*, "Parashat Kedoshim": "If I am not for myself—that is to say, if I am not myself perfected first to transform myself from the materialistic to the idealistic—that the ego or I should change and become nothing, then who will be for me? . . . Who of others would be for me, would approach me and my level, since I did not repair things first for myself?"

121. *Keter Shem Tov*, p. 5.

A country once had occasion to carry on a difficult war. In this land there was a great hero on whom the people relied entirely in its struggle. The hero was well equipped with various weapons and carried on the battle courageously. The enemy, however, was shrewd and quietly stole the hero's weapons. Then the hero no longer had wherewith to fight, and the people of the country who had depended wholly on him were taken captive along with him.[122]

It is obvious that the Baal Shem Tov perceived himself as the "mighty hero," the *tzaddik* of the generation. In certain moments of ecstasy he felt himself organically intertwined with God, experienced in himself the personality whose profundity and exaltedness works on, and influences, the eternal being and ceaseless becoming of the cosmos. In the world-view of this mystic the boundaries between waking and dreaming, between reality and thought, were erased, for in the real his exalted eye saw only the ideal and the desired, and in lifeless, rigid matter only languishing sparks that yearn for the heights and await liberation. Extremely interesting in this respect is the letter that he wrote from Medzhibozh to his brother-in-law, Rabbi Abraham Gershon of Kutow in Jerusalem[123]—a letter in which he reports in all details two of his *aliyyot neshamah* (ascents of the soul). The first took place on Rosh Ha-Shanah in 1746, and the second three years later, on Rosh Ha-Shanah, 1749.

On Rosh Ha-Shanah of the year 1746 I pronounced the incantation for *aliyyat neshamah,* as you know, and in my vision I saw marvelous things such as I have not seen since I reached my mental maturity. And what I saw and learned when I rose thither is not to be related and not even to be described orally. When I returned to the "Lower Paradise" *(Gan Eden Ha-Taḥton),* I saw souls of living and dead persons, some of which were known to me and some unknown. Without number, these souls wandered from one world to the other with great, marvelous, and indescribable joy. And many wicked persons also repented and were forgiven for their sins . . . All of them together pleaded with me insistently and said: "God has bestowed upon you great understanding, that you might grasp and know about these matters, and so you will rise with us and support and help us." And because of the bliss that I saw among them, I decided to rise with them. And in my vision I saw how the Satan Samael rose to accuse

122. *Toledot,* "Parashat Kedoshim"; *ibid.,* "Parashat Emor."

123. This letter was supposed to have been transmitted to the Baal Shem Tov's brother-in-law by his disciple Jacob Joseph Ha-Kohen, who was planning to travel to Jerusalem. The journey, however, did not take place, and the letter remained with Jacob Joseph who, many years later, published it at the end of *Ben Porat Yosef.*

with great joy, the like of which has never been. And he obtained verdicts of destruction for numerous souls that were to be slain with bizarre deaths. Then a deathly terror seized me, and I literally offered up my life and begged my teacher and master[124] to go with me, because it is fearfully dangerous to rise to the upper worlds, for since I came to consciousness I had never had occasion to rise to such heights. And I rose from one level to another until I entered the hall of the Messiah, where the Messiah studies Torah with all the Tannaim and the *tzaddikim*, and also with the Seven Shepherds.[125] And there I saw a great, immeasurable bliss but did not know what it signified. I thought it was perhaps about my departure from the world, but I was given to understand that I was not yet to die, because there above they take pleasure in my effecting unifications below with the aid of their sacred Torah . . . I then asked the Messiah, "When will the lord come?," and he answered: "Know that when your teaching will be known and revealed throughout the whole world . . . and others will also be able to make unifications and ascents like yourself, then all the *kelipot* will be destroyed and the hour of acceptance and help will arrive." And I marvelled at this and was grieved that the time is yet so long, for when can this happen? But because while I was there I learned three kinds of formulas *(segullot)* and three holy "names" . . . I was consoled and thought to myself: Perhaps thereby my contemporaries will also be able to come to this level and state, like myself. They also will become suited for ascents of the soul such as mine. But I was not given permission, as long as I live, to reveal this.

Further on the Baal Shem Tov tells of the second ascent of the soul which occurred in 1749. At that time the Haidamack movement in the Ukraine was strengthened, and many Jewish communities were destroyed. The Baal Shem Tov writes of this in his letter.

On Rosh Ha-Shanah 1749 I had an ascent of the soul, as is known, and saw a great arraignment, such that the Satan Samael was virtually given permission to destroy whole lands and communities. And I offered up my soul and prayed: "Let us fall into the hand of God, but let us not fall into the hand of man!" And permission was given that, instead of this, there should be great sicknesses whose like had never been in all the land of Poland or in any of the other lands that are close to us. And so, indeed, it was; sickness spread immeasurably. And I decided with my fellowship to recite *Ketoret* quite early in order to nullify the decree. Then it was revealed to me from heaven:

124. An allusion to Ahijah Ha-Shiloni (see above, p. 39).
125. Meaning the patriarchs Abraham, Isaac, and Jacob, then Moses and Aaron, Joseph the righteous, and King David.

"You yourself have chosen to fall by God's hand. What, then, do you wish to nullify?" . . . Since then I have not recited *Ketoret* and not prayed for this. Only on Hoshanna Rabbah did I go to the synagogue with all the people and say *Ketoret* once, so that the pestilence might not spread in our region.—And so, with God's help, we were successful . . .

It is said that after the great poet Dante Alighieri completed the first part of his *Divine Comedy,* the Italian women would point him out with their fingers and say with great reverence: "There is the man who descended into the deepest abysses of hell and came back to us." With no lesser respect did the "fellowship" of Medzhibozh look upon the Baal Shem Tov who made such "ascents of the soul," sat at the same table with the Patriarchs and Seven Shepherds, and spoke directly with the Messiah son of David. And the impression the Baal Shem Tov made with his teaching on his disciples, the students and rabbis, became even greater by reason of the fact that they saw before themselves a simple *baal shem*—not a brilliant scholar, not a clever swimmer over the sea of the Talmud. This was a true revelation, an extraordinary transvaluation of values.

Filled with enchantment, they set out over the world to tell of the great miracle, to reveal their master's teaching.

CHAPTER THREE

The Disciples of the Baal Shem Tov

The Baal Shem Tov's disciples—His successor Rabbi Dov Baer, the Maggid of Mezhirech—From Medzhibozh to Mezhirech—The sources of the Maggid's teachings—*Likkutim Yekarim*, *Likkutei Amarim*, *Or Torah*, and *Or Ha-Meir*—Pantheistic conceptions in the philosophy of the founders of the Hasidic movement—The doctrine of *tzimtzum* (contraction or withdrawal) and the purpose of *maaseh bereshit* (the work of creation)—Love and *tzimtzum* as a "complete unity"—The mission of the people of Israel—The *tzaddik* in the role of the High Priest on Yom Kippur—The *tzaddik* and the *adam be-fo'al* (realized man)—Theoretical tzaddikism—The first battle against the Hasidim; the social foundations of this struggle—The excommunication-booklet, *Zemir Aritzim Ve-Ḥorvot Tzurim*—Jacob Joseph Ha-Kohen, the founder of Hasidic literature; his battle against the rabbis—The significance of his *Toledot Yaakov Yosef*.

IT IS related of the Baal Shem Tov that he once addressed God with this prayer: "Master of the Universe, it is known and revealed before You how filled to overflowing my heart is, and there is no one to whom I can reveal all this." "That I sometimes speak words of Torah to others," he declared on another occasion, "is only from the superfluities that rise above the edges, as a vessel filled with liquid above the spout pours out a certain part of the overflow." Like every innovator or founder of new systems and philosophies, the Baal Shem Tov experienced loneliness and believed that he lacked the proper successor to whom he might entrust everything he felt and thought.

Each of the Baal Shem Tov's well-known disciples, notes the

historian of Hasidism, Mendel Bodek, received from him "according to the root of his holy soul,"[1] i.e., according to the level of the disciple's own spirit, but not the master's entire teaching. Israel's own son, Tzevi Hirsch, had a very slight understanding of his father's significance. Typical is the story related by *Shivḥei Ha-Besht* that on the day of the Baal Shem Tov's death, all his disciples stood at his bed-side and his son, Herschele, was not there; he was asleep. When he was awakened and brought to his father's bed-side and the latter began to speak words of Torah to him, the son said: "I do not understand what you are saying."[2] Mendel Bodek, who is not chary of the greatest praise for each of the Baal Shem Tov's disciples, when mentioning the master's only son, must content himself with the remark that the latter throughout his life "walked humbly with God, conducted himself like a simple man, and his righteousness was not known to anyone."[3] The Baal Shem Tov's successor, his spiritual heir and the leader of the movement founded by him, was the Maggid of Mezhirech, the preacher Rabbi Dov Baer, who became his associate and follower only in the last years of his life.

Very few precise details of the Maggid's life are known. From all the legends produced in Hasidic circles about him and his encounter with the founder of Hasidism, it can only be determined that before Dov Baer met the Baal Shem Tov he followed the same path as all the rabbis and scholars of that era. Born in Lukacz, a little town in Volhynia,[4] he studied both the "hidden" and the "revealed" Torah day and night, and when still quite young, as related in *Keter Shem Tov* (II, p. 30), was renowned as a great dialectician and scholar in the Talmud and rabbinic codes, as well as in the wisdom of the Kabbalah. An ardent devotee of Rabbi Isaac Luria's Kabbalah, he followed the way of asceticism and would frequently fast from Sabbath to Sabbath. As town preacher (in the Volhynian towns of Mezhirech, Dubno, Korets and Rovno), he would often, in his sermons, summon his listeners to mortification of the flesh, penitence and *tikkun* (correction).

Characteristic of his outlook at that time is the following story related in his name by his disciple, Rabbi Wolf of Zhito-

1. *Seder Ha-Dorot Ha-Ḥadash*, folio 10b.
2. *Shivḥei Ha-Besht*, 41.
3. *Seder Ha-Dorot Ha-Ḥadash*, folio 7b.
4. The year of his birth is variously given in several sources—by Dubnow c. 1710; by Horodetzky, 1704.

mir. In his youth, when the Maggid was a *melamed* or teacher in a village, he once sat in a corner of a room. A certain Polish landowner entered with a hussy—a beautiful woman with breasts in extreme décolletage, as the manner of such women is. Unconsciously the Maggid glanced at the beautiful woman with bared breasts, and immediately a great sorrow rose in his heart. He then began to revile the evil in his heart in the following way: The inception of her creation derives from her father's and mother's seed. Thence come her beauty, her whiteness and rosiness. And whence came their seed? From their ugly and disgusting foods, such as snakes, crayfish, and the like. It is from this that the seed and, consequently, her empty beauty and charm derive. And he pondered the disgusting circumstances so long that he began to vomit in their presence. The landowner thereupon ordered him thrown out.[5]

It is interesting that the Maggid himself, when in his later years he became the recognized leader of the Hasidim, quotes in one of his sermons[6] the Baal Shem Tov's teaching that is in such sharp contrast to his own erstwhile views:

> When a man sees a beautiful woman, let him think whence this beauty comes to her. If she were dead, she would not have this lovely face. This being so, it derives from the divine power that inheres in her. It is this power that gives her face its beauty and color; hence, it follows that the root of beauty is divine power. And so, why should I be attracted to, and yearn for, only a part? Better to unite with the root of all worlds, which is the primal source of beauty.

Of the meeting of the Maggid with the Baal Shem Tov, various legends, from which it is not difficult to derive the kernel of truth, are related in *Shivḥei Ha-Besht*[7] and in *Keter Shem Tov.*[8] From his constant fasting, the Maggid's body became so weakened that he could no longer walk without the assistance of another and had to lie in bed. Some of his friends then advised him to seek a cure from the Baal Shem Tov who, at that time, was already renowned throughout the entire region for his formulas and remedies. In the beginning Israel regarded the Maggid, as he did many other clever scholars, with a certain irony, conducted himself like a "common man," and told

5. *Or Ha-Meir*, beginning of "Parashat Ḥayyei Sarah" (we quote following the Warsaw edition of 1883).
6. *Or Torah*, 76 (we quote following the Lublin edition of 1883).
7. *Or Torah*, 13.
8. *Ibid.*, II, 30.

simple stories and popular proverbs. But the Kabbalah of Rabbi Isaac Luria was the common ground on which these two men could approach each other. The Baal Shem Tov believed it extremely desirable to win this profound Kabbalist to his fellowship, to bring him to the awareness that he had been wandering lost all his life, to show him that "his learning was without soul."[9]

The Baal Shem Tov not only cured the Maggid's body and diseased legs; he also effected a total revolution in his philosophy and liberated his soul from leaden melancholy, from the fear of sin. He managed to persuade the ascetic preacher that God need not be served with fasting and mortification of the flesh but precisely through joy and cheerfulness. Rabbi Dov Baer, relates *Keter Shem Tov,* then sent home the servant who had accompanied him on his journey to the Baal Shem Tov and himself remained "and studied great and profound wisdoms with him." Thanks to his strong character and organizing abilities, he became, after the death of the Baal Shem Tov, the leader of the new movement and contributed much to its spread and rapid growth. The center of Hasidic teaching passed, after the founder's death, from Medzhibozh to Mezhirech, from Podolia to Volhynia.

Like the Baal Shem Tov, so the Maggid published no writings in his lifetime. A skillful preacher, Dov Baer presented his teaching to his listeners in the form of sermons "from month to month and Sabbath to Sabbath."[10] A vivid portrait of how the Maggid used to give his homilies on the Sabbath at table and how ingeniously he thereby interpreted various verses of the Bible is given to us in his *Lebensgeschichte* (Chapter 19) by Solomon Maimon who, in his youth, made a pilgrimage to Mezhirech to learn about the newly risen Hasidic movement. Dov Baer himself did not write his sermons, but he was very desirous that they not be lost and that his disciples write them down and transmit them to future generations. Of this, his disciple Solomon of Lutsk speaks at length in the preface to *Likkutei Amarim.*

He relates that many of the Maggid's disciples would write down his sermons, but they often abbreviated them and also very frequently did not transmit the substance of the profound words correctly but interpreted them according to their own understanding. He himself did not undertake to write down

9. *Ibid.*
10. See the title-page of *Likkutei Amarim.*

the master's holy words, for he was apprehensive that he also would not transmit them with proper accuracy. Once the Maggid asked him why he was not writing down his sermons. When Solomon explained his reasons for not venturing to do this, the Maggid replied: Nevertheless, it would be well that they be written down somehow, "so that they might be a reminder for the service of the Creator Blessed be He." When the disciple asked him why he desired this so much, the Maggid replied, basing himself on a Biblical verse: "Is, then, what King David asked (Psalm 61:5) a little thing in your sight: 'I will dwell in Thy tents forever *(olamim)?*' That is to say, I wish to dwell in Thy tents in both worlds" [the word *olamim*, commonly translated "forever," may also mean "worlds"].

Nevertheless, Solomon of Lutsk did not fulfill his master's wish for many years after the latter's death. Only after Jacob Joseph Ha-Kohen, in his works *Toledot Yaakov Yosef* and *Ben Porat Yosef*, published the Baal Shem Tov's letters and many of his statements did Solomon also decide to familiarize the broader world with his own master's spiritual legacy. From all the manuscripts known to him in which the Maggid's sermons were written down, he chose the best, the one which the venerable Rabbi Ze'ev Wolf of Grodno in Lithuania had written, introduced certain corrections into it, and published it in Korets in 1784 under the double title *Likkutei Amarim* and *Maggid Devarav Le-Yaakov.*[11] The work was quite successful and from 1784 to 1792 went through three editions. Solomon of Lutsk himself, however, notes in the introduction that this collection of the Maggid's sermons is "only a drop of the sea of his great wisdom." It is therefore not surprising that, aside from the printed *Maggid Devarav Le-Yaakov*, numerous manuscripts and copies of Dov Baer's teaching circulated among the Hasidim.

In 1792 Samuel ben Jehudah Leib Segal Bodek of Lemberg published a collection, *Likkutim Yekarim,*[12] in which he quotes numerous sayings of the Maggid of Mezhirech and refers frequently to circulating "documents" and "holy writings" in which many "marvelous secrets" of the Maggid are noted.[13] Once he even concludes with the remark, "And I will not here give of the interpretations that are to be found in the writings

11. The closing letters of the three words *Maggid Devarav Le-Yaakov* indicate the Maggid's name, Dov.

12. The name of the collector is not indicated on the title-page, but on the second page in the three rabbinic *haskamot*. Dubnow's suggestion that *Likkutim Yekarim* appeared anonymously is hence not altogether correct.

13. *Likkutim Yekarim*, folio 25b (end); *ibid.*, 27a; *ibid.*, 28b.

of the righteous teacher Dov Baer, may his memory be for a blessing for the life of the world to come, because they are very profound and exalted and each word requires a large commentary."[14]

In 1804 a new collection of the Maggid's sermons and sayings, *Or Torah*, which Dov Baer's disciple, Isaiah of Dunovitz, wrote down in his day, appeared in Korets. This rendering is more extensive than that of Solomon of Lutsk and is distinguished from *Likkutei Amarim* not only by its style but also by its completely different order. While in Solomon's edition the sermons are printed without any system whatever, in *Or Torah* they are organized according to the order of the verses of the Bible and the statements of the Talmud, Midrashim, and *Zohar*.

Several of the Maggid's disciples in their own works quoted a great many sayings of their master that are missing from both the collections just mentioned. Especially important in this respect is *Or Ha-Meir* by Rabbi Wolf of Zhitomir. The sources just listed provide more or less adequate material for a knowledge of the personality and world outlook of the Baal Shem Tov's spiritual heir, the second leader of the nascent Hasidic movement.

First of all, the following characteristic detail must be noted. The Baal Shem Tov's disciple, Jacob Joseph Ha-Kohen, whenever he quotes the words of his master, always says: "I heard from my teacher" or "I heard in the name of my teacher." It is different in the case of the Maggid Dov Baer. Neither in *Likkutei Amarim* or in *Or Torah* is the Baal Shem Tov given the title *mori*, "my teacher." On the few occasions that the Maggid mentions the Baal Shem Tov, he does so only with the phrase, "Rabbi Israel Baal Shem Tov, may his memory be for a blessing, said" or "Rabbi Israel Baal Shem Tov." However, a great many of Israel's sayings, and indeed of the most important of them, are quoted in the Maggid's sermons—but not in the name of their author and without any mention of him.

This is by no means accidental. These men were too different in their character, their sentiments, and even in their philosophy. Only in his middle years did Rabbi Dov Baer, the scholarly ascetic, turn to the way which the wandering village teacher and exorciser, Israel ben Eliezer, with his marvelous sensitivity to the people, had intuitively laid down. The Baal Shem Tov managed, through the great moral force of his personality, to turn the melancholy scholar away from the path of

14. *Ibid.*, folio 24b.

asceticism, but the Maggid grasped the richness of the Baal Shem Tov's philosophy only with his mind and not with his heart, with his keen thinking but not with ardent feeling.

The Maggid's doctrine is founded on the basic idea that is the focus of the Baal Shem Tov's entire philosophy, namely, that the world is not only God's creation but also bears divinity in itself: "It is from Him and in Him" and "There is no place void of Him."[15] Dov Baer does not tire of repeating in his sermons that God "fills all worlds and is in all worlds."[16] The Holy One Blessed Be He bears in Himself all worlds, is over and under all worlds, fills all worlds, and is the place of all worlds.[17] The understanding man, teaches the Maggid, knows that "the whole world is filled with God;" and how greatly to be deplored is the person who takes literally the statement of the Bible and believes that "God has established His throne in the heavens," and the whole world lies empty, void, and dead before His eyes.[18]

Dov Baer interprets in extremely ingenious fashion the well-known words of the philosophical pessimist of the Bible, Koheleth, "For God is in heaven and thou art on earth; therefore, let they words be few" (Ecclesiastes 5:2): He who does not understand that God fills all worlds, permeates all worlds, surrounds all worlds, and that there is no place void of Him, but believes that God is above, in the heavens, and he, man, is on the earth—such a man may not speak much, for what can he accomplish with his words, what can his words repair or correct?[19] Even in corporeal matters—the Maggid repeats the Baal Shem Tov's saying—God is hidden, and this is the meaning of the phrase, "the whole earth is full of His glory."[20]

Here it is necessary, however, to note one important point. Some scholars especially stress the pantheistic conceptions in the philosophy of the founders of the Hasidic movement. But one must take account of the fact that in the Baal Shem Tov and in the Maggid of Mezhirech these ideas are closely associated with concepts that are distinguished in the most decisive way from the pantheistic philosophy. From the point of view of pantheism, there can be no talk of any distinction or barrier between God and nature, between matter and spirit.

15. See above, pp. 36ff.
16. *Or Torah*, 121.
17. *Ibid.*, 44.
18. *Likkutim Yekarim*, 23.
19. *Or Torah*, 106.
20. *Ibid.*, 104.

This absolute identity, however, is not the *cause* of the universe; it is in fact the universe itself, the God-universe-unity, the universal, absolute *du partzufin* (dual face, or configuration).

Such a notion is totally inconsistent with the philosophy of the founders of Hasidism. To be sure, they were also firmly persuaded that the world is permeated with God, that it is "of Him and in Him" and that "there is no place void of Him." But God is *beyond* the world, and the world is His creation. Hence, God existed before the world. Indeed, the Maggid of Mezhirech several times repeats the idea that "God decided to create the worlds."[21] He speaks also of the "primordial will to create the worlds"[22] and says that "all the worlds came into being through will."[23] This means that the creation of the world is a *free* act on the part of the deity. "Obviously," declares the Maggid, "the world cannot be considered praise or glory for God, for He is the Infinite, and all the worlds, in comparison with Him, can have no value whatever."[24]

Vast also is the difference between the exponents of pantheistic philosophy and the founders of Hasidism in regard to the question of the role and significance of matter. In Spinoza, for example, extension and thought, i.e., matter and spirit, are the two co-equal divine attributes that man can understand. If in the Baal Shem Tov a phrase such as "there is no difference between matter and form"[25] may still be found, in Dov Baer of Mezhirech matter is a thing of slight value. To be sure, the Maggid notes that "God is arrayed even in all corporealities." In every material thing there are also divine "sparks," and man is called to liberate these sparks from the *kelipah* or husk, from the material. The material, Dov Baer insists, is "dross," and the form, the beauty, "is the spirituality and life of this vessel."[26] It is, after all, well known, he explains, that matter is the lowest of all levels, but because there is no place that is outside of God, it is, *nevertheless*, divine.[27]

Closely linked with this is the doctrine of *tzimtzum* (contraction or withdrawal) which occupies an extremely important position in the Maggid's philosophy. However, we must note

21. *Likkutei Amarim*, folio 23b; *ibid.*, 39a.
22. *Likkutei Amarim*, 29.
23. *Or Torah*, 97.
24. *Likkutei Amarim*, 24 (we quote following the Lemberg edition of 1862).
25. *Toledot*, "Parashat Bo."
26. *Or Torah*, 76.
27. *Likkutei Amarim*, 43.

one very significant detail that is not sufficiently elucidated in the collections that provide us with the opportunity to obtain some knowledge of his doctrine. We have indicated that, in the Maggid's view, the creation of the world is a free act of will on the part of the divine omnipotence. In both collections, however, we find two very pregnant sayings. The first is, "The Holy One Blessed Be He is called rest *(menuḥah)*, for movement has no relationship to Him." Movement is attributable only to a thing "within the boundaries of time and place," but God is the Infinite "and He does not move from place to place" and is not within the limitations of time. Even more typical is the second saying of Dov Baer: "In regard to the *Ein Sof*, or Infinite, it is not proper to speak of will."[28] This statement perhaps justifies the conjecture that the Maggid, like Menaḥem da Fano and Jonathan Eybeschütz,[29] also took the position that it is not the "First Cause" but the "God of Israel," the prototype of the ten *sefirot*, who is the Creator of the world. Perhaps this is one of the "wondrous mysteries" in the Maggid's doctrine of which the author of *Likkutei Yekarim* speaks, and the compilers who wrote down the Maggid's sermons considered it improper to reveal this mystery and therefore quoted their master's saying without commentary.

On the other hand, the mystery of *tzimtzum* is discussed at length.[30] "God contracted or withdrew Himself and created the worlds."[31] "In this world everything is complete *tzimtzum*," declares the Maggid.[32] Were it not for *tzimtzum*, he notes, the worlds could not exist, because they could not endure the overwhelming divine light.[33] Everything that exists in the world was created through *tzimtzum*.[34]

In the previous chapter we indicated that the Baal Shem Tov perceived in the concept of *Elohim* the powers of nature. For his part, the Maggid declares, *Hineh ha-tzimtzum nikra Elohim*, "Withdrawal, or contraction, is called *Elohim*." The divine light that is diminished and weakened through barriers and

28. *Or Torah*, 82; *Likkutei Amarim*, 7; *Or Torah*, 4; *Likkutei Amarim*, 15.

29. See our *History*, Vol. VI, pp. 198ff.

30. Also in the name of the Baal Shem Tov, the following statement is transmitted: "And the Holy One Blessed be He made numerous contractions or withdrawals through many worlds, so that there might be unity with man who was unable to bear His radiance" (*Keter Shem Tov*, 5).

31. *Or Torah*, 76.

32. *Ibid.*, 30.

33. *Or Torah*, 29, 52.

34. *Ibid.*, 30.

garments is named *Elohim.* Along with this he explains in a very remarkable way the words of the Torah, *Bereshit bara Elohim,* commonly translated "In the beginning God created." The phrase, according to the Maggid, really means, "In the beginning *Elohim* was created," i.e., first the contraction or withdrawal of the light of the *Ein Sof,* or Infinite, took place.[35]

The Maggid's thesis concerning *tzimtzum* is congruent with his solution to the problem of the purpose of the world's creation. Dov Baer several times repeats the idea that the Baal Shem Tov had expressed in the following statement:

> The attribute of *Malchut* (kingship) is in our hands and associated with us. That is to say, by the fact that we recognize God's greatness and kingship, He attains His perfection with the attribute of *Malchut,* for without the people there is no king and only through the people does the royal splendor disclose itself.[36]

The purpose of the creation of the world, explains the Maggid, is that the attribute of *Malchut* might be revealed. "Because there is no king without a people," he says in another place, "God contracted His glory."[37]

The Maggid also repeats[38] the Baal Shem Tov's idea that was expressed as a commentary to the Biblical words, "The righteous shall flourish like a palm tree": There are two kind of *tzaddikim* (perfectly righteous men), and both are complete *tzaddikim.* The difference between them consists in this: one is a *tzaddik* only for himself and "does not influence others through his righteousness"; such a *tzaddik* is likened to a cedar tree that bears no fruit. But there is another kind of *tzaddik*—one who strongly influences others and "increases good in the world." This type of *tzaddik* is likened to a date tree that brings forth many sweet fruits. The latter *tzaddik* is of a far higher level.

We encounter here, in the founders of Hasidism, the very idea expressed in Jehudah Abravanel's lovely words when speaking of the highest revelation of the active, creative love that bestows and influences, the love of God for the world:

35. *Ibid.,* 68.
36. *Keter Shem Tov,* 7: "And the quality of kingship is from our side and in our hands —that is to say, that we recognize His greatness and His kingship, and then He is perfected in the quality of His kingship, for there is no king without a people, because through the people the kingship is revealed."
37. *Or Torah,* 70; *Likkutei Amarim,* 15, 39.
38. *Or Torah,* 87; *Likkutim Yekarim,* 35.

"The fruit-bearing tree is lovelier and more perfect than that without fruit, and the living stream that fructifies and is in constant motion is incomparably more beautiful than standing, even though crystal-pure, water."[39] The idea of Israel Baal Shem Tov that "the influence of the divine spring streams incessantly and its intent is to do good" is developed further by the Maggid of Mezhirech. God, who is the acme of perfection, Dov Baer teaches, has incorporated, out of His great goodness and infinite love, His divine thought in created worlds, so that there might be those who would receive the divine influence or abundance. But no creature is capable of receiving the wondrous abundance of light, the incessant stream of active, divine light. Therefore, God, in order to create the worlds, "withdrew or contracted Himself," as it were.

The contraction, the Maggid repeatedly emphasizes, thus took place out of *love*. "Out of love did God create the worlds."[40] Love and *tzimtzum*, Dov Baer explains, are "a complete unity," for out of love, out of the active, divine love, the worlds that can receive the divine light "only through *tzimtzum*" were created.[41] In this connection the Maggid interprets in his own fashion the Biblical verse, "For the Lord God *(Adonai Elohim)* is a sun and a shield": Just as a man's eye can receive the light of the sun only through a covering (shield), so the light of divinity *(behirut Adonai)* can only be received through a separating veil, in the form of *Elohim*, i.e., through *tzimtzum*. *Adonai Elohim*, Dov Baer adds, denotes love and fear, i.e., love veiled in fear.[42]

As with the Baal Shem Tov, so with the Maggid of Mezhirech the conception of the goal and purpose of the work of creation is closely connected with the idea of the cosmic significance of the human personality. In the case of the Maggid, however, the role of man, the individual, is much more strictly linked with the idea of the cosmic role of Israel than it is in the Baal Shem Tov. God and the Torah are, after all, one; hence, the Torah, to be revealed, also required *tzimtzum*. "God Blessed Be He had to contract His Torah so that its light might shine over all the worlds."[43] But the only bearer of the Torah is Israel. On Mount Sinai the holy covenant, the great revela-

39. See our *History*, Vol. IV, p. 19.
40. *Or Torah*, 105.
41. *Likkutei Amarim*, 18; *Or Torah*, 29.
42. *Likkutei Amarim*, 105.
43. *Or Torah*, 45: "God Blessed be He required the contraction of the Torah in order that He might make the light of His Torah shine throughout all the worlds."

tion, when Israel recognized God as its king, took place. Israel alone exemplified the principle of God's kingship *(Malchut Shamayim)* and acclaimed Him king and ruler over the world and human society. God declared Israel "a kingdom of priests," for this people alone actualizes the *Malchut Shamayim* in the world.

For this reason, explains the Maggid, creation is also for the sake of Israel. "God," he explicitly declares, "decided to create the worlds for the sake of Israel."[44] Were it not for *tzimtzum*, these worlds would have no existence and Israel would also not have been.[45] Israel, Dov Baer emphasizes, is the principle *(ikkar)* of life, and the various peoples of the world obtain the essential elixirs of life from it.[46] This idea about the great mission that Providence has designated for the Jewish people, an idea which Rabbi Isaac Luria had already expressed in his day,[47] is frequently reiterated by the Maggid in his sermons. "The souls of Israel are the *ikkar*, not the peoples of the world; but these peoples have a share in Israel, and from it each draws life."[48]

The role of the human personality, of the *Jewish* personality, occupies the focal point in the Maggid's theosophical worldview. The divine attribute of kingship is in Jewish hands, for only through the fact that the Jews acknowledge God's greatness and revere His kingship does He attain His perfection.[49] But man's understanding is limited. We cannot reach the nature of deity,[50] the Maggid declares, and the glory of God's essential being we do not grasp.[51] "Man's thought is in no way capable of understanding the *olam ha-binah*, the world of divine thought."[52] "The purpose of the creation of the world," Dov Baer teaches,[53] "is that we might raise the worlds to their primordial source"—the source that we grasp only according to our understanding.

In this connection, he interprets in his own way the well-known Talmudic statement, "He who makes his name great loses his name" (*Avot* 1:13): Before the Holy One Blessed Be He

44. *Likkutei Amarim*, 23, 39.
45. See *Or Torah*, 29.
46. *Ibid.*, 33; *Likkutei Amarim*, folio 8b.
47. See our *History*, Vol. V, p. 75.
48. *Or Torah*, 33.
49. See above, p. 72.
50. *Or Torah*, 98.
51. *Likkutei Amarim*, folio 7a.
52. *Or Ha-Meir*, "Parashat Vayyetze."
53. *Or Torah*, 101.

created the world, His kingship was not recognized, for there is no king without a people; but since His wisdom, His greatness, and the infinity of His power cannot be grasped by all the worlds, He carried through, as it were, one withdrawal or contraction after another, so that the world might be able to endure His light. Hence, we have the right only to call Him by the name *Adonai*, i.e., Lord and Ruler, for we understand merely a very small level of the worlds; we only grasp His will, as it were, to reveal Himself as Lord and Ruler. But the Tetragrammaton, the Ineffable Name, in which His essence is veiled—that we cannot comprehend. This is the meaning of "He who makes his name great loses his name": Because God, as it were, wished to reveal Himself as Lord and Ruler, His real name had to remain hidden and veiled.[54]

God discloses Himself in the world only in that form in which man apprehends Him. As man represents God, the Maggid declares, so *is* He, i.e., in *that* form does He reveal Himself to the world.[55] As a man appears in front of a mirror, Dov Baer explains, so his form is reflected toward him. Such is also the case with God, as it were: As man reveals himself before God, so God reveals Himself before man.[56] This is the meaning of the legend that when the Jews crossed the Red Sea "God appeared to them like a young man, but at Mount Sinai, when they already had more refined notions and were worthy of receiving the Torah, he appeared to them like an old man."[57] *Tzimtzum* and love are a total unity. Out of love, God created the world through *tzimtzum*, because only through *tzimtzum* can man grasp divinity. As a father, out of love, speaks with his beloved little son in childish language so that he, with his childish mind, might understand his words, so man's infantile notions and conceptions about God are also pleasing to Him.[58]

Here we touch upon the central point of the Maggid's philosophy. We human beings, he teaches, are able to comprehend merely the lowest level even of the worlds created through *tzimtzum;* we can understand God only in the aspect of Lord and Ruler, but the Ineffable Name, which designates the essence and nature of divinity, is incomprehensible to us.

54. *Likkutei Amarim,* folio 46b; *Or Ha-Meir,* the Scroll of Ruth.
55. *Or Torah,* 51, 52ff.
56. *Likkutei Amarim,* folio 4b: "As a man gazes at himself before the mirror, so his face is reflected toward him. Thus it is also, as it were, with the Holy One Blessed be He: As a man shows himself before Him Blessed Be He, so He is revealed to him."
57. *Or Torah,* 113, 114; *Likkutei Amarim,* 48.
58. *Likkutei Amarim,* 41.

Therefore, he adds, we do not grasp the upper worlds except through transcendence of corporeality and accession of spiritual power.[59] And the symbol of "spiritual power," he explains, is thought, which leads to *devekut* or cleaving to God, to removal from corporeality. Dov Baer does not tire of repeating the Baal Shem Tov's dictum that the essence and origin of everything is the idea, thought. "Thought," he teaches, "is the principle and root of all worlds; it is the source of all, and from it all things came into being." The Biblical phrase, "Let us make man in our image," is explained by Dov Baer as meaning "in that image and form in which he was inscribed in thought."[60]

The Baal Shem Tov's saying, "In the place where man thinks he is, there is he completely," is also repeated by the Maggid[61] (he does not, however, as his way commonly is, mention his teacher's name). "Thought is a higher level than speech," Dov Baer declares.[62] In connection with this, he interprets in his own fashion the Biblical statement: "And I am of uncircumcised lips" (Exodus 6:12): When a man is at a high level, the category or state of speech becomes too constricted for him, i.e., he is then no longer capable of expressing his experience in words.[63] To teach Torah to others, the Maggid explains to his disciples, a man must rise to such a state that only his listeners feel and hear "that the world of speech speaks in him," but he himself must not hear his voice. He must ascend to the level "where he does not feel anything of himself." When he begins to hear his own words, he should cease at once.[64]

Man is the only creature in the world who is illumined with the light of thought. The Jew is the only one who, thanks to the Torah, has the right conception of God the Creator. Therefore, "when a man stands before the Holy One Blessed Be He, all the worlds stand, and the angels sing a song of praise."[65] But we already know that even the Israelite can grasp God only in the aspect of Lord *(Adonai)*, but not His essence, the Ineffable

59. *Ibid.*, 46.
60. *Or Torah*, 4.
61. *Ibid.*, 29: "Wherever the thought of a man thinks, there he is." See also *ibid.*, 50; *Likkutei Amarim*, 18, and *ibid.*, 104: "Man is a part of God on high, and when his thought cleaves to the heights, he can know what is done on high."
62. *Or Torah*, 78.
63. *Ibid.*, 32.
64. *Or Ha-Meir*, "Parashat Tzav;" *ibid.*, "Parashat Koraḥ."
65. *Or Torah*, 110; *Likkutei Amarim*, at the end.

Name. Nevertheless, the Maggid notes, at a certain moment, on the holiest of days, on the Sabbath of Sabbaths, the Day of Atonement, "in which there is no eating or drinking," there was one man, the High Priest, who through "transcendence of corporeality and accession of spiritual power," attained such an exalted level that he was able "to grasp the hammer of the Mind that is above the worlds." Therefore on this day the High Priest pronounced the Ineffable Name, "which is the name of the essence of God."[66]

The Maggid was firmly persuaded that at present also there are chosen individuals who, through transcendence of corporeality, can attain the level of the High Priest on the Day of Atonement. These elect few are the *tzaddikim,* or perfectly righteous men of the generation.

We noted in the previous chapter the enthusiasm with which the Baal Shem Tov speaks of the universal role of the *tzaddik.* But the founder of Hasidism deems it necessary to insist, in this connection, that not only do the common people require the *tzaddik* but the *tzaddik* also requires men of lower degree. They complement each other; one must work on the other. According to the Baal Shem Tov's philosophy, every man is suited, at certain moments of spiritual enthusiasm, to weave himself into the divine eternity, and a common stockingmaker who lives all his days "from the honest labor of his hands" may attain such an exalted level that the entire community is sustained through his merit.[67]

It is different, however, with the Maggid Dov Baer. We have here not the man of the people who walks with cane in hand and pipe in mouth over the streets and marketplaces and tells parables and proverbs to simple village Jews and women. The Baal Shem Tov's disciple and successor, the scholar and dialectician, was a typical intellectual aristocrat, permeated with the spirit of "elitism." Maimonides in his day was thoroughly convinced that the truly "actualized" or "realized" man *(adam be-fo'al),* the man at the summit of perfection, is he who has mastered all sciences and is engrossed in the supernal worlds. And the only task of the multitude of common mortals is to serve the "realized man," to provide for his needs so that he may engage quietly and without hindrance in speculation and the quest for philosophical truth.[68] In the view of the Maggid

66. *Likkutei Amarim,* folio 46b.
67. See above, pp. 51–52.
68. See our *History,* Vol. I, p. 148.

of Mezhirech, the "realized man" is the *tzaddik*, who is also absorbed in the upper worlds—not, however, through the aid of the natural sciences and philosophical speculation but only through transcendence of corporeality, through cleaving to God and religious enthusiasm.

Many of the Maggid's sermons are really nothing but paeans to the crown and master of the world, the *tzaddik*. "Only thanks to the *tzaddikim* and out of God's love for them," Dov Baer declares, "was the world created."[69] The world exists only for the sake of the *tzaddik*, and only for his sake did "the Holy One withdraw or contract Himself," so that the worlds might be able, as it were, to endure Him.[70] The Torah of the *tzaddik* is a plaything for God.[71] God created the world so that He might have pleasure from the *tzaddik*.[72] The will of the *tzaddik* is the will of God, for—the Maggid explains—the Holy One Blessed Be He "contracts" His wisdom according to the understanding of the *tzaddik*, just as a father adapts himself to the notions of his beloved child.[73] God thinks what the *tzaddikim* think, for His thought reveals itself most clearly through the *tzaddik's* thought. "If they think with love, they bring the Holy One Blessed Be He into love;" only through their love is God's love disclosed.[74] The souls of the *tzaddikim* are the limbs of the *Shechinah*. Everything is in the *tzaddik's* hand.[75] "The *tzaddik* annuls the decrees of the Holy One Blessed Be He."[76] The *tzaddik* can call forth changes in the order of nature whenever he wishes.[77]

Great are the *tzaddikim*, who transform divine judgment into divine mercy.[78] The works of the *tzaddikim* are greater then the work of creation, for in the work of creation something *(Yesh)* was created out of nothing *(Me-Ayin)*, but the *tzaddikim* transform the *Yesh*, the something—i.e., from all common things, even corporeal things, they raise the holy "sparks" to the state of *Ayin*, the divine Nothingness.[79] It is

69. "For because of the love with which God loved the *tzaddikim* and gloried in them, He created the world . . . and on account of this He created the worlds" *(Or Torah*, 80, 117; *Likkutei Amarim*, 7).
70. *Or Torah*, 32; *Likkutei Amarim*, 24, 41.
71. *Or Torah*, 14.
72. *Ibid.*, 32, 95; *Likkutei Amarim*, 17.
73. *Or Torah*, 25.
74. *Ibid.*, 98.
75. *Ibid.*, 60.
76. *Ibid.*, 26.
77. *Ibid.*, 40; *Likkutei Amarim*, 38.
78. *Or Torah*, 127.
79. *Ibid.*, 132.

written, "The Lord rejoices in His works;" this means that the Master of the universe rejoices in His best creation—the *tzaddikim.*[80] The well-known phrase of the Psalms, "Day unto day uttereth speech," is interpreted by the Maggid in this manner: One day boasts to another of the glorious deeds of the *tzaddikim.*[81] "When the *tzaddik* stirs himself with reverence," Dov Baer teaches, "he stirs reverence and repentance in the heart of all Israel."[82] "The *tzaddik,*" he adds, "can raise all men with himself."[83] In this lies the profound meaning of the words, "For a just man falleth seven times and riseth up again" (Proverbs 24:16).

Whenever the *tzaddik* falls, it is only for the sake of rising, so that he may lift more "sparks" with himself.[84] Hence, no one should be surprised that the *tzaddik* falls from his level and at times speaks profane words. This, the Maggid explains in the style of the Baal Shem Tov, is like a prince who goes about among villagers to search for a treasure hidden with one of them. He must dress like a peasant so that it will not be recognized that he is a prince, and they may reveal to him where the treasure is. So the *tzaddik* also speaks profane words, but he links these words, as it were, to God.[85]

Maimonides' "realized man," the man of the zenith of perfection, keeps as far as possible from the multitude and thinks only of how to avoid the injury it may cause him when he comes into contact with it.[86] The Maggid's *tzaddik,* on whom the world rests, however, is the guardian of the multitude and raises all men with himself. "The elevation comes through the *tzaddik.*"[87]

To be sure, the Maggid develops in his teaching only a system of *theoretical* tzaddikism. The *tzaddik* may not think in his prayer of actual, earthly needs. His whole purpose and essence when he undertakes to pray is only "for the sake of the *Shechinah* that is the place of the world."[88] As we shall subsequently see, however, some of the Maggid's disciples drew a logical inference from their master's doctrine, and from *theoretical* tzaddikism passed over to *practical* tzaddikism. If the

80. *Ibid.*, 73.
81. *Or Ha-Meir, Derush* for Pesaḥ.
82. *Or Torah,* 84.
83. *Ibid.*, 127.
84. *Ibid.*, 84, 123.
85. *Ibid.*, 97.
86. See our *History,* Vol. I, p. 148.
87. *Or Torah,* 71.
88. *Or Ha-Meir,* "Parashat Shemot."

tzaddik can do everything, if he is capable of "making changes any day he wishes" and may even "annul the decrees of the Holy One Blessed Be He," he can provide man with all his needs—"life, children, sustenance."

This transition was made by Hasidism only later. But in the last year of the Maggid's life a bitter struggle against the new movement erupted, a struggle which for decades divided the entire East European Jewish community into two hostile camps.

To describe this thirty-year war between the Hasidim and Mitnagdim is beyond the scope of our project.[89] Our task is only to determine the resonance this struggle found in Jewish literature and to estimate the influence it exercised on ideological tendencies and the cultural development of the Jewish community in eastern Europe. In this connection it must be noted, first of all, that the struggle was by no means a purely religious one. In fact, the major part in it was played by secular, social motifs. We noted in an earlier volume[90] that the process of dissolution that gripped the Polish kingdom with its backward and withered order of life in the seventeenth and eighteenth centuries was felt most strongly in the defenseless and ruined Jewish community. The foundations of Jewish autonomy and of Jewish social and communal life were profoundly shaken. The debts of the impoverished communities grew tremendously, and to pay these debts, as well as to buy off the local secular and religious officials so that they would not persecute the Jewish populace so intensely and not manifest their power and wickedness against it through all kinds of libels and slanders, the *parnassim* and "notables of the city," i.e., the leaders of the Jewish community, had to impose a large poll tax and other levies on every member of the community.

At the head of the community council *(Kahal)* were the rich and powerful men who had influence with the Polish landowners and in the courts of the rulers and officials. These leaders of the *Kahal*, on obtaining power, would imitate the nobles and oppress the poor masses. Gradually, as the decline of the state organism proceeded, the community council was transformed into an oligarchy[91] which brutally utilized its power to oppress

89. The struggle is most thoroughly described in Dubnow's *Geshikhte Fun Khasidism*, Berlin, three volumes, 1930, translated by Z. Kalmanovitch, and in P. Marek's work published in the twelfth volume of *Yevreyskaya Starina* (1928).

90. Vol. VI, pp. 135ff., 217ff.

91. The historian Bershadski notes in his well-known work *Litovskiye Yevrei*, St. Petersburg, 1883, p. 16: "During the course of the entire eighteenth century the ruling class

and exploit the masses of the people in the most shameless way. In apportioning the taxes, the leaders of the *Kahal* used to engage in all kinds of duplicity. They would exempt themselves and their associates from levies and impose everything on the broad strata of the populace. The general public, which painfully felt the burden of the enormous taxes, began to carry on a struggle against the leaders of the community with their unjust levies and inequitable collection of the state and community imposts.

As has been noted, leading the *Kahal* were the rich and powerful who enjoyed influence among the landowners and in the courts of the rulers and officials. The men of wealth, however, had to share their power with another group. While wealth brought power, Torah and scholarship constituted the most assured way leading to both power and honor. Learning and competence in Talmudic knowledge played such a dominant role in Jewish life in Poland in the eighteenth century that Solomon Maimon considered it possible to divide the Jewish populace into the following three classes: unlettered persons engaged in business and in all sorts of trades and other work; learned men who make the Torah their profession; and scholars who devote their lives exclusively to study, are not engaged in any profession, and are maintained at the expense of the commercial-industrial class. The second class consisted of the rabbis, rabbinic judges, and the like. The third class consisted of the "prodigies" who, with their extraordinary skill and great expertise and brilliance in study, evoked great reverence among the unlearned.[92] Very frequently rich men would purchase for their sons-in-law, who were students and "prodigies," a rabbinic position; in this way "Torah and wealth" were united in the family.

The leaders of the community, the monied and Torah aristocracy, endeavored to preserve all power in their hands. In many communities franchise limitations were frequently instituted for the artisan class, so as not to grant its members the ballot and so that they would have as little say as possible in communal affairs.[93] The artisans attempted to fight for their rights but had little success in their struggle. The leaders of the

of Jewish society *(Kahal)* was recruited from a limited circle of families, united by the consciousness of the solidarity of their interests and, above all, by familial relationships."

92. *Lebensgeschichte*, 6.

93. See P. Marek in *Yevreyskaya Starina*, XII, 83.

Kahal, or community council, were, after all, respected by the officials and their people, and so were able to do what they wished. This led the disenfranchised members of the community to such bitterness that in several places (e.g., in the community of Shavli) they addressed to the government a statement to the effect that they had no need of the heads of the *Kahal* or the rabbis, who know only how to rob the poor and take the last morsel of bread from their mouths.[94]

But now suddenly a new movement arose that ventured to create a revolution in the firmly established order. The Baal Shem Tov directed the arrows of his sarcasm against those who "in truth study only the 'commandment of men learned by rote' (Isaiah 29:13) that they might seem wise," those who study Torah only to sharpen the mind, so that they may be considered scholars and accorded honor. The Baal Shem Tov placed feeling, the flame of devotion, above scholarship, faith above study and investigation. A simple artisan who obtains sustenance from the honest toil of his hands and prays with devotion and intention *(kavvanah)* was, for him, more valuable than the arid, prideful scholars of whom the Biblical verse says, "Woe to those that are wise in their own eyes."

The leaders of the community, the influential men and scholars, perceived in this new movement the threat of a revolution attempting to wrest power out of their hands, to effect a revaluation of all social values. The simple Jews, the common people and artisans, saw in the followers of the Baal Shem Tov their loyal helpers and protectors. Only so are explicable the bitterness and hostility with which the leaders of the community and most of the rabbis attacked the Hasidic movement as soon as it had spread so far that it became a noticeable factor in communal life.

In accord with the fashion of that era, when everything wore a religious vesture, this struggle against the new movement was veiled in a *Shulḥan Aruch* mantle and declared "a war for the sake of God," and the battle slogans bore a purely religious character. But the religious battle motifs that were set forth were very weakly grounded and not particularly convincing. The Hasidic circles could not be accused of moral laxity, as the Frankists had been. The suspicion that they inclined toward the false messiah was also without foundation, for it was precisely the Baal Shem Tov who, far more than Rabbi Jacob Emden and the other rabbis, with all their excommunications

94. *Ibid.*, 89–90.

and persecutions, brought it about that the Frankists and Sabbatians lost their last influence in Podolia, Galicia, and the entire Ukraine.

It is therefore worth dwelling on the proclamation with "the great and terrible ban of excommunication" that the *parnassim* and rabbis of the community of Brody issued on the twentieth of Sivan, 1772 against the new "sect." In this proclamation written in a mixed language, half Yiddish, half Hebrew, are collected the worst crimes and sinful deeds with which the Mitnagdim charged the Hasidim. One of the major accusations is that the sect "has instituted new and strange customs, different from those of the whole people of Israel, which are contrary to our Torah and the *Gemara* and the earlier and later codes." It is particularly noted, as if this were an impermissible "new and strange custom," that the Hasidim organize separate prayer conventicles for themselves and pray "with different rites." And it is further explained in what the different rites consist. The Hasidim do not pray according to the Ashkenazic Rite but according to the Sephardic Rite, "from the prayerbook of the holy Rabbi Isaac Luria."

It is clear that the Sephardic Rite and the prayerbook of Isaac Luria did not belong to the "new customs, different from those of the whole people of Israel," for this rite was accepted in the Sephardic communities and, furthermore, from the proclamation itself, it becomes obvious that even in the city of Brody itself there was at that time a "*shtibl* beside the *kloyz* of our congregation" and there "for many, many years now men have been praying from the *siddur* of Rabbi Isaac Luria, may his memory be for a blessing." The *parnassim* and rabbis of Brody had nothing against this and speak of the Jews who pray in this *shtibl* with great respect.

The rabbis complain no less of the fact that the Hasidim "make for themselves honed slaughtering knives, about which there is nothing to be found in the entire Talmud and all the earlier and later codes, and of which all the slaughterers say that it is impossible to slaughter with them."[95] But one of the chief authorities in the camp of the Mitnagdim, the well-known Rabbi Ḥayyim Volozhiner, later publicly declared that he saw no prohibition against the honed slaughtering knives and reported, along with this, that the same view was expressed by his teacher, Elijah the Gaon of Vilna.[96]

95. *Zemir Aritzim*, 13 (we quote following Dubnow's reprint in *He-Avar*, II, 1918).
96. See Rabbi Shneur Zalman's letter in *Bet Rabbi*, folio 40.

It is for these "sinful deeds" that the *parnassim*, together with the rabbis, deemed it necessary to declare in their proclamation that "we must put on the garments of vengeance, ferret them [the Hasidim] out and root them up, destroy their memory from the earth, and pour coals upon their heads, together with bans, curses, and excommunications." But it was not in the separate prayer groups, nor in the Sephardic Rite, nor in the outcries and bizarre movements made by the Hasidim in prayer that the danger of this "sect of the suspected ones"[97] lay. The "ugly deeds" of the "sect" consisted mainly in the fact that the people, the artisans and other democratic elements, obtained in the teaching of Hasidism an ideological weapon, a justification and support in their obdurate battle for equal rights against the "important men," the *parnassim* and leaders of the community.

As the struggle between the Maimunists and their opponents in its day found it literary echo, first of all, in the form of proclamations, appeals, and public letters, so it was also in the struggle between the Hasidim and the Mitnagdim. Already in 1772, as soon as the first controversy about the Hasidim broke out, there appeared in the little Volhynian town of Oleksenitz a collection under the mellifluous title, *Zemir Aritizim Ve-Ḥorvot Tzurim.*[98] The collection appeared anonymously, but the historian Dubnow has expressed the quite correct conjecture that its arranger and editor was the scribe of the community of Brody, Jehudah Leib ben Mordecai.

A fiery opponent of the Hasidim, this scribe collected all the documents written in 1772 against the new "sect": *Iggeret Kena'ot* of the community of Vilna, the proclamation of the *parnassim* and rabbis of Brody, the *takkanot* (ordinances) of the community of Lesnaya against the Hasidim, the letter which the community of Vilna sent to the community of Brest-Litovsk, and the open letter of the leaders of the community of Vilna to all the Lithuanian Jewish communities with a special accusation against the sect of the Hasidim who "call themselves by the name Mezhirecher and Karliner." To these documents the editor added his own anti-Hasidic tract, written in a highly bombastic, rhetorical style. From the sea of rhymed sentences and fragments of sentences, rhetorical phrases and puns, one can barely obtain the following grievous "sins" on the part of

97. *Kat Ḥashudim;* remade from the word *Ḥasidim* (in the letter which the *parnassim* of Vilna and its rabbis sent to the rabbi of Brisk, Abraham Katzenellenbogen.

98. Printed with the participation of the communities of Vilna and Brody (see Dubnow, *Geshikhte Fun Khasidism,* Vol. I, p. 211).

the Hasidim: they are not fond of the "revealed" Torah and are always concerned with the "secret" Torah; they throw themselves about in praying and cry so loudly that "their voice is heard at a distance;" they sing table songs with clapping of hands and dancing; they do not mourn the exile but only "rejoice and are happy, eat and make holiday."

The collection *Zemir Aritzim Ve-Ḥorvot Tzurim*, which, according to a report in a letter from the Mitnagdim of Vilna, was circulated "to all the dispersions of Israel," created a great sensation. But, at first, the Hasidim did not dare to come forward with a public reply, so distressed and intimidated were they by the bans and proclamations with which the communities of Lithuania and Galicia assailed them.[99] They merely employed the defensive strategem of everywhere buying up the copies of the excommunication collection and burning them. This they carried through so thoroughly that only two copies of the entire edition have survived.[100]

Only eight years later did the members of the Hasidic movement feel sufficiently strong to issue forth publicly against the Mitnagdim, not merely to defend themselves against the enemies' attacks but themselves become the aggressors and assail the hostile camp with sharply pointed arrows dipped in hatred and contempt. During this whole period the Hasidic doctrine was mainly an oral teaching, transmitted from mouth to mouth. Only a few copies of the teaching of the Baal Shem Tov and the Maggid of Mezhirech used to circulate from hand to hand.[101] But in 1780 a whole compendium of Hasidic doctrine, *Toledot Yaakov Yosef*, was published simultaneously[102] in two neighboring cities, Korets and Mezhirech.

The author of this work was one of the Baal Shem Tov's favorite disciples, the rabbi of Polonnoye, Jacob Joseph Ha-Kohen. Jacob Joseph was only a few years younger than his teacher.[103] He was descended from a very distinguished family

99. The situation of the small Hasidic circles in the Lithuanian communities was especially critical at that time. Several of the major leaders of the Hasidim, such as Rabbi Menaḥem Mendel of Vitebsk, Rabbi Israel of Polotsk, and Rabbi Abraham of Kalisk even left Lithuania and, with numerous followers, settled in Palestine.

100. One of these was in the hands of the historian Dubnow, who reprinted the text in the journal *He-Avar*, II, 1918.

101. These are undoubtedly the "strange writings" and "manuscripts" about which the open letter of the community of Vilna relates that they were found among the "sect" and were burned publicly at the pillory before the service for welcoming the Sabbath.

102. Dubnow, *Geshikhte Fun Khasidism*, Vol. I, p. 226.

103. Jacob Joseph died around 1782 as a very old man. "And he was extremely old," notes *Shivḥei Ha-Besht*, folio 21b. The same thing is repeated by the author of *Seder Ha-Dorot Ha-Ḥadash*, folio 10b.

and, when still quite young, was already renowned as a great dialectician and an expert both in matters revealed and secret. He soon occupied the rabbinic office in Shargorod and led the same kind of life as other scholars of his time, devoting himself greatly to *pilpul*,[104] immersing himself in the Kabbalah of Rabbi Isaac Luria, and carrying on frequent fasting.

Hasidic legendry relates that at first the rabbi of Shargorod regarded the amulet-writer and exorcist known as the Baal Shem Tov with contempt. Once Rabbi Jacob Joseph came very early, as was his custom, to the synagogue to pray with the congregation. To his great amazement, however, he found an empty synagogue with only the sexton sitting in a corner. The sexton explained that all the people were in the marketplace around the Baal Shem Tov, listening to him tell stories and witticisms. The rabbi was astounded. He immediately invited the Baal Shem Tov to visit, entered into conversation with him, and from then on became one of his most faithful disciples.

The community soon became aware that its rabbi was inclined toward the new "sect," and therefore began to persecute him to the point where he had to leave Shargorod and became rabbi in Raschkow. There apparently he lived in great poverty, for a Hasidic legend relates that when the author of *Toledot* was president of the rabbinic court in Raschkow the angels complained to the Baal Shem Tov: "Why are you silent when the rabbi of the holy community of Raschkow is without a livelihood!"[105]

It was not easy for the scholarly ascetic to accept the teaching of the founder of the Hasidic movement. From the letter of the Baal Shem Tov mentioned above,[106] it may be seen very clearly that when Jacob Joseph was already his disciple, he still held to his erstwhile ascetic way and carried on fasting and mortification of the flesh. Finally he became one of the Baal Shem Tov's most loyal disciples and apostles and the founder of Hasidic literature.[107]

His major work, *Toledot Yaakov Yosef*, is divided according to

104. In his *Ben Porat Yosef* are printed several of his *ḥillukim*, or subtle distinctions, that he composed in his youth ("in the days of his adolescence when he was studying in the *yeshivah*").

105. *Shivḥei Ha-Besht*, folio 32a.

106. See above, p. 46.

107. Shortly after *Toledot*, his *Ben Porat Yosef* was published (Korets, 1781), and in 1782 his *Tzafenat Pa'ne'aḥ* appeared, also in Korets. His *Ketonet Passim* was printed posthumously (Lemberg, 1866).

the *sidrot*, or portions of the Pentateuch assigned for reading each week, but the material in this comprehensive book is assembled without any order whatsoever. The same subject is treated many times over and frequently even in the same words. In one place ("Parashat Shemot") the author himself confesses, "I wrote this without order and did not properly adapt each word to the subject." A discussion is frequently broken off in the middle, and the author at once proceeds without rhyme or reason to another subject. It is, therefore, difficult to agree with the historian of Hasidism, S.A. Horodetzky, that the author of *Toledot Yaakov Yosef* was endowed with a powerful literary talent.[108] But one virtue he did possess. He had a militant temperament, and where he settles accounts with the opponents of his master's doctrine, he becomes emotive, his style obtains thrust and weight. One feels the courageous battler with heavy hammer in wrathful hand. Jacob Joseph is conscious that on him lies the duty to avenge all the persecutions and excommunications, the venomous proclamations and summonses, with which the enemy ruthlessly attacked his comrades and his beloved master's teaching. And he repays the enemy in full measure.

The author of *Toledot* speaks with scathing irony of the scholars who are so arrogant because they have studied much Torah.[109] He concludes that even one who has studied the entire Torah is still not a wise man or sage *(ḥacham)* but a scholar *(lamdan)*. For a *ḥacham* is only he who intends through study of Torah "to unite himself with God's holy name," which is, after all, the chief thing and the ultimate purpose of life.[110] The scholars, says Rabbi Jacob Joseph, claim everything according to the law. They argue: Because I have studied a section of the *Gemara* with *Tosafot* and the like, I deserve a reward.[111] When the *yetzer ra* (evil inclination) persuades one of the common people to commit a transgression, *Toledot* sarcastically declares, that person does not know of any subtleties or evasions. He confesses that he did not behave properly and thereby does not bring anyone into temptation. Among the scholars, however, it is quite different. When a scholar commits even the greatest transgression, he will endeavor to prove to you that he is doing a *mitzvah*, a good deed. He seeks sanctions

108. *Ha-Ḥasidim Veha-Ḥasidut*, I, 109.
109. *Toledot*, "Parashat Vayyetze."
110. *Ibid.*, introduction; *ibid.*, "Parashat Vayiggash" and "Parashat Shofetim."
111. *Toledot*, "Parashat Va'era."

for his deeds in the Torah and distorts the law so as to show the reason why it is permissible to do so.[112]

It is written in the Bible: "And you shall choose life, that you may live, to love the Lord your God . . ." In recent generations, Jacob Joseph laments, hearts have become petty. Men always wish to make of the Torah a crown, to boast and aggrandize themselves through it. If a person learns a *halachah* (law), he boasts of it; if he studies further, he boasts even more. If he studies the codes, he becomes exceedingly great in his own sight and removes himself from God. So the scholars "break their feet," stride from one city to another, and study in the *yeshivot.* This, it appears, is what the Biblical verse "Wherefore should you be stricken any more" (Isaiah 1:15) means: The more you strike your feet to go and study in the *yeshivah,* "you rebel more and more," i.e., the farther you remove yourselves from God.[113]

The well-known verse of the Song of Songs, "Seize for us the little foxes that spoil our vineyards," is interpreted by *Toledot Yaakov Yosef* as follows: The little foxes that spoil our vineyards are the rabbis who pursue money.[114] He who occupies himself with communal concerns, *Toledot* complains, soon obtains a great fortune. We see with our own eyes the conduct of the rabbis and leaders who concern themselves with communal matters, conduct "that is indescribable."[115] Jacob Joseph speaks wrathfully of the rabbis appointed by the officials and rulers of the city; these rabbis act "against God and His anointed one."[116] It is written, "You shall appoint a king over you." But what is a king among us? —A rabbi. The interpretation, therefore, is: You yourself are to appoint a king over you. Chose one for yourself who does not pursue glory, for such a person is assuredly a pious man. Otherwise, if you do not yourself choose, there will come one who will seat himself by force on the rabbinic chair; and "he who runs after this is certainly a vile man."[117]

Toledot relates an interesting story of the transformations sustained by the long-standing custom that the rabbis at Ḥanukkah time should travel around among the villages to visit their residents. In earlier generations, Jacob Joseph notes,

112. *Ibid.*, "Parashat Shofetim."
113. *Ibid.*, "Parashat Va-Yeḥi."
114. *Ibid.*, "Parashat Bo."
115. *Ibid.*, "Parashat Ve-Zot Ha-Berachah."
116. *Ibid.*, "Parashat Naso."
117. *Ibid.*, "Parashat Shofetim."

rabbis always acted for the sake of heaven, and so they instituted this custom of touring the villages also for the sake of heaven. In the city the rabbis were constantly occupied with their Torah in the *yeshivot* and with other religious matters; only on the days of Ḥanukkah, which are vacation time, did they have leisure to travel to the villages and guide the village Jews in questions of morality, in the right way concerning desecration of the Sabbath, matters of ritual slaughtering, and many other things. The rabbis did all this for the sake of God and did not receive so much as a penny from the villagers. In later generations, however, the rabbis who traveled to the villages to supervise conduct there found for themselves authorization to accept gifts from the villagers as recompense for desisting from their occupation, since they had to tear themselves away from their livelihood for the journey. But reverence for God in the villages became ever slighter, and so, in time, the rabbis ceased to pay any attention to the conduct of the villagers but only traveled around at Ḥanukkah time to collect gifts for themselves. Later the officials imposed on the villagers a special tax which they had to send as "Ḥanukkah money" to the rabbis, so that the latter would no longer have to take the trouble to tour the villages to obtain it.[118]

The author of *Toledot Yaakov Yosef* cannot forget the persecutions which his "sect" had to suffer at the hands of the rabbis and *parnassim* of the communities. The scholars, he wrathfully exclaims, are "wise to do evil," but wish to know nothing of doing good. They only stir up strife and controversy.[119] They are Jewish demons. Jacob Joseph, who witnessed the seven-year rabbinical struggle between the parties of Rabbi Jacob Emden and Rabbi Jonathan Eybeschütz, cries out bitterly: Rabbis contemn each other; they wound each other with the sword of their tongues. Each wishes to display his great cleverness and is ready to trample the other only to show that he is greater. Every one shouts: I should reign, I am a greater scholar! The *erev rav* (mixed multitude) of the Bible, *Toledot* angrily declares, are the scholars, those who are wise to do evil, who have separated the common people from the *tzaddikim* of the generation.[120]

The animosity which the scholars bear to the *tzaddikim* derives from their envy at the fact that the latter are so loved by

118. *Ibid.*, "Parashat Tzav."
119. *Ibid.*, "Parashat Ki Tetze."
120. *Ibid.*

the people.[121] The struggle of the rabbis against the leaders of Hasidism is declared in *Toledot* to be a "war of Amalek," through which "the soul of the *tzaddikim* and the Hasidim is bowed down to the dust and the men of violence have prevailed." It is written, "The Lord is at war with Amalek." In every generation Amalek carries on war ostensibly in God's name and produces a "division among the pious," separating the people from the *tzaddikim* of the generation.[122] The *Gemara* relates, writes the author of *Toledot,* that Jerusalem was destroyed only because scholars were reviled and angels of God were shamed. This means, he adds, Jerusalem was destroyed through the scholars, who are called "false prophets," as is written: "Thy prophets have seen vain and foolish things for thee" (Lamentations 2:14).[123]

Jacob Joseph Ha-Kohen sets the *tzaddikim* of the generation, led by his teacher the Baal Shem Tov, in complete opposition to the scholars, those "who are wise to do evil." As we have noted, the chief importance of *Toledot Yaakov Yosef* consists in the fact that it first presented the Baal Shem Tov's doctrine and laid the foundation of Hasidic literature. The ideas the author expresses in his own name have no independent significance, for they are really nothing more than a commentary or paraphrase of the Baal Shem Tov's ideas.

Toledot Yaakov Yosef produced an enormous sensation not only in Hasidic circles but also among their opponents, the Mitnagdim. The sharply polemic tone of the work especially irritated the rabbis. Their anger was intensified by the fact that the enemy who permitted himself to attack the scholars and rabbis so sharply was himself a rabbi. As soon as the work arrived in Vilna in the summer of 1781, a proclamation was issued in all the synagogues at the decision of the rabbis and leaders of the community—a proclamation in which, among many other bans, it is declared that every man must "push away with both hands" the people who call themselves by the name Hasidim.

Go announce it. They are banned and excommunicated and separated from the whole congregation of Israel. And, of course, one is not permitted to associate or speak with them. Also the people who belong to this accursed sect in our community are put under the great

121. "Parashat Vayiggash."
122. *Ibid.*, "Parashat Shofetim."
123. *Ibid.*, "Parashat Ki Tetze."

ban, so that they must move out of our community with their wives and children. This also is decreed: that no one, whether of our community or of Shnipishok and of Antokol and of those who accept our authority, may lease or rent them any dwelling. And whoever violates this is himself excommunicated and banned, and let all the curses fall on his head. And with him who obeys it will be well, and the blessing of God will come upon him.[124]

The leaders of the Vilna community were not content with this and dispatched agents with a summons signed by the Gaon Elijah and many other rabbis and *parnassim* to other communities, calling upon them also to issue forth with a strict ban against the Hasidim. But the renewed campaign of 1781 was even less able than the first battle of 1772 to stifle the Hasidic movement, for in the course of these nine years the movement had become stronger and more widespread. Indeed, in the proclamation we have just discussed the rabbis of Vilna must declare that "the affliction (the Hasidic movement) has spread to all the dispersions of Israel, and especially in the land of the Ukraine there are *tens of thousands* of such unclean persons."

Because the new movement spread to various lands, it lost its original unitary character and, under the influence of various environments, assumed differing forms. Of this in the next chapter.

124. See Dubnow, *Geshikhte Fun Khasidism*, Vol. I, p. 232.

CHAPTER FOUR

Tzaddikism and Ḥabad

From theoretical tzaddikism to practical tzaddikism—Elimelech of Lyzhansk and his *No'am Elimelech*—The manifesto of practical tzaddikism—"The *tzaddik* decrees and God fulfills"—Two ways of Hasidism—The Rabbi of Lyady, Shneur Zalman—In the heat of controversy—Shneur Zalman's hatred for Napoleon—His death—The significance of *Tanya*—The problem of *tzimtzum* in Shneur Zalman's explication—*Or Mitlabesh* and *Or Makkif*—God as both immanent and transcendent—Shneur Zalman's extreme idealism—The purpose of the "work of creation"—"The world is created for the sake of Israel"—The three garments: thought, word, and act—The significance of study of Torah and observance of the *mitzvot*—The doctrine of the three categories: *Ḥochmah*, *Binah* and *Da'at* (ḤaBaD)—Two kinds of love and fear—*Ahavat Olam* (everlasting love) and *Ahavah Rabbah* (great love)—Two states in man's heart—The highest degree of love is "beyond the state of knowledge and understanding"—The Kabbalist overcomes the scholar—*Tanya* on the role of the *tzaddik*—Shneur Zalman on the secular sciences.

IN THE previous chapter we discussed the theoretical tzaddikism which occupies such a prominent place in the theosophical system of the Maggid Dov Baer. We observed how the Maggid stressed that the bond between the *tzaddik* and the people must be a purely ideal one. The *tzaddik* may not have in mind concrete, practical needs with his prayer; his only desire and purpose must be the *Shechinah*, "which is the place of the world."[1] But real life is stronger than abstract, ideal

1. See above, p. 79.

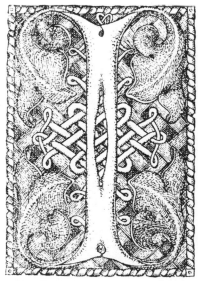

theories; it triumphantly lays its impress on these and fills them with its specific demands and requirements.

In the previous chapters we noted the causes that converged to make the movement created by the Baal Shem Tov extremely congenial to the masses of the people. But the profound theosophical speculations of the Maggid on the cosmic role of man in general and of the *tzaddik* in particular could interest only the elect few who were thoroughly familiar with the theoretical Kabbalah and the romantic world of Jewish mysticism. The broad strata—the ignorant villagers, tavern- and inn-keepers, merchants, small shopkeepers, artisans, beggars, and *Luftmenschen* in the southern provinces (the Ukraine, Volhynia, Podolia, and Galicia)—longed, however, for actual aid and support and dreamed of a guide who would be close and comprehensible and stand by them in their great distress.

If the *tzaddik* is "one who can do everything," if he is so beloved of God that he can nullify the harshest decrees, if he can alter "the work of creation," then let him show "what he can do," let him disclose the great miracles, let him—above all—provide his Hasidim with a livelihood and free them from all plagues and afflictions! The economic situation of the Jewish masses was extremely precarious; the sources of livelihood were based only, as it were, on a miracle. The Jewish populace was defenseless and powerless against the persecutions and slanders of its religious and political enemies, against the slightest caprice of a crazed landowner or nobleman. Hence, the people waited with all the ardor of their believing souls for one who could manifest great wonders, who possessed the power necessary to be their protector and provider.

A definitive response to the demands of the masses was provided by the disciple of the Maggid of Mezhirech, the Galician Elimelech of Lyzhansk,[2] in his *No'am Elimelech,* which first appeared two years after its author's death (1788).

No'am Elimelech may, with full right, be called "the manifesto of practical tzaddikism." Like *Toledot Yaakov Yosef,* so *No'am Elimelech* is written in the form of a commentary on the Pentateuch. The entire text of the five books of the Torah is interpreted as a "Song of Songs" in honor of the *tzaddik* and his marvelous deeds. It is, for instance, said in the Book of Genesis,

2. Born in 1717, died in 1786. In his youthful years, the Hasidic sources relate, the *tzaddik* of Lyzhansk "studied Torah in the way of the scholars," and only under the influence of his brother Zusya of Hanipoli did he become the disciple of the Maggid (see *Maaseh Tzaddikim*).

"And God saw the light, and it was good." *No'am Elimelech* explains that the "good" consisted in the fact that the light revealed by God is designated "to be a help and support to the *tzaddik* in raising the sparks," for the Master of the universe "desires precisely the work of the *tzaddikim.*"

The level of the *tzaddik*, Elimelech teaches, is higher "than the level of the angels."[3] "The *tzaddik* has the power to bind together all the worlds."[4] These worlds are under his authority, and he may do with them what he pleases.[5] The *tzaddik* can accomplish everything. He can even bring about the advent of the Messiah.[6] "The *tzaddik* draws abundance to the worlds."[7] "Through the *tzaddik* bitter is turned to sweet."[8] "As the *tzaddik* decrees and says, so it will be."[9] The *tzaddik* transforms judgment into mercy, and "if death has been decreed for a man, he can nullify the decree and change it to life."[10] The *tzaddik* can atone for the sin of the whole generation.[11] It is written, "the first-born of thy sons": this means the *tzaddik*, who is already sanctified in the womb of his mother, and it is he who is called "a son of God Blessed Be He."[12] The *tzaddik* can attain such a level that he sees without eyes and hears without ears.[13] "God regards the world through the eyes of the *tzaddikim.*" The *tzaddik*, through his holy mouth, can bring about "all mercies and grace."[14] "The *tzaddik* decrees and God Blessed Be He fulfills."[15]

God has blessed the *tzaddik* with the gift of being able "to give life to all worlds through the power of the divine portion which he has obtained from above."[16] It is written, "The Lord is good to all": God's goodness is the divine portion with which the *tzaddik* is endowed and with which he influences "the whole world." It is precisely in the influence of the *tzaddik* on

3. *No'am Elimelech*, "Likkutei Shoshanah."
4. *Ibid.*, "Parashat Shemot."
5. *Ibid.*, "Parashat Tetzavveh."
6. *Ibid.*, "Parashat Mishpatim"; see also "Parashat Vayyeshev": "The *tzaddik* alone, through his holy deeds, can accomplish everything."
7. *Ibid.*, "Parashat Balak."
8. *Ibid.*, "Parashat Terumah."
9. *Ibid.*, "Parashat Be-Ḥukkotai."
10. *Ibid.*, "Parashat Aḥarei Mot."
11. *Ibid.*, "Parashat Kedoshim."
12. *Ibid.*, "Parashat Mishpatim."
13. *Ibid.*, "Parashat Shemot."
14. *Ibid.*, "Parashat Be-Ha'alotecha."
15. *Ibid.*, "Parashat Mi-Ketz."
16. *Ibid.*

all worlds that the meaning of the words "And His mercies are over all His works" lies, for if God should Himself be, as it were, the influencer, the real world *(olam ha-maaseh)* would not be able to receive the stupendous influence. Only when the influence flows through the mediation of the *tzaddik* "are we able to receive it."[17] All the mercies which God performs for the world are always done through the hands of the *tzaddik.*[18] The *tzaddik* is the mediator and broker; he receives the influence from above and distributes it to all.[19]

The chief instrument wherewith the *tzaddik* effects his great wonders is the word. "Out of every word that proceeds from the *tzaddik's* mouth an angel is created."[20] When the *tzaddik* begins to speak, a great impression is made on all the worlds, "and this is a paradigm of redemption."[21] The words proceeding from the *tzaddik's* mouth radiate to the heavens.[22] The essence of the *tzaddik's* life is attained through prayer, for through it the *tzaddik* unites with the Creator.[23] In the power of prayer the *tzaddik* can nullify all decrees; the Holy One Blessed Be He decrees and the *tzaddik* nullifies.[24] But, *No'am Elimelech* insists, no alteration whatever in God's unitary and limitless will arises thereby.

One must bear in mind that "no evil is created at God's command," but man, who is connected with all the worlds, breaks his divine connection through sin and thereby falls into grave peril. Here the *tzaddik* comes to his aid; through his prayer he once again binds the sinner to his erstwhile source,[25] for with his prayer the *tzaddik* creates new heavens.[26] How does the *tzaddik's* prayer have such a colossal effect? To this *No'am Elimelech* replies: The Torah, after all, was given out of love alone, as it is written, "Who chooses His people Israel in love." God elected Israel through love, and the *tzaddik* is also pure love. And so all the letters of the Torah are purified through the prayer of the *tzaddik* who loves all men. Indeed, the verse of the Psalms (119:40), "Thy word is very pure; there-

17. *Ibid.*
18. *Ibid.*, "Parashat Be-Ha'alotecha."
19. *Ibid.*, "Parashat Bo"; see also "Likkutei Shoshanah."
20. *Ibid.*, "Parashat Shelaḥ"; see also "Parashat Va-Yishlaḥ."
21. *Ibid.*, "Parashat Yitro."
22. *Ibid.*, "Parashat Ha'azinu."
23. *Ibid.*, "Parashat Vayyera."
24. *Ibid.*, "Parashat Vayyetze."
25. *No'am Elimelech*, "Likkutei Shoshanah."
26. *Ibid.*, "Parashat Vayyetze."

fore thy servant loveth it," indicates this; everything is out of love.[27]

No'am Elimelech constantly reiterates that the *tzaddik* does not think of himself but of the good of all and is prepared to sacrifice himself for the sake of Israel.[28] The *tzaddik* must be freely available to all Jews. He must always be prepared to benefit each individual.[29] He must be ready even "to go down to hell" to attain his goal of effecting the good of Israel.[30] In this connection *No'am Elimelech* stresses that there are two kinds of *tzaddikim.* The first are those who are removed from this world and completely engrossed in the supernal worlds. The entire function of this kind of *tzaddik* is to purify and "correct" his soul, in order "to raise it to its root and place of origin."[31] But there are also *tzaddikim* who always think and worry only about the troubles of Israel, and their goal and all their thoughts are simply to call down benefits on the world, to bring "blessing, mercy, life, and everything good."[32]

It is clear that the second kind of *tzaddik* is the more important, and only *tzaddikim* "who have a bond with the whole of Israel" provide the Jewish people "with all their needs."[33] The *tzaddikim* of the first kind are ascetics who afflict themselves and fast, while the others eat in holiness and purity for the sake of God's service. It is the latter *tzaddikim* "who have the power to influence and decree according to their will." They provide the world with the three major joys: children, life, and sustenance.[34] *No'am Elimelech* teaches that for the *tzaddik* to influence the world, he must enjoy the life of *this* world.[35] The *tzaddik* who wishes to affect the world must descend from his high level; he must come down to the generality of Israel, so that he may be able "to remove from them all evils and humiliations."[36]

This idea that the *tzaddik* "descends from his level for the good of Israel" is frequently repeated in *No'am Elimelech.* If the

27. *Ibid.*, "Parashat Va-Yishlaḥ"; see also "Parashat Vayiggash," where it is several times repeated: "The Sabbath is only love; fear must come from love."
28. *No'am Elimelech*, "Parashat Ha'azinu," "Parashat Ḥukkat."
29. *Ibid.*, Parashat "Shelaḥ."
30. *Ibid.*, "Parashat Balak."
31. *Le-shorashah ule-mekom maḥtzavtah.*
32. *Ibid.*, "Parashat Shemot."
33. *Ibid.*, "Parashat Vayyetze."
34. *Ibid.*, "Parashat Va-Yikra"; see also "Parashat Shemot."
35. *Ibid.*, "Parashat Vayyera"; see also "Parashat Toledot."
36. *Ibid.*, "Parashat Toledot"; see also "Parashat Shemot."

tzaddik had no defect whatever, how would he be able to rule over the *kelipah*, or husk?[37] Most people, we read in *No'am Elimelech*, are so steeped in corporeality that they cannot raise themselves to the service of God. For this reason, God in His great mercy sends some sort of sin to the *tzaddik* so that he may also come to "littleness," and when he strengthens himself to rise once again to his previous level he thereby also lifts the entire people. If the *tzaddik* were free of the least sin, he would have no relationship to our sinful world. How, then, could he have any influence on it? But when he is caught in a transgression, he repents and therewith also redeems the world. In this lies the meaning of the words, "Happy is the generation whose prince sins."[38]

But the old principle of *do ut des*, "yourself give if you wish that others should give to you," is not forgotten in *No'am Elimelech*. The *tzaddik* does, indeed, "contain all Israel." He raises all the base deeds committed by Jews and brings them to holy levels.[39] "The world cannot endure without *tzaddikim.*" "Everything is dependent on the *tzaddik.*" "No influence comes except through the *tzaddik.*" "The *tzaddik* is blessing himself." The *tzaddik* performs great miracles: he heals the sick, frees captives, gives prosperity, and blesses man with life, sustenance, and children.[40] The *tzaddik* with his great righteousness brings it about that, even in our bitter exile, we find favor among the nations of the world.[41] The *tzaddik* is dear and sweet "with all kinds of sweetnesses."[42] Etc., etc. But to derive all this from the *tzaddik*, one must bind oneself closely to him. "Israel must be joined with the *tzaddik.*"[43] If the *tzaddik* wishes to bestow his influence on a person, to bless him with prosperity and the like, he must link that person's soul to his own.[44] To benefit from the *tzaddik's* blessing and great influence, one must *believe* in him and agree with him in all things.[45]

One must also be concerned about the *tzaddik* in this world

37. *Ibid.*, "Parashat Va-Yeḥi."
38. *Ibid.*, "Parashat Va-Yikra"; see also "Parashat Naso."
39. *Ibid.*, "Parashat Vayyetze."
40. *Ibid.*, "Parashat Vayyera," "Parashat Terumah," "Parashat Tetzavveh." Characteristic also is the following passage: "It is written of Abraham, 'And he lifted up his eyes and saw three men.' The *tzaddik* realized that he was obliged to endow Israel with three things—life, sustenance, and children."
41. *Ibid.*, "Parashat Ḥukkat."
42. *Ibid.*, "Parashat Ki Tissa."
43. *Ibid.*, "Parashat Devarim."
44. *Ibid.*, "Parashat Mi-Ketz."
45. *Ibid.*, "Parashat Lech Lecha," "Parashat Be-Shallaḥ," "Parashat Balak."

and see to it that he has "plenty of money."[46] Through giving gifts to the *tzaddik, No'am Elimelech* teaches, a man "is bound with a lasting bond" to him, and the evil inclination no longer has any power to bring him to sin; on the contrary, he is hallowed through the *tzaddik.* "Great is the deed of one who gives to the perfect *tzaddik,*" Elimelech of Lyzhansk notes. Then, he assures us, the world is sated with everything good, "with abundance and blessing, mercy and life, children and prosperity, and peace without end."[47] The "perfect *tzaddik,*" he adds, does not in any way think that the gifts given to him are for his own good and benefit; his only intention is that thereby "a good influence for all Israel" will be aroused, and his sole desire is "to see the joy of Israel, when they do not lack anything good."[48] One must remember that the *tzaddik's* only function is, after all, "to raise and establish the *Shechinah.*"[49] The material blessings that he receives are "for the sake of spirituality." Even in eating and drinking he raises the holy sparks. Even when he speaks material, profane words, it is all for the sake of the Creator.[50]

Typical is the following passage. It is written in the Torah (Numbers 15:24): "And it shall be, if anything be committed by ignorance without the knowledge (lit., the eyes) of the congregation." The eyes of the congregation, declares *No'am Elimelech,* means the leaders of the people. But when the eyes of the congregation, i.e., its leaders, follow an evil way, God in His great mercy has compassion on His people Israel and sends them great *tzaddikim* who are always concerned about the entire body of Israel, and these, with their prayers, "sweeten" all judgments over Israel and change them to mercy.[51] Hence every man is obliged "to study the deeds of the *tzaddik.*"[52] It is a duty to relate stories about the great *tzaddikim* and their righteous qualities.[53] And he who permits himself to utter harsh words against the *tzaddik, No'am Elimelech* admonishes, acts, as it were, as if he had blasphemed God, and the severest punishment will come upon him.[54]

The work of the Galician Elimelech was, as we have already

46. *Ibid.,* "Likkutei Shoshanah."
47. *Ibid.,* "Parashat Pekudei."
48. *Ibid.*
49. *Ibid.,* "Parashat Be-Ha'alotecha."
50. *Ibid.,* "Parashat Toledot," "Parashat Vayiggash," "Parashat Va'era," "Parashat Shelaḥ," Parashat Re'eh."
51. *Ibid.,* "Parashat Shelaḥ."
52. *Ibid.,* "Parashat Ki Tissa."
53. *Ibid.,* "Parashat Bo."
54. *Ibid.,* "Parashat Shelaḥ."

noted, very well suited to the requirements of the numerous lessees, innkeepers, merchants, small shopkeepers, and all the various kinds of brokers and *Luftmenschen* in Galicia and the Ukraine.[55] But the nascent Hasidic movement refused to content itself with the ignorant masses of the southern provinces. It also ventured to spread its influence over the northern provinces of White Russia and Lithuania. Its energetic emissaries and propagandists boldly invaded the key citadel of rabbinic scholarship, Vilna, and managed to obtain devotees and followers among the associates of the Gaon of Vilna himself.

It is clear that here Hasidism had to come forward with other ideological baggage than for the village Jews of Galicia and the Ukraine. The great Maggid's disciple, Elimelech of Lyzhansk, based himself on his master's teaching concerning the universal role of the *tzaddik*, and on the basis of this teaching created his system of practical tzaddikism. At the same time, the Maggid's brilliant scholarship, spiritual and intellectual aristocratism, and theosophical metaphysics were skillfully utilized by his youngest and best loved disciple, Shneur Zalman, the acknowledged leader of the Hasidim in White Russia and the founder of the new way of Hasidism which obtained renown under the name *Ḥabad*.

Shneur Zalman, the founder of the Hasidic dynasty Shneurson, was born in 1747 in the White Russian town of Liozna into a distinguished family. His father Baruch, a scholar, traced his descent from the famous Maharal of Prague. At the age of twelve the young Shneur Zalman was already renowned as a prodigy, and at the age of fifteen he was married. Living with his father-in-law in Vitebsk, he spent day and night in study of Torah. Among the *Ḥabad* Hasidim there are various legends about the enormous diligence and extraordinary capacities of their founder. At the age of eighteen he was already famed as one of the greatest scholars in Talmudic literature. In order better to understand certain questions discussed in the Talmud, Shneur Zalman devoted a great deal of attention to astronomy and mathematics. This information he drew exclusively from Hebrew sources, such as Joseph Solomon Delmedigo's *Elim* and other works,[56] for he understood no languages other than Yiddish and Hebrew.

But Shneur Zalman was not satisfied merely with the "revealed Torah." Somewhere in the deep chambers of the soul of

55. It is worth noting that in the times of Elimelech of Lyzhansk approximately one-third of the Jews of Galicia consisted of villagers and rural residents.

56. On this see Borenstein's *Simat Ayin*, pp. 20–21, supplement to M. Teitelbaum's *Ha-Rav Mi-Ladi U-Mifleget Ḥabad* (1913).

this great dialectician and scholar, a tender, poetic strain palpitated. He used to sing the prayers with his own melodies, drawn from the depths of his heart, for the melody, he would say, springs out of the magic of the heart and soul.[57] Thus he could not be satisfied with Talmudic literature alone and immersed himself in the "esoteric wisdom." He discovered profound mysteries in Isaiah Horowitz's *tikkunim* to the prayerbook and declared that prayer is "the foundation of the whole Torah." Then he heard of the Maggid of Mezhirech, who was great both in "the revealed" and in "the hidden" and was following his own new way. It is very probable that Shneur Zalman, as well as the young Solomon Maimon, was familiarized with the new Hasidic movement by one of the energetic emissaries and propagandists whom the Maggid Dov Baer dispatched to various provinces.

A Hasidic legend relates that at first Shneur Zalman "stood at the crossroads," not knowing which way to go—whether to Vilna, the major city of scholarship, or to Mezhirech, the capital of Hasidism. "I heard," a Hasidic legend relates in his name, "that in Vilna they study well and in Mezhirech they pray well. In Vilna the chief thing is study, and in Mezhirech the service of the heart. As far as studying is concerned, I can do that on my own well enough, but I have devoted myself very little to the service of the heart." Shneur Zalman thereupon decided to seek the way of life in Mezhirech. Like Solomon Maimon, his contemporary, the prodigy of Liozna, had no money for expenses, and set out on foot for Mezhirech.

The Maggid Dov Baer soon recognized in the young scholar and "seeker" the future leader in Israel; hence, he drew him very close to himself and, as the Hasidic sources relate, handed over to him "all the secrets of his wisdom." Shneur Zalman became an intimate friend of the Maggid's only son, who is known, because of his total removal from this-wordly interests, by the name Abraham "the Angel" *(Malach)*. Abraham was an ardent Kabbalist and also inducted his young friend[58] into the profound mysteries of the Kabbalah. From then on (this was about 1767) Shneur Zalman would occasionally hasten home to his household for a short stay, but the rest of the time he spent with the Maggid Dov Baer and accompanied him on his travels to Rovno and Hanipoli.[59]

57. To the present day among the Ḥabad Hasidim there is a great love for "the *rebbe's* melody," a melody without words in which the Hasidim perceive a profound mystery, a "supernatural attachment, or cleaving," to the holy *sefirot*.

58. Shneur Zalman was seven years younger than Abraham "the Angel."

59. The Maggid spent the last years of his life in Hanipoli and also died there.

The Hasidic legend that Shneur Zalman turned away from the road leading to the learned city of Vilna and set out on the way leading to Hasidism is not, in fact, quite correct. The scholar of Liozna attempted to combine both ways. In this he was aided by his teacher, Dov Baer himself. On the latter's advice Shneur Zalman undertook his first major work, the writing of a commentary to the *Shulḥan Aruch*, more correctly, the production of a new *Shulḥan Aruch*, in which all the laws and precepts given in the original *Shulḥan Aruch* are interpreted and explained in easily comprehensible fashion, so that "those who, because of the burden of earning a livelihood, cannot devote much attention to study of Torah" may also easily find every necessary law. In reaching decisions about the laws Shneur Zalman was a strict constructionist. We must, he admonished, faithfully follow the words of the Scribes and their strict interpretations in all details, as well as all the severities in the *Gemara* and the rabbinic codes.[60]

Shortly after he completed the first part of his *Shulḥan Aruch*, *Oraḥ Ḥayyim*, the first battle against the Hasidim erupted, and the leader of the movement, the Maggid Dov Baer, died. Thereupon tumultuous years of excommunications and persecutions commenced for the Hasidim. Shneur Zalman, who had a calm and sedate nature, attempted unsuccessfully to allay the controversy. When the eldest of the Maggid's disciples, Rabbi Mendel of Vitebsk, decided to leave his home to settle in Palestine, he, together with his young colleague Shneur Zalman, traveled to Vilna to see the Gaon and demonstrate to him personally that he was "suspicious of pure men," that the Hasidim are upright Jews and do not violate any law or negative commandment of the Torah. But the fanatical Rabbi Elijah slammed the door in their faces and refused to see them, because there is an explicit law in the *Gemara* (*Sanhedrin* 38b) that "it is forbidden to carry on converse with heretics" and one may not look on their form.

Three years later, when Shneur Zalman was already in fact the acknowledged leader of all the Hasidim in White Russia,[61] he issued an open letter to his followers which begins with the words, "I will speak peace."[62] In this letter he begs the Hasidim as far as possible not to irritate their opponents and to remove

60. *Likkutei Torah*, "Parashat Mattot."

61. Shortly after Rabbi Mendel of Vitebsk moved away to Palestine, Rabbi Shneur Zalman settled in Mogilev and in a short time went from there to his native town of Liozna. According to Hasidic legendry, Shneur Zalman finished the entire Talmud for the sixteenth time in Mogilev.

62. Published in *Bet Rabbi*, 33–34.

themselves from controversy. But the letter could be of only slight avail. In the following year (1781) a new struggle against the Hasidim broke out.[63] It was not only Jacob Joseph HaKohen with his *Toledot Yaakov Yosef* who brought this about. When one reads the documents describing the first controversy of 1772, it seems that purely ideological motives are involved: the rabbis and community leaders fought against the new "sect" because they suspected it of Sabbatian and Frankist heresy. But in the year 1780–81 we already find among the battlers against the Hasidic movement the schemer and informer Avigdor who purchased the rabbinic office in Pinsk from a Polish nobleman.[64] His hatred for Hasidism stemmed from his fear of losing his post, and he therefore addressed to the Gaon of Vilna a denunciation of the Hasidim and portrayed them as apostates and pernicious heretics.[65]

Even more clearly do the social factors of this struggle appear in its later period, in the closing years of the eighteenth century, when the major target of all the attacks of the Mitnagdim was the leader of the White Russian Hasidim, Shneur Zalman, who, as a result of his great organizing ability and extraordinary authority as a scholar, obtained tens of thousands of new followers for the Hasidic movement in Lithuania and White Russia.[66]

In the 1780's the battle against the Hasidim was weakened by political factors. At that time the disintegration of the Polish kingdom proceeded apace. The three neighboring countries wrested entire provinces from it, and the compact community of Polish Jewry was thereby divided into four parts. The largest segment of the Baal Shem Tov's disciples, however, still remained in the moribund Polish state. This significantly diminished the struggle against the Hasidim, for at the slightest sign of danger the Hasidic leaders and their adherents could move to a neighboring province which was under a different government. This situation, however, changed in the middle of the 1790's after the total collapse of the Polish kingdom.[67] Except for Galicia, all the other former provinces of Poland hav-

63. See above, pp. 90–91.

64. Avigdor himself notes in his petition to the Senate (*Yevreyskaya Starina*, 1910, pp. 276–277): "I leased the rabbinate of Pinsk in Lithuania for a good sum of money from the master of the city."

65. See Teitelbaum, *op. cit.*, pp. 34–35.

66. In the 1790's the number of Shneur Zalman's followers is supposed to have attained one hundred thousand.

67. Rabbi Shneur Zalman himself indicates this in one of his letters (see *Bet Rabbi*, p. 72; see also ibid., p. 53).

ing significant Hasidic communities came under the sovereignty of the czarist regime. This brought it about that when the battle against the Hasidim was renewed in 1796, it quickly assumed completely new forms. The Mitnagdim no longer appealed merely to the Jewish communities or fought only with the weapon of excommunications. They also applied for aid to the governmental authorities, sending to relevant agencies denunciations and complaints about their enemy, whom they wished to conquer and destroy with the aid of the new power.

As is generally known, the beginning of the controversy which erupted in 1796 was linked to two events. The Hasidim gave out a rumor to the effect that the Gaon of Vilna regretted his earlier persecution of the Hasidim. When the Gaon learned of this and issued a public denial, the Hasidim tried to persuade people that the denial was falsified and that the Gaon had not written it. At that time also Shneur Zalman's *Tanya* came off the press. In several of its expressions the Gaon of Vilna perceived blasphemy. Bitter opponents of Hasidism among the Gaon's associates contributed not a little to this, and soon (October 2, 1796) the Gaon issued a wrathful open letter to the communities of all the larger cities directed against those who "transgress the Torah and interpret it not according to the law," and demanded of all that they "take vengeance for the desecration of the Torah whose beauty these wanton men have cast to the ground; let no one have mercy on them, but let all issue forth with the sword of vengeance against these persons who destroy the holy covenant."

When the leaders of the *Kahal* in Minsk received the Gaon's wrathful summons, they at once appointed a special commission to work out the harshest measures against the Hasidim. They informed other communities about the measures they decided upon with the characteristic remark that in their struggle against the Hasidic "sect" they could rely on the power of the government: "We have the opportunity of persecuting the Hasidim for, with God's help, we have obtained for this the authorization of the great ruler, our governor-general."[68]

The Gaon of Vilna, who was removed from all worldly concerns, honestly looked upon his battle against the Hasidim as a "war for the sake of Heaven." His intent was simply to protect the sacred Torah from those who "deliberately misin-

68. See Marek, *op. cit.*, *Yevreyskaya Starina*, XII, p. 147.

terpret it." But those who had personal scores to settle with the Hasidim and their leaders knew very well how to exploit this.[69]

The anti-Hasidic struggle assumed new forms as soon as Elijah of Vilna died. Immediately after the aged Gaon was buried, a rumor was spread in Vilna that the Hasidim were delighted and dancing with joy at the news that their great opponent was no more. The prudent and calm leader of the Hasidim, Rabbi Shnuer Zalman, immediately following the Gaon's death, circulated a proclamation to his followers admonishing them not to dare issue forth with mocking words against the deceased.[70] This, however, was of no avail. The leaders of the Vilna community soon dispatched to St. Petersburg a denunciation against "a new Jewish sect," which was represented in it as *politically* dangerous and whose prime leader was noted as the rabbi of Liozna, Rabbi Shneur Zalman.[71] By order of the authorities the rabbi was arrested in September, 1798 and taken to St. Petersburg.

The imprisonment of Rabbi Shneur Zalman produced a tremendous sensation in Hasidic circles. Sixty thousand rubles were quickly collected and Hasidic intercessors proceeded with the money to St. Petersburg. The funds collected for "redemption of the captive" contributed significantly to expediting the trial in the "secret chancellery." From Shneur Zalman's written replies to the questions put to him, it was not difficult for Paul I's officials to convince themselves that the ideas which this Hasidic rabbi and his collaborators were disseminating bore no political character. On the nineteenth of Kislev (December) the rabbi was released from the Peter-Paul Fortress of St. Petersburg.[72] With great joy Shneur Zalman informed Rabbi Levi Yitzḥak of Berdichev and Rabbi Baruch

69. Rabbi Shnuer Zalman himself apparently understood this. Therewith is explicable the fact that when he complains in a private letter about the Gaon "who proclaimed the nonsinfulness of the shedding of the blood [of the Hasidim] like water in the year 5532," he considers it necessary to point out in his summons to his Hasidim: "For it is clearly known to us that not from him [the Gaon] did the words go out—God forbid—to deal with us high-handedly, and all the days of his life this offense and transgression through error did not come from the master—God forbid" (*Bet Rabbi*, p. 71).

70. See his letter in *Bet Rabbi*, p. 72; "After the death of the rabbi, the Gaon of Vilna of blessed memory, I wrote a fearful warning to all the loving brotherhood not to speak any evil words at the bier of the sage, not a shadow of ill repute and not a fraction of dishonor, under the strictest possible prohibition."

71. As his collaborators are mentioned there: Rabbi Levi Yitzḥak of Berdichev, Rabbi Ḥayyim Ḥaykl of Amdur, Rabbi Asher of Stolin, and Rabbi Shelomoh of Karlin.

72. To this day the Ḥabad Hasidim celebrate banquets on the nineteenth of Kislev in memory of this event.

of Medzhibozh in a letter about the great miracle that had occurred with him: sitting in the fortress, he was reciting the Psalms, and when he came to the verse, "He hath redeemed my soul in peace," the door was unlocked and he was given the news that he was free.[73]

The joy, however, was quickly marred. The Hasidim refused to forgive the Mitnagdim for the persecutions they had suffered and joined forces in Vilna with the democratic elements which had for years carried on a stubborn battle against the leaders of the *Kahal*.[74] In this way they managed in February, 1799 to bring down the leaders of the *Kahal* and close the *bet din*, or rabbinic court. In new elections they placed their candidates in office and set at the head of the *Kahal* one of their friends, Meir Raphaels. The former leaders of the *Kahal*, however, refused to surrender, and here the rabbi of Pinsk, Avigdor ben Ḥayyim, came to their aid. This avaricious man was hated in Pinsk by the masses and no less so by the Hasidim, who regarded him as a bitter enemy. With their combined forces they at last managed to drive the despised rabbi from Pinsk. Avigdor joined the former heads of the *Kahal* in Vilna, and together they attacked their opponents.

Travelling to St. Petersburg, Avigdor lodged a complaint against the community of Pinsk which had deprived him of his rabbinate. In a lengthy memorandum he set forth in nineteen points, with quotations from Hasidic literature, various charges against the "new Jewish sect" that he claimed posed a serious threat to the empire and to society. Represented as the leader of this highly dangerous sect is the rabbi of Liozna, Shneur Zalman. Avigdor finally achieved his goal. In October, 1800, a directive was issued from St. Petersburg to the governor of Moghilev to arrest Shneur Zalman and bring him to St. Petersburg. Once more the leader of the White Russian Hasidim was locked up in the Peter-Paul Fortress, had to carry on a disputation with Avigdor, and was compelled to give written replies to all the charges against him. This time again the rabbi managed to demonstrate that the charges were of a purely personal character and that the teaching of the founder of the Hasidic movement was absolutely free of political "sedition." He also wrote a long letter to the Emperor Paul I in which he introduced a mass of quotations from the Bible and Talmudic literature to prove that everyone is obliged to subject himself

73. See *Bet Rabbi*, p. 70.
74. See our work, "Milḥemet Ha-Kahal Beha-Rav Ha-Aḥaron" in *He-Avar*, II.

to, and fulfill the commands of, the king. At the end of the letter he expresses his firm assurance that the emperor will recognize his innocence and humbly accepts beforehand the czar's verdict "as the judgment of the king of high."[75] Rabbi Shneur Zalman was soon freed, and after Paul's unexpected death quickly obtained permission to leave Petersburg and return home.

Shortly after this, Shneur Zalman left his birthplace and settled in the town of Lyady, where he spent his last years. It is under the title "the rabbi of Lyady" that the founder of *Ḥabad* Hasidism is known in history. To put an end to the struggle between the Mitnagdim and the Hasidim, Shneur Zalman traveled to various cities to visit the most important rabbis and scholars of his time, such as Moses Ḥafetz, Joshua Zeitlin, and others, and endeavored in personal conversation to prove that the teaching of Hasidism is not to be suspected of any noxious ideas, and that it contains no threat to the Torah and the community of Israel. At that time the Hasidic movement became so strong that the Mitnagdim themselves had to reckon with it as a significant communal power. This compelled them to lay down their weapons and make peace.

But the rabbi of Lyady, who by temperament and character was always a peacemaker, was fated to spend his life in an atmosphere of strife. After the Mitnagdim ceased to persecute him, he suffered much from his own colleague, Rabbi Abraham of Kalisk, who by character and world-view had to come into conflict with the always sedate and thoughtful author of *Tanya.*[76] Rabbi Shneur Zalman was destined to spend the last year of his life under the thunder of the great European war then raging, and he died in a strange place, a castaway Russian village in the distant fields of Kursk.

In 1812 when the war between France and Russia broke out and Napoleon's triumphant armies crossed the Niemen River, the leaders of Hasidism were divided, according to their sympathies, into two camps. The rabbis who lived in the Polish provinces, such as Elimelech of Lyzhansk and Yaakov Yitzḥak of Lublin, sided with Napoleon and prayed that his generals

75. For a discussion of the "old *rebbe*'s" second arrest and Avigdor's denunciations, see J. Hessen's work on the religious struggle in *Voskhod*, 1902; Marek, *op. cit.*, pp. 153–162; Teitelbaum, *op. cit.*, I, 90–122, 166–182, II, pp. 185–200; Dubnow, *op. cit.*, II.

76. For a discussion of the conflict between Rabbi Shneur Zalman and Rabbi Abraham of Kalisk see Teitelbaum, *op. cit.*, I, Chapter 15; A.W. Brawer's article "Al Ha-Maḥaloket Bein Ha-R. Shneur Zalman Mi-Ladi Ve-R. Avraham Mi-Kallisk" (*Kiryat Sefer*, I, p. 144).

would triumph. One must take into consideration that in the Duchy of Warsaw created by Napoleon (in 1807) equal rights were decreed for all citizens *without distinction of faith*. The Jews of Poland, therefore, had to regard "the great Napoleon" with much sympathy. Only a few rabbis, such as Israel of Koznitz, looked with hostility on Napoleon out of fear that the victory of revolutionary France might lead Jews to apostasy and denial of God. This view was also taken by the leaders of Hasidism who lived in the Russian provinces.

Most hostile of all to "the great Corsican" was the rabbi of Lyady. He was firmly persuaded "that as soon as France triumphs, apostasy will spread among Jews" and that Napoleon is "Satan, who is the greatest antagonist of the good, and all of whose striving is only for evil." When he learned that Moses Meisels was friendly to the French army, he wrote one letter after another to him and admonished him to remain loyal to his fatherland and do everything for the welfare of the Russian empire. Typical is the following letter:

> On the first day of Rosh Ha-Shanah, before *Musaf*, it was shown to me (from heaven) that if Bonaparte triumphs, wealth will increase among Jews and their fate will be improved, but the hearts of the children of Israel will be separated and removed from their Father in heaven. If our Czar Alexander prevails, poverty will increase among Jews, to be sure, and their fortunes will decline; on the other hand, the hearts of the children of Israel will unite with their Father in heaven.[77]

The son of the rabbi of Lyady, Dov Baer, also stresses in his letter[78] to the same Moses Meisels that his father was strongly convinced "that the Jewish religion is best protected under the regime of Czar Alexander." He also indicates in this letter how energetically his father propagandized among his followers and urged them to cooperate with the Russian army against the French in all ways, including espionage.[79]

77. Teitelbaum, *op. cit.*, I, 156.
78. Printed several times.
79. Also in the *kol kore*, or summons, which the rabbi of Lyady addressed to the Jews in White Russia after he fled from Lyady, it is repeated that the Jews, out of gratitude for all the benefits which the Russian government has conferred upon them, should collaborate with all their powers with the Russian army, spying out and informing the Russian generals betimes about the number and location of the enemy army—in short, "doing everything that can remove whatever danger from our beloved Czar Alexander I and bring use to his empire and our fatherland" (first published in Saul Ginsburg's *Otechestvennaya Voina*, pp. 59–61). From the whole style of this summons it is not difficult to conjecture that the text was written in the staff-room of the Russian generals, and the completed summons was given to the rabbi of Lyady to sign.

Napoleon's victorious regiments, however, came ever closer. When they captured Borisov, which is quite close to Lyady, Rabbi Shneur Zalman took his entire family and fled with the Russian army. For months the sixty-six year old rabbi had to drag himself from village to village in the winter cold which had broken out very early, until he became ill on the way and died in the village of Piena in the district of Kursk on the fifteenth of Kislev.

The "old rabbi of Lyady" is known in the history of Jewish culture as the founder of a unique form of Hasidism bearing the name *Ḥabad.* He developed his teaching most fully in his important ethical-theosophical work *Likkutei Amarim,* better known under the title *Tanya.*[80] This work, which became very renowned, is not a unitary creation but a collection of various booklets. In the first period of Hasidism's efflorescence, the acknowledged leaders of the movement were true "guides of the generation" and teachers of the way. With the growth and territorial expansion of Hasidism, the leaders were no longer able to have frequent personal intercourse with their followers and admirers, and the latter therefore used to address written inquiries to them on all kinds of communal and religious-ethical matters. The leaders would reply to these questions in public, or open, letters and booklets[81] which were immediately duplicated in numerous copies, and thus circulated throughout the entire region. But the copyists would very frequently make mistakes or, for various reasons, introduce changes into the text. Hence, Rabbi Shneur Zalman decided to publish his "sayings" and "replies" in a separate book. Most important is the first part of his work, which consists of two sections, "Sefer Shel Beinonim" and "Shaar Ha-Yiḥud Veha-Emunah."[82]

80. The title *Tanya* derives from the first word with which both parts of the work begin. We have employed the Shklov edition of 1814. Shneur Zalman's sermons, which he gave in the form of commentaries to the Pentateuchal lections of the week, were not written down by the rabbi himself. This was done by his brother Jehudah Leib and by his children, who published them under the titles *Likkutei Torah* and *Torah Or.*
81. This is indicated by the author of *Tanya* himself in the preface to his work: "These booklets that are called by the title *Likkutei Amarim* . . . All of them are responsa to numerous questions which the men of our fellowship ask as advice constantly, each one according to his stature, to seek counsel for their souls in the service of the Lord." Also Rabbi Zusya of Hanipoli notes in his *haskamah* of the year 5556 (1796) that since the booklets spread among Jews in many copies from the hands of various writers, and since, as a result of the large number of the various copies, many errors crept in, the author was forced to bring these booklets into print.
82. The first edition (1796) consisted merely of these two works, and only in the later editions were added "Iggeret Ha-Kodesh," "Iggeret Ha-Teshuvah," and "Kuntres Aḥaron."

The author humbly declares in the preface that the content of his *Likkutei Amarim* is taken from various works composed by "exalted and holy writers." But this is not quite correct, for out of the various and often contradictory elements, out of the separate sayings and thoughts, he managed to build a complete structure, a unique theosophical-ethical system. In the creator of this structure a great master and a marvelously keen and brilliant mind are discernible. To be sure, this structure, built on the threshold of the nineteenth century, in the era of revolution and enlightenment, seems quite old-fashioned and medieval. But responsibility for this lies not so much with its author as with the narrow, backward environment in which he had to live and work.

Not without reason was the young Shneur Zalman so dear to the old Maggid of Mezhirech. Like his teacher, the disciple was utterly devoted to scholarly rabbinism, espoused the strictest observance of the commandments, and held faithfully and firmly to the slogan that "study of Torah is equal to all the commandments." Like the Maggid also, Rabbi Shneur Zalman wished to warm the cold, rigidified structure of rabbinism with mystical fire, with the ardor and flame of the Baal Shem Tov's teaching.

As with the Maggid, so also in the philosophy of Rabbi Shneur Zalman the problem of *tzimtzum* (the divine contraction or withdrawal) occupies an extremely important place. And just as his teacher had done, so Shneur Zalman interpreted Rabbi Isaac Luria's teaching about *tzimtzum* in a way different from the majority of Luria's disciples. According to Ḥayyim Vital's *Etz Ḥayyim*, Luria gave the following portrait of the creation of the universe: When the *Ein Sof* (Infinite) decided to create worlds so that His name and deeds might be revealed, "He contracted Himself," i.e., He concentrated His infinite light in the center. In the midpoint a vacuum or empty space was formed, and in this space God "radiated, created, completed, and brought forth all the worlds."[83] But the Maggid of Mezhirech gave the *tzimtzum* doctrine of Rabbi Isaac Luria a different explanation. He could not agree[84] with the idea that "God contracted Himself" and left an empty space *(makom panui)* for the worlds, because this is inconsistent with the fundamental teaching of the founders of the Hasidic movement that "there is no place void of Him." We have

83. See our *History*, Vol. V, p. 71.
84. *Maggid Devarav Le-Yaakov*, p. 21.

quoted[85] the Maggid's saying to the effect that God created the worlds through *tzimtzum* out of love. Since the worlds would not have been capable of bearing the stupendous influx of the divine light, God, as it were, contracted Himself, i.e., *weakened* His infinite light through barriers and garments. And it is this weakened, veiled light that is called *tzimtzum*, which, according to the Maggid's explanation, is identical with the Biblical concept of *Elohim*. Through this *tzimtzum* the worlds were created.

The author of *Tanya* also takes this position. He believes that one cannot explain the concept of *tzimtzum* in such a manner that a "removal of space to the sides" occurred in the light of the *Ein Sof*, for the *Ein Sof* is, after all, not subject to the limitations of time and place. It is also written, "I, the Lord, change not." In God no change occurred with the creation of the world.[86] Hence, it is clear that by the concept of *tzimtzum* one cannot understand a movement from one place to another; what is meant is only the veiled condition in which the divine light reveals itself.[87] With profundity and great brilliance the rabbi of Lyady discusses in his *Tanya* the sharpest contradictions and difficulties which the ancient Kabbalists of the generation of Ezra and Azriel[88] had already struggled to reconcile and explain—how from the *Ayin* (nothing) is born the *Yesh* (something), how from the infinite comes the finite, the limited, and the ephemeral.

The author of the *Tanya* stresses that, in regard to the problem of knowledge of God, he adopts the view of Maimonides that the conceptions man can have of divinity must be limited to negative attributes.[89] Shneur Zalman several times repeats that no creature can grasp the mystery of the creation of something out of nothing or have the slightest conception of the nature of the Creator and His thought.[90] "The Torah speaks in the language of men," declare the sages of the Talmud. The

85. See above, p. 73.
86. *Tanya*, 48: "As for what is written, 'I, the Lord, change not,'—that means that there is no change at all. As He was alone before the creation of the world, He alone will be after the creation, without any change in His essence or in His knowledge, for in His knowledge of Himself He knows all the creatures, for all are from Him."
87. *Likkutei Torah*, "Va-Yikra," 102; *ibid.*, 90 (we quote according to the Vilna edition of 1878).
88. See our *History*, Vol. III, pp. 13ff.
89. *Likkutei Torah*, "Pekudei," 7, 12.
90. "Iggeret Ha-Kodesh"; "Shaar Ha-Yiḥud Veha-Emunah," 49; "Sefer Shel Beinonim," 24.

language of men, however, is so pallid and poor that it cannot provide a true and accurate conception of the nature of the objects and phenomena which surround man and fill the space of the world. Man employs word-images and word-symbols. But how is it possible to present in images and signs any conception of that which has no form or image? How can one speak of divine qualities and attributes when all the designations and similes in human language are adapted only to human perceptions and ideas? These reflect human feelings and desires, but the nature of God is altogether different; He is absolutely other than human.

One must bear in mind—Shneur Zalman, basing himself on Maimonides, repeats—that men designate completely different conceptions with the same word. We employ, for example, the expressions "thought," "word," and the like in regard to both man and God, while in reality we have to do here with totally different conceptions. When we use the expression "speech" or "word" in regard to man, we understand by it the word born and expressed through man's thought which, by means of sound, is separated from the speaker and transmitted to another. But what is designated by the concept of "word" or "speech" in regard to God is the revelation, the passing from potentiality to actuality, from the state of hiddenness to disclosure, of the divine light. This revelation is also called the ten *sefirot*, through which all the worlds were created and animated.

All the *tzimtzumim* through which the worlds were created are merely in the state of *hester panim* (hiding of the face),[91] for in the divine itself no *tzimtzumim* and concealments occur, and both darkness and light, as well as all the *tzimtzumim* and garments, are not separated from God. He remains to eternity "the only and single One" *(Yaḥid U-Meyuḥad)*. Even now, after the creation of the world, as it is said in the Torah, *Adonai Hu Elohim*, "the Lord is *Elohim*." God and *Elohim*, which is the mirror-image of nature (*Elohim* in *gematria* is equivalent to *ha-teva*, "nature") are one and inseparable, "without any change whatsoever."[92] The change is only from the point of view and from the limited conceptions of the "recipients," i.e., from the side of men.

91. A mystical expression which is already to be found in the *Zohar*.

92. "Sefer Shel Beinonim," Chapters 20–21; "Shaar Ha-Yiḥud Veha-Emunah," Chapter 6: " 'The Lord He is God' *(Adonai Hu Elohim)* means that these two names are actually one . . . for the name of God does not conceal and contract except for the worlds below, but not as regards the Holy One Himself, since He and His name *Elohim* are One."

With great subtlety the author of *Tanya* disposes of the philosophical question whether divinity is immanent or transcendent, i.e., whether God is the external or internal First Cause of the world. In his view divinity is both simultaneously; it is *in* the world and also *beyond* the world. "God Blessed be He," declares Shneur Zalman, "does indeed permeate all the worlds in equal measure,"[93] but men can grasp and bear the divine light only through marvelous *tzimtzumim* wrapped in heavy veils, until the abundance of the divine light passes over from the state of "infinity" to the state of "boundary and limitation." There can be no comparison whatever between these limited human concepts and the actual divine nature, and the light the creatures receive according to their perceptions is such an incomparably small ray of the infinite light that there can be no analogy or relationship between them.[94] Hence, the author of *Tanya* stresses with particular sharpness the vast distinction between *or mitlabesh* and *or makkif*, between immanent light and transcendent light.[95]

In reality, "the Holy One Blessed be He fills all worlds equally," and Shneur Zalman admonishes, "You must not even think that the heavens with all their stars and the earth with its creatures are a *davar nifrad mi-penei atzmo*,"[96] for "God Blessed be He fills the whole universe."[97] From this point of view, the divine light which "fills all worlds equally" is an *or mitlabesh*, an immanent light. The conceptions, however, which the "recipients," the creatures, have of the world and of the divine light permeating it are "literally like nothing." These limited human perceptions are, in comparison to the divine First Cause, "nullified in relation to actual being," just as a weak ray of light amounts to nothing when compared with the soul's rich world of feelings.[98] In regard to these limited human conceptions, God "is separate and distinct from the worlds," and His infinite light is in the state of *sovev u-makkif* (surrounding and embracing). It is transcendent, *above* and *beyond* the world.[99]

93. "Sefer Shel Beinonim," Chapter 40: "The Holy One Blessed be He fills all the worlds equally."
94. "Sefer Shel Beinonim," Chapter 48: "Shaar Ha-Yiḥud Veha-Emunah," Chapter 6.
95. *Ibid.*, Chapter 23 and Chapter 48.
96. "An independent, separate thing."
97. "Shaar Ha-Yiḥud Veha-Emunah," Chapter 6.
98. "Sefer Shel Beinonim," Chapters 23–44 and 46; "Shaar Ha-Yiḥud Veha-Emunah," Chapter 6.
99. "Sefer Shel Beinonim," Chapter 46: "For the Holy One Blessed be He is extrinsic

The idealistic nature of Shneur Zalman's philosophy appears even more clearly than in the case of the Baal Shem Tov and the Maggid of Mezhirech. "With our corporeal eyes," he teaches,

we can in no way grasp God's power and His breath that are revealed in the creation of the world. If we were able to note and grasp all this, we would no longer see any material things. We would then understand that all this really amounts to nothing in relation to the living spirit which is in all material things and without which all these are literally nothing.[100]

We would understand, he repeats, that all material things—even stones, earth and minerals—are in reality "not things in themselves." They owe their entire existence only to the sparks of life with which they are endowed by God, and without these they return to the womb of non-being.[101] The pious rabbi of Lyady had no conception of the fact that, in his view of the material world, he came in his own way to the same conclusions as the Irish bishop George Berkeley and the great Scottish skeptic David Hume.

In what does the purpose of *maaseh bereshit* (the creation of the world) consist? The author of *Tanya* is firmly convinced that everything in the world was created for the sake of a definite goal and purpose. Like his teacher, the Maggid of Mezhirech,[102] Shneur Zalman sets forth the same reason: "There is no king without a people."[103] The purpose of all the *tzimtzumim* and stages of creation, he teaches, was to create man, who must carry on warfare with the material of his body, struggle against the *sitra aḥara* (the other side, the demonic), unite himself through free choice with the light and reject the

---

to the worlds and configuratively surrounds all the worlds, so that He cannot be clothed or contained in them." *Ibid.*, Chapter 23: "The will of God Blessed Be He, who is called 'surrounding all the worlds,' for He is in the configuration that He cannot be clothed or contained inside the worlds, but He vivifies and gives light from above in the configuration of surrounding or embracing . . . For all the worlds, the supernal and the lower, are reckoned as nothing by Him, so that He does not clothe Himself with them but surrounds all the worlds in the configuration of embracing."

100. "Shaar Ha-Yiḥud Veha-Emunah," Chapter 3.

101. "Sefer Shel Beinonim," Chapter 38.

102. See above, pp. 74–75.

103. "The purpose of the creation of the world is for the sake of the revelation of God Blessed Be He, and there is no king without a people" ("Shaar Ha-Yiḥud Veha-Emunah," Chapter 7). "The purpose of the development of all the worlds is that the glory of the Lord may fill all the earth" ("Sefer Shel Beinonim," Chapter 49).

darkness, raise his soul and all the powers of his body "to the Lord alone." Everything is for the sake of love for man here below, in order to raise him to God.[104]

But, as with the Maggid of Mezhirech,[105] so also with his disciple the role of the person, of the individual, is intimately associated with the cosmic role of the community of Israel. God, declares Shneur Zalman, contracted His infinite light and clothed it in the form of the limited world out of love for His people Israel, to bring this people close to Himself and to include it in His unity.[106] The congregation of Israel, the source of all Jewish souls, is the *Shechinah.*[107] Every individual, we further read, must bear in mind his enormous responsibility. He is obliged to say: For my sake was the world created; I must repair and improve it. Along with this, however, he must not forget that the mother of his divine soul is the community of Israel, the source of "the souls of all Israel."[108]

We indicated in the previous chapter[109] the motivation of the view held by the Maggid of Mezhirech: God and the Torah are, after all, one; hence, the Torah also, in order to be revealed, required *tzimtzum.* However, the sole bearer of the Torah is the people of Israel; therefore, the creation of the world is also for the sake of Israel alone. This thesis is developed by the author of *Tanya* into a complete system.

Man can fulfill his mission—to raise the world to God, to "illuminate the darkness with the divine light" and to fill the world with God's glory—through the aid of "three garments:" thought, speech, and act. Thought and speech are the study of the Torah, and act is the fulfillment of the six hundred thirteen commandments of the Torah.

Here the typical scholar and rabbinic codifier appears before us. Shneur Zalman does not tire of repeating that "there is no good but Torah,"[110] that "the study of Torah is equal to all the commandments,"[111] that "the virtue of one who engages in study of Torah is superior to all the commandments."[112] Man

104. "Sefer Shel Beinonim," Chapter 36, Chapter 49.
105. See above, p. 73.
106. "Sefer Shel Beinonim," Chapter 19. See also *Torah Or*, "Shemot": "The purpose of the creation of the world is for the sake of Israel."
107. *Ibid.*, Chapter 37.
108. *Ibid.*, Chapter 41.
109. See above, pp. 73ff.
110. "Sefer Shel Beinonim," Chapter 14; *Likkutei Torah*, "Pekudei," and in numerous other places.
111. "Sefer Shel Beinonim," Chapter 5.
112. *Ibid.*, Chapter 23.

cannot grasp God's thought. Hence God veiled His wisdom and will in the Torah through the mystery of *tzimtzum*,[113] and in the hour when man occupies himself with the words of the Torah his soul unites with "the word and thought of the Holy One Blessed be He."[114] Each individual law about what is permitted and what may be eaten, about non-liability and innocence—all this is a revelation of God's will.[115]

Of no lesser importance, according to the philosophy of *Tanya*, is fulfillment of the commandments of the Torah. In definite contradiction to the statement quoted above that the study of Torah is equal to all the commandments, Shneur Zalman declares, "There is greater virtue in fulfilling the commandments than in study of Torah."[116] God, we read in *Tanya*, contracted His infinite wisdom and His will "in the six hundred thirteen commandments of the Torah and in their laws."[117] The Infinite and His wisdom, Shneur Zalman affirms, are one, and no mortal can grasp them. But through numerous *tzimtzumim*, God's wisdom descended from one level to another in the chain of the worlds until it incorporated itself in material things, and these are the six hundred thirteen commandments of the Torah.[118]

"The essence of the revelation of the *Shechinah* is in practical commandments," the author of *Tanya* repeats.[119] The commandments are the disclosure of God's will that is embodied in all the worlds; these, the highest as well as the lowest worlds, all draw abundance and life from the commandments fulfilled by men below.[120] All the worlds, both the highest and the lowest, are dependent—we further read—on every command-

113. *Ibid.*, Chapter 47.
114. *Ibid.*, Chapter 23.
115. *Ibid.*: "For all the laws are the details of the inner emanations of the Divine Will itself. For thus God Blessed Be He decided that this thing is permitted, or *kasher*, or exempt, or innocent, or the opposite." See also Chapter 52: "And the laws themselves are of the attributes of the *Ein Sof* Blessed Be He."
116. The author of *Tanya* himself dwells on this contradiction and also attempts to resolve it (*Likkutei Torah*, "Parashat Ba-Midbar," in the last explanations).
117. *Ibid.*, Chapter 4.
118. "Sefer Shel Beinonim," Chapter 52.
119. *Siddur* "Shaar Tefillah"; see also "Sefer Shel Beinonim," Chapter 17: "The love of the Lord is to cleave to Him through observing His commandments and His Torah, and this is the whole [duty of] man."
120. "Sefer Shel Beinonim," Chapter 23: "For the commandments are inwardly the will of the Most High and His true wish with which all the worlds, the upper and the lower, are clothed, to give life to them; for all vitality and abundance is dependent on the observance of the *mitzvot* in the lower worlds."

ment that is performed.[121] Through his fulfillment of the commandments of the Torah, man unites with the light of the *Ein Sof.*[122] Through its observance of the commandments, Israel redeems the world.[123]

Study of the Torah and observance of the commandments, however, have slight value when they are carried through without *kavvanah,* inner concentration and devotion.[124] But *kavvanah,* declares *Tanya,* is dependent not on the heart alone; it does not derive merely from impulse and emotion. Here Shneur Zalman appears before us not as the scholar and codifier who produced his own *Shulḥan Aruch* but as a Kabbalist and creator of his own Hasidic system. Earlier[125] we quoted the Baal Shem Tov's words to the effect that the highest degree of faith is found in the man who possesses two qualities: he bases himself on the tradition of the fathers, and he has also convinced himself of the truth of his faith through his own searching. The feeling and passion of the heart, we read in *Tanya,* must be controlled by the understanding of the mind. Enthusiasm cannot make a man suited "for grasp of divinity" if it is not accompanied by clarity of understanding. One must have both—the flame of the heart and the logical theories of the mind. One must *know* the divine power that rules all the worlds, and this knowledge is attained with the aid of the human understanding that *seeks* God and immerses itself in speculation about Him.

Man's soul, *Tanya* teaches,[126] consists of two parts: *sechel* (mind) and *middot* (attributes or qualities). *Sechel* includes the three levels of *ḥochmah* (wisdom), *binah* (understanding), and *da'at* (knowledge). *Middot* are the love of God and the reverence and fear of God's greatness. *Ḥabad* (an acronym for *ḥochmah, binah* and *da'at*) are the birth-giving mothers and source from which the *middot* derive. In the soul of the man who does not immerse and bind his thought and understanding "in the greatness of the Infinite Blessed be He," true love and reverence for God will not be born; instead "vain imagin-

121. *Tanya,* last "Kuntres": "And all the worlds, the upper and the lower, are dependent on the precise performance of one commandment."

122. "Sefer Shel Beinonim," Chapter 37 and Chapter 46; see also *Torah Or,* "Parashat Shemot," "Parashat Va'era."

123. "Sefer Shel Beinonim," Chapter 31.

124. "Sefer Shel Beinonim," Chapter 38 and Chapter 40.

125. See above, Chapter Two, p. 54.

126. In another place ("Sefer Shel Beinonim," Chapter 1), the author of *Tanya* notes that man's soul consists of two elements—the "animal soul" and the "divine soul."

ings" will be created. Indeed, for this reason, *da'at* or knowledge "is the existence and living breath of the *middot.*"[127] The *middot* are according to the degree of reason, *Tanya* repeats;[128] the mind rules the heart.[129] "The service of the heart is according to knowledge *(da'at).*"[130] However, Shneur Zalman insists along with this, the essence of *da'at* is not merely knowledge, not simply to know of God's greatness from books of speculation, but to immerse oneself in God's greatness, to let one's own thought penetrate into God with all the power and strength of the heart and mind, until the thought is solidly bracketed to God with a bond as strong as that wherewith one binds himself firmly to a material thing that he sees with his corporeal eyes.[131]

Here we touch upon the most interesting point in the philosophy of Rabbi Shneur Zalman. We have seen how through *binah* and *da'at,* the last two links of the trinity of *Ḥabad,* love and reverence for God are born in the human soul. The Maggid of Mezhirech had already insisted in the sharpest fashion that true love for God is only a result of fear, of great reverence for God.[132] If man has total reverence for the Creator, love will thereby also awaken in him.[133] But fear or reverence must express itself not in terror of punishment,[134] not as in a man who is afraid of a "ravenous bear," but must be an "exalted fear," an "embarrassed fear," i.e., it must be the feeling of profound reverence and astonishment before the majesty of God that a man experiences when he begins to be ashamed of his littleness and vanity.[135] The author of *Tanya* also bases himself on this idea. He, too, declares that "without the preliminary stage of fear, one cannot attain to love."[136] It is written, "And thou shalt serve the Lord thy God": in order that the service may be "perfect," every man must serve God

127. "Sefer Shel Beinonim," Chapter 3 and Chapter 16.
128. *Ibid.*, Chapter 6.
129. *Ibid.*, Chapter 12.
130. *Ibid.*, Chapter 34.
131. *Ibid.*, Chapter 42. See also *ibid:* "The chief thing is to accustom his knowledge and his thought constantly to be fixed in his heart and mind, so that everything that he sees with his eyes, the heaven and the earth and all that is therein—all are external garments of the King Blessed Be He, and thereby he will always remember their inwardness and their vitality."
132. *Or Torah,* p. 28; *Likkutei Amarim,* 18.
133. *Likkutei Amarim,* 23.
134. *Or Torah,* 77.
135. *Ibid.*, 60.
136. "Sefer Shel Beinonim," Chapter 19, Chapter 43.

according to two states and levels—both in the state of a servant and in the state of a son. Basing itself on the statement of the *Zohar*, "Fear and love are two wings . . . and fear is included in love," *Tanya* also compares fear and love to two wings. Just as a bird cannot fly with only one wing, so fear alone is merely the one wing with which it is not possible to rise to the heights, and love, too, is only the one wing with which one cannot ascend there. One must serve God not merely as a servant or as a son but combine both conditions.[137]

But there are two kinds of fear and two kinds of love. There is, first, a "natural fear" *(yirah tiv'it).*[138] In every "man of Israel," declares *Tanya*, a treasury of "reverence for God" is hidden in the depths of "the understanding of his heart." This treasury is first brought from potentiality to actuality with the aid of the second link in the above-mentioned trinity–*da'at*. Through *consciousness* the treasuries of the natural "understanding of the heart" are first raised to the state of the clear idea that all things above and below, everything that one's eyes perceive in the heavens and on earth, are merely "external garments of God Blessed be He," as it is written, "The whole earth is full of His glory."[139] But the state of knowing that the whole earth is filled with God's glory is, in Shneur Zalman's view, not the supreme level. There is still another level of reverence of God, and this is "exalted reverence, inward reverence," which attains the state of *ḥochmah* (wisdom), the third and highest element of *Ḥabad*. It is written, "Who is wise?—He who can foresee events (*ha-nolad;* literally, "what may be born"), i.e., the wise man is one who sees from whence everything is *born* and knows that everything derives from the *Ayin* (nothing) and is transformed into *Yesh* (something) through God's word and "through the breath of His mouth." Thereby he understands that the earth and all the heavens with their luminaries are, in relation to God's word, like nothing at all, and are nullified in relation to reality, as the illumination of a ray of light is nullified in comparison with the stupendous light of the sun itself.[140]

Love for God is also divided in *Tanya* into two levels: *ahavah tiv'it* (natural love) or *ahavah rabbah* (great love), and *ahavah*

137. *Ibid.*, Chapter 41, and numerous other places. The author of *Tanya* in this connection manifests great knowledge in various psychological and ethical matters.

138. This is also called by Shneur Zalman *yirah tata'ah* (lower fear).

139. "Sefer Shel Beinonim," Chapter 42.

140. *Ibid.*, Chapter 43.

sichlit (intellectual love) or *ahavat olam* (everlasting love). Everlasting love comes from *tevunah ve-da'at* (understanding and knowledge), through thinking oneself into the marvelous greatness of God who fills and embraces all worlds. Through this consciousness, love for God is strengthened in man; it does not wish to unite with any material thing nor with any other spiritual entity in the world, but only with God, who is the source of life.[141] But higher than this "intellectual love" which is based on *binah* and *da'at* is the simple, natural love *(ahvah tiv'it)* that is also great love *(ahavah rabbah).*[142] "Natural love," *Tanya* repeats, "transcends the knowledge that conceptualizes and understands, and is higher and more exalted than knowledge. It is like the love of a child—a love that is not conscious, not illuminated and grounded "in conception and understanding" and through logical, intellectual reasons. The child does not understand in what the fatherhood of his father really consists and why he should love him, but his whole soul is closesly bound, without any conscious reason, to the soul of his father; and this bond is so powerful that he yearns ceaselessly for his father and cries for him, convulsed in weeping.[143]

Yet this love, too, is not the supreme state of love. There is still another state, the author of *Tanya* declares, "which transcends the worth of all others as gold overshadows silver with its value."[144] There are, according to Shneur Zalman, two states in man's heart. One is external *(beḥinah ḥitzonit);* this is the passion or emotion which derives from *beḥinat ha-binah veha-da'at* (the state of understanding and knowledge), immersing oneself by means of thought in the grandeur of the *Ein Sof.* The other state is an inner one, hidden in the profoundest depths of the heart. The love which streams from these depths and of which it is said in the Song of Songs (8:6), "Its flashes are flashes of fire," is "beyond the state of knowledge and understanding." Man possesses it *be-hese'aḥ ha-da'at* (with diverted attention, without consciously knowing it). It is a gift which man receives from God, an act of God's grace that transcends *binah* and *da'at.* This is the reflection of the truly divine light that is revealed in the highest element of the trinity,

141. *Ibid.*

142. *Ibid.*, Chapter 44: "For the two states of love consist of the state of mighty, exalted, and great love, with mental fear and trembling; for this is the love that is called above by the name "eternal love" *(ahavat olam).*

143. *Likkutei Torah*, "Parashat Ba-Midbar;" see also "Iggeret Ha-Kodesh," folio 14b (according to the Shklov edition of 1814).

144. "Sefer Shel Beinonim," Chapter 18 and Chapter 44.

ḥochmah, which is the crown of all the emanations and divine qualities, the vessel of the light of the *Ein Sof.*

The Jewish people, however, is bound in an everlasting covenant with the Torah, which is the revelation of divine wisdom and which it receives as an inheritance from its fathers, transmitted from generation to generation. For this reason it is written, "for the word is very nigh unto thee," and the Jews were commanded, "Ye shall be holy." They are rendered holy by the fact that in the soul of "every man of Israel" there is a reflection of the *Ein Sof,* as it were, in the form or state of *ḥochmah.* This is the meaning of the words: "Wisdom *(ḥochmah)* preserves the life of him who has it" (Ecclesiastes 7:12). And *ḥochmah, Tanya* repeats, is "above understanding and perception."[145] It is, however, their source. Indeed, for this reason it is called *ḥochmah,* which signifies *koaḥ mah,*[146] a hidden power that is incomprehensible and not cognizable by human perception. It is the garment and vessel of the *Ein Sof's* light, "which thought cannot grasp."

Hence, we read in *Tanya,* every member of the Jewish people which carries forward the long chain of the fathers' heritage and whose progenitors were likened to the divine "chariot"[147]—even women and ignorant persons, even the least worthy and the sinners[148]—sacrifice themselves for the sanctification of God's name and frequently suffer grievous afflictions in order not to deny the one God. These boors and ignoramuses offer themselves up not because they grasp and understand the greatness of God. They do so without reflection and logical theories, without "any argument and reason." They act thus and not otherwise because it is impossible for them to deny the one God, to turn away from him. As a result of the long chain of tradition, God shines in the depths of everyone's soul; He shines in the state of *ḥochmah* which is beyond knowledge and the reason that perceives and understands.[149]

145. In another place (*Likkutei Torah,* "Parashat Va-Yikra," in the explanation to "do not hold back salt") the author of *Tanya* concludes: "For the soul itself is above the essence of the intellect."

146. A play on words.

147. "These, these are the *merkavah.*" For a discussion of the mystical significance of the *merkavah,* see our *History,* Vol. II, pp. 58–59.

148. Typical is the following passage in *Tanya*: "And at times sinners of Israel reincarnate extremely exalted souls that were in the depths of the *kelipot*" ("Sefer Shel Beinonim," Chapter 18).

149. *Ibid.,* Chapter 18–19 and Chapter 25; *Torah Or,* "Parashat Shemot."

The Kabbalist in Shneur Zalman triumphs over the codifier and scholar; mystical passion tears through the artificial web of cold, intellectual theories. Only when we read these pages of *Tanya*, which are written in a difficult, unpolished style but in which not only a fine scholar and brilliant mind but a great personality is so clearly discernible, do we understand wherein the extraordinary propagandizing power of the rabbi of Lyady consisted.

We must note one other important point in Shneur Zalman's philosophy—his attitude toward the role of the *tzaddik*. The *tzaddikim*, in his view, are superior to the angels, because the angels are not given free choice,[150] and "whoever unites himself with a sage, it is as if he united with the *Shechinah*."[151] In every generation, we read in *Tanya*, sparks "of the soul of Moses our teacher" descend and clothe themselves in the body and soul of the "sages of the generation, the eyes of the community," who teach the people to know and understand the greatness of God and to serve Him with the whole heart and soul.[152] But, along with this, it is indicated in *Tanya* that in *every* "soul of the house of Israel" there is something "of the state of Moses our teacher." Shneur Zalman also repeats that the highest state of love is "equal in *every soul* of Israel and is our inheritance from our ancestors,"[153] and he asserts that even in the soul of a "boorish and completely ignorant man" the holiness of the Sabbath and the festival shines just as in the soul of the *tzaddik*, for all of us have the same Torah."[154]

When some of Shneur Zalman's disciples began to apply to him with requests concerning their material needs, as if he were a miracle-worker who, as they hoped, would be able to influence the "upper worlds," he protested publicly against this in his booklet "Iggeret Ha-Kodesh," which he distributed among his followers. There was never, he here asserts, a custom among Jews to ask advice of scholars regarding material affairs. Even the Tannaim and Amoraim, to whose wisdom all mysteries were revealed, were not addressed with such questions, for it was known that they were not prophets who could predict what will happen.[155] In total antithesis to the teaching of *No'am Elimelech*, the rabbi of Lyady declares that when any-

150. "Sefer Shel Beinonim," Chapter 39; "Shaar Ha-Yiḥud Veha-Emunah," Chapter 11.
151. *Ibid.*, Chapter 2.
152. *Ibid.*, Chapter 42.
153. *Ibid.*, Chapter 44.
154. *Ibid.*, Chapter 46.
155. "Iggeret Ha-Kodesh," 18–19.

one finds himself in distress and grievously afflicted, it would be better for him to turn directly to his Father in heaven and not seek any righteous intercessor,[156] for God is a merciful Father.

In general, *Tanya* is permeated with complete optimism. "Evil does not come down from on high and everything is good," Shneur Zalman affirms.[157] But since men do not understand "the greatness of His goodness," they think it is evil. Because God is "only good," *Tanya* teaches, "the principal thing is that man should rejoice and be glad always." For this reason we also encounter in it a number of times the Baal Shem Tov's favorite teaching, "the *Shechinah* rests only in the midst of joy." On the other hand, in opposition to the Baal Shem Tov's doctrine, Shneur Zalman insists that the joy must be only "the joy of the soul" and that man's body must be "contemptible and despised in his sight."[158]

In closing, one further point must be touched on. Several scholars of Hasidism conclude that *Tanya* "may quite properly sustain comparison with the best works of the medieval Jewish thinkers." Such a statement, however, is not altogether correct, for one must take into consideration that the authors of *Sefer Ha-Kuzari*, *Moreh Nevuchim*, and *Or Adonai* stood at the summit of the culture of their time. This cannot be said of the author of *Tanya*. Shneur Zalman grew up in a community which, like a collective Ḥoni Ha-Me'aggel, had been somnolent for generations. Despite the fact that he drew his mathematical and astronomical knowledge from Joseph Solomon Delmedigo's *Elim*,[159] he still held, at the threshold of the nineteenth century, to the old Ptolemaic system. A contemporary of Lavoisier, he continued to operate with the "four elements;" living a hundred years after Newton, he still had no conception of the nature of the seven basic colors.[160] A typical son of a backward milieu, Shneur Zalman regarded the secular sciences with defi-

156. On the other hand, however, the author of *Tanya* does not tire of indicating the great importance of giving charity, and that one must aid with material assistance all needy members of the community. "Israel is not redeemed except through charity," the rabbi of Lyady repeats several times (see *Tanya*, Chapter 37; "Iggeret Ha-Kodesh," folios 2, 4; *Torah Or*, "Parashat Shemot").

157. *Iggeret Ha-Kodesh*, folio 8b.

158. "Sefer Shel Beinonim," Chapter 32.

159. See above, p. 100.

160. See *Torah Or*, end of "Parashat Vayyetze." It was precisely the author of *Kedushat Levi* who did know that "from white *all colors* are made" (see *Kedushat Levi*, "Likkutim").

nite contempt. He concludes that to occupy oneself with "external wisdoms" is generally a vain thing." It makes sense to familiarize oneself with them only if one can use them "for the service of God."[161] Shneur Zalman therefore rules in his *Shulḥan Aruch* that if one has already studied through the entire Torah, he is still forbidden to study the "wisdom of the gentiles." Merely on occasion is the Jewish scholar permitted to concern himself with the sciences, and only in case he may learn from them matters of Torah and reverence for God.[162]

On this question both wings of the Hasidic movement—White Russian *Ḥabad*, and Volhynian and Galician tzaddikism—were in agreement. Such a view necessarily led to a sharp conflict with the Haskalah movement, of which we shall have occasion to speak in later chapters.

161. "Sefer Shel Beinonim," Chapter 8.

162. See M. Teitelbaum, *Ha-Rav Mi-Ladi U-Mifleget Ḥabad*, II, p. 17.

CHAPTER FIVE

Lovers of Israel;
LEVI YITZḤAK OF BERDICHEV AND NAḤMAN OF BRATZLAV

The standard-bearers of "love for Israel"—Mosheh Leib of Sasov—Ze'ev Wolf of Zbarazh, Menaḥem Mendel of Kosov, and Meir of Peremyshlyany—Levi Yitzḥak, the rabbi of Berdichev, and his *Kedushat Levi*—The "eyes of God" as man's creation—Love as the primary attribute of God and the cornerstone of the world—Love of Israel and love of the Creator—Everything in the world is filled with God's love—The cosmic role of the Jewish people—The *tzaddik* must always speak favorably of Jews—Redemption for the whole world—Liberation from fear of the seven departments of hell—The Baal Shem Tov's great-grandson Rabbi Naḥman of Bratzlav—Rabbi Naḥman's career—His philosophy—Questions to which there is no answer—The world is created for the sake of mercy and requires mercy—Two kinds of heretics—Rabbi Naḥman's struggle against the rationalists—Simplicity and sincerity without subtleties; the "wisdom of holiness"—The great state of joy—The melody of the world—The supreme state of silence—The melody of "Rosh Amanah"—The role of the *tzaddik;* the *tzaddik* in the state of Moses the Messiah—The tales of Rabbi Naḥman of Bratzlav.

WE HAVE observed that the Baal Shem Tov's doctrine was transformed among his disciples, and that in the Hasidic movement in the second generation after his death two major currents were clearly formed: on the one side, practical tzaddikism; on the other, the Ḥabad Hasidism of White Russia. In the southern provinces, where Jacob Frank in his day had declared war on the melancholy, servile Jewish way of life and dreamed of the glory and splendor of the Christian nobility with their beautiful palaces and dazzling luxuries, a unique Jewish aristocracy was formed with its own "courts," with carriages decorated with silver and gold, with numerous servants and thousands of admirers who, like faithful slaves, obeyed the commands of their "lord," the *tzaddik*, the incarnate symbol of "the foundation that is in the *sefirah* called *Tiferet* (Beauty)," and whose power is limitless in both worlds. On the other side, in the northern regions of White Russia and Lithuania, the protagonists of Ḥabad made a bold attempt to warm frigid, congealed rabbinism with mystical fire, with the fervor and flame of the Baal Shem Tov's teaching. They would not and, perhaps, could not acknowledge the fact that the teaching thereby lost much of its unique charm and primordial power.

Among the standard-bearers of the Hasidic movement, however, there were those who sought faithfully to realize in life the teaching of the founder in its pristine form. These men set as the foundation of their lives the Baal Shem Tov's doctrine about "love for the Creator" and "love for Israel."[1] To be sure, such romantic dreamers did not succeed in gaining dominance in the movement, but they were inscribed in the heart and memory of the common people, who lovingly and gratefully adorned their names with garlands of beautiful, tender legends.

We shall here mention only a few of them, first the remarkable Mosheh Leib of Sasov (near Brody), whose name is always accompanied by the term *Ohev Yisrael*, "lover of Israel," and whose life was one long chain of touching and gentle human love. I first learned the true meaning of love of Israel, Mosheh Leib of Sasov declares, from a simple village gentile. The villager was sitting in a tavern with some of his friends, and when he had become somewhat intoxicated he asked one of them: "Do you love me or not?" The other answered: "I love you very much." The man then said to him: "You say you love me, and yet you do not know what I lack; when one truly loves another he knows all his needs and requirements." To this his friend made no reply. Therefrom, concludes the *tzaddik* of Sasov, I first properly understood that love for Israel means to feel all

1. See above, p. 43ff.

the needs of Israel, to suffer all its pains, to share its afflictions.[2]

The most moving stories are told about the devotion with which this *tzaddik* would manifest his love for children suffering from leprosy, how he would dress their wounds with his own hands, smear their boil-covered heads with salve and say, "He who cannot bring himself to suck with his own mouth the pus and blood of sick Jewish children's boils has not even attained to half the level of true love for Israel."[3] A Hasidic tale relates that once, on the eve of the Day of Atonement, the entire congregation was already gathered in the synagogue but Rabbi Mosheh Leib had still not arrived. However, he had once for all decreed that they must not wait for him to commence the service, and so they began the *Kol Nidrei* without him. Only when the prayers were already half over did the rabbi appear. The Hasidim greatly desired to know the reason. They learned that while he was on the way to the synagogue for *Kol Nidrei*, he heard a child crying. Turning to the house from which the cry was coming, he saw through the window that no one was there; the mother had gone to the synagogue, and the child was wracked with crying. The *tzaddik* took pity on the child, picked it up, and played with it until it fell asleep. Only then did he go to *Kol Nidrei.*[4]

The *tzaddik* of Sasov once was visited by the *tzaddik* of Zhydachov who wished to observe the behavior of the Sasover at the hour for reciting the midnight prayers lamenting the exile of Israel. The most marvelous stories were told about Mosheh Leib's conduct of these prayers.[5] What the Zhydachover saw that night at the Sasover's is marvelously related by Peretz in his magnificent story "If Not Higher," and we need not retell it here.

Especially typical of the *tzaddik* of Sasov is the following tale that is even somewhat inconsistent with the traditional Jewish way of life. Rabbi Mosheh Leib was extremely fond of the commandment of accompanying brides to the marriage canopy and used to involve himself a great deal with the weddings of poor young women. At one such wedding, relate the Hasidim, the Sasover was extremely merry while accompanying the bride to the canopy with the musicians. The musicians

2. *Maaseh Tzaddikim*, 35 (Lublin edition, 1900).

3. *Seder Ha-Dorot Ha-Ḥadash*, 33–36 (Lemberg edition, 1865); see also *Maaseh Tzaddikim*, 38.

4. *Maaseh Tzaddikim*, 35.

5. *Maaseh Tzaddikim*, 37–38.

played and the *tzaddik* danced, rejoicing the bride and groom. I would wish, the *tzaddik* then said, that at my funeral, when my body is brought to burial at the cemetery, the musicians play the same wedding tune. The *tzaddik's* wish was in fact fulfilled. On a winter's day, when the Sasover was to be buried, a sled carrying musicians who were supposed to go to a wedding stood several versts from Sasov. Suddenly the horses tore themselves from the spot and flew like an arrow out of a bow, coming to a stop just at the cemetery where the *tzaddik* was about to be buried. When the musicians saw the great crowd at the cemetery and learned who the deceased was, they recalled Rabbi Mosheh Leib's words at that wedding. The rabbinic court was consulted and ruled that the wish of the *tzaddik* must be fulfilled. And so the Sasover was buried to the sounds of the wedding tune.[6]

In close spiritual affinity with the *tzaddik* of Sasov were such unique personalities as Ze'ev Wolf of Zbarazh (the son of the Baal Shem Tov's well-known disciple, Yeḥiel Michael of Zlochov), Menaḥem Mendel of Kosov, and Meir of Peremyshlyany. Ze'ev Wolf of Zbarazh would never permit anyone to raise a whip over a horse "out of pity for living things."[7] Once one of his associates whom he respected highly came to him and complained strongly about his partner and requested the *tzaddik* to punish the latter. "Do you think," Ze'ev Wolf said, "because your comrade is not one of my friends, I love him less than you? God forbid. My love for every Jew is equal. Why then should I be angry at your partner?"[8] Another time in winter the *tzaddik* was travelling with a coach driver to the celebration of a circumcision in a severe frost. Arriving at the house, Ze'ev Wolf at once entered but quickly remembered that the coach driver had remained outside in the cold with the horses. No one observed that the *tzaddik* soon left the house and told the driver to go in for a while and warm himself. The driver said that he could not leave the horses for fear of having them stolen. The *tzaddik* answered: "Go into the house for a while and warm yourself; in the meantime I will watch the horses." The driver at first declined, but when the *tzaddik* insisted he agreed and went into the house. There he warmed

6. *Kehal Ḥasidim Ha-Ḥadash*, 58 (Peremyshlyany edition, 1902).

7. Of Moseh Leib of Sasov it is also related that he used to go about to the fairs and, when he would see a bound calf or a sheep on a wagon, he would promptly bring a bucket of water to quench the animal's thirst, so that it should not suffer pain.

8. *Seder Ha-Dorot Ha-Ḥadash*, 24.

himself, was given refreshments, and completely forgot that the *tzaddik* was waiting for him outside with the horses. So a rather long time passed. In the house they could not understand where the *tzaddik* had disappeared until they went out into the street and found him half frozen with the horses. Astonished they asked him: "Rabbi, what are you doing outside?" He answered simply: "I sent the driver into the house to get warm and I stayed to watch the horses, and he has not returned yet."[9]

Once, relates *Seder Ha-Dorot Ha-Ḥadash*, the wife of the *tzaddik* of Zbarazh had a quarrel with her maidservant. The women had certain complaints against each other, and both set out for the rabbinic court for adjudication of their dispute. The wife then saw that the *tzaddik* took his coat and was preparing to go with them. She said to him: "You need not go; I shall be quite able to present the case myself." "No," answered the *tzaddik*, "I am not going for your sake, but for the sake of your servant, the orphan girl, to protect her interests." *Seder Ha-Dorot Ha-Ḥadash* further relates that in town a group of young men were spending whole nights playing cards. Some persons came to the *tzaddik* and complained of this debauchery. However, the *tzaddik*, who used to judge all men favorably, answered: "It is clear that Jews wish to serve the Creator not only by day but also by night, and so they accustom themselves to stay up all night; when this becomes a matter of habit for them, they will certainly repent completely and serve the Creator day and night."

No less typical are the stories that are told about the *tzaddik* Menaḥem Mendel of Kosov. The root of all things, he used to say, is love for Israel, and the most marvelous tales are told of the devotion with which he would aid people in distress.[10] Characteristic of his attitude is the following story: Once one of his friends, a devoted disciple and a very rich man, came to him. The *tzaddik* carried on a friendly conversation with the man and asked him incidentally: "Do you know such and such a teacher who lives in your town and is also one of our Hasidim? How is he getting along there?" The rich man was silent, for he knew nothing of the poor teacher who lived in a back alley at the edge of town. The *tzaddik* then asked him a second time about the teacher, and the man of wealth confessed: "I do not know him; I have never had anything to do with him, and

9. *Ibid.*, 24.
10. See *Maasiyyot Meha-Gedolim Veha-Tzaddikim*, 13–15; *Seder Ha-Dorot Ha-Ḥadash*, 34–35.

I did not even know until now that this man was living in my town." The *tzaddik* replied softly:

You ought to be ashamed of yourself. Look, God has given you the privilege of being a rich man, and you wish to know nothing of your brethren. You are men who share the same view, you are both my Hasidim, and one does not know of the other. How is it that you do not concern yourself? How is it that you are not interested in knowing how your poor brethren live in your town, so that you might share their trouble, aid and support them in any way you can. God has blessed you with great wealth so that you might be a chieftain and leader, so that you might help poor people and provide for their welfare. It is shameful that you do not even know how this teacher who belongs to the same camp as yourself is getting on. Why, he might perish of hunger and cold, die before his time, and you would know nothing of it! If you wish to be a real human being, you must take the situation of your brethren close to your heart. The poor man who goes about naked and unshod must be no less important to you than the man of great wealth."[11]

Of Meir of Peremyshlyany it is told that he would bring non-Jews near to himself equally with Jews, making no distinction between them. "This," he would say, "I learned from God Blessed be He. Of Him it is written, 'Thou hearest the prayer of every mouth.' Hence, for God there is no distinction between one faith and another, for He desires the heart."[12]

These unique "lovers of Israel" engaged in literary activity only to a very limited extent, and the compositions they did write are of slight significance.[13] But they also had their theoretician—the author of *Kedushat Levi*, the well-known Rabbi Levi Yitzḥak of Berdichev. Levi Yitzḥak ben Meir was born in Zamosc[14] into a prominent family. His father was a scholar, and Levi Yitzḥak in *Kedushat Levi* frequently refers to his interpretation of various passages in the Torah. As a boy Levi Yitzḥak was already renowned as a prodigy of learning[15] and when still a very young man served as preacher in Pinsk. In the first years after the death of the Baal Shem Tov, the

11. *Seder Ha-Dorot Ha-Ḥadash*, 35.

12. *Maasiyyot Meha-Gedolim Veha-Tzaddikim*, 28. For other stories about the *tzaddik* of Peremyshlyany, see ibid., 23–24, 28, 31–32.

13. Mosheh Leib of Sasov did write a small composition on the Torah entitled *Likkutei Ramal*, and Menaḥem Mendel of Kosov composed a book entitled *Ahavat Shalom*.

14. The year of his birth has not been established (in Dubnow, circa 1740).

15. Even such a bitter opponent as the author of *Zemir Aritzim* must recognize that Rabbi Levi Yitzḥak is "full of Torah."

preacher of Pinsk became interested, apparently as a result of the propaganda of the Maggid Dov Baer's emissaries, in the new Hasidic movement. Covertly, so that the community might not know and suspect him of heresy, he began to travel to Mezhirech where he became familiar with the teaching of the Baal Shem Tov and the Great Maggid.

In 1771 Levi Yitzḥak was elected rabbi by the community of Pinsk. A year later, however, the persecutions of the new sect began. The Gaon of Vilna issued his excommunications, and in the communities of Lithuania men eagerly searched and rummaged after the covert followers of the "heretical" movement. The community of Pinsk also uncovered the secret that its rabbi belonged to the "sect," and he was promptly deprived of his office.[16] The severe persecutions of the Hasidim compelled him to leave Lithuania and he settled in Zelechow in the "government" of Shedletz. There, too, he had to suffer a great deal from the Mitnagdim. In 1782 he was compelled to carry on a public disputation with the well-known opponent of Ḥasidism, the rabbi of Brest-Litovsk, Abraham Katzenellenbogen.[17] He obtained peace and great honor only when he settled in the 1780's in Berdichev, where he became the recognized leader of the Hasidim of Volhynia, as well as the hero of numerous popular legends.

In his way of life and conduct Rabbi Levi Yitzḥak of Berdichev was quite similar to the founder of the Hasidic movement. Wearing his *tallit* and *tefillin*, he loved to carry on conversations with simple people about everything in the world,[18] for he was fond of repeating the saying of the Baal Shem Tov: "God may be served in all kinds of ways, not merely through prayer but even through weekday conversations in the marketplace." He also held fast to the Baal Shem Tov's idea that God may be served only in joy. Levi Yitzḥak liked to travel about with his comrades through the neighboring towns and villages, to visit one of his disciples with his whole retinue. Here, first

16. No small role was played in this connection by the above-mentioned Avigdor (*supra*, pp. 103, 106).

17. As a continuation of this disputation, the rabbi of Brest-Litovsk in 1784 issued a public disputation letter "in honor of the rabbi, our master, our teacher, Levi Yitzḥak, the president of the rabbinic court of the holy community of Zelechow," with complaints against the Hasidim and their system. The letter is preserved in David of Makow's *Shever Poshe'im* (see below) and a Hasidic collection *Maḥshevot Kesilim* (see *He-Avar*, Vol. II, "Chassidiana," 31; *Devir*, I, 297; S. Dubnow, *Geshikhte Fun Khasidism*, I, 248–254).

18. See *Seder Ha-Dorot Ha-Ḥadash*, 16.

of all, the mystery took place: he would pray with such enormous enthusiasm that all around him were astonished and filled with dread. Later the noisy banquet at which the *tzaddik* would rejoice with all the people, and they would serve God with song and dance, began. Levi Yitzḥak's gentle converse with men, his love and devotion to the common people, his marvelous simplicity, and the fervent trust with which he would appeal in his prayers to the Guardian of Israel and the Creator of the world made him the most popular personality in the region.

Levi Yitzḥak presented his philosophy, his credo, in his *Kedushat Levi*, a collection of sermons which he was wont to give on the Sabbath at the "third meal."[19] As far as the fundamental question that constitutes the focus of Hasidic literature —the purpose of the creation of the world—is concerned, he bases himself on the doctrine of his teacher, the Maggid of Mezhirech, to whom in fact he quite frequently refers.[20] But in him this doctrine obtains a different explanation and is irradiated with gentle, loving beams.

It is known, Rabbi Levi Yitzḥak declares, that all the worlds were created for the sake of the terrestrial world in which man serves God,[21] since the state of divine kingship reveals itself only in the fact that man serves God in the earthly world. Only through man is God associated with the title King, for there must first be a people that acknowledges the king as monarch over itself. And it is a cardinal principle in the service of the Creator that man must always remember that all his movements, all his deeds, make an impression above.[22] *We* make God reign over us, and this is the purpose of the creation of the world—that His royal power may be revealed.[23] But God must conduct His world according to the powers of the recipients, i.e., the creatures, and not according to the power of the *Ein Sof*, or Infinite.[24] The Ineffable Name has no relationship to any attribute, any measure or boundary.[25] Only through *tzimtzum* (contraction or withdrawal) was the first power emanated, and

19. First published in Slavuta, 1798.

20. "I heard from the *tzaddik*, my master, my teacher and my rabbi, Dov Baer, whose soul is in the treasuries on high" (*Kedushat Levi*, "Parashat Lech Lecha"); "I heard from my holy teacher, the holy light, the Maggid, our master, our teacher, Dov Baer ("Parashat Vayyetze"); and many other places besides.

21. *Ibid.*, "Parashat Bereshit."

22. *Ibid.*, "Parashat Shelaḥ."

23. *Ibid.*, "Likkutim."

24. *Ibid.*, "Parashat Ki Tissa."

25. *Kedushat Levi*, "Likkutim" to "Parashat Bereshit."

that is the category that we call *Elohim* and *Adonai*. But the name *Adonai* points to the attribute of kingship; hence, He is called *Elohenu*, "our God." The Bible says: "I am the Lord your God," for all the causes, everything that occurs, is for our sake, for the sake of man.[26]

This anthropocentric idea is further developed in *Kedushat Levi* in a very remarkable way. Man, declares Rabbi Levi Yitzḥak, is the measure of all values, the criterion of all categories, states, and levels. If man with his eye does good in the world, the eye is inscribed in the upper worlds. These are the *einei Adonai*, the eyes of God, according to man's conceptions. But if—Heaven forbid—man's eye does evil, the divine eye above remains closed and locked. The same is true of man's ear. By calling to God with his prayers, man creates in the heights the hearing ear that receives human cries and petitions. This is the deeper meaning of the Talmudic statement "Know what is above you." This statement is to be understood as meaning: Everything above is created *through you*.[27]

As with the Maggid Dov Baer, so with his disciple Rabbi Levi Yitzḥak of Berdichev the individual is merged with the collectivity, with the concept of *Kenesset Yisrael*, the community of Israel. The revelation of divinity is, after all, the Torah; and the Torah was accepted and fulfilled only by Israel. "The soul of Israel is the body of the Torah;"[28] hence, the people of Israel is the incarnation of deity in the world. The author of *Kedushat Levi* does not tire of repeating: "It is known that in truth all the worlds were created only for the sake of Israel; it is the chief factor that caused the creation of the universe,"[29] and "The foundation of all the worlds is the community of Israel."[30] To be sure, *Kedushat Levi* notes, it may be asked: What relationship is there between God and the sons of man? Are

26. Ibid., for "Shabbat Naḥamu."

27. *Ibid.*, "Parashat Metzora": "So that when a man does good with the eye, then the eye is engraved above . . . And this is the meaning of the verse 'The eyes of the Lord are turned to the righteous.' Viz., whence are they the eyes of the Lord? On this it says: From the *tzaddikim* who do good with the eye. Therefore there is an eye above. And as for His ears, viz., whence are they His ears? This is said about 'their cry,' meaning from the fact that they cry to God Blessed Be He . . . And this is the meaning of our sages of blessed memory: "Know what is above you"—viz., what is above all is from you, for what you do below is engraved on high. And you should know that there is an eye that sees and an ear that hears, that is to say, that the eye that is above sees and the ear that is above hears. *And whence does the eye or the ear come above? It is from your deeds that you perform.*"

28. *Kedushat Levi*, "Parashat Ba-Midbar."

29. *Ibid.*, "Parashat Va'era," "Parashat Bereshit."

30. *Ibid.*, "Parashat Vayyetze."

there not so many ministering angels who praise and glorify the Creator of the world? But the Creator is by nature the *constantly* creative power. The Creator, *Kedushat Levi* teaches, "created everything and is everything," and His influence is never interrupted, for at every moment He spreads His great influence and abundance on His creatures, on all worlds and on all the heavenly palaces *(heichalot).*[31] He constantly influences and bestows because, Rabbi Levi Yitzḥak explains, He desires that there be someone capable of receiving His influence and abundance.[32] The Holy One Blessed be He is, indeed, called "the great, mighty, and fearful." It is, indeed, said of Him that "to Him praise is seemly," and yet the words of His people Israel find favor in His eyes, and even from the lowliest of the lowly, from him who is on the bottom-most stage, God derives great pleasure.[33]

In the view of the author of *Kedushat Levi,* God bestows good upon Israel continuously, and it is His pleasure, as it were, that Israel obtain abundance from Him, just as our sages said: "More than the calf desires to suck, the cow wishes to give suck."[34] And the pleasure derives from the fact that God "has no perfection until Israel receives from Him and He bestows upon them."[35] The pious and reverent Rabbi Levi Yitzḥak always stresses that everything happens through God's free will. Nevertheless, he actually adopts, albeit unconsciously, the view of Ḥasdai Crescas that God *must* by nature unceasingly bestow and influence and that His full perfection is disclosed only in His being the *Creator,* the constant source of streaming influence. God bestows only the good; from Him "no evil comes to the worlds." That which to us here below seems evil, Rabbi Levi Yitzḥak explains, leads in truth only to good, and he whose eyes are opened and who penetrates into the heights knows that everything is for good.[36] For the revelation of deity, after all, is out of pure *love.* Even the fact that God destroyed the Temple and that Jews are in exile, Levi Yitzḥak teaches, is certainly a benefit for them.[37]

31. *Ibid.*, beginning of "Parashat Bereshit."
32. *Ibid.*, for Rosh Ha-Shanah.
33. *Ibid.*, "Parashat Va-Yeḥi."
34. *Ibid.*, "Parashat Naso."
35. *Ibid.*, "Parashat Vayyere."
36. *Kedushat Levi,* "Parashat Ḥukkat." See also *ibid.*, for Rosh Ha-Shanah. God forbid that from Me [from the *Ein Sof*] evil should go forth; everything is dependent on the quality of the recipients"; *ibid.*, "Parashat Pekudei,": "The main thing is that God Blessed Be He sends evil to Israel so that from this there may come good for Israel."
37. Explanation to the Scroll of Lamentations.

The pages of *Kedushat Levi* glow with joyous optimism, based on the consciousness that "the love of the Creator Blessed be He is there," that in everything the divine love is experienced.[38] In relation to God there can be no talk of limits or of attributes and qualities, for He is the Infinite *(Ein Sof)*. But when He, "with His unitary, simple will," decided that the quality of love was to be disclosed, in order "to love Israel," He emanated the category or state of love, and this is called *olam ha-atzilut*, the "world of emanation." Later His will decided to create all the worlds and to reveal His divinity in the world, and this is called *olam ha-beriah*, the "world of creation." This, *Kedushat Levi* adds, was predetermined in "the thought that His love should be disclosed in all of them [the worlds],"[39] for the beginning of the revealed divine thought is love.[40]

As *No'am Elimelech* is the "Song of Songs" celebrating the *tzaddik* and his wonders, so *Kedushat Levi* is the "Song of Songs" of love for Israel, which is hallowed and ennobled through the connection with God's love and love for God. Love—this is the root and principle. It permeates the entire world; it is the primordial cause of the "work of creation." Out of love was Israel, and everything in the world, created. Hence, *Kedushat Levi* repeats, the attribute of love was emanated from the Creator into the world "only that God might be loved."[41]

A man is forbidden to say that there is anything in the universe in which the divine breath is not felt; he must immerse himself in the inner qualities of the thing and he will perceive in it the sparks of love, after which he must take these sparks and serve God with them.[42] The service of the priest in the Temple, even when he performed the ritual and offered the sacrifices, *Kedushat Levi* observes, was not perfect if he was not imbued with love for Israel, for every priest who is not filled with love for his people offers worship of no value, because the Holy One Blessed be He created everything out of love—love for Israel.[43] Love, in Rabbi Levi Yitzḥak's view, is the vessel for the divine light; and even physical desires are also a vessel for love, and through them man arrives at love of the Creator.[44]

38. *Ibid.*, "Parashat Mishpatim."
39. *Ibid.*, "Parashat Beshallaḥ": "And this was first in His thought, that He would reveal His love in all of them."
40. *Ibid.*, for Shavuot.
41. *Kedushat Levi*, for Shavuot.
42. *Ibid.*, "Parashat Terumah."
43. *Ibid.* "Parashat Tetzavveh": "For every priest who has no compassion for the people, his cultic service is nothing."
44. *Ibid.*, "Parashat Noaḥ."

In contrast with his teacher, the Maggid Dov Baer, who taught that love of the Creator comes only through fear of God,[45] the author of *Kedushat Levi* teaches that there are two kinds of servants of God: one serves Him out of love, the other out of fear. And the difference between them is this: He who serves out of fear feels himself an isolated being who dreads something that is higher and stronger than himself, but he who serves out of love is as if he were nothing at all. He completely forgets his own ego,[46] for true love is that in which man attains total transcendence of all of his qualities, serves God with all his limbs and movements, and forgets himself completely.[47] Fear separates, love unites.[48] He who serves out of love is in "the state of pleasure" but he who serves out of fear is in "the state of shame."[49]

Even *yirat ha-romemut*, the fear which derives from great reverence for God "who is glorious and exalted," and which brings one to the level of *sur me-ra*, "turning away from evil," derives from *middat ha-tzimtzum*, the quality of contraction or withdrawal. It leads to restraint and isolation. But there is another state in which man loses his sense of personal existence and "does not think of himself at all." Then he obtains ardent enthusiasm for the Creator of the world and love for Him. Prayer also derives from the quality of love. Only through love does one obtain the level of enthusiasm at the hour of prayer. When man pours out his petition in the surrender of his soul and body, transcends his own being, and "unites with the life of the *Ein Sof* Blessed be He," then the divine light of the *Ein Sof* flows down on him.[50]

It is a cardinal principle, *Kedushat Levi* asserts, that one who serves out of fear is in the category of a servant but one who serves out of love is in the category of a son. And Israel accepted the Torah out of love.[51] The festival of Shavuot, celebrating the giving of the Torah, is also the symbol of the quality of love.[52] God furthermore redeemed the Jews from

45. See above, pp. 73, 118. *Kedushat Levi* even quotes the Maggid's saying about two categories of fear—fear of punishment and fear of majesty ("Parashat Kedoshim").

46. *Kedushat Levi*, "Parashat Lech Lecha."

47. *Ibid.*: "But the true love is that which a man needs to pour out from all his qualities and to feel God Blessed be He in all his limbs and movements so that nothing remains to him himself."

48. *Ibid.*, "Likkutim."

49. *Ibid.*, "Parashat Pineḥas."

50. *Ibid.*, "Parashat Vayyetze."

51. *Ibid.*, "Parashat Yitro."

52. *Ibid.*, for Shavuot.

Egypt through the state or category of love. "I call you my children," He declared in His great mercy.[53]

"God is to be served out of love," *Kedushat Levi* repeatedly proclaims.[54] But there are two levels or degrees of love. There is one kind of person who loves God totally because God accepts our human service, rewards us, and recompenses every man according to his deeds. For this fulfillment of God's will much good is prepared. But there is also a very different and far more exalted degree of love. There are those who love God solely because of His love for men, even if no reward were in the offing. Because of God's great love alone is He precious to us. Because He chose Israel out of great love, He is dearer to us than anything else.[55] Such a love, *Kedushat Levi* affirms, is like the love of a bridegroom "who kisses his bride on the mouth," not like those who kiss an official's hand in the expectation that, in exchange for this token of affection, the hand "will give us a good reward."[56]

This, Rabbi Levi Yitzḥak exclaims emotively, is the basic purpose of our life and the desire of our hearts: to sacrifice ourselves with all our spirit and soul for the sake of the love of our Creator. And how dear, sweet, and precious to us are all the afflictions that come upon us. We are ever prepared to go through fire and water, because precisely through these afflictions is His great name sanctified and revered.[57] Love, *Kedushat Levi* asserts, exalts and hallows. Certainly, the author adds, the angels in their holiness are higher than the children of Israel, but when the Holy One manifests His love for Israel, then, because of this love, Israel is superior even to the most exalted angels.[58]

Typical of Rabbi Levi Yitzḥak is his attitude toward the miracles of the Torah. Not the miracle itself, we read in *Kedushat Levi*, arouses a feeling of joy in us; the joy derives from the fact that in the miracle God's love for Israel is revealed. It is

53. *Ibid.*, "Parashat Yitro."
54. *Kedushat Levi*, "Parashat Mase'ei", and in many other places.
55. *Ibid.*, "Parashat Va-Yeḥi": "Those who love God Blessed be He because of His love for us alone, and even if no reward were drawn to us through all the love of God for us alone—they are beloved and pleasant and delightful; and because of His love alone do we love with a perfect love, and because of the love of God alone who chose His people Israel in love, He is more beloved to us than anything else." See also *ibid.*, "Parashat Va'era": "And a man ought to serve the Creator not for the sake of any benefit to himself at all, but only that the Creator may have pleasure from him."
56. *Ibid.*, *Derushim* for Pesaḥ, Song of Songs.
57. *Ibid.*, "Parashat Shemot."
58. *Ibid.*, "Parashat Be-Shallaḥ."

written: "This is the day:" this is the promise of great joy and bliss, the manifestation of God's love for His chosen people.[59] Because the Jewish people is hallowed through the divine love, declares Levi Yitzḥak, "no man is permitted to speak an evil word about Israel"; one must "speak only favorably of Israel."[60] As had the Baal Shem Tov in his day, so Rabbi Levi Yitzḥak regarded with great indignation the preachers who constantly berated the people. The Jews who do not, as do the angels, fulfill the will of God perfectly are to be judged favorably because they are, after all, burdened with the cares of earning a living. For this reason Moses our teacher also begged God that "he might stand as the guide of Israel to argue constantly in its favor."[61] So, Levi Yitzḥak adds, the *tzaddik* of the generation must also behave. The *tzaddik*, we read in *Kedushat Levi*, is always small in his own estimation.[62] Love for God is for him more precious than all the pleasures of the world to come,[63] and his only purpose all the days of his life is to bestow "an abundance of blessing," to bring down "mercy and grace upon Israel," and to pray constantly to God "for the welfare and blessing of Israel."[64]

Rabbi Levi Yitzḥak was a man who practiced what he preached. Hasidic literature is filled with wonderful tales of the marvelous deeds of the rabbi of Berdichev, about his heartfelt prayers of protest in which he would argue with God for his beloved Israel,[65] demonstrate his people's innocence, and show how greatly the common folk deserve to be judged favorably. Once Levi Yitzḥak saw a wagondriver dressed in his prayer-shawl and phylacteries smearing grease on the wheels of his wagon. The anger with which a rabbi of the school of the author of *Kav Ha-Yashar* would have fallen on the "crude ignoramus" and "sinner in Israel" can be imagined, but Rabbi Levi Yitzḥak looked on and exclaimed with enchantment: "Master of the universe, see what a precious folk your people Israel is; even when they smear the wheels of a wagon they pray to You!"

"All Israel serve the Creator," Levi Yitzḥak declares, but one

59. *Kedushat Levi*, "Likkutim."
60. *Ibid.*, "Parashat Bo."
61. *Ibid.*, "Parashat Pineḥas."
62. *Ibid.*, "Likkutim."
63. *Ibid.*, Song of Songs.
64. *Ibid.*, "Parashat Be-Shallaḥ."
65. Rabbi Levi Yitzḥak's *Kaddish*, known to all, with the introduction "I, Levi Yitzḥak the son of Sarah of Berdichev, have come before you to plead for the community of Israel," may serve as an illustration of his unique debates with God.

must not—God forbid—think that "if they did not serve, they would not be redeemed." The rabbi's optimism was so great that he was sure that, even if Israel were at the lowest level and not fit to be redeemed, God in His great mercy and grace would, nevertheless, send redemption.[66] Redemption, however, will come not for Jews alone but for all the world. The giving of the Torah was an act of grace not merely for Israel but for the whole world.[67] However, because the Jews accepted the Torah in love, they are in the supreme category of "nothing" or "non-being" *(Ayin).* The peoples of the world, however, refused to accept the Torah, and so they are in the lower state of "being" *(Yesh)* and cannot attain the superior level.[68] The holiest souls among the gentiles converted and united with Israel—for example, Ruth the Moabitess, who was privileged to be the progenitress of the redeemer.

In every contact that a Jew has with a gentile, in every conversation with him, he awakens the holy sparks that are "in the gentile."[69] In the "time to come," in the messianic era, Levi Yitzḥak exclaims with emotion, "all the nations will proclaim God Blessed be He as king over themselves."[70]

In considering *Kedushat Levi,* it is worth dwelling on one other motif which is actually characteristic of the Hasidic movement in general but manifests itself with special clarity in Rabbi Levi Yitzḥak's philosophy. When, in the sixth volume, we portrayed the cultural condition of German-Polish Jewry in the eighteenth century, we underscored the dominance in that era of the idea of "reward and punishment," the dread of the seven departments of hell that hung like a somber, leaden cloud over the horizon of the ghetto. The Baal Shem Tov and his disciples—and this is one of their great merits—neutralized this dread, rent apart the oppresive melancholy, and drove away the hosts of evil spirits which lay in wait for man at every step of his way. Already in the Baal Shem Tov's teaching, reward and punishment play a very minor role. It suffices for one to regret in his heart the sin he has committed for that sin to be erased and for the individual to become cleansed and exempt from punishment.[71]

66. *Ibid.,* "Parashat Bo."

67. *Ibid.,* "Parashat Yitro."

68. *Ibid.*

69. *Ibid.,* for Shavuot. Rabbi Levi Yitzḥak refers in this connection to Rabbi Isaac Luria and his doctrine about the mission which the Jewish people has to fulfill among the nations of the world.

70. *Kedushat Levi,* "Parashat Balak."

71. See above, p. 47–48.

The flames of hell which danced demonically on every page of *Shevet Musar* and *Kav Ha-Yashar* disappear, as if through a magic exorcism, in the literature of Hasidism. They are not denied, but simply forgotten; very little interest is taken in them. This is most clearly noticeable in Rabbi Levi Yitzḥak's *Kedushat Levi,* which is thoroughly permeated with the profoundest optimism. The severest punishment for a transgression is seen by *Kedushat Levi* in the fact that thereby the individual who has committed it loses the pleasure of fulfilling what is commanded. There is not, the rabbi of Berdichev declares, any special reward for the fulfillment of the commandment; the entire reward consists in the fact that "one commandment brings another in its train."[72] That we so eagerly await the coming of the Messiah, *Kedushat Levi* asserts, is not for the sake of the material goods that we shall obtain as reward, but for the sake of the fact that only then shall we properly comprehend the greatness of the Creator.[73]

In this liberation from deathly terror before the black hosts of destroying angels and the flames of the seven departments of hell, in this dispelling of distress and sorrow through the encouraging slogan that God can be served by man only through joy, lay one of the major causes of the triumph that the early Hasidic movement gained in the Jewish world.

Rabbi Levi Yitzḥak was a harmoniously integral nature who looked with childlike, mystical eyes and with a heart overflowing with joyful trust on God's world that is "entirely good." His sharpest antithesis is represented by his younger contemporary, Rabbi Naḥman of Bratzlav.

In the cradle of the Hasidic movement in Medzhibozh lived the Baal Shem Tov's beloved daughter Hodel, whom popular imagination surrounded, along with her father, with a garland of imaginative legends. She bore two sons who, as the Baal Shem Tov's grandsons, played a certain role in the Hasidic world—Rabbi Ephraim of Sudylkow (the author of *Degel Maḥaneh Efrayim*) and Rabbi Baruch of Medzhibozh. Hodel also had a daughter named Feiga who was married to Simḥah, the son of the Baal Shem Tov's well-known disciple and admirer, Naḥman of Horodenko. In 1772 Feiga gave birth to a son and named him after his grandfather from Horodenko. This scion of the founder of Hasidism belonged to those extraordinary spirits who are crowned with a wreath of thorns, whose fate is an incessant struggle with themselves, with the tragic con-

72. *Kedushat Levi,* "Parashat Be-Ḥukkotai."
73. *Kedushat Levi, Derush* for Shavuot.

tradictions of life, and whose only faithful companion on their sorrowful life's way is pain, veiled in a dark mantle of solitude.

Nature endowed the Baal Shem Tov's little great-grandson generously: with a rich, unbridled imagination, a spark of the true poet, a restless spirit which pondered and quested indefatigably after the hidden and concealed, a tender, sensitive heart that carried in itself the agony of the world, the sufferings of a whole generation. The child grew up in the mystical environment of Medzhibozh, the center of Hasidism, where all the air was filled to overflowing with the most remarkable miracles and extraordinary stories about the Baal Shem Tov and his Hasidim. Rabbi Naḥman himself later told his disciples of the bated breath with which he used to listen, as a child, to the miracle tales which the old *tzaddikim* and the ardent Hasidim used to tell in the house of his parents when they came to Medzhibozh to pray at the grave of the Baal Shem Tov.[74]

Even as a six-year-old child Naḥman already attempted to carry the yoke of a pious man and endeavored to fast. Every Sabbath eve he ran to the ritual bath and from there, dressed in Sabbath clothes, he would hasten to the study house and with childish steps stride back and forth, waiting impatiently until he would experience the holiness of the Sabbath and the palpitation of the additional soul with which a Jew is endowed on this day. Years later he told his disciples how once, as a child on a Sabbath eve, he clung to a reading-stand in the study house and with great trembling listened to one of the adult Hasidim fervently sing the Song of Songs and how the singing soon passed over into sobbing and weeping; and he also, the six-year-old child, looking at the Hasid, poured out his fervent prayer before God and wept bitter tears. Often in the evening little Naḥman would run to the grave of the Baal Shem Tov and beseech his great-grandfather to help him and bring him close to God.[75] To fulfill the Biblical verse "I have set the Lord always before me" he would endeavor with closed eyes to represent to himself the Ineffable Name. He was not content with the statutory prayers but loved to converse with God in an isolated corner in plain Yiddish, in the *teḥinnah*—language of his mother. He studied with great diligence not only the Talmud and Kabbalah, but the Bible,[76] *Ein Yaakov*, and "morality books" as well. Especially precious to him was *Shaarei*

74. *Maggid Siḥot*, 55.
75. *Ibid.*, 5.
76. His love for the Bible was also great in his later years, and he frequently admonished his Hasidim, or disciples, to go over the whole *Tanach* (*Maggid Siḥot*, 75).

Tziyyon,[77] whose simple, spiritual prayers he found highly congenial.

At the age of thirteen young Naḥman was married and went to live in the house of his wealthy father-in-law in the village of Husyatin, not far from the town of Medvedovke. The lovely region around the village made a powerful impression on the poetic soul of the youthful mystic. The echo of this impress is discernible in many of the sayings preserved in his books. He had a small boat in which he used to cross the little river near the village and then swim to a hidden corner to spend long hours. He would also ride on a horse deep into the forest, leave the horse there, and remain alone in the thickness of the forest to pour out his feelings in ardent prayers to the Creator. His prayers were not the canonized ones from the *Siddur Ari* but improvised in plain Yiddish. Later he was to teach his disciples that one should pray to God in *Leshon Ashkenaz* (Yiddish).[78] When a man prays on the open field, the Bratzlaver would tell his disciples, the little grasses mingle with his prayers, help him, and strengthen him in his supplication.[79] Every word is then a whole world. When a man prays, it is as if he were gathering flowers, blossoms, and the loveliest petals, and weaving from them the most magnificent garlands.[80]

In his later years also Rabbi Naḥman would speak with great emotion to his pupils of the marvelous power of man's prayer. "Prayer is in the category of pure miracle. It is beyond nature, beyond time. It is a phenomenon that stands at the pinnacle of the world."[81] The level of prayer is tremendously lofty, loftier than study of Torah (*Maggid Siḥot*, 40). When a man isolates himself and pours out his yearning and pain before God, then the *Shechinah* for its part also pours out its yearning and pain before him and consoles and calms him.[82] A prayer which comes from the heart is the category of *hitgalut malchuto* (revelation of God's kingship).[83] The divine, which is in the category or state of *or ha-ganuz* (hidden light), reveals itself as a result of man's prayer.[84] It is good, the Bratzlaver asserts, to make of

77. See our *History*, Vol. V, pp. 66, 80, 81.
78. *Likkutei Moharan*, II, No. 25; *Maggid Siḥot*, 72.
79. *Ibid.*, No. 11.
80. *Ibid.*, I, No. 65.
81. *Ibid.*, No. 9, No. 93.
82. *Likkutei Moharan*, I, No. 259.
83. *Ibid.*, No. 49.
84. *Ibid.*, No. 15.

the whole Torah one prayer.[85] In his later years, when Rabbi Naḥman once passed Husyatin with its lovely fields and meadows with one of his disciples, he recalled the youthful years that he spent there and with intense emotion exclaimed: "O how good it was then for me! At every step there I felt the taste of paradise, and whenever I was alone in the forest or field, upon my return the world appeared to be completely renewed —indeed, like a totally different world."[86]

In 1798, when Rabbi Naḥman was already recognized as a *tzaddik* and had numerous disciples, he decided to do what his great-grandfather had not been able to do—pilgrimage to Palestine. The journey lasted more than a year and was adorned by his disciples with all kinds of stories and legends.[87] The land of the patriarchs made an enormously powerful impression on the young mystic. "All the vitality that I have," he would later say, "derives from the fact that I was in *Eretz Yisrael.*" Returning from the long journey, Rabbi Naḥman settled in Zlotopola. The well-known "grandfather of Shpola," however, was greatly irked by this; he regarded the young *tzaddik* as an intruder who settled in the vicinity of his capital without his consent. The "grandfather" was apprehensive that this would affect his income, inasmuch as many of his disciples might abandon him to go over to the Baal Shem Tov's great-grandson. A series of persecutions and intrigues thus began. This grieved Naḥman who, in 1802, left Zlotopola and settled in Bratzlav, where he spent his most fruitful years.

Not without reason has he gone down in history under the name "the Bratzlaver." To be sure, during his years in Bratzlav Naḥman had to suffer a great deal from numerous *tzaddikim* who could not forgive his ironic words about the "false leaders who make themselves great with the title rabbi; they undertake to be guides of the world and cannot even lead themselves." On the other hand, in Bratzlav Naḥman also acquired his most dedicated disciples. There he met the man who forever forged his name together with the name of the teacher whom he idolized—Nathan ben Naftali Herz of Nemirov.

Rabbi Nathan of Nemirov was a scholar and a "man of language." Previously he had been a Hasid of Chernobyl, but upon becoming acquainted with Rabbi Naḥman, he became his eternally devoted pupil and servant. Even after his death the Bratzlaver boundlessly dominated his disciple's world out-

85. *Ibid.*, II, No. 25; *Maggid Siḥot*, 55.
86. Hillel Zeitlin, *Rabbi Naḥman Mi-Braslav*, 44.
87. See *Maggid Siḥot*, 8–22.

look, all his thought and action.[88] "If I came to Bratzlav only to bring Nathan close to me," Rabbi Naḥman was later to say, "this would have been quite sufficient." Nathan became not only Naḥman's disciple but also his faithful and indefatigable secretary. He used to write down not merely his master's sermons but also every saying and conversation of his, for he was firmly convinced that in each word of his teacher's holy mouth the profoundest mysteries were hidden. Everything that Rabbi Nathan wrote down from his teacher's speech he later published for the world. This devoted pupil and admirer endeavors to render not only what his teacher taught but also *how* he spoke his teaching and his words of instruction to his pupils. The Bratzlaver said of himself, "Every word of teaching is for me washed with tears."[89] In the tone in which he would present his instruction, in every gesture and movement of his hand, lay so much painful tenderness and exalted feeling that the effect on his pious listeners was enormous.

When Rabbi Naḥman was thirty-five, the first clear symptoms of the tuberculosis which removed him prematurely from the world appeared. He spent a rather long time in Lemberg seeking a cure from the professors there, but this proved of little avail. In 1810, after Passover, a great fire broke out in Bratzlav, and Naḥman's house burned down. He thereupon settled in the neighboring town of Uman, which had always attracted his imagination. He used to say that the martyrs who perished at the hands of Chmielnitzki's armies and of Gonta's Haidamacks begged him to be close to them and to pray for them. Hence he settled in a house opposite the cemetery, to be nearer these martyrs. Soon he joined them. Rabbi Naḥman came to Uman a dying man; the disease progressed rapidly, and on the fourth day of Sukkot, 1810, he expired.

We have observed that Naḥman's faithful disciple, Nathan of Nemirov, assumed loving care for his master's literary legacy, preserved it in writing, and published it. Nevertheless, it is no simple matter to obtain quick familiarity with Rabbi Naḥman's world of ideas, and this not merely because his secretary wrote down his teaching without any order or system. One must bear in mind that the *tzaddik* of Bratzlav who died so young was not a solidly established thinker or moralist with a definite world outlook. He was in perpetual conflict through-

88. Very characteristic in this respect are Nathan's numerous letters to his son Isaac that have been preserved.
89. *Maggid Siḥot*, 52.

out his life; he searched not only with speculative thought but with a heart that bled constantly, with all the nerves of his deeply sensitive soul. Hence, the tragic antitheses, the conspicuous—though, to be sure, largely apparent—contradictions. Moreover, it must be taken into consideration that this man, who was endowed with a rich imagination, the spark of a true poet, and a questing spirit, grew up in a purely mystical milieu. He was raised and educated on the Kabbalist literature in which philosophical ideas and overwhelming poetic symbols and images are combined with all kinds of *notrikon, gematriot,* magical names, and word-play. One therefore also has not infrequent occasion, in his case, to seek flashes of thought and pearls created out of tears and sorrow under a mass of sand and splinters.

As with all the major theoreticians of Hasidism,[90] so with Naḥman an extremely important place is occupied by the fundamental question of the purpose of creation. With him, however, this question obtains a very specific elucidation. We noted[91] that the theoreticians of Hasidism gave Rabbi Isaac Luria's doctrine of *tzimtzum,* or contraction, a unique explication, insofar as they believed that one cannot understand the concept of *tzimtzum* to mean that "a removal to the sides" of the light of the *Ein Sof* or Infinite occurred and a "free space" was left for the worlds; such an understanding, in their view, would have been inconsistent with the statement "I, the Lord, change not" and with the fundamental thesis of the Baal Shem Tov that "there is no place void of God." The Maggid of Mezhirech especially insisted that "*tzimtzum* comes because of love," that God "created all the worlds" out of love, and that love and *tzimtzum* are "a total unity."[92] On this thesis the optimistic world-view of the Baal Shem Tov and of Rabbi Levi Yitzḥak of Berdichev were based. But where the theoreticians of Hasidism perceived solid ground and a clear solution to the fundamental problem, the restless thinking of the rabbi of Bratzlav saw only the great question mark, the insoluble enigma.

Rabbi Naḥman also proceeds from the Baal Shem Tov's position that there is no place void of Him. "God," he would frequently repeat, "is with you, in you, near you." It is clear that in all things, in all acts and all thoughts, "God—as it were

90. See above, Chapter Three, pp. 71ff; Chapter Four, pp. 110ff; Chapter Five, pp. 132–134.
91. Above, p. 111.
92. Above, p. 73.

—is incorporated."[93] "From all things," Naḥman explains to his disciples, "God's splendor calls out—even from the common tales the gentiles tell, for 'the whole earth is full of His glory.' "[94] You must know, he points out, that even a person all of whose dealings are with gentiles can have no excuse to say that he cannot serve God because he is always in a benighted environment, for our sages have long ago shown that in all material things, in all the languages of the various peoples, deity may be found; for without deity all these would have no vitality or endurance, as it is said in the Bible: "And Thou givest life to all" (Nehemiah 9:6).[95]

But the Bratzlaver realized quite well that this Hasidic doctrine about the divine omnipresence contradicts Rabbi Isaac Luria's "mystery of *tzimtzum,*" of God's contraction or withdrawal. He quotes the passage from Ḥayyim Vital's *Etz Ḥayyim* in which it is explained that when the *Ein Sof* wished to create the world, there was no place for creation, for everything was the *Ein Sof* or, rather, the *Ein Sof* was everything. God therefore withdrew the light to the sides, and through this withdrawal arose the empty space in which the *middot*, the attributes, and time disclosed themselves; and the creation of the world consists in these.

This "empty space," Rabbi Naḥman adds, was, indeed, absolutely essential for creation, for without it there would have been no place in which the world could have been produced. Nevertheless, this idea of *tzimtzum* and the appearance of the "empty space" is quite impossible for the human mind to grasp, except perhaps in the future when the redeemer will come, for two utter opposites are associated in the idea: *Yesh* (something) and *Ayin* (nothing). When we say that the "empty space" arose through *tzimtzum*, it is implied that the *Ein Sof* withdrew his divinity thence, i.e., that divinity, as it were, is not present there, for otherwise there would have been no empty space; everything would have been simply the *Ein Sof*, and no place would have existed for the creation of the world.[96] In reality, however, deity is also present there, for "God fills

93. *Likkutei Moharan*, I, No. 56.

94. *Maggid Siḥot*, 36.

95. *Likkutei Moharan*, I, No. 32.

96. *Likkutei Moharan*, I, No. 64: "And this empty space was necessary for the creation of the world, for without empty space there would have been no place for the creation of the world . . . and this contraction or withdrawal of the empty space is impossible to understand and grasp, save in the time to come (i.e., in the hereafter), for in connection with it one must speak of two antinomies, Being *(Yesh)* and Nothingness *(Ayin)*. For the empty space is through contraction. God, as it were, contracted His

and embraces all the worlds." There can be no point in which divinity is not present. Thus the whole problem of "empty space," which is so closely linked with the problem of creation, remains insoluble until "the days of the Messiah."

To this great *ignorabimus* the rabbi of Bratzlav very frequently returns in his conversations with his disciples. He constantly insists that there are problems and questions to which man can give no clear answers, for the answers merely lead one to a labyrinth of new questions, new difficulties, and insoluble problems. As a profoundly loyal believer, Naḥman was firmly persuaded of the truth of the Jewish tradition concerning the non-eternity of the universe, the idea that the world was created at a definite time. But there was a skeptical side in him, and he therefore declared openly that the thesis that God created the world out of free will is purely a matter of faith, for through reason it is difficult to understand the creation of the world in time. Indeed, the heretics deny it because it cannot be grasped by reason.[97]

The same thing is true of the universal role of the Jewish people. Like all the other theoreticians of Hasidism, Naḥman teaches that "the entire world was created only for the sake of Israel"[98] and that "every Jew is literally a divine part from above,"[99] for "the Holy One Blessed be He, the Torah, and Israel are all one."[100] But here also the skeptic in the *tzaddik* arises, and he frankly declares: We are called a peculiar, chosen people *(am segullah)*, but ordinary reason cannot understand how God elected one people from among all the peoples as a holy nation; this is "beyond nature, beyond human reason."[101] Here, Naḥman asserts, there can be only one answer: Be silent; so the divine will decided. And the state of silence is beyond speech, for the word can explain nothing here, and it is foolish to raise questions to which there is no answer. In this matter silence is wiser than all wisdoms and sciences.[102]

But it is not only the problem of "empty space" in the crea-

---

divinity thence, and there is, as it were, no divinity there. For if there were no empty space and the *Ein Sof* were all, there would be no place for the creation of the world at all . . . And therefore it is impossible to understand at all the category of empty space until the time to come."

97. *Likkutei Moharan*, II, No. 8.
98. *Ibid.*, I, No. 17.
99. *Ibid.*, No. 49, No. 259.
100. *Ibid.*, No. 251.
101. *Likkutei Moharan*, I, No. 21.
102. *Ibid.*

tion of the world that, according to the Bratzlaver, is insoluble. The question of the purpose and goal of the creation of the world also remains without resolution. We have observed that the Maggid of Mezhirech insisted that God created all the worlds out of love, and that love and *tzimtzum* are a complete unity. This was also the firm belief of Rabbi Levi Yitzḥak of Berdichev. The *tzaddik* of Bratzlav, however, does not speak at all of love, but of mercy. "God created the world out of mercy." "The Holy One Blessed be He," Rabbi Naḥman explains to his disciples, "is full of compassion and the whole world is full of compassion, and He is very favorably disposed to the world."[103] But wherein does compassion for the world consist? To this Rabbi Naḥman gives an extremely melancholy reply. The world is full of agony, suffering, sorrow, and affliction.[104] No one in the world has a good end.[105] Even the rich and powerful must concede that "the world is filled with sadness and pain."[106] It is written in the Bible: "But man is born to trouble, as the sparks fly upward" (Job 5:7). This refers to everyone without exception; all, great and small, are born to suffering and are filled with wrath and afflictions.[107] Everyone, Rabbi Naḥman declares with bitter irony, says that there is *olam ha-zeh*, the present world, and *olam ha-ba*, the world to come. As far as *olam ha-ba* is concerned, we all believe it exists. It may also be that somewhere in some world there is also *olam ha-zeh*, but here we have true hell. All are constantly in great affliction; there is no *olam ha-zeh*.[108]

The pious *tzaddik* even attempts to console men: Know that all human troubles and agonies derive merely from lack of understanding, for one who understands knows that everything is under the providence of God; then he suffers no afflictions and feels no pain.[109] But this answer does not satisfy even Rabbi Naḥman himself. It is possible, he says, that for God all the diseases and afflictions also come from compassion, for it

103. *Ibid.*, II, No. 51.
104. *Maggid Siḥot*, 49.
105. *Ibid.*, 35.
106. *Ibid.*, 83.
107. *Likkutei Moharan*, II, 43.
108. *Likkutei Moharan*, II, 43. It is worth noting here that, like Rabbi Levi Yitzḥak of Berdichev and the other theoreticians of Hasidism, the Bratzlaver also occupies himself very little with the problem of reward and punishment, of Hell and Heaven. And when Leviathan is mentioned by him, the explanation immediately follows: "Leviathan—this is the state of kingship" (*Likkutei Moharan*, II, No. 7).
109. *Ibid.*, I, No. 250.

is certain that everything God does to man or brings upon man, even the most grievous sufferings, are nothing but mercy. We implore, however, that He give mercy into our hands, for we do not understand His mercy, and we cannot receive this mercy of His. Let God hand His compassion over to us, that we ourselves may have compassion upon ourselves.[110]

Not without reason does Rabbi Naḥman's pupil, Nathan of Nemirov, remark so frequently that his teacher was always in conflict with himself. "He fell away from this, then began again, then fell away again."[111] The mystic Naḥman, who experienced God with every tremor of his soul, perceived in all the doubts and questions he himself raised pure heresy and blasphemy. Indeed, he quotes the Talmudic legend that when, at the hour of Rabbi Akiba's tragic death, the question was raised: "This is Torah, and is this its reward,?" the answer came: "Be silent; so God has decreed." To be silent, not to demand an answer to the enigma—this is superior to speech.[112]

Full of tragic import is the statement of Rabbi Naḥman: "A man may give a great cry and no one hears a sound."[113] Hence, his constant battle against speculation, against the external wisdoms or sciences which, in his view, lead men to heresy. But the Bratzlaver deems it necessary to note that one must distinguish two kinds of heresy. The first kind derives from the "external wisdoms" and the natural scientists, who deny free will,[114] declare nature "the mother of all living things,"[115] and express the heretical idea that the world must be, that it exists not because of God's free will but as the product of necessity, of iron regularity.[116] In this kind of heresy, Rabbi Naḥman concedes, there are "sparks of holiness," a reflection of the divine light, for even in this denial "the life of God is incorporated."[117]

110. *Ibid.*, II, No. 62.
111. *Shivḥei Ha-Ran*, 8.
112. *Likkutei Moharan*, I, No. 64.
113. *Maggid Siḥot*, 26.
114. *Likkutei Moharan*, II, No. 7.
115. *Ibid.*, No. 216: "Know that the philosophers call nature the mother of all living things."
116. *Ibid.*, I, No. 52. In this connection the following point is interesting. Rabbi Naḥman endeavors to show that the philosophers are mistaken and only God is a necessary existent, while all the worlds are merely "possible existents." His arguments, however, finally lead to the conclusion that, in a certain sense, the world is also "in the state of necessary existence."
117. *Maggid Siḥot*, 48.

There is also, however, a very different kind of heresy. Naḥman frequently mentions those "who are wise to do evil," the "light-headed among the people" with whom he had occasion to meet and carry on conversations.[118] The "light-headed among the people" are the rationalistically-minded enlighteners for whom there are no enigmas; they explain everything through common sense, whereas he, Naḥman, is thoroughly convinced that the supreme level of knowledge is not-knowing and not-understanding.[119] With a contemptuous smile he tells his disciples how one of the "light-headed" boasted before him that he was "learned in the languages of the gentiles" (*Maggid Siḥot*, 78). Naḥman, the mystic and skeptic, who was not of this world, considered this "foolish talk." These heretics, he indignantly declares, speaking of the rationalistically-minded *maskilim* or enlighteners, display sciences that are not sciences at all, ask questions to which there can be no answer. In their arguments and ideas no "sparks of holiness" inhere, for they are not of the category of the "breaking of the vessels" *(shevirat ha-kelim)* where "divine life" still remained, but of the "empty space" which is, "as it were, utterly devoid of divinity."

It is of these heretics, Naḥman notes, that it is said in the Bible: "All who come to her will not return."[120] Thus the Bratzlaver strongly assails the "speculators" and "deniers" who interpret the whole Torah according to their sciences or wisdoms and their heresy. They declare all the stories told in the Torah merely parables and allegories, and explain all the commandments rationally, rejecting observance of them.[121] Hence, he issues forth sharply against Maimonides' rationalist doctrine[122] and admonishes his pupils "not to look at all into the books of the speculators and of philosophy." He indicates that they ought to remove themselves from the speculative books which the "great men among our brethren of the household of Israel" wrote, for these are extremely injurious to faith.[123]

118. He was, incidentally, well acquainted with the renowned *maskil* of Uman, Ḥaykl Hurwitz, and his son Hirsch Baer, who was later a professor at Cambridge, used to read to the rabbi of Bratzlav certain passages of the German classics (see *Die Zeitschrift*, p. 470, *Sion*, 1861, p. 179).

119. "And know that this is the purpose of knowledge. For the purpose of knowledge is not to know . . . and they do not enter into union and they do not know" (*Likkutei Moharan*, I, No. 24).

120. *Likkutei Moharan*, I, No. 64.

121. *Ibid.*, II, No. 19.

122. *Ibid.*

123. *Likkutei Moharan*, II, No. 44; *Maggid Siḥot*, 29; *ibid.*, 30.

The Bratzlaver does not tire of repeating to his disciples that the chief thing and the acme of perfection is to serve God in sincerity and utter simplicity, without any wisdoms or sciences, and that the greatest of all wisdoms is not to be wise in any way.[124] Well it is with him, he would tell his disciples, who every day "eats" several chapters of the Mishnah, "drinks" several chapters of the Psalms, and "clothes himself" with many commandments, for "beyond this, all is vanity."[125] He himself, Rabbi Naḥman assures them, attained his level only in consequence of the fact that he behaved like a "common man" and recited a great many Psalms in simplicity.[126] The essence of Judaism is plainness and sincerity, without wisdoms.[127] One must also serve God and fulfill His commandments with sincerity and simplicity, without sciences, without subtleties, and without all the strictures and fine points which only lead to melancholy.[128] Sincerity without science and subtlety, faith without speculation, not to wish to inquire and search—these, he constantly repeats, are the principal things. But in the heart of every man resides a speculator and skeptic, and he must be expelled.[129] One must believe in God on faith alone, without speculation;[130] the essence of faith is to believe in God "without signs and wonders."[131]

The chief thing in knowing God is to do this only through perfect faith.[132] He who lives in faith, even if great afflictions and troubles come upon him, can console himself that God will have mercy upon him and the afflictions will be only for his good and his atonement. But the man of speculation who has no faith, when stricken by some catastrophe has no one to turn to and nothing wherein to find comfort.[133] There is nowhere to flee except to God and His Torah.[134] Better to be "a simpleton believing everything," and also believing the truth, than to be a wise man and a denier of everything—God forbid.[135]

Sincerity and simplicity alone! Nevertheless, the Bratzlaver

124. *Likkutei Moharan*, II, No. 47.
125. In Nathan's letters to his son Isaac.
126. *Maggid Siḥot*, 59.
127. *Likkutei Moharan*, II, 19.
128. *Ibid.*, II, No. 47.
129. *Maggid Siḥot*, 29.
130. *Ibid.*
131. *Ibid.*, 49.
132. *Ibid.*, 69.
133. *Ibid.*, 29, 36, 48.
134. *Maggid Siḥot*, 83.
135. *Ibid.*, 49.

deems it necessary to warn that "even in sincerity it is forbidden to be a fool."[136] He, who asserted that he was in the category of a *prostak*, a common man, declares that the chief thing for man is knowledge and one who has no knowledge is not of the civilized human species.[137]

Thought is extremely exalted, declares Rabbi Naḥman and adds, "It is necessary to guard thought greatly" (*Maggid Siḥot*, 33). Man's mind is his soul. Every Jew must always think himself into the mind or reason of everything, associate himself with the wisdom and reason inherent in everything, and thereby approach God. As long as men are not illumined with the light of knowledge and do not understand and sense the power of its divinity, "they are not men at all."[138] For the essence of man is reason; hence where reason searches, there is the whole man, and the more a man knows, the more firmly is he bound up with the root, i.e., with God.[139]

This sounds almost Maimonidean, and at first blush it may be difficult to understand why the Bratzlaver was such a bitter opponent of Maimonides' rationalist doctrine. However, one must bear in mind that the mystic Naḥman understands by "knowledge" and "recognition of God" something other than the thinker of Aristotle's school. Not without reason does he stress that only where the wisdom of philosophy ends does true wisdom, i.e., the wisdom of the Kabbalah, begin,[140] and that where one does not understand through reason he must have faith. But Rabbi Naḥman asserts that there is something higher even than faith, and this is "holy wisdom" (*ḥochmah de-kedushah*).[141] This religious philosophy cannot be grasped with the aid of cold reason but only through intuition, supported by a powerful imagination.

It was difficult for the Bratzlaver, who never went through any philosophical school, to express his complicated worldview in clear propositions. It was even more difficult for him to avoid certain inconsistencies and to establish his universe of ideas through logical arguments. He therefore felt with special poignancy the crudeness of the word which silences the deep-

136 *Ibid.*, 35.

137. *Likkutei Moharan*, II, No. 7.

138. *Ibid.*

139. *Ibid.*, I, No. 81: "For the chief thing in man is reason, and therefore in the place that reason thinks, there the whole man is, and the more one knows, the more is he included in the root, i.e., in God Blessed be He."

140. *Maggid Siḥot*, 71.

141. *Ibid.*, 29.

est and most intimate things. Not through philosophical theories, not through overly subtle and tortuous explanations, he therefore contends, can one solve the great enigma of the world, for "silence is a state beyond the word." Wordlessly, immersed in oneself, one must feel in the hidden corners of the soul the divine mystery of mankind. "When a difficulty about God arises," the Bratzlaver teaches, "be silent;" through this silence, your own thoughts will find the explanation for your difficulty.[142] With *closed* eyes, he declares, one must contemplate the purpose of the world,[143] and with *wakeful* ears listen to the marvelous melody of the world. This melody-motif occupies, as we shall see further, an extremely important place in his philosophy.

One must not forget, Naḥman admonishes his disciples, that the things of this world are worth nothing.[144] The *yetzer ra*, the evil inclination, is like one who strides around among men with a closed hand, and no mortal knows what is in it. The *yetzer ra* is deceitful and asks everyone: What do I hold in my hand? Each person imagines he holds precisely what he desires, and so all run after him. And when he opens his hand, all see that there is nothing there. Thus the *yetzer ra* deludes the world.[145]

All the desires of the world, the Bratzlaver further says, are like the beams of sunshine which penetrate through the dust of the air into a room; when one wishes to take hold of them, he gropes in vain and nothing remains in his hand.[146] Nevertheless, Rabbi Naḥman sensed that in this world which is filled with pain and sorrow, in this world which is like hell, a wondrous magic, a reflection of the divine light which trembles in every creature and glistens in every obscure corner, is hidden. The ascetic and mystic of the castaway little town of Medzhibozh had, after all, a spark of the true poet in him, and so he perceived with his poetic eye not only the world's agony and tears but also the beauty hidden beneath the agony. He heard the marvelous symphony of the cosmos in which he sensed the revelation of the divine glory, the garment of the *ḥochmah dekedushah*, the holy wisdom.

According to the Bratzlaver's philosophy, the supreme thing

142. *Sefer Ha-Middot*, "Emunah."
143. *Likkutei Moharan*, I, No. 65.
144. *Maggid Siḥot*, 35.
145. *Ibid.*, 24.
146. *Maggid Siḥot*, 24.

in the world is the beauty of the melody. "The sound of the melody," he taught, "is the three basic colors of the rainbow; the sound of the melody is the garment of the *Shechinah.*"[147] For "melody is a great and exceedingly exalted thing; its loftiness cannot be calculated."[148] One must know music, Rabbi Naḥman ever reminds his disciples, to understand how to put together the tones scattered everywhere and construct out of them the melody, i.e., to create the joy, the prophetic spirit, that is the utter antithesis of sadness; for only when the prophet hears the melody through which the musician creates complete joy does the spirit of prophecy awaken in him.[149]

Of the Bratzlaver his pupil Rabbi Nathan relates "that he would very frequently sing one of his own melodies. While singing it he would begin to dance, and he who has not seen Rabbi Naḥman's dancing has in his life never seen anything good." Naḥman, who always carried in his heart the pain of the world and was himself filled with sadness, constantly preached to his disciples that "one ought ever to be in joy and to serve the Lord with joy."[150] "And jump once more with joy!," he always encouraged his disciples.[151] One must remove himself as far as possible from sadness and be careful always to be in a happy frame of mind.[152] "Let man ever strengthen himself in joy," the Bratzlaver repeats, "for sadness is extremely noxious."[153] A laughing face heals a man.[154] It is a great commandment to be always in joy and to strengthen oneself and drive away sadness and melancholy with all one's powers.[155] The highest virtue is to encourage oneself, to pursue melancholy and bring it into the state of joy, i.e., to transform it and all afflictions into pure happiness.[156] From one who is in sorrow God removes Himself;[157] hence, every man ought to be

147. *Likkutei Moharan,* I, No. 54.
148. *Maggid Siḥot,* 78.
149. *Ibid.*
150. *Ibid.,* No. 222.
151. This is several times repeated in Nathan's letters to his son Isaac. Characteristic is the following passage in Nathan's letter written at the conclusion of the Sabbath of "Shemot," 1836: "For we need especially to strive to break that melancholy which does more harm—God forbid—than everything else. O, do not fear, my dear child! Do not fear! God is with you in truth. Remember what our master and teacher of blessed memory said: 'God is great. Men do not at all know . . .' "
152. *Ibid.,* No. 282.
153. *Ibid.,* II, No. 51.
154. *Maggid Siḥot,* 32.
155. *Ibid.,* II, No. 24.
156. *Ibid.,* II, No. 23.
157. *Sefer Ha-Middot,* "Atzvut."

strongly admonished ever to abide in joy. The man who is privileged to be in such a state is guarded by God Himself.[158] The wicked, declares the Bratzlaver, sing mainly "melodies of wailing and sorrow."[159] Through the melody of a man one can recognize "whether he has taken upon himself the yoke of the Torah."[160]

When the patriarch Jacob dispatched his ten sons to Joseph in Egypt, relates Rabbi Naḥman, he sent along with them the melody of *Eretz Yisrael*, of Palestine, and this is the secret of the words of Jacob to his children: "Take of the *zimrat* ["best fruits," but understood by Naḥman as *zemirat*, "song"] of the land" (Genesis, 43:11). For you must know, he explains, that every place has its own melody, and every blade of grass has its own song, and through the grasses that flourish and grow out of the earth a melody is produced. Hence, every shepherd has his own special melody according to the grasses growing where he pastures his flock.[161] Thanks to melody, the spirit of man rises above all other creatures of the earth. Melody liberates man "from the spirit of the beasts," raises his spirit to the heights, while the spirit of the beasts remains rooted below.[162]

Rabbi Naḥman was once walking with one of his disciples over a field near Zlotopola and said to his companion:

O that you might have the privilege of hearing the singing of the paeans and praises of the grasses and plants! Every little blade of grass sings a paean to God without any extraneous motives, without any strange thoughts, without any consideration of recompense. Ah, how good, how lovely it is when one hears this song of the grasses; it is good to be pious among them![163]

"How precious and lovely," he says elsewhere, "it is to go out at the beginning of spring in the fields when nature awakens from its sleep and to pour out a prayer to God there. Every fresh blade of grass that grows, every little flower—all merge themselves with the prayer, for they also yearn and long for

158. *Maggid Siḥot*, 26. The following point is also worth noting. The ascetic Naḥman of Bratzlav who, in his youth, mortified his flesh and fasted so much warns his disciples: "One must have great compassion on his own body, as it is written: 'Hide not thyself from thine own flesh.' One must refine the body in order that the soul may transmit to it the ideas and conceptions that it has attained" (*Likkutei Moharan*, I, No. 22).

159. *Ibid.*, I, No. 226.

160. *Ibid.*, II, No. 1.

161. *Ibid.*, II, No. 63.

162. *Ibid.*, No. 63.

163. *Maggid Siḥot*, 60.

God."[164] The poet awakens in the Bratzlaver and he exclaims feelingly:

There are fields on which trees and plants of marvelous beauty grow, and the splendor of these blooming fields is impossible to describe. Happy is the eye that can see all this, for all the trees and plants are in the state of holy souls which grow and flourish there. And there are so many other naked souls wandering about lost beyond the boundary of the blooming fields and waiting for correction or repair *(tikkun)*.[165]

The mystic and poet perceives the whole cosmos woven together in one web. You must know, Rabbi Naḥman says to his disciples, that the world is like a spinning top. Everything is in continuous motion and ceaselessly changes its form. A man is transformed into an angel, and an angel into a man. The same is true with all other entities in the world. Everything is in perpetual movement and alteration; one thing is transformed into another. There is a constant ascent from below to above and descent from above to below, for everything derives from one root and everything is a perfect unity.[166]

God, says the Bratzlaver, never creates the same thing twice, for everything is changed, everything ceaselessly alters its form.[167] And Rabbi Naḥman—he also, is in perpetual motion. He is the indefatigable seeker, for, as he explains, "I cannot abide at one level."[168] It is not good, he says, to be old.[169] One must always renew himself,[170] for only through continuous renewal, through ceaseless striving, is the most exalted and loveliest thing in the world, the melody, created and revealed.

You must know, he constantly teaches his disciples, that every wisdom in the world has its own song and melody; through this song the wisdom in question discloses itself. According to its state and aspect, every wisdom has its melody

164. *Ibid.*, 48.
165. *Likkutei Moharan*, I, No. 65. Elsewhere (*Maggid Siḥot*, 66) the rabbi of Bratzlav again mentions the "naked souls" on which there should be so much compassion because they cannot find any vestment or garment. They wander, unfortunately, between two worlds; they cannot raise themselves to the heights nor descend below.
166. *Maggid Siḥot*, 31.
167. *Ibid.*, 36.
168. *Ibid.*, 63.
169. In one of his letters to his son Isaac, Nathan of Nemirov writes: "And everything is contained in what he of blessed memory warned in a loud voice and scolded us and said as follows: 'It is not permitted to be old.' "
170. *Maggid Siḥot*, 35.

which belongs to it alone. Even the wisdom of heresy has its own melody. And the higher the level of the wisdom, the more exalted is its melody. Each religion also has its own melody; even the false religions of the peoples who serve idols have their individual melodies. The highest religion, which is more exalted than all the wisdoms and faiths of the world, i.e., the religion in the light of the *Ein Sof* that embraces all worlds, has its own individual song also. And it is loftier than all the songs and melodies in the world, and all the songs and melodies of all the wisdoms draw nourishment from this supreme and peerless melody. Higher than everything else is the melody of faith, and in the Messianic Age, when all the peoples will be enlightened "to call upon the name of the Lord," heresy and unbelief will cease in the world and all will believe in the Infinite God.[171] Then the profound words of the Song of Songs (4:8) will be fulfilled: "Come, look from the top of Amanah" (*Rosh Amanah*, which Naḥman here translates as the "peak of faith"). The song that derives from the supreme faith, the song attained by the godly man Moses, who spoke with God and gave the chosen people the Torah, will resound. Moses was the first to reach the state of silence that is higher than the word and to penetrate into the mystery of "Be silent; so has He decided."[172] In the state of silence that is beyond all words is the supreme and loveliest melody created, the melody of *Rosh Amanah*, the melody which can redeem even the souls fallen into the deepest abysses of heresy that derive from "the empty space."[173] And this is the secret of the words: *Az yashir Mosheh*, "then Moses will sing" [Rabbi Naḥman translates the verb as future rather than as past]. Then, in the Messianic Age, the redemptive and liberating song of Moses, the man of God, will resound.[174]

But every generation has its representative and leader who is in the state of Moses-Messiah. Here we encounter the teaching of Naḥman of Bratzlav on the *tzaddik* of the generation. Naḥman speaks with no less hostility than Jacob Joseph Ha-Kohen of Polonnoye about the "arrogant scholars" who fight against the *tzaddikim* and regard them with arrogance and contempt. This quarrel, he declares, is of the same character as that be-

171. In the time to come (i.e., in the hereafter), the Bratzlaver repeats, "all will know the Lord—even the idolatrous peoples of the world" (*Likkutei Moharan*, I, No. 21).

172. See above, pp. 147, 149.

173. See above, pp. 146–147.

174. *Likkutei Moharan*, I, No. 64. See also *ibid.*, II, No. 8.

tween Jacob and Laban. Jacob is the *tzaddik*, and Laban the conceited scholar who is the "son of Lilith," the "Jewish demon." His learning is only to make himself great and carry on controversies. As far as such a scholar is concerned, "a carcass is better than he."[175] If the Mitnagdim revile the truly pious, this is only because they have studied with scholars who are unfit, with "Jewish demons."[176] One can be a scholar, Rabbi Naḥman adds, and at the same time a thoroughly wicked man. And he who thinks that to be a scholar is the principal thing is in the state of Aḥer (Elisha ben Abuyah) who "cut down the plants" [i.e., became a heretic], for Torah without good deeds is worthless.[177]

The pillar of the world, the true leader of the generation, Naḥman teaches, is the *tzaddik*. However, his concept of the role of the *tzaddik* is quite different from that of Rabbi Elimelech of Lyzhansk. The Bratzlaver saw in the *tzaddik* not primarily the miracle-worker but the conscience of his generation. "The *tzaddik* cannot push away from himself even one who has sunk into all the 'forty-nine gates of uncleanness.' On the contrary, he brings the most vile and unclean person even closer to himself, is more gentle to him, and treats him with greater tenderness and compassion." Rabbi Naḥman would fly into a rage when any of his disciples begged him to pray for a livelihood, or when the Hasidim would tell of his miracles and wonders. "I do not understand," he would say at such times,

> how you have the heart to trouble me with such foolishness. I am like one who strides day and night over the desert and wishes to make an inhabited place out of it. For the heart of each of you is like a neglected wilderness; in it there is no little corner for the *Shechinah*. I am always rummaging and searching, for I wish to repair your hearts so that the *Shechinah* may rest in them.

Rabbi Naḥman was therefore displeased with the conduct of many of the *tzaddikim* of his time. "Now," he complains to his disciples, "false masters of names *(baalei shemot shel sheker)* have multiplied greatly."[178]

There are leaders who are crowned with the title rabbi. In reality they cannot even train themselves, not to speak of train-

175. *Likkutei Moharan*, I, No. 12.
176. *Ibid.*, No. 28.
177. *Ibid.*, No. 31.
178. *Maggid Siḥot*, 38.

ing others; yet they presume to lead the world.[179] In former times, Naḥman ironically declares, the *tzaddikim* used to be poor and humble; now they are rich.[180] Wealth, in his view, is one of the things that corrupt men. A truly good man, he says, is very far from riches;[181] and the wealth the *tzaddikim* possess harms them greatly.[182] When Naḥman was told of the miracles of the Galician *tzaddikim*, he replied with a skeptical smile[183] and incidentally related an anecdote about a king who had two sons, one wise and the other foolish. The king put the fool in charge of all of his treasures; the wise son, however, received no post but sat alone in the king's palace. It was hard for the people to understand why the son who was not wise had an official appointment and all men came to him, both those who contributed and those who received from the accumulated treasures, while the wise son held no position at all. To this the king replied: Does it require such great brilliance to take treasures that are prepared and distribute them? The wise son always sits near me and constantly conceives new ideas, gives me perspicacious advice which I would never have thought of. Indeed, it is thanks to him and his counsel that I have conquered countries and lands of which I had previously not even known. And from this come all the treasures which the not very clever treasurer takes already prepared and distributes. Thus it is evident that the wise man, the counsellor, is far more important than the treasurer.[184]

These sarcastic words of the Baal Shem Tov's great-grandson enraged some of the contemporary *tzaddikim* and rabbis, and they persecuted him and his followers with no less bitterness and intensity than the Mitnagdim of the Vilna Gaon's school had previously persecuted the "Karliner."[185] Their hostility

179. *Likkutei Moharan*, I, No. 61.

180. *Ibid.*, No. 200.

181. *Maggid Siḥot*, 23.

182. *Ibid.* The great magnates, he says elsewhere, are almost all crazy, for money makes them mad (*Likkutei Moharan*, II, No. 64).

183. *Likkutei Moharan*, I, No. 186.

184. *Maggid Siḥot*, 53.

185. To give some notion of the hatred with which several *tzaddikim* persecuted the Hasidim of Bratzlav even after the death of their *rebbe*, it suffices to quote several lines from the summons of the rabbi of Savran to his disciples: "Let this make known in all the earth that there have arisen the Hasidim of the Bratzlaver instead of their fathers, a breed of wicked men, sinners and seducers of multitudes. Therefore, I admonish those who heed my authority to remove these wicked men with all kinds of removals. You shall not intermarry with them, for they are forbidden to enter into the congregation of the Lord, and a teacher from the community of the Bratzlaver shall not teach your children Torah, for it will turn into heresy inside him. The slaughtering of a ritual slaughterer of the Bratzlaver is invalid. There shall be no precentor for the congregation

was increased by Naḥman's proud statement that he was the true *tzaddik* of the generation who is in the state of Moses-Messiah.[186] The same process which had once taken place in the soul of the mystic and poet Moses Hayyim Luzzatto[187] occurred in a certain sense in Rabbi Naḥman of Bratzlav. Luzzatto sensed in himself extraordinary powers but did not know what they signified. He thought that he, the darling of the Muses, was accompanied by a heavenly messenger and that he heard the voice of a *maggid*, or mentor-angel. This man of poetic revelation and of the penetrating, eagle eye of the gifted artist believed that he had attained the state of "unveiling of the eyes" in consequence of his ascetic life and his profound fathoming of the mysteries of the Kabbalah.

The Bratzlaver, with his enormous imaginative power, with his poetic spark and restless, searching spirit, felt that he was incomparably higher than many of the famous *tzaddikim* of his day with their miracles and preachments. He was sure that he was the true *tzaddik* of the generation who had been appointed by Providence to be the faithful guardian and pointer of the way for all who wander lost over the confused labyrinths of life. The *tzaddik*, Naḥman teaches, is forever searching and inquiring in order to uncover the divine will, for in every object, in every creature, God's will is expressed. The *tzaddik* seeks and endeavors to grasp this hidden divine will.[188]

"The *tzaddik* is the man in whom is the spirit," says the Bratzlaver. This means that the *tzaddik* carries in himself the "spirit of God" that "hovered over the face of the waters," the "spirit of life" that renews and redeems the world.[189] Every

from this group of wicked men, for his prayer is an abomination. In short, make every effort to destroy all their means of livelihood. One who would have compassion on them is forbidden to be himself shown compassion, and God will send blessing on all the work of the hands of everyone who heeds my words, and he will have eternal life as his reward" (*Ha-Melitz*, IV, 127). In the article from which we quote these words a melancholy picture of the persecutions which the Hasidim of Bratzlav had to endure even fifty years after their master's death is given. Rabbi Naḥman, for his part, reacted very little to the attacks of his adversaries. Unperturbedly he noted to his Hasidim: "They, the adversaries, have carved themselves out a figure of a man [that is to say, they have an altogether false notion of him] and make war on him" (*Maggid Siḥot*, 63). Interesting details about the persecutions which the Hasidim of Bratzlav had to suffer are also found in Nathan's letters to his son. Nathan relates how in Ladizin they broke the windows in the house where he stopped on his journey. In his house a troop of soldiers was billeted, and he frequently repeats in his letters: "Lo, the billet still stands in my house and I have no idea when it will depart."

186. *Likkutei Moharan*, I, No. 9, No. 118.
187. See our *History*, Vol. VI, p. 181.
188. *Likkutei Moharan*, I, No. 47.
189. *Ibid.*, No. 8.

Jew, Naḥman declares, knows only one motif of the melody that resounds throughout the expanse of the world, but the *tzaddik* knows the entire melody. He attains the state of Moses, "which is the state of silence," the supreme state that is "beyond speech."

"Ephemeral is the loveliness and splendor of the whole world," says Rabbi Naḥman, "but the genuine *tzaddik* is the incarnation of the beauty and nobility of the world. And when this beauty is disclosed, the eyes of the world are opened and it begins to understand true beauty. Hence, everyone should strive to be as close as possible to the *tzaddik*."[190] "The chief and fundamental thing," he repeats, "is that everything is dependent upon binding oneself to the *tzaddik* of the generation."[191] Know, Rabbi Naḥman teaches, that one must go to the *tzaddik* to find what is lost, for before a man's birth he is told what he must do and achieve in the world, but as soon as he is born he forgets everything he was taught. The *tzaddik*, however, seeks and finds all the lost things of the world. He instructs each man and reminds him to what purpose he was born and what he must accomplish.[192] It is not possible to attain the truth otherwise than by being as close as possible to the *tzaddik* and following the paths he points out.[193] Men, says the Bratzlaver smilingly, do not understand why one should go to the *tzaddik* and hear the Torah from his mouth; can one not himself read ethical instruction and pious books? No, there is a vast difference between the person who learns from a book and one who hears the living word from the teacher's mouth and whose soul comes into intimate contact with the teacher's breath. The person who looks into the face of the *tzaddik* does not need to speak a word to sense at once how his own countenance is steeped in darkness.[194]

Rabbi Naḥman, however, is not content with this and sets forth a completely new requirement which is in fact alien to Jewish tradition and smacks of Catholicism. There are, he says, three states through which one comes close to the *tzaddik*, and the highest of them is "the state of confession," of revealing one's entire soul to him.[195] Nathan of Nemirov, indeed, relates that every one of Rabbi Naḥman's intimates had, first of all, to

190. *Likkutei Moharan*, II, No. 67.
191. *Ibid.*, I, No. 10; *ibid.*, No. 123: "The chief thing, and the most important of all, is to bind oneself to the *tzaddik* of the generation."
192. *Ibid.*, I, No. 188.
193. *Ibid.*, No. 7.
194. *Ibid.*, No. 19.
195. *Ibid.*, No. 8.

confess to his master, to give an account of all his acts, everything he had done and thought.

People believe, Rabbi Naḥman told his disciples, that if the *tzaddik* is great, he does not regard common mortals at all, since he is so far removed from the weekday world. But this is a grave error. On the contrary, the greater the *tzaddik*, the more he can consider and understand the events of the world.[196] Every Jew must feel a certain pain every day, but the greater a man is, the more intense his pain.[197] Only one who has profound compassion and sacrifices himself for the sake of Israel can be a leader,[198] for the world has need of such compassion.[199] But let no one think, the Bratzlaver insists, that the true *tzaddikim* are so great because they were born with great souls. Everyone can attain their level.[200] "Every Jew may reach the level of the *tzaddikim*,[201] because Moses our teacher who represents the supreme level that man can attain is incarnate in him."[202] Everything depends on free will; even in the lowest depths of hell one can draw near to God. Every person in the world, Naḥman teaches, can attain the superlative level; it depends entirely on his own free choice.[203] Every Jew, even the least and lowliest who is at the bottom-most level, he further declares, is also "able to return to God."[204] It sometimes happens, the Bratzlaver teaches, that the true *tzaddik* is a common man, one who is called a *prostak* and "does not reveal or explain any Torah."[205] And yet precisely in this lies his greatness, for he thereby gives life to the common people and elevates them.[206]

Rabbi Naḥman, who was unhappy when miracle stories about rabbis were told, nevertheless frequently indicated to his disciples that to relate stories about the *tzaddikim* is a noble act. This is the state of *gadlut de-moḥin*, "greatness of mind." Through telling stories about *tzaddikim*, he asserts, the light of the Messiah is brought down to earth and much darkness and many troubles are removed from the world.[207] But, he adds,

196. *Likkutei Moharan*, II, No. 61.
197. *Ibid.*, No. 77.
198. *Ibid.*, No. 7.
199. *Ibid.*, I, No. 105.
200. *Maggid Siḥot*, 61.
201. *Likkutei Moharan*, I, No. 97.
202. *Ibid.*, II, No. 26.
203. *Maggid Siḥot*, 7.
204. *Ibid.*, 54.
205. *Likkutei Moharan*, II, No. 78.
206. *Ibid.*
207. *Sefer Middot*, "Tzaddik."

one must know how to tell the story.[208] And the *tzaddik* himself must clothe his teaching in the garment of tales; we know that the Torah itself is veiled in stories, "for it was not possible to reveal it in its true form."[209]

Thus the poet in Rabbi Naḥman, despite all obstacles, overcame the *tzaddik* and found a creative path for himself. In the last years of his brief life he sought a "garment" for his teaching, in order to transmit it to his disciples in images and symbols. Thus his imaginative and image-filled wonder-tales, which constitute the first lovely page of neo-Yiddish artistic literature, were created. "I shall begin to tell stories," Rabbi Naḥman declared to his disciples.[210] These stories, unfortunately, have not come down to us in their original form, for the Bratzlaver did not write down his tales but *told* them to his disciples, and his loyal disciple, Nathan of Nemirov, wrote them down from memory only later.

Rabbi Nathan was a scholar and a Kabbalist but without the slightest poetic sensitivity, and he was very little suited properly and faithfully to retell such unique, richly imaginative tales. He did not understand them, but only believed that the profoundest mysteries are concealed in them. Thus he wrote commentaries to the tales, and these commentaries show how little he grasped the extraordinary products of his teacher's inexhaustible imagination. It should therefore occasion no surprise that, under his unskilled fingers, these tender creatures lost part of their charm and some of them became quite crippled. Thus, for example, the imaginative and colorful story of the wise man and his son with lamed feet is transmitted in distorted form. And in the case of the story of the king who carried on wars, Rabbi Nathan himself indicates that he forgot the end and that "it is not written down well as he, Rabbi Naḥman, told it."

The Bratzlaver expressed his desire that the stories which he related to his disciples in plain Yiddish be published with a Hebrew translation.[211] His pupil Nathan fulfilled the wish five

208. *Likkutei Moharan*, I, 234.

209. *Ibid.*, No. 164.

210. See second introduction to *Sippurei Maasiyyot.*

211. In modern times S.Z. Setzer attempted to demonstrate that Rabbi Naḥman's tales, which were told in Yiddish, were written down by Nathan of Nemirov in Hebrew, and the printed Yiddish text is "a translation from a Hebrew text which is itself a translation from the very Yiddish speech into which it was later translated." That this conjecture hangs in thin air with little ground under it, and that Setzer's arguments are very weak and in addition filled with contradictions, has been discussed at length by S. Niger in his thorough work *Rabbi Nakhman Braslaver Un Zayne Sippurei Maasiyyot.*

years after his master's death, and in 1815 issued Rabbi Naḥman's tales, accompanied by a Hebrew translation. This translation was mocked by the writers of the Haskalah period for its "vulgar" language. Joseph Perl wrote parodies on it, and even in more recent times the historian of Hasidism, Simon Dubnow, deemed it necessary to deride the "linguist" Nathan of Nemirov and his ignorant translation. In point of fact, the clumsy language of the Hebrew translation is not at all indicative of Nathan's ignorance but of the inordinate respect he had for every word of his teacher. In the Hebrew works that he published, as well as in his hundreds of still unpublished letters, Nathan demonstrated that he wrote Hebrew considerably better than many other scholars of his time. But he considered it necessary to translate his master's stories in the same way as, in the Middle Ages, the Torah was translated into *Leshon Ashkenaz.* Because of their reverence for the sacred text, the medieval translators faithfully followed the word-order of the Hebrew original, were afraid either to add or drop a single word, took no account whatever of the spirit and character of the language into which they were translating, and paid little attention to the fact that, through the slavish word-for-word rendering, the sentence construction became heavy and wooden and the content was not infrequently obscured and made difficult to understand.[212]

The pious Nathan of Nemirov sought in his master's stories "stupendous mysteries" and "divine revelations."[213] In every statement of the tales he perceived the profundest meanings and intentions, and he believed that by altering even a single word and failing to transmit them as they came forth from the master's mouth, he would be "greatly detracting from the work." To be sure, as we have already noted, Nathan himself did not accurately transmit the text and thereby, indeed, "greatly detracted from the work."[214] But what he committed to memory and wrote down on paper he endeavored to translate verbatim with the most painstaking fidelity.

Rabbi Nathan preserved the thirteen tales of the Bratzlaver and transmitted them to the reading public.[215] Most of these

212. See our *History,* Vol. VII, pp. 94–95.

213. *Maggid Siḥot,* 57.

214. First introduction to *Sippurei Maasiyyot.*

215. (1) The story of the king with the princess; (2) the story about an emperor and a king who had no children; (3) the story about a certain sage; (4) a tale about a king who issued a decree of apostasy; (5) a tale about a king; (6) a story about a king and a wise man; (7) a tale about a king who carried on wars; (8) the rabbi and his only son; (9) a

bear a general character. Indeed, only one, the story about the rabbi and his only son, has a purely Jewish content. This is a typical Hasidic story telling of a scholarly rabbi whose keen subtleties and commonplace prayers cannot satisfy his only son, who is endowed with a gentle, sensitive soul. The son is attracted to a Hasidic *rebbe*, a *tzaddik*, because only the *tzaddik* can refresh his languishing heart. But the Mitnagdic rabbi cannot bear this and interposes all kinds of obstacles. Finally, the son's soul flickers and expires out of longing for the source of fresh life, the Hasidic *rebbe*.

Full of acid irony is the story of the wise man and the simple man. The literature of Haskalah is rich in satires and lampoons directed against the Hasidim and their *rebbes*. The story of the wise and simple men is a clever satire produced by the "opposite side" in the Hasidic camp. Rabbi Naḥman here maintains his fundamental thesis that one must approach the phenomena of life only with simplicity and sincerity, and that the enterprise of the rationalist "speculators" who wish to analyze everything through their reason is foolish and misguided. They think everything in the world can be fathomed and explained through common sense, but the Bratzlaver argues that "things happen that are the contrary of speculation and cannot be explained through human logic."[216] When a man, Rabbi Naḥman suggests, relies only on his reason and wisdom, he may fall into many errors and snares.[217] He therefore tells a story of two friends, one a simple man and the other a sage who had attained much knowledge. He relates how the first, with his simplicity and sincerity, walks with sure steps over the tortuous pathways of life, while the wise man with his speculation and doubts is hurled from one trouble to another and falls into the deepest swamp.

An interesting point is worth noting here. Whereas the *maskilim* in their satires portray their opponents in black colors only—all the *tzaddikim* are, for them, hypocrites, swindlers, and frauds—Rabbi Naḥman of Bratzlav portrays his antagonist, the "sage," as a decent person who wishes only to attain the truth but seeks it in false ways. The most poignant element in the satire is the fact that Rabbi Naḥman here struggles not

---

story about a wise man and a simple man; (10) the story about the town merchant and the poor man; (11) the story about a prince and the son of a servant; (12) the story about the prayer leader; (13) a tale about seven beggars.

216. *Maggid Siḥot*, 31.

217. *Likkutei Moharan*, II, No. 12.

only against the "speculators" and rationalists of his age but also against the "speculator" and skeptic residing in himself. His pupil Nathan of Nemirov tells of the anguished cry that Rabbi Naḥman once uttered before his Hasidim: "When one falls into the mud, he cries and cries and cries!"[218] But this cry was transformed into a satire, into an act of liberation. Through mocking laughter at the overly subtle "sage" who is so deeply sunk in mud, he wishes to free himself from the "sage" and "speculator" still hidden in himself.

Rabbi Naḥman of Bratzlav did not tell his tales in a vacuum. There was always a definite cause, some specific event, that moved him to illustrate it to his listeners with a story. So, for example, his disciples were once sitting and talking of Napoleon's great victories that were taking place at that time, and they expressed their astonishment that a common mortal of low estate should become so exalted and be crowned emperor. "Who knows," Rabbi Naḥman replied, "from whence his soul derives? Souls also are sometimes exchanged." And at once he began to relate his remarkable story of the king's son and maidservant's son who were exchanged for each other.

On another occasion, when he heard that Nathan of Nemirov had written to another disciple that he should always be joyous, Rabbi Naḥman declared: "I will tell you how men once were joyous." And he immediately commenced to relate the story of the seven beggars, the story that is the crown of his tales, one of the loveliest and profoundest stories in Jewish literature.[219] In it, through the life-wisdom of the six beggars,[220] the *tzaddik* who was also a thinker and poet renders his innermost world of ideas, attained through innumerable sufferings and the most painful doubts. The *tzaddik* and poet is firmly persuaded that only through the way of suffering does one attain the highest and noblest, that the world's agony and the pitch-black night are permeated with rays of divine light and beauty. One need only have eagle's eyes to see them. Small and petty are the requirements of daily life, and clangorously dissonant is the tumult of the noisy regions of life; but he who has a sensitive hearing perceives the wondrous melody resounding in the cosmos, perceives with the trembling strings

218. *Maggid Siḥot*, 53.

219. The story of the seven beggars was reworked in modern times by Jonah Speavack in dramatic form—*Rabbi Nakhman Bratzlaver in Geshtalt Fun Zayn "Mayse Mit Di Zibn Betlers,"* Vilna, 1932.

220. The story of the seventh beggar is missing. It was not told by the Bratzlaver.

of his heart the immense joy that springs out of the deep pain of the world.

To provide some notion of the style of this marvelous tale, we here give part of the story that the third beggar, the stutterer and stammerer, who is in reality "not a stammerer at all but, on the contrary, a very good speaker—something that is extremely surprising," tells. The stammering beggar says,

> I go about and gather all truly saintly persons and bring them to the man of genuine grace, the great man; and he, the man of true grace, spins time from them. . . . Everything has a heart and the world as a whole also has a heart. The heart of the world is a complete form with a face and hands and feet. Now, the toe-nail of the world's heart is more tender than another man's heart itself. And there is a certain mountain on which stands a stone, and out of the stone flows a spring. And the mountain with the spring stands at one end of the world, and the heart of the world stands at the other end. And the heart stands over against the spring and yearns and longs constantly to come to the spring. And the longing and yearning of the heart for the spring is stupendously powerful, and the heart always cries that it may come to the spring, and the spring also yearns for the heart. And the heart has two debilities—one because the sun wearies it greatly and burns it, and this magnifies the other debility, which the heart suffers because of its longing and yearning for the spring. And it always cries that it may come to the spring, for the heart constantly stands over against the spring and cries out greatly in longing for the spring. When the heart needs to rest a bit, a large bird comes and spreads its wings over it and protects it from the sun. Then the heart rests a while. But even when it is resting, it still looks at the spring and yearns for it. Now if it longs so greatly for the spring, why does it not go to it? Because when the heart wishes to approach the mountain on which the spring is, it no longer sees the top of the mountain and cannot see the spring, and as soon as it does not look on the spring, it expires, for the very life of the heart derives from the spring. As long as it stands over against the mountain it sees the peak on which the spring is, but as soon as it wishes to approach the mountain it no longer sees the spring and can no longer look upon it and it may—God forbid—perish. And if the heart should—God forbid—perish, the world itself would be destroyed, for the heart is the life of everything, and how could the world have any existence without the heart? Therefore the heart cannot approach the spring but always stands over against it and longs and cries that it wishes to come to the spring. And in the spring there is no time, because the spring is not in time but beyond it. But then, how, can the spring be in the world? The spring's existence in the world derives only from its being given a day as a gift by the heart. And when the day wishes to end, as soon it goes away the spring will no longer have any time

and will depart from the world. And if the spring would not be, then the heart would also—God forbid—perish, and the whole world would be annihilated. Therefore, when the day approaches its end, the heart and the spring begin to take leave of each other and commence to speak parables and poems and songs to one another, exceedingly beautiful songs and poems with great love and great longing—the heart to the spring and the spring to the heart. And the man of true grace supervises this and watches over it. As soon as the day comes to its end and is about to depart, the man of true grace comes to its aid and grants the heart another day and the heart gives the day to the spring. And as the day arrives from whence it comes, so it also goes with parables and lovely songs in which there are all wisdoms.

And all the time which the man of true grace has, adds the stammering beggar, comes to him through me, for I always wander about and gather all the genuinely pious, from whom time comes, and bring them to the man of true grace.

CHAPTER SIX

Hasidic Tales; ATTACKS ON THE MOVEMENT

Two kinds of Hasidic tales—Collections of Hasidic tales—Their echo in modern literature—Tract literature in opposition to the Hasidim—The Maggid of Slutsk, Israel Loebl; his *Sefer Ha-Vikkuaḥ* and *Glaubwürdige Nachricht*—David of Makow and his *Zemir Aritizim* and *Shever Poshe'im*—The estranged are reconciled—Irenic tones in the polemic literature

THE TALES of Rabbi Naḥman of Bratzlav are an utterly unique phenomenon, produced on the threshold of the nineteenth century but under circumstances reminiscent of ancient times. These tales were not written down by their author, nor did he polish their form and style. Indeed, he was not aware that he was a poet and creator of artistic works, that he was one of those who revealed the treasures about which he dreamed and for which his soul yearned—the treasures of the beautiful and noble, which glisten throughout the space of the world, in everything that bears the stamp of God's creation. Like a folk-singer of ancient days, Naḥman improvised his tales, recited them before his listeners, and thus transmitted them to others and allowed them to wander over the world.

Whereas these tales are the fruits of individual creation and bear the clear impress of the single poet, an enormous number of tales and legends whose author is the entire Hasidic community and which are typical products of anonymous popular creativity were produced in the same milieu. Every historian of culture must recognize that this plethora of legends and miracle tales demonstrates most clearly the enormous power with which the Hasidic movement worked on the spirit and mood of the Jewish masses.

We have observed how frequently Rabbi Naḥman of Bratzlav reminded his disciples that it is a great thing to tell stories about the *tzaddikim*. On this point he was in agreement with the other *tzaddikim* of his generation, and the Hasidic masses fulfilled the wish of their leaders with strong enthusiasm. At the very time when the Berlin Haskalah was attempting to propagandize its rationalist philosophy and to struggle against everything that smacked of "mysticism," the followers of the Hasidic movement devoted themselves with no less diligence to the creation of myths and braided garlands of imaginative legends around their beloved heroes, the *tzaddikim* of the age.[1]

Nathan of Nemirov indicates in the first introduction to *Sippurei Maasiyyot* that only those tales that are completely new and that were produced by the imagination of Rabbi Naḥman of Bratzlav were permitted to enter this collection. But Naḥman would also, at times, take a story which had long been circulating among the people and tell it in such a reworked and altered form that it obtained a totally new appearance.[2] The stories and legends that the Hasidic masses produced may also be divided into these two categories. We have elsewhere[3] in-

1. Typical in this respect is the story which is told in *Adat Tzaddikim* (24–28) how the Baal Shem Tov, before his death, called together all his disciples and designated with what kind of livelihood each should occupy himself. One named Rabbi Jacob, who had served the Baal Shem Tov for a long time, he admonished: "You shall travel around over all places where my name is known and there relate stories about me; from this you will have a living in abundance." It is further related how Rabbi Jacob fulfilled the Baal Shem Tov's testament when he heard that in Italy lives a rich man who pays a ducat for every story told about the founder of Hasidism. This story is associated with another tale which properly demonstrates the Baal Shem Tov's greatness, and Rabbi Jacob is so richly recompensed by the wealthy man for the last story that it suffices him for all of his life.

2. "And also at times he would tell a story of the stories that are told in the world, but he added much to them and changed and corrected the tales, so the plot was completely altered from how they are told in the world. But of these stories, only one or two were written in this book, and all the other tales are completely new and have never been heard before."

3. *YIVO-Bleter*, Vol. III, 332–335.

dicated how the well-known story of Moses' argument with God, written down in Leib bar Moses Melir's *Lange Megile*,[4] was transformed into a Hasidic legend in which Moses and God are changed into the Maggid of Mezhirech and the Baal Shem Tov. In similar fashion the remarkably beautiful story about the shepherd with his extraordinary prayer from the medieval *Sefer Ḥasidim*[5] was altered in the Hasidic environment. The same thing happened with many other stories.

The Hasidic movement, however, also produced a very large number of its own tales and legends about its favorite heroes. In the same year in which *Sippurei Maasiyyot* of Rabbi Naḥman of Bratzlav was published (1815), there also appeared in four editions[6] *Shivḥei Ha-Besht*, a legendary biography of the founder of Hasidism in which the author, the ritual slaughterer Dov Baer, the son-in-law of the Baal Shem Tov's secretary, collected the hundreds of legends produced in Hasidic circles in the course of two generations. All these miracle tales, the imaginatively rich and poetically beautiful as well as the crude and barbaric, are transmitted as actual, trustworthy events.

Sippurei Maasiyyot as well as *Shivḥei Ha-Besht* enjoyed immense success.[7] But the garland of legendry was extended further. Popular imagination produced new miracle stories that were transmitted orally from generation to generation until they were collected in special works: *Maasei Tzaddikim*, *Mifalot Tzaddikim*, *Divrei Tzaddikim*, *Adat Tzaddikim*, *Sefer Ha-Dorot Ha-Ḥadash*, *Pe'er Mekuddashim*, *Kehal Ḥasidim Ha-Ḥadash*, *Maasiyyot Meha-Gedolim Veha-Ḥasidim*, *Maasiyyot U-Maamarim Yekarim*, and many others. Whole generations were raised on these anthologies, which were several times reprinted. Their influence is discernible also in modern literature. Hence, we consider it necessary to give the contemporary reader some notion of this unique popular poetry.

In these anthologies there are a few tales taken from older sources and rendered in altered form. To this scattered array

4. See our *History*, Vol. VII, pp. 124ff.
5. See our *History*, Vol. II, pp. 47–48.
6. Two in Hebrew (in Kapust and Berdichev), and two, those of Letichev and Oster, in Yiddish. In 1816 a new edition of *Shivḥei Ha-Besht* appeared in Yiddish in Novy Dvor, and a year later (1817) the translator of *Milḥamah Ve-Shalom*, Eleazar Paver (see our *History*, Vol. VII, p. 334), issued his translation of *Shivḥei Ha-Besht* in Zolkiew (see *Kiryat Sefer*, XII, 129).
7. In the course of less than two years *Shivḥei Ha-Besht* appeared in five editions, and over six thousand copies were sold (see Joseph Perl, *Megalleh Temirin*, 23, 123, 230).

belongs, for example, the extremely complicated and highly imaginative story of hospitality to travellers which is found in the collection *Mifalot Tzaddikim.*[8] It is also quite probable that it is from older stories that the adventure-filled tale of the pious Hasid who was also a very poor man is taken. This tale relates how everything the man undertook turned out badly and how he applied to the Maggid of Koznitz and asked the latter to give him some advice as to how he might provide for his family and himself. The Maggid told him that there was good fortune for him only in one enterprise—theft. The tale further relates how the words of the *tzaddik* were fulfilled.[9] In some of the tales the typical narrative style of the old legends is still preserved. For example, in the marvelous story about the *tzaddik* Elimelech of Lyzhansk: "Now we leave the Jew, the lessee of the estate, and turn to the young Count Potocki."[10]

The majority of these anthologies include all kinds of miracle stories about well-known *tzaddikim* and their disciples. Many of the legends are woven around the chief hero of the Hasidic movement, the Baal Shem Tov. We present as illustration only two of these.

Everyone knows, relates *Maaseh Tzaddikim,* of the journey which the Baal Shem Tov took to the Holy Land, where he wished to visit the saintly author of *Or Ha-Ḥayyim.*[11] On the way great hindrances and troubles came to him from God, and so he once fell into melancholy, and because of the intense hardships and cares that he suffered, the holy spirit departed from him and he suddenly fell from all his high levels. The Baal Shem Tov then reflected: "What is to be done?—I shall serve the Creator of the world like all ordinary mortals." He had with him a book of Psalms, and so the whole time he travelled on the ship to Istanbul he recited songs and praises to God like a common man, until he came to Istanbul with his daughter Hodel. They arrived in the city in great poverty and distress. It was then the month of Nissan, a few days before Passover. What did the Baal Shem Tov do? He went to one of the local houses of study, spent the night there, and prayed *be-katnut ha-moḥin* (in smallness of mind). Two days before the festival the godly woman Hodel went to the river to wash a shirt for

8. Before the story is the following comment: "A story that I heard orally from the mouth of a reliable man who saw [it] with his eyes in the precious book *Sefer Hachnasat Oreḥim* that is to be found in the state library of Vienna."

9. *Kehal Hasidim Ha-Ḥadash,* Story No. 205.

10. *Pe'er Mekuddashim,* 41.

11. The well-known mystic Rabbi Ḥayyim ben Moses Attar (1696–1743).

the holy day for her saintly father. Standing at the river, she remembered the situation in which she and her father found themselves, that they were naked and bare, had neither *matzot* nor wine nor anything else for the festival, but that all this was nothing compared to the fact that the holy spirit had departed from her father, as had all of his high degrees, and that he was lying "in smallness of mind" in the house of study "like one of the common multitude."

This caused her great anguish. She began to weep, and the tears poured from her eyes without cease. Just at that time a very rich man passed by on a ship. He saw how the righteous, godly woman was weeping bitter tears, and he had compassion on her and asked her: "My daughter, why are you weeping?" At first she was silent but when he begged her once more to tell him what was the matter—perhaps he might be able to help her in some way—she told him what a holy father she had and what had happened to them. The rich man then said to her: "Go, my daughter, go at once to your father and tell him that I invite him to my house for the entire festival." And he wrote down for her exactly where he lived so that she might come to him with her father. Hodel went at once to her father and told him all this. On the eve of Passover, following the afternoon service, the Baal Shem Tov set out to go to the rich man, who lived in a splendid palace. As soon as the Baal Shem Tov crossed the threshold, saw the splendor of the rooms and the extraordinary beauty of all the appurtenances and furnishings, his heart was filled with joy and his face lit up. The rich man conducted him into a marvelously beautiful chamber, asked him to be seated, and entertained him with some excellent wine. As the Baal Shem Tov drank one glass and then another, his heart became even merrier. The "smallness of mind" to which his worries and troubles had brought him departed from him and he returned to his erstwhile high levels. The Baal Shem Tov then said to his wealthy host that he would like to rest awhile so that later, at the *seder*, he might tell of the Exodus from Egypt with refreshed strength. He lay down, immediately fell asleep, and slept till ten o'clock at night.

The rich man, who was waiting for the Baal Shem Tov with the *seder*, became perturbed and asked: "What has happened to our guest? We must look and see what he is doing." He took a light and entered the Baal Shem Tov's room. There he saw that the latter was sleeping but that rivers of tears were pouring from his eyes. With great astonishment the man remained rooted on the spot and saw how the tears kept streaming and the Baal Shem Tov's face changed every minute. Suddenly the Baal Shem Tov uttered a cry and woke from his sleep. He washed his hands, recited the evening prayers, and then all sat down to the *seder.* The Baal Shem Tov recited the Haggadah with such fervor and his face was so radiant that the rich man understood that a holy man was sitting before him. After the *seder* the host asked his guest what the rivers of tears which he had shed in his sleep signified and why he had awakened with such a cry. The Baal Shem Tov told him that he had had an "ascent of the soul" and there, in the "upper worlds" heard that a terrible decree had been issued against the entire community of Istanbul. Many would be expelled and the rest would be slain and destroyed.

And so I began weeping and begging them to nullify this bitter decree. But my petition was not accepted. Then I undertook to sacrifice myself for our brethren so that they might not perish and be driven out by enemies and oppressors. Only when I was ready to sacrifice myself was great compassion aroused. The decree was annulled, and because I was prepared, out of love for the people of Israel, to sacrifice myself, my soul was returned to me as a gift and I awakened from sleep. Tomorrow, at the morning prayers, you will learn the whole truth.

And so it was. In the morning all the Jews in the synagogue wondered why the two most prominent representatives of the community did not come to the service. They waited for them a long time, but the men arrived only at the conclusion of the service and with great joy related that they were just coming from the sultan's court and that a great miracle had occurred there. One of the counsellors, who was extremely wicked and a Jew-hater, was about to persuade the sultan to issue a decree of expulsion against all the Jews but they, the Jewish representatives, with the help of God found favor with the sultan's mother and, thanks to her, the decree was annulled and the wicked counsellor severely punished.[12]

Of a very different character is the second story. A certain villager used to pray on the High Holy Days in the Baal Shem Tov's *bet ha-midrash.* This villager had a boy with a very dull mind, whom it was not possible to teach even to recognize the shape of the letters, to say nothing of praying or studying Torah. Hence, the father was accustomed not to take his son

12. A second version of the story is to be found in the collection *Maasiyyot Meha-Gedolim Veha-Tzaddikim,* 33–38 (we quote according to the Warsaw edition, 1890).

with him at the High Holy Day season. It was, after all, embarrassing to bring into the synagogue a boy who could not even recite the prayers. But when the son became *bar mitzvah*, the father took him along on Yom Kippur; he was afraid that if he remained in the village without supervision he might, as a result of his great ignorance, take food on the holy fast day. The lad had a little whistle which he used to blow in the fields while herding the flocks. He took this whistle along with him, hiding it in the pocket of his trousers. The father knew nothing of it.

The boy sat in the study-house throughout the holy day. All the people were praying, while he alone said nothing, for he did not know even the alphabet. At the *Musaf* service the boy said to his father: "Father, I have with me my whistle, and I want very much to blow on it." The father was horrified, rebuked his son, and angrily said to him: "Don't you dare do such a thing!" The father could not take the whistle away from the boy because it was an object that, according to the law, could not be touched on the holy day. Following the afternoon service the lad again implored his father: he could no longer be silent, he must blow at least once. When the father realized how intensely the son yearned to blow his instrument, he asked him where he was keeping the whistle. The boy pointed to his trouser pocket. The father thereupon took hold of the pocket with his hand, grasping it firmly so that the lad should not be able to reach the whistle. In the meantime the congregation had begun to recite the *Neilah* service. In the midst of the *Neilah* prayers the boy suddenly tore the pocket with the whistle away from his father's hand, seized the whistle, and through the house of study, over the heads of the amazed congregation, a powerful, triumphant blast resounded.

The Baal Shem Tov, who was leading the congregation in prayer, greatly curtailed the service, contrary to his custom, after the blast. Following the evening service he explained that the boy had helped him immensely and had raised all the prayers to heaven with his act. "For," the Baal Shem Tov added,

> this boy was unfortunately unable to pray. Throughout the sacred day he listened to Jews praying before God, and the holy spark that flickered in him flared up with a bright flame. In another person this flame is expressed in the words of prayer. This lad, however, knew nothing and could not express his great ardor other than through a blast from his whistle. And the more the father prevented him from

fulfilling his ardent wish, the stronger the flame of enthusiasm flared up in him until he could no longer endure it and expressed all his intense desire through his blast. And because this was done from a pure heart, without any external motives but only for the sake of God, the pure breath of his mouth was eagerly accepted. For God desires the heart and, along with the boy's blast, all the other prayers also rose.[13]

Tales such as this about the marvelous power of sincere prayer circulated in very large numbers in the Hasidic milieu. Typical is the following story connected with the name of the lover of Israel, Mosheh Leib of Sasov. The *tzaddik* Rabbi Feivish of Balshvetz related that when he came to Sasov he heard that a letter had just arrived from Berdichev with the news that Rabbi Levi Yitzḥak was ill and begged the *tzaddik* of Sasov to pray for him and to remember him especially at the time of his "dances" on the evening of the holy Sabbath. Rabbi Mosheh Leib bought an expensive pair of new shoes especially for the dancing. Rabbi Feivish relates that Rabbi Mosheh Leib's dances on this occasion were extremely exalted, indeed, truly "things from above;" in every movement mighty "unifications" were hidden. The whole room was filled with light, and the entire "family on high" danced with the *tzaddik*. The thing was literally not to be grasped by the mind.[14]

That such a joyous, fervent dance may sometimes be more important than the holiest prayer is exemplified by the remarkable story of the birth of Rabbi Israel of Koznitz,[15] whose parents were common but decent, pious people. Rabbi Israel's father was a very poor man and once, on the eve of the Sabbath, did not have a single coin for the needs of the sacred day. He was unwilling to take any dole or to ask for charity, and so decided that he preferred to go hungry on the Sabbath rather than request anyone's help. In order not to witness his wife's anguish he spent all of Friday in the synagogue. The poor woman, having nothing to prepare for the Sabbath, began at least to tidy and clean the house in honor of the sacred day. Then a miracle occurred. In a hidden corner she found a pair of gloves which she had received as a gift in better times long before but which had been lost for a long time, so that she did not know what had become of them. The gloves were decorated with golden buttons. She at once took them to the goldsmith and made generous purchases for the Sabbath.

13. *Kehal Hasidim Ha-Ḥadash*, Story No. 18.
14. *Maaseh Tzaddikim*, 37.
15. *Adat Tzaddikim*, 5–8.

After the service for welcoming the Sabbath her husband came home from the synagogue, thinking that he would find a darkened room without even a loaf of bread over which to recite a blessing. To his amazement, he saw that the room was bright and the table laden with all sorts of good things. When his wife told him the miracle that had taken place, he wept for joy and praised God for His mercies. His happiness was so intense that he seized his wife by the hand and began to dance with her. The same thing occurred after each course. Three times the couple danced happily in gratitude and praise to God for His great kindness. The Baal Shem Tov, with his holy spirit, saw how the couple were dancing, took great pleasure in it, and chuckled loudly. He assured his pupils that when these simple people were dancing, the whole "family on high" rejoiced and danced with them.

Not all of the Hasidic tales deal with the greatness of the *tzaddikim*. Many of them were created for the sake of their moral—to teach something, to illustrate a certain point. In *Maaseh Tzaddikim*, for instance, a story is told of how a woman once came to the rabbi of Apt to request advice on an important matter.[16] The *tzaddik*, with his holy spirit, immediately realized that this woman had not long before committed a grievous sin. As soon as she crossed the threshold the rabbi cried: "Harlot, harlot, how have you the impudence to come to me after committing such a sin? Leave the room at once!" But the woman answered him with these words:

> The Creator of the world is long-suffering even toward the wicked. He does not demand immediate payment of His debt from them, and does not reveal their sin before anyone, so as not to shame them and to give them opportunity to repent, whereupon He will not turn His countenance away from them. But the rabbi of Apt sits on his chair and cannot restrain himself for a moment and immediately discloses what the Creator kept hidden!

The rabbi replied: "No one has ever overcome me in my whole life, save this woman." From these words, *Maaseh Tzaddikim* notes, a man may obtain a lesson regarding the extent to which the commandment of loving Israel and of judging every person favorably must be carried.

Other tales are interesting in so far as they present a very clear picture of the philosophy that dominated the Hasidic environment. Once, relates *Kehal Ḥasidim Ha-Ḥadash*, the Em-

16. *Maaseh Tzaddikim*, 40–41.

peror Franz Joseph[17] issued such a cruel decree in Galicia that the whole land literally trembled. At that time in the city of Lyzhansk, in the study-house of the holy *tzaddik* Rabbi Elimelech,[18] a prominent Hasid, a distinguished and very pious man by the name of Rabbi Feivel, was staying. This Rabbi Feivel awoke at night from sleep, went in to the *tzaddik* Rabbi Elimelech, and said to him:

Rabbi, I come to you with a legal matter. There is an explicit teaching in the Mishnah that he who is half slave and half free may not marry a maidservant, because he is no longer a slave, but he also cannot marry a free woman, because he is still half a slave. God Blessed be He has said of Israel: "You are my slaves." Why, then, are we compelled to bear the yoke of Franz Joseph with his evil decrees, when we are indentured to God?

So Rabbi Feivel argued before the holy *tzaddik* with great ardor in the middle of the night.

Rabbi Elimelech replied: "Your arguments are quite cogent, but a lawsuit is not tried in the middle of the night." In the morning there came to Lyzhansk three *tzaddikim*, the *maggid* of Koznitz, the rabbi of Lublin, and the rabbi of Apt, all three of whom were Rabbi Elimelech's pupils. The *tzaddik* was happy to see them and invited them to dinner. In the middle of the meal Rabbi Elimelech summoned Rabbi Feivel and said to him: "Tell these guests of the legal matter with which you came to me at night." Rabbi Feivel said: "I have not now the fervor that I had last night and cannot now present my arguments." Rabbi Elimelech then said to him: "I give you the power of speech, so that you may speak with the same fervor as last night." Rabbi Fievel thereupon expressed his arguments before the *tzaddikim* with great ardor and with truly flaming power.

After the three *tzaddikim* had heard his arguments, the rabbi of Apt opened his holy mouth and said:

The custom is that after one has listened to the arguments of the litigants, both parties must go out. Therefore, Rabbi Feivel, be good enough to leave, and You, Master of the universe, should, according to the law, also leave the courtroom. But how can we demand that You depart from us when the whole world is filled with Your glory, and all our bliss consists in the fact that You dwell among us sinful men. But we tell You openly that we will not have any partiality in this case and will issue a just verdict.

17. The name is erroneous. The emperor Joseph II is meant here.
18. The author of *No'am Elimelech.*

After the meal the three *tzaddikim* immersed themselves in the legal question whether the Emperor Franz Joseph had the right to issue such a severe decree which affects the entire Jewish religion and whether this decree must be accepted. The *tzaddikim* explored the matter with great dialectic ingenuity, searched *Ḥoshen Mishpat* and all the other books of the law, and came to the conclusion that Rabbi Feivel was, indeed, right. They then wrote down the verdict and sealed it with their three signatures. Three days later came the tidings that the decree had been annulled.[19]

Maaseh Tzaddikim[20] relates that the rabbi of Apt heard that a common villager from a neighboring village was a "performer of saving acts" *(poel yeshuot)* and that whoever applied to him obtained help or healing. This was a source of great surprise to the rabbi, and he suspected that perhaps the *sitra aḥara* (the other side, or the demonic) had something to do with this. So he went to the village and stopped for a night's rest in the hostelry of the villager. Unobtrusively he observed the conduct of the villager and saw a common Jew selling whisky, changing money, reciting his prayers without any special concentration, sleeping soundly the whole night through. The *tzaddik* remained astonished. In the morning he summoned the villager and told him that he was the rabbi of Apt, commanding him to reveal his secret and to explain how he was privileged to be a *poel yeshuot.*

The villager declared that he deserved this only because of his great confidence in God. He related how he once had to bring the landlord payment for his rent but did not have a single penny. Nevertheless, he was not anxious, for he firmly trusted that God would not forsake him. And so it was. At the last minute God in His great compassion sent him the necessary sum through a stranger who concluded a deal with him, whereby he obtained the possibility of paying the landlord on time. "So," the villager related,

> I have been helped many times. Once I lost my entire fortune. As is my way, I was quite calm and happy in my great trust that God would not forsake me. The members of my family, however, strongly urged that I should, for God's sake, travel to the city and there find a suitable partner with whom to carry on business. At first I did not

19. *Kehal Hasidim Ha-Ḥadash,* Story No. 62. An interesting tale on the same theme—how the grievous oppression of the candle and meat-tax was nullified as a result of the *tzaddik* of Zhidachov and the local "Purim Rabbi"—is told in *Pe'er Kedoshim* (there the Purim Rabbi is called "Kehal Purim").

20. *Maaseh Tzaddikim,* 31–33.

even wish to hear of this, but the members of my family pressed me so urgently that I finally agreed and set out for the city to seek a partner. En route, on the green, open field, my heart was again filled with happy trust in God, and out of the depths of my heart I prayed to Him: "Master of all worlds, You oversee everything that exists. You give sustenance to every living creature. Accept, then, my petition. I am now in grievous distress. My household compels me to seek a partner, a mortal man who comes from dust, who is here today but it is doubtful whether he will still be among the living tomorrow. I beg You, God: better You be my partner. Send me Your blessing, and everything that I earn I will divide into two equal parts. From one part I will support my wife and children and the other part will be dedicated to God. I will distribute it among poor people and scholars who sit and study Torah." After this prayer, when I put my hand in my pocket, I found a silver coin there. I returned home at once and told the members of my family that I had acquired as my partner a very rich man who, for luck, had temporarily given me a silver coin. That same day I purchased a little merchandise with the coin and God favored me with His blessing and sent me great abundance. I made myself two little chests, and all the money that came to me I divided into two parts: half in the chest intended to support my family, and the rest in the chest designated for poor people and needy scholars. I myself sit at the register and do not rely on any of my family out of fear that perhaps one of them will, God forbid, betray the partnership. Hence I sleep the whole night through so that I have the strength to remain all day in the hostelry to be faithful to the partnership and to distribute God's half, as is proper. This is my work for God.

When the rabbi of Apt heard this, he said to those who accompanied him: "Why are you surprised at the power of this man? God Himself is his partner."[21]

At the same time as the unique product of naive, child-like wonder and enchantment—the legend and tale literature—was created in the Hasidic world, the Mitnagdic camp produced its arrows poisoned with hostility and wrath in the forms of tracts, summonses, argumentations, bans, excommunications, etc. In an earlier chapter[22] we dwelt on the tract entitled *Zemir Aritzim Ve-Ḥorvot Tzurim* which was written at the time of the first attack by the Gaon of Vilna on the "noxious sect." The tract literature became considerably more extensive in the last and sharpest battle against the Hasidim which broke out in the years 1797–1800.

21. *Maaseh Tzaddikim*, 31–33. The story is also given in a somewhat altered form in *Adat Tzaddikim*, 22.
22. See above, pp. 84–85.

In this connection the first person who must be mentioned is the energetic and temperamental *maggid* of Slutsk, Israel bar Jehudah Loebl. He had been a *maggid*, or preacher, in the communities of Moghilev and Reisen (to 1787), as well as in Novogrudok. Since he was known as an ardent opponent of the Hasidic movement,[23] the Mitnagdim of Vilna, at the command of the Gaon, appointed him an itinerant preacher and commissioned him to attack the Hasidim in various places through polemical speeches and sermons. Israel Loebl fulfilled his mission with genuine dedication. On his travels through Lithuania, Poland, and Galicia he had to suffer a great deal from the Hasidim, who persecuted him intensely and several times gave him a severe flogging. He carried on his propaganda work with tireless enthusiasm, not contenting himself merely with preaching and oral disputations. While the Gaon was still alive,[24] Loebl began his *Sefer Ha-Vikkuaḥ*, a bitter tract against the Hasidic movement and against the major *tzaddikim* of that era. It appeared in Warsaw several months after the Gaon's death.[25]

The historical significance of Israel Loebl's *Sefer Ha-Vikkuaḥ* lies in the fact that in it are printed for the first time the Gaon's summons of the month of Sivan, 1796 "to those who tremble at the word of the Lord," the inquiry of the heads of the community of Minsk, and the Gaon's reply to "the children of Israel who tremble," written in pained anger. This reply is justly entitled in *Sefer Ha-Vikkuaḥ* "the reply of Elijah, the zealot who was zealous for the Lord of hosts."

Typical is the tone in which the long introduction to *Sefer Ha-Vikkuaḥ* is written. The Mitnagdic preacher lists virtually all the sects which ever existed among the Jews, from the time of the Sadducees to Shabbetai Tzevi and the Frankist movement. All this, laments Israel Loebl, was still not enough, and

23. Loebl's hatred for Hasidism was associated also with purely personal motives. His own brother fell into the "net" of the Hasidim, and Loebl's effort to "save" him from it was unsuccessful.

24. The *haskamot* to *Sefer Ha-Vikkuaḥ* are dated: Rosh Ḥodesh Sivan and 22 Menaḥem Av, 5556.

25. Because the Hasidim very diligently bought out this edition and promptly burned the copies they collected, *Sefer Ha-Vikkuaḥ* is now extremely rare. We have utilized a complete copy located in the manuscript collection in the Asiatic Museum of Leningrad (No. 407). On the title-page is inscribed: *Sefer Vikkuaḥ La-Ḥoker Ha-Nesher Ha-Gadol Ha-Rabbani Ha-Mufla Morenu Ha-Rav Yisrael Maggid Meisharim Be-Kammah Kehillot Baal Meḥabber Sefer Atar Yisrael Ve-Takkanat Ha-Mizbe'aḥ Asher Kinne Kinnat Adonai Tzeva'ot Neged Ha-Emunah Ha-Ḥadashah Hemah Ha-Kat Naḥash Ha-Kadmoni Ha-Mechannim Atzmam Be-Shem Ḥasidim La-Sur Mi-Darkam Oreḥot Akalkallot Ve-Lo Li-Netot Mi-Darchei Avoteinu Ha-Kedoshim U-Leha-Shome'a Yinam.*

so there appeared one "who was called among the Hasidim Rabbi Israel Baal Shem Tov. Then trouble after trouble surrounded us. After his death, he [the Baal Shem Tov] was even more successful than when still alive. He hated God's Torah and in his heretical books marked out an altogether new path that is utterly opposed to our Torah. For his purposes he preached bizarre interpretations even of the Ten Commandments." After him his pupils arose. They formed one band and made the scholars the target of their arrows. "They pursue and persecute and bite like mad dogs; they do not rest day or night but cover the scholars with mockery." I, declares the *maggid* of Slutsk, have considered this "sect" and became convinced that there is not among them a single decent person. Even of the best among them it has been said: They blaspheme God's word! They violate the whole Torah. They are a sect of scoffers, of flatterers, of liars and slanderers. This is what the better among them are; the worse are robbers and murderers, and every word they speak is falsehood and vanity. To this, evidence is borne by all the communities in which there are adherents of this "wicked and vile sect."

Israel Loebl complains further that the Hasidim hate us more than the nations of the world. They allow the shedding of our blood like that of cattle and wild beasts. Among them it is permitted to kill Mitnagdim, to flog them and inform against them, as they have done in the case of the distinguished rabbinic scholar Rabbi Shalom of Lubavitch, and the great Rabbi Jacob of Shklov and—to distinguish the living from the dead—the great rabbi of the community of Wolpa whom they wanted to kill in the mountains and whom they stripped and forced to go into the city naked. So they did also to the deceased *maggid* of Horodno, and the late *maggid* Yitzhak Ḥayyim who was a righteous preacher and teacher in Rogachev. They also wanted to flog me many times. It is impossible to recount their wickedness. "And I must look on and see," complains the author of *Sefer Ha-Vikkuaḥ*, "how all the wise and able men of our generation are witnesses to this and remain silent." For this reason he considers himself obliged "to attack them with all kinds of stratagems."

In this Israel Loebl bases himself on two authorities. "We know," he points out, "of the command issued in an authenticated document by the saintly Gaon, Rabbi Elijah of Vilna, that it is a great duty to struggle against them with all kinds of cunning." But he also considers it necessary to base the entire matter on a very different "command." "I," Loebl declares, "have seen written the law of the Czar, may his glory be exalted and his honor increase, to whom every important matter comes—and it is also printed in the statutes—that at the present time no man may make any new religion." And he says further: "Since it is an order of the Czar himself that there not be any new religion, then surely everyone is especially obliged to devote himself and carry through this command."

Apparently at that time the Mitnagdic circles heard a rumor to the effect that Czar Paul I was making an investigation of the Masonic lodges (the Illuminati and others) whom he suspected of sympathy with the liberal ideas of the French Revolution. It occurred to the Mitnagdim that this suspicion might also be exploited in the Jewish world, that the Hasidim might be included among the suspect "sects," and the government might deal with them "according to the law." "Therefore," Israel Loebl triumphantly exclaims, "I summon all the rabbis of this sect, i.e., Rabbi Samuel of Amdur,[26] and Rabbi Mordecai of Lechewich,[27] Rabbi Zalman of Lyady, and Rabbi Mottl of Chernobyl, to enter into a public disputation with me and my colleagues, the noble and prominent men who are zealous for the Lord." And he warns his opponents not to take the emperor's command lightly—"especially," he adds, "since we are privileged to have a Czar who does not respect persons, is not partial, takes no bribes, and does no evil; he is a lord who listens to the words of truth, and his officers also follow his ways." The *maggid* of Slutsk admonishes his antagonists that if they harm him or any of his collaborators, they must realize that this will also be a rebellion against the law of the government and the ordinance of the Czar, "may his glory increase." "The fanatical Mitnagdim," justly remarks the historian of the Hasidic movement, Simon Dubnow, when quoting Loebl's introduction, "began to speak in the tone of policemen."[28]

In the meantime, pending the public debate with the Hasidic rabbis, Loebl published his *Sefer Ha-Vikkuaḥ* in which a "true Talmudist" carries on a disputation with "Zimri who is known by the name Hasid." It may easily be imagined that the Hasid comes out of this debate bruised and battered. In general, the author of *Sefer Ha-Vikkuaḥ* rarely lets him speak. He comes off with very brief ripostes. Mainly the "true Talmudist," i.e., the

26. At that time a well-known Hasidic leader in the circle of Grodno.

27. One of the most important Lithuanian *tzaddikim* in the circle of Slutsk.

28. S. Dubnow, *Di Geshikhte Fun Khasidism*, II, 140–141.

Mitnagdic Loebl, argues and pours sulphur and brimstone on the "wicked and vile sect."[29]

In the same year as *Sefer Ha-Vikkuaḥ* appeared in print (1798), the energetic propagandist Loebl published another tract entitled *Ta'avat Tzaddikim,* also in the form of a debate between a Mitnaged and a Hasid. A year later he printed in Frankfurt-am-Oder a German tract with the long title *Glaubwürdige Nachricht von einer neuen und zahlreichen Sekte unter den Juden in Polen und Litauen die sich Chassidim nennt, und auf die Menschheit empörenden Grundsätzen und Lehren.* This tract was reprinted in the journal *Sulamith* (1807) and the Frenchman Gregoire utilized it in his *Histoire des sectes religieuses.* However, even such a determined opponent of Hasidism as Heinrich Graetz must admit that Loebl "may not always be believed implicitly" because he is "in factual details not very reliable."

Israel Loebl also had a courageous fellow-battler. Several months after *Sefer Ha-Vikkuaḥ* appeared in print, another tract against the Hasidim was published under the title *Zemir Aritzim.* This tract appeared anonymously, but Dubnow[30] and the bibliographer Samuel Wiener[31] have shown that the author was the *maggid* David of Makow who died in 1815. Typical is the style of *Zemir Aritzim.* The *maggid* of Makow is a great lover of rhetorical flourishes and figures of speech. Practically the entire work is written in rhymed verses and fragments of verses.[32] As a result, the thought is not infrequently obscured

29. According to David of Makow, the Hasidim wrote a response to *Sefer Ha-Vikkuaḥ* (see *Zemir Aritzim,* folios 12–13): "For I certainly heard that the Hasidim in their stiff-neckedness continue in their rebellion and plan to print some book telling evil tales, devious and straying, concerning the distinguished Torah scholar. . . . our master Rabbi Israel of Slutsk . . . and lo, if I had seen that book, a supplement of the New Testament, I would have hit him on his head, that is to say, with many arguments . . . but because this book of dust and ashes, preaching wickedness, has not been finished as yet and I do not know the nature of this unborn [transgressor] and all the details of the foolishness in it." Apparently this counter-document carried the title *Mul Maggid Peti* (see *ibid.,* folio 13a; folio 15b: "but the book *Mul Maggid Peti*"). Whether the document appeared in print is unknown to us.

30. See S. Dubnow, *Geshikhte Fun Khasidism,* Supplement No. 3.

31. *Kohelet Mosheh,* 439.

32. As an example we present the title-page of *Zemir Aritzim* in translation: "The book *Zemir Aritzim* (The Cutting Down of the Vicious) to cut out all the thorns and thorn-bushes that have arisen in the community of the Jews, a sect who call themselves by the name of Hasidim; they became thorns and schismatics, their righteousness was like a filthy cloth; their prayers were with thunder and lightning, filled with violence and the treachery of deceivers. They are more rapacious than wolves of night, charlatans and worthless healers, tearing and devouring like locusts. They have changed the order of worship in every word, without reason or cause, without direction and without any path. They have abandoned the Torah which gives light to those who study it. Therefore, I, the young man who sits in the dust at the feet of the disciples

and the effect of the violent attacks the author launches against the Hasidim whom he so despised is weakened.

There is literally no crime of which *Zemir Aritzim* does not hold the Hasidim guilty. Their hands are full of robbery, they steal and lie. They bring misfortune and ruin with them. The ignorant Hasidim are compared to the "destroying angels." They know nothing, understand nothing, and grope in darkness. He who calls himself a Hasid bites and kills like a venomous serpent. The company of the Hasidim is the true "valley of demons." They are all sinners and make others to sin.[33] "Who does not know," the author of *Zemir Aritzim* exclaims emotively,

> that the members of this sect have overthrown and ruined everything? Their whole intent is gradually to uproot and destroy the Jewish faith. They have made the Torah of Moses and the Talmud of Rabina and Rav Ashi a mockery. Day and night I mourn over the destruction of the Torah. It was the crown of the people of Israel, their ornament and beauty. Now the accursed Hasidim, these wild boars of the forest, have corrupted and besmirched its splendor.

Everything I have written about them, adds the *maggid* of Makow, is only a tiny portion, for no amount of time will suffice to list all their deeds. Hence, everyone who carries the fear of God in his heart is obliged to persecute and oppress them with all kinds of oppressions, to strengthen himself to deracinate them, so that no root or branch of this vile company will remain, as it is said, "And you shall destroy their name." "I am astounded at the shepherds of Israel, the rabbis and the sages of the generation," the fanatical *maggid* exclaims,[34] "who lead and guard the Jewish community, the 'scattered sheep of Israel.' " They have the right and power to issue forth against

---

of the wise and heeds the authority of the Gaon, our master and our teacher, Elijah of blessed memory, arose. And I printed this little book to be a memorial for all generations, so that they be not like the Hasidim, a generation of confusion, and that they may teach, every man his neighbor, to say: 'Know ye the Lord,' and they may set for themselves path-marks to walk in the ways of our fathers, for they keep faith with us and are in covenant with us. The Lord is our King, He will help us. In the year 5558 from creation."

33. "They work violence with their hands. They steal and lie and conceal things in their vessels, pillage and destruction [are] in their paths . . . The foolish Hasidim, men of the Kabbalah, are like demons, and the Torah and the testimony are abandoned and orphaned . . . They do not know and do not understand, they walk in darkness . . . He who is called by the name *Ḥasid* and *Parush* bites like a serpent and discharges poison like a viper . . . And the community of the Hasidim are called the valley of demons . . . Sinners and those who make others sin."

34. *Zemir Aritzim*, folio 6a; folio 15a.

the violators. Why, then, are they silent, keep their hands in their pockets, and stand at a distance? They ought to have cried out in the Jewish camp that men should assemble to save themselves from the danger; they ought to have issued an edict to the effect that it is obligatory to cast every volume of the noxious Hasidic books into the fire. These books should be burned, so that no memory of them remains. No Hasidic book may be kept in any Jewish house, for it can cause great injury beyond the possibility of repair. Of this it is written: "All who come to her will not return and will not attain the pathways of life."

I, the *maggid* of Makow exclaims, can no longer endure this. The Hasidim will not frighten me with their clamor. I have firmly decided to issue forth against them fearlessly. Let men greater than I learn how one must struggle on behalf of the "zeal of the Lord of hosts," how these wicked men must be pursued with all the forces at one's command. One may have no mercy on them. They must be driven out of the Jewish community and live outside its camp. One must not allow them to lodge overnight. It is forbidden to intermarry with them or bring them to burial, for they have violated all the laws of the Torah.[35]

The fanatical *maggid* expresses his hope that God will help him attain his goal: to root out the Hasidic sect, so that no memory of a single Hasid shall survive. He also hopes that God will strengthen the hearts of the scholars and rabbis that they also may issue forth against the Hasidim and persecute and annihilate them, so that their name may be erased forever. Then our eyes will light up and our hearts will be rejoiced, as King Solomon says, "When the wicked are destroyed, there is rejoicing."[36]

It is not only the rabbis and leaders of the generation who must participate in the "holy war." The whole people must do so. And David of Makow turns to the "people of the Lord," urging them to strengthen themselves to root out the Hasidim, so that no remnant of them survives.[37]

35. "And from me the great men will see and learn by inference from minor to major to be zealous with zeal for the Lord of Hosts with all their strength, and to persecute them in every way, and to have no compassion upon them, and to drive them out from every settled place, so that they may be outside the camp of Israel; and it is forbidden to give them lodging overnight; you shall not intermarry with them or be kind to them; you shall not give them a resting place in the land, for they have altered the law and violated *Torot.*"

36. *Zemir Aritzim*, folio 12b.

37. *Ibid.*, folio 7a.

The *maggid* pours out all his wrath against the founder of Hasidism. The Baal Shem Tov, he declares, was a man without understanding and knowledge, "a withered leaf, dried stubble." Would that he had been brought to burial immediately after his birth. For this man removed the crown of the pure and sacred Torah. With his words he undermined the foundations of the faith. He misled hundreds and thousands; he taught them to be cavalier in observance of the Torah and its commandments. Everyone who bears the name Jew is therefore obliged to trample the Baal Shem Tov's books *(Keter Shem Tov* and *Tzava'at Ha-Rivash)* like dust in the streets and to burn them.[38] With no less hostility does David of Makow speak of the *tzaddikim* of his generation, especially of the *maggid* of Koznitz and the well-known *tzaddik* Rabbi Isaac of Lublin. He portrays the *tzaddikim* of that time as ignorant, crude, and extremely avaricious men who defraud the common people, take gifts from miserable beggars, extort the last penny from them, themselves live in wealth and comfort, and grow fat at the expense of the poor, deluded people.[39]

After publishing *Zemir Aritzim*, the *maggid* of Makow was by no means minded to conclude his battle against the Hasidim whom he so despised. In *Zemir Aritzim* he notes[40] that he is collecting material for a second part that will be entitled *Shever Poshe'im* in which he will, at greater length and with numerous arguments from the words of the sages and the holy *Zohar*, expose the wild follies and base deeds of these "wicked men." From 1798 to 1800 the author of *Zemir Aritzim* assiduously gathered material for the promised second part, which he published in 1800. The rich material collected in *Shever Poshe'im* may be divided into two parts. The first was written by the author himself, and in it he argues with the *tzaddikim* of his time—Shneur Zalman of Lyady, Elimelech of Lyzhansk, Michael of Zolochev, Mottl of Chernobyl, and many others—criticizes *Toledot Yaakov Yosef*, and attacks the Hasidim and their behavior with harsh invectives. The second, more important part is a collection of documents (letters, proclamations, summonses of rabbis and communities, and the like) dealing with the battle against Hasidim during the period 1772–1798. These documents have an important value for the history of the controversy between the Mitnagdim and the Hasidim.

38. *Zemir Aritzim*, "Moda'a Rabba," folio 3b; folios 4–5, 8, 11b, 16 (at the end).
39. *Ibid.*, folio 7a, 9a, 10a, 11a, 12.
40. *Ibid.*, folio 8b, 13a.

The *maggid* of Makow, however was no longer able to disseminate his polemic work in print and therefore requests, at the end, that his manuscript be diligently copied and the copies "be distributed among Jacob and spread among Israel." This wish was, in fact, fulfilled. Copies of David of Makow's work were energetically circulated under various titles: *Shever Poshe'im*, *Zimrat Am Ha-Aretz*, and *Zot Torat Ha-Kena'ot*.[41]

David of Makow lived for another fifteen years after completing his *Shever Poshe'im*, but he no longer carried on polemics against the Hasidim. The pious Mitnaged became convinced in his old age that the Hasidim are no such threat to the preservation of Judaism as he had thought. He also realized that a new and dangerous power which wished to destroy the old way of life had appeared in the Jewish quarter. Already in his *Zemir Aritzim* he notes: "We see that, unfortunately, heretics and deniers who were unknown in former times have now multiplied among us."[42] And David of Makow's fellow-battler Israel Loebl, at the time of printing his German pamphlet against the Hasidim in Frankfurt-am-Oder (1799), obtained the opportunity to become familiar with the "Berlin Haskalah." An especially powerful impression was made on him by David Friedländer's well-known *Sendschreiben* to Teller (see our *History*, Volume VIII, pp. 116ff.) Indeed, Loebl in Frankfurt itself that same year published a battle-document entitled *Even Boḥan* on which he wages war not against the Hasidim and their *tzaddikim* but against the "new heretics" who deny the "practical *mitzvot*."[43]

Soon the erstwhile enemies, the Mitnagdim and Hasidim, issued forth together against their common enemy, Haskalah. Those who had been far apart came closer, and this development found its resonance in literature. New books of disputations were written—disputations between the Mitnagdim and the Hasidim, but a completely different tone resounds in these than in, for example, Loebl's *Sefer Ha-Vikkuaḥ*, or in the disputations between the rabbi of Brest-Litovsk and Rabbi Levi Yitzḥak of Berdichev.

41. We have employed two copies of David of Makow's work, one under the title *Zimrat Am Ha-Aretz*, located in the manuscript collection of the Asiatic Museum in Leningrad, and the second, more complete one, under the title *Zot Torat Ha-Kena'ot*, which was in the Kaufmann manuscript collection in the library in Leningrad of the Society for the Dissemination of Enlightenment and Culture Among Jews.

42. *Zemir Aritzim*, folio 16b.

43. We have not had opportunity to become familiar with this battle-document. We know of it only from Benjacob's *Otzar Ha-Sefarim* (No. 46) and of the quotations which are given in Graetz, *Geschichte der Juden*, Vol. XI, second edition, 1900, p. 551.

Characteristic in this respect are two disputation works, both of which have the title *Vikkuḥa Rabba.* The older of these, which apparently circulated in manuscript copies[44] for a long time with insignificant variations, was first published under the title *Matzref Ha-Avodah* in 1858 and several years later (1866) under the new title *Vikkuḥa Rabba.* The work is written in the form of a letter which a disciple of the Gaon of Vilna, Benjamin Ze'ev of Slonim, and a disciple of Rabbi Levi Yitzḥak, Joseph of Nemirov, wrote to each other in 1786. This is already "a war in peace." The erstwhile opponents wish to be reconciled, try hard to understand each other, to grasp each other's outlook on the world. The Mitnaged ends with "these are the words of his colleague and friend," and the Hasid with "these are the words of his lover and friend."

Written in an even more irenic tone is the second *Vikkuḥa Rabba,* which was first published in 1886[45] but was undoubtedly composed much earlier. This work is composed in the form of an oral discussion between a Mitnaged and a Hasid. The Mitnaged poses fifty questions and the Hasid presents fifty replies to them. Both parties speak very amicably; the Hasid calls the Mitnaged "my friend" and assures him that he loves him "with everlasting love," and the Mitnaged declares the Hasid to be his dearest friend, whom he loves wholeheartedly. The dialogue concludes with the Hasid's assurance that the disputation was carried on not for the sake of victory but "to obtain perfection and knowledge."

44. A beautifully written copy of this work was found in the library in Leningrad of the Society for the Dissemination of Enlightenment and Culture among Jews. We believe S. Wiener's conjecture (*Kohelet Mosheh*, 394) that *Vikkuḥa Rabba* was composed by Jacob Bachrach of Bialystok.

45. On the title-page is noted: "Brought to the press by Moses Aaron Gliksman."

CHAPTER SEVEN

Elie Halévy, Solomon Löwisohn, and Shalom Cohen

The first German-Jewish journal, *Sulamith*—Assimilationist tendencies—Not a nation but a religious community—Napoleon and the Jewish question—Elie Ḥalfon Halévy and his poem—The "swan-song"—"Israelites," not "Jews"—Solomon Löwisohn and his work—Löwisohn's paean to beauty and the "daughter of beauty"—The significance of his *Melitzat Yeshurun*—Löwisohn's tragic death—Shalom Cohen—His *Mishlei Agur* and *Matta'ei Kedem*—The renewed *Ha-Meassef*—Cohen's allegorical drama *Amel Ve-Tirtzah*—Cohen's years of wandering—His move to Vienna—A forum for the Hebrew word.

IN THE second volume of our work we noted the great difference between the cultural situation and world outlook of Spanish Jewry, on the one hand, and the Jewish community of France, on the other, in the first half of the thirteenth century. "These," we there stress, "were not only two separate but also two hostile worlds." Even greater, however, was the difference between the world outlook and cultural tendencies of the bearers of Haskalah and those of the Hasidic world at the threshold of the nineteenth century: on the one side, striving for European culture and education, contempt and hatred for the old-fashioned, backward Jewish way of life, and a vast self-disparagement before the external Christian-European civilization and the rationalist world-view; on the other side, mystical fervor, transcendence of corporeality, refusal to recognize any boundaries between the imaginative and the real, and utter contempt for the alien, non-Jewish world—for practical knowledge, for the "external wisdoms" or sciences.

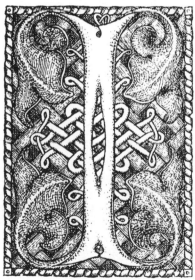

While the theoreticians of Hasidism spoke with intense fervor of the universal role of Israel, among the bearers of Haskalah and enlightenment, assimilationist tendencies, which in the larger German communities assumed the form of an epidemic of conversion, were strengthened. Whereas the Hasidic movement evoked a whole literature not only in Hebrew but also in Yiddish, the language of the masses, among the circles of the "enlightened," their Hebrew forum, the journal *Ha-Meassef,* inevitably succumbed, and its place was taken by a magazine published in the language of the *Vaterland,*[1] a magazine called *Sulamith* (Leipzig, 1806).

Sulamith itself dwells on the factors that necessitated the failure of the "excellent journal" *Ha-Meassef.* It indicates that for the "clear-sighted," i.e., for the cultured and learned, *Ha-Meassef* was no longer a "requirement." Pious and orthodox men of learning, on the other hand, considered it sinful to read such works, especially when the pietists and "ultra-holy" took special pains to see to it that *Ha-Meassef* forfeit all credibility in the circles of Jewish readers. Others, again, who would gladly have perused such an "enlightened" journal could not read *Ha-Meassef* because they "were not learned in the Hebrew language."[2]

The editors of the journal, David Fränkel and Joseph Wolf, note in both their programmatic articles that a new age in history is dawning. The law of righteousness now dominates the moods of all nations; the barriers and partitions that until now have separated one people from another have been broken through as a result of the spirit of culture and tolerance; humanity and fraternity are presently on the lips of all and deeply inscribed in every heart. In respect to Jews also, no exceptions are now made. Men are beginning to feel and understand that a great injustice has been perpetrated against them. The times are now past, thank God, when the concepts of "man" and "Jew" were understood to be totally heterogeneous.[3]

The spread of humanitarianism, we are further informed, is the loveliest ornament of our time; it renders mankind happy with its beneficences. It is the source from which the most beautiful flower—genuine fraternal love—now blooms. And

1. In *Sulamith*, Hebrew poems, as well as short prose articles, were printed from time to time for those who were fond of them.

2. *Sulamith*, I, 29.

3. *Ibid.*, 6–7.

when fraternal love fills the hearts of men, tolerance occupies the most honored place in society. *Sulamith,* the editors declare, sets as its task the dissemination among the Jewish people of "genuine culture and humanitarianism . . . clarification of the concepts of nature, art, and the social relationships of men," so that the Jews may also be able to employ for their benefit "the happy mood in which enlightenment and culture have placed the souls of men" and to "spread over the nation" blessing and joy.[4]

The editors, however, promptly declare along with this that *Sulamith* "will least of all be concerned with political matters," whether in regard to the Jewish people or any other nation. Of human rights for the Jewish community that were denied them, the editors do not venture to speak forthright words. They are content with allusions and hints. They merely hope that, as a result of "the development of the intensive capacity for education of the Jews," they will be in a position to understand and properly feel the good "about which our age has to rejoice," and then the children of Israel will also be able, "enchanted and grateful," to approach the exalted memorial which history erects for the "enlightened rulers of our time" and write on it the inscription: "To you [i.e., the enlightened rulers] we pledge our hearts—to you, who are imbued with the spirit of humanism and liberalism and have again endowed the degraded people with their lost rights."[5]

The editors of the German-Jewish journal assert that the grandchildren of "those oppressed Jews" now enjoy the bliss of living under enlightened, idealistic, and humanitarian rulers, who deem it their sacred duty to render their subjects happy through all possible means, and also to guarantee the existence of the Jews and to consider them equal with all other subjects of the kingdom.[6]

This lovely, blissful idyll, however, was suddenly shattered by a Christian clergyman in an open letter to the editors of *Sulamith.*[7] The writer disdained indirection and allusion and spoke frankly. He notes that the just-mentioned "grandchildren" still live with the same civic disabilities as their "oppressed" grandfathers. The condition of the Jews, writes the

4. *Ibid.*, 10, 18. Also in the sub-title of *Sulamith* it is noted: "A journal for the advancement of culture and humanitarianism within the Jewish nation."
5. *Ibid.*, 11.
6. *Ibid.*, 23.
7. *Ibid.*, 148–152.

Christian correspondent, is deplorable. Excluded from all civic branches of industry and from all the higher and more respected "services of the state," even driven out of the auditoriums designated for enlightenment and science, the Jews are compelled to engage only in occupations of trade and exchange. Moreover, the correspondent notes, they are burdened with oppressive special taxes which are very frequently further associated with mockery and degradation. And he lists on two full pages all the special Jewish taxes and levies, all the insults and indignities that the German Jews had to suffer. This letter of the Christian clergyman constitutes the only pages of a whole year of *Sulamith* in which the civic disabilities of the German Jews of that day are openly discussed.

Quite in the spirit of David Friedländer, *Sulamith* speaks in a series of articles of the "abuses and the crude and absurd ceremonies of the Jews." In former times, *Sulamith* laments, the number of religious statutes and precepts was quite small, "for at that time there were still no rabbis—as in our times—who increased the number of laws endlessly through distortion of good sense."[8] The journal does not weary of reiterating that it battles for "pure religiosity," for "genuine religiosity and higher morality."[9]

The contributors to *Sulamith* realize quite well that in the epidemic of conversion the largest number of victims are intelligent Jewish females to whom Judaism and the Jewish world outlook in general are absolutely alien. For this reason, in fact, they devote a great deal of attention to the religious education of the modern Jewish woman. They endeavor to explain to their readership that "religious sentiments ennoble woman in extremely high degree." They often deplore the fact that the Jewish woman knows so little of "pure Jewish belief" and of Jewish history.[10] The journal also very frequently addresses itself to the female reader, the "worthy co-religionist" and "dear sister." In a large number of letters written especially to a "respected woman of the Jewish faith" it is noted that the supreme duty of all Jewish parents is to be concerned for purposefully organized schools for their daughters, schools wherein their religious sentiment will be aroused from earliest youth.[11]

8. *Ibid.*, 172.
9. *Ibid.*, 27, 38, 39, 216ff.
10. *Ibid.*, 216, 219ff.
11. *Ibid.*, 487.

Another point is here worth noting. The editor Joseph Wolf still speaks of the "Jewish nation," but the other editor David Fränkel very rarely uses the term "nation" in regard to the Jewish community. He speaks mainly of "bearers of the Jewish religion," "those related by religion," and "co-religionists." From the second year of its publication, when David Fränkel remained the sole editor, the assimilationist tendencies of *Sulamith* became more marked. Contemporary political and social circumstances contributed not a little to this. We dwelt at length in a previous part of our work[12] on the sharply assimilationist drives which dominated the Jewish intelligentsia of Germany at the threshold of the nineteenth century. At the time when, in the pious circles of the Hasidim, Jews looked with contempt on the foreign environment and regarded the Jewish people as the center of the world, the young Ludwig Börne tells in a letter to Henriette Herz of the Jewish students at the university: "Here in Heidelberg some Jews of fine family are studying. It is remarkable, however, that these persons take all possible pains to keep it a secret that their great-grandfather limped.[13] One never sees two young Jewish persons walking together or even speaking to one another."

At the time Börne wrote his letter (1807), events occurred in triumphant France which further strengthened the assimilationist tendencies in Jewish intellectual circles. As a result of the Revolution, the French Jews obtained civic equality and were no longer compelled to purchase human rights through apostasy and baptism. But it was precisely the Revolution which contributed not a little to the fact that the Jews of France wished to demonstrate to the whole world that Jews are by no means a nation but a religious community. The activists and protagonists of the French Revolution were the masses of the urban bourgeoisie. In their battle for power and rights these strata first felt themselves a *national* community, a *people.* The Revolution tore the Jews out of their civic disabilities and isolation, and the liberated felt themselves France's grateful sons.

Since in such an ethnically unified land as France the concept of nation merged with the concept of state,[14] the Jews dwelling there considered themselves Frenchmen. As early as

12. See our *History,* Vol. VIII, Chapter Four, from p. 105 to the end of the chapter.
13. This means: They are descended from the patriarch Jacob who limped on one foot after his wrestling at night with the angel.
14. See our *History,* Vol. VIII, Chapter Four.

1791, immediately after the decree granting Jews equal rights was published, the courageous battler for the emancipation of the Jews, Berr Isaac Berr, in his summons to his brethren, deemed it necessary especially to note: "Thanks to God and the supreme power of the people, the nations recognize us not merely as citizens but also as Frenchmen." Some ten years later his son, the talented orator Michael Berr, declared in his summons to all Europeans of the Jewish faith that he "felt himself at heart more a Frenchman than a Jew."[15]

In explaining these tendencies a special significance accrues to a poetic work in Hebrew published by a fellowcitizen of Michael Berr's, Elie Halfon Halévy, that same year (1801). A German Jew,[16] learned in Talmudic literature, Elie Halévy moved in his youth to Paris where he was *ḥazzan*, or cantor, in the synagogue and a teacher of Hebrew. In his new home Halévy learned French thoroughly. The great events following the outbreak of the Revolution made him an ardent French patriot; and when the First Consul of France, the brilliant Napoleon Bonaparte, concluded a temporary peace (in 1801) after his remarkable victories, Elie Halévy expressed his feeling of joy and patriotic enthusiasm in his poem *Ha-Shalom*, consisting of forty-nine five-line stanzas. This is really an "occasional poem" which the *ḥazzan* composed to be sung at the solemn assembly in the Great Synagogue after the declaration of peace. In the *ḥazzan*, however, slumbered a true poet, and unexpectedly, perhaps even for the author himself, he produced a masterpiece that inscribed his name in the history of neo-Hebrew poetry.

Halévy's poem was welcomed with great enthusiasm. It was published along with a German and French translation and with greetings from the well-known orientalist Sylvestre de Sacy.[17] Already in the first stanza the influence of the two different cultures in which the poet lived is clearly noticeable. Following the aesthetic taste of contemporary French literature, with its fondness for the traditions of classical culture and the Graeco-Roman legends and heroes, the Hebrew poet begins with an invocation of the Muses, the goddesses of song, requesting that they endow his poem with harmony and grace. But along with this he also addresses the "sweet singer," the

15. See Graetz, *Geschichte der Juden*, Vol. XI, p. 221.

16. Born in Fürth circa 1760.

17. Halevy's poem is reprinted in Fürstenthal's *Ha-Meassef*, 1829, pp. 216–226 and in S.P. Rabinowich's *Kenesset Yisrael*, II, last section, cols. 19–28.

poet of the Psalms, asking that the Psalmist lend him his harp or equip his instrument with its marvelous strings. The historian Heinrich Graetz is so charmed by Halévy's ode, in which he perceives "genuine, golden poetry," that he declares the author of *Ha-Shalom* superior to Solomon Ibn Gabirol, Jehudah Halevi, and Moses Hayyim Luzzatto.[18]

This, of course, is an enormous exaggeration. The influence of two completely different cultures disrupts the harmony of the poem to a certain degree. Some of the images come out overly artificial, and the cold polishing of art is more discernible in them than the flame of poetic inspiration. But the poet's feeling for the stupendous events bears him along; he forgets the classical models and metaphors and creates for himself. He forges verses poured from steel in which are felt the storm of the revolution, indignation over the servitude and degradations that men had lived through, and triumphant jubilation over the fact that the enemy had been shattered and the masses of the people, filled to overflowing with youthful forces, had come to power. After a hiatus of generations triumphant tones of patriotism were heard again in Hebrew poetry. The poet who had come from Germany declares his new home the "loveliest of all lands." He regards the French as "the daughter of my people." With deep indignation Halévy laments that, before the Revolution, "base men bound my people and my land[19] in chains." And the powerful stanzas in which the poet portrays the grievous condition of France under the *ancien régime* conclude with the words:

"My friends, were I to tell you all that happened
To the loveliest of kingdoms throughout the days of
trouble,
You would shed tears like a river, your heart would melt
like water."

A particularly strong impression is made by the verses in which the poet portrays the victorious march of the young Napoleon and his legions. Halévy succeeds in rendering the enormous power of the regiments armored in steel and filled with courageous desire for battle, led by their brilliant general, before whom all nations tremble. The praises and laudations with which the poet greets Bonaparte are not merely the com-

18. *Op. cit.*, Vol. XI, 1900, p. 218.
19. I.e., France and the French people.

mon incense of stock patriotic fashion; in them genuine astonishment before the extraordinary man and his tremendous deeds, thanks to which the great miracle occurred with France, is felt:

Yesterday considered a maidservant by peoples and princes,
Today the crown of the daughters; princes bow before thee.

The poet sees in the First Consul of France not the inheritor but the faithful protector and proponent of freedom and civic equality. He regards Bonaparte not merely as the "friend of conquest" but also as the "friend of wisdom."

After Elie Halévy wrote his poem he lived more than twenty-five years longer (he died in November, 1826). He was one of the founders of, and contributors to, the weekly *Israélite Français*[20] which appeared in 1817–1818, published a textbook *Limmudei Dat U-Musar* (Metz, 1820),[21] and also left in manuscript a Hebrew-French dictionary.[22] But he wrote no more Hebrew poems. His *Ha-Shalom* was the swan-song of Hebrew poetry on the soil of France. The headlong process of assimilation was too unfavorable a soil for Jewish national poetry.

The hero Bonaparte, so enthusiastically celebrated by Halévy, could not, with his historical sense, believe that the distinction between the French Jews and the rest of the population was the same as that between Catholics and Protestants. He decisively rejected the view that the Jews are merely a religious sect and declared that the Jews must be considered a separate nation, a "nation among other nations."[23] To persuade himself that the Jews of France may be considered true French citizens, Napoleon first wished to obtain from them a declaration to the effect that they were prepared to assimilate completely. To this end he convened, in 1807, the famous "Sanhedrin" in which a series of questions were put before the Jewish representatives, questions unified by one concept: emancipation must be purchased at the cost of assimilation. The Jewish "notables" had no alternative but to give their assent.

The same phenomenon was repeated at that time on the other side of the Rhine, in Germany. We have observed[24] that,

20. Graetz, *op. cit.*, 218.
21. W. Zeitlin, *op. cit.*, 134.
22. J. Klausner, *op. cit.*, 286.
23. *Il faut considerer les juifs comme nation et non comme secte. C'est une nation dans la nation.*
24. See our *History*, Vol. VIII, p. 117.

after the publication of the edict granting Jews civic rights (1812), David Friedländer declared: "The Jews have no home other than the land which has recognized them as citizens with equal rights. The Prussian Jews love their fatherland, and the German language is their mother tongue; they need no other." And when a German professor came forth with anti-Semitic attacks, the principal of the Frankfurt Jewish school, Michael Hess, in his reply[25] categorically declared: "The Jews are not a people at all; they are to be considered simply a religious confession."

Especially interesting in this respect is an article published in *Sulamith*[26] under the title "Über die Namen der Israeliten." Some thirty or forty years ago, the author asserts, when Germany assumed the task of liberating itself from superstition, from all the defects impeding the final victory of humanitarianism, people came, in connection with the question of the Jews, to the conclusion that, to improve the condition of the "Israelites," they must in no case be regarded as a nation; on the contrary, all the national customs and usages that have remained in their midst must be removed from them as far as possible. They must live like true Germans, according to German laws and customs. Recently, however, *Sulamith* complains, men have appeared "who endeavor to show that Jews are still a *nation.*" These men make a great outcry when anyone expresses the indisputable truth that the German Jews of today belong to the German people, just as do Germans of the Catholic, Protestant, or Reformed faith."

Filled with fear before the national "ego," before self-consciousness, because this might—God forbid—hurt the cause of civic emancipation, *Sulamith* asserts that the term "nation" in regard to the Jews is not only politically nefarious but morally so as well. An uncultured Jew may come to the conclusion that he must remain "national," i.e., live apart and be loyal to his old habits and customs. The fact that the Jews are declared a nation, *Sulamith* repeats, is precisely as "unjust, false, noxious, and pernicious" as calling them "Jews" *(Juden).* The term Jews is not of religious but of political-geographic derivation, and since the kingdom of Judea no longer exists there are obviously no more Judeans or "sons of Judah." The Jews of today are merely a religious group and must therefore be called by no name other than "Israelites."

25. *Freimüthige Prüfung der Schrift des Herrn Prof. Rühs über die Aussprüche der Juden an das deutsche Bürgerrecht,* 1816.
26. Volume VI, 145–152.

It is clear that, given such strong and outspoken assimilationist tendencies, the large German centers were extremely unfavorable soil for the development of neo-Hebrew *belles lettres.* To be sure, at that time Jewish poets appeared in Berlin and Vienna who sought to produce works in Hebrew. These, however, were men who came from other countries that had a compact Jewish settlement still closely linked with the old world-view and way of life. Of these young poets Solomon Löwisohn and Shalom Cohen must be especially noted.

Solomon Löwisohn was born in the Hungarian city of Mor in 1789. Apparently his father Jehudah Loeb ben Jacob was something of a *maskil,* for he was not content with having his son obtain extensive knowledge of Talmudic literature in the Jewish schools; he was also concerned that he become proficient in the Bible. At the age of twelve the young Solomon began to attend the school of the local Capuchin monks in which he studied mathematics, German, and the fundamentals of Latin. Shortly thereafter Solomon became acquainted with a Christian student from Budapest, and the two friends struck a unique bargain; the student from Budapest taught him Latin, while he taught the other boy Hebrew. The intellectually curious Solomon also devoted himself intensively to self-education and was greatly aided in this by a local Jew, the wealthy and cultured Solomon Rosenthal, who permitted him the use of his well-stocked library.[27] The young man's difficult economic situation forced him to engage for a time in teaching children. As soon as he had accumulated a little money, however, he set out to study in Prague at the famous *yeshivah* located there.[28] But he soon left the *yeshivah* and went over to the university, where he studied Greek, Syriac, and modern languages.

In 1810 Löwisohn published in the revived *Ha-Meassef* the first chapters of his philological work *Siḥah Be-Olam Ha-Neshamot.* The following year he published the complete work in Prague in the form of three conversations between the famous grammarian David Kimḥi and the participant in Mendelssohn's Torah commentary, Joel Brill (Loewe). A year later Löwisohn published his second philological work, *Bet Ha-Osef.* Especially interesting in the work is the last chapter on the origin of the language of the Mishnah. In complete opposition

27. See Klausner, *op. cit.,* 233.

28. In 1809. This date can be determined on the basis of the fact that in his first work, published in *Ha-Meassef* in the summer months of 1810 *(Nissan-Av),* he is identified as Solomon Löwisohn of Prague.

to Isaac Satanow's view,[29] Löwisohn puts forth the thesis that the language in which the Mishnah is written was not the spoken language of the people of the Mishnaic era, since the masses of the people then spoke Aramaic, but an artificial, specially created language of the learned Tannaim, who employed it in their academies and schools. This work of the youthful philologist was so well received[30] that it was reprinted as an introduction to the 1815 Vienna edition of the Mishnah.[31]

Already in *Bet Ha-Osef*, in which Löwisohn speaks of *temunot ha-melitzah* (poetic or rhetorical figures),[32] it is obvious that we have before us not an arid grammarian but a philologist with a poetic sensitivity. Less than two years later, when Baruch Jeiteles,[33] with whom Löwisohn was friendly, died (December, 1813), the young scholar mourned the premature death of his friend and patron in a lovely elegy, "Shir Misped,"[34] in which the work of an authentic poet is apparent. About a year later (1815) Löwisohn left Prague and settled in Vienna where he occupied the post of chief proofreader in Anton von Schmid's famous Hebrew press. In the same year he completed his masterpiece *Melitzat Yeshurun*, on the spirit and form of Old-Hebrew poetry (published in Vienna in 1816; reprinted in 1831).

In the fourth volume of our work (pp. 97–98) we noted that Messer Leon of Mantua, a child of the Renaissance era and an

29. See our *History*, Vol. VIII, Chapter Seven.

30. The young Samuel David Luzzatto writes in 1820 to I.S. Reggio with enthusiasm: "From the day that I saw the book *Meḥkerei Aretz* of Rabbi Solomon ben Levi, this man was precious in my eyes. And when I saw what he transcribed there from his book *Bet Ha-Osef* on the matter of the definite article with some of the proper nouns, his worth became even greater in my sight, and I longed greatly to see this book, and after the time when the Lord chanced to bring his book *Melitzat Yeshurun* into my hands my love for him increased greatly, and when I saw the things that he transcribed here also from his book *Bet Ha-Osef* and when I saw him mention his essay on the 'world of souls,' my soul yearned to see these two works, as a hind pants for streams of water. And now, how shall I repay you, my friend, for all the kindness you have shown me in quenching my thirst, for in truth I found in them good and comforting things? I found? No, not so, for from beginning to end they are all filled with new and pleasant things. They are sweeter to my palate than the choicest honey, and today I know that besides me there is another redeemer for the holy language . . . Would that he might be given to me as a brother" (*Iggerot Shadal*, No. 22).

31. Some thirty years later Adam Ha-Kohen Lebensohn, along with Jehudah Behak, reprinted both of Löwisohn's works with many notes under the title *Meḥkerei Lashon.*

32. *Meḥkerei Lashon*, 58–66.

33. See our *History*, Vol. VIII, p. 103.

34. The elegy is not published, but rather large fragments from it are quoted in *Melitzat Yeshurun*, 1816, folios 24b, 53a, 62a, and 80b.

admirer of Cicero and Quintilian, was the first Jewish scholar who ventured to consider the Bible not merely as "holy writ," as a divine and sacred work, but also as one of the most remarkable of literary monuments, as a collection of supreme artistic achievements. He attempted to show in his *Nofet Tzufim* that, in the realm of elegant style and emotive oratorical art, the prophets and Biblical historians must be acknowledged the foremost masters. The rays of the Renaissance era set; they were covered over by the leaden clouds of religious and political reaction. *Nofet Tzufim* was completely forgotten, as was its author Messer Leon, with his enthusiasm for ancient rhetoric and oratory.

Bible exegesis became steeped in mysticism and in "secrets of secrets," and the creators of Hasidism ingeniously sought and found their favorite thoughts and revelations in the most varied texts of the Bible. But now, like Messer Leon in his day, the European-educated, twenty-five-year-old Solomon Löwisohn appeared and attempted on his own account to carry through what the author of *Nofet Tzufim* had not been able to do. Not Cicero and Quintilian of the antique Roman world were Löwisohn's teachers and guides but the brilliant Johann Gottfried Herder with his classic work *Vom Geiste der hebräischen Poesie.*[35] Another important difference must be noted. Messer Leon was a philologist and rhetorician. Löwisohn was also a philologist but, above all, a poet. When Heinrich Graetz mentions the influence of Herder's work on Löwisohn he remarks quite justly, "The beauty and sweetness of Hebrew poetry, its nobility and simplicity, was felt more profoundly by Löwisohn than by Herder, for it was closer to him and more his own."[36]

Messer Leon wrote a rhetorical work in heavy, highflown language, but Löwisohn produced a study of the principles and forms of Old-Hebrew poetry which was itself truly a masterpiece, illuminated with the rays of genuine poetic inspiration, of authentic poetic brilliance. The introduction to *Melitzat Yeshurun* is magnificent. We have noted[37] that the Meassefim endeavored to display to the European world the beauty of the Biblical language. Solomon Löwisohn sought to celebrate for the Jewish world, in the language of the Bible and in brilliant verses, *beauty* itself. In the classical Book of Proverbs, wisdom

35. First published in Dessau in 1782–1783.

36. *Op. cit.*, 411.

37. See our *History*, Vol. VIII, pp. 75ff.

declares that it is the foundation of the world, but the young Bible-exegete declared beauty to be the living breath of the universe.

In free verses rich in imagery and unfettered by rhyme,[38] the poet sings his inspired hymn to beauty and its marvelous daughter, poetry. All corners of the universe are filled to overflowing with the tones of this modest "daughter of beauty." Its rhythmic sounds are heard in every tremor of man's soul. It is the joy and consolation of all human hearts. In the silence of the night, in the trembling rays of the moon, in the rush of the storm-wind, in the colossal force of the angry waves of the sea, in the mighty crash of the falling iceberg, in the modest murmur of the hidden spring, in the waving of a flower bathed in the rays of the sun—everywhere its melody is heard, its living breath felt.

The author of *Melitzat Yeshurun* sets himself the task of disclosing "the wondrous treasures of the daughter of beauty that are collected in the book of books." In poetic language abounding in imagery he seeks to familiarize the reader with poetic forms, to explain the significance of various technical terms.[39] All this Löwisohn illustrates in the most successful way with numerous quotations from the Bible. But he is not content with quotations; he also takes entire poems, such as the extremely ancient Song of Deborah and the Song of Moses at the sea, and analyzes them according to his poetic principles. Moses' song does not interest him as a hymn and paean to the Creator for His great miracles but only as a poetic work, a treasure of apt metaphors and images. The same is true of the Song of Songs, in which all the commentators had sought the profoundest mystical secrets. Löwisohn considers the Song of Songs exclusively as a poetic work, an incomparable love-story,[40] and declares that the poem in the third chapter "Al Mishkavi Ba-Lailot," (On My Bed at Night) is one of the most beautiful love-songs in world literature.[41] To show more clearly that he considers the Bible only as a literary work of peerless poetic value, Löwisohn introduces, along with quota-

38. Luzzatto's poetic introduction to *La-Yesharim Tehillah* served as a model for Löwisohn.

39. E.g., metaphor, irony, allegory, hyperbole, antithesis, personification, trope, hypotyposis, and many others.

40. Herder, with his work *Lieder der Liebe* (1778), undoubtedly served Löwisohn as a model. There also it is noted that the Song of Songs must be considered exclusively as a love-poem and that no mystical allusions are to be sought in it.

41. *Melitzat Yeshurun*, 37 (we quote according to the first edition).

tions from the Bible, examples from various Hebrew and even European poets, such as Horace and Shakespeare.

One other point is worth dwelling on. Modern philology shows that many so-called metaphors and poetic expressions were originally, many centuries ago, not metaphors at all but considered real phenomena by the men who lived at that time. When, for example, the eighteenth Psalm portrays God thundering from heaven—"the Highest *(Elyon)* gave forth His voice . . . He sent out His arrows and spread them abroad"—this, for the author of the Psalm, is no more than a poetic metaphor. But it is beyond doubt that many generations earlier the people actually believed in a God named Elyon who shouts and hurls his arrows in great wrath. The same is true of such expressions as "Out of the room comes the whirlwind" (Job 37), "And he flew on the wings of the wind: (Psalms 18), and "He brings the wind out of His treasuries" (Psalms 135:7). Certainly in ancient times men actually imagined that the storm-wind is hidden in the treasuries of the gods in special rooms, and that the wind is really borne on wings; all this was, in the consciousness of these men, a real fact. Generations later, concepts changed and certain beliefs died out. The old expressions, however, remained, but now merely as metaphors, as images and poetic similes.

In Löwisohn's time philologists understood little of the transformations sustained by verbal images in human history, but he, with his fine sensitivity, knew how to elucidate the actual historical nature of numerous metaphors and poetic images. When, in Proverbs (Chapter 17) it is said, "Her house is the way to Sheol, going down to the chambers of death," or when Isaiah (22:16) calls out to Shebna, "What hast thou here, and whom hast thou here, that thou hast hewed thee out a sepulchre there, as he that heweth him out a sepulchre on high, and that graveth an habitation for himself in a rock?," Löwisohn points out[42] that the "great of the people," the rich and prominent, in Biblical times used to carve out in the mountains special caves, beautifully adorned, in which the deceased members of their family were buried. On the quotation from Isaiah (Chapter 2), "And they shall go into the holes of the rocks and into the caves of the earth for fear of the Lord and for the glory of His majesty," Löwisohn comments:

you must know that the land of Judea and its environs consists only of mountains and stony peaks. In them are long, deep caves that

42. *Melitzat Yeshurun,* 83.

protect men from the broiling sun, and in time of trouble the inhabitants would conceal themselves in these caves from the enemy, as happened, for instance, at the time of the wars the Jews carried on with the Philistines or when David had to hide from Saul.[43]

"It is worth calling your attention, dear reader," Löwisohn notes,[44]

> to the fact that you cannot properly sense and grasp the whole power and poetic beauty of the images in the Bible unless you have first thoroughly explored the nature and character of the land of Canaan and its vicinity, and the customs and qualities of men among the Oriental peoples. For one encounters in the Bible numerous metaphors and similes which derive either from things and objects that are found in the land that is very remote from our way of life, or from the customs and attributes of Oriental peoples which are quite different from the order of life that we see among the peoples in whose midst we live.

Löwisohn in fact set himself the task of giving the Jewish reader this requisite information, and in the fall of 1817 completed his geography of the Bible, *Meḥkerei Aretz*,[45] which achieved great success. Two years after *Meḥkerei Aretz* was published it appeared in German translation,[46] and in 1839 Jacob ben Solomon Kaplan of Minsk reprinted Löwisohn's work with many supplements and notes in Vilna under the altered title *Eretz Kedumim*. A year after *Meḥkerei Aretz* appeared, Löwisohn completed his German work *Vorlesungen über die neuere Geschichte der Juden*. By *neuere Geschichte* Löwisohn understands the era from the time after the destruction of Jerusalem by the legions of Titus until modern times. The historian Heinrich Graetz warmly praised this work of the young scholar;[47] he considered it necessary especially to note that while, at that time, every Jewish enlightener who wrote in German deemed it proper to mock the Talmud, Löwisohn speaks with great respect of this colossal monument of Jewish culture.[48]

43. *Ibid.*, 97.
44. *Ibid.*, 30.
45. Published in Vienna, 1819.
46. *Biblische Geographie mit einer Karte des Schauplatzes der Bibel*, Vienna, 1821 (see Zunz, *Gesammelte Schriften*, Vol. I, p. 198).
47. *Op. cit.*, 411.
48. In this connection Graetz quotes the following passage from Löwisohn's *History:* "The Talmud, a gigantic structure of mental acuity and sense, immeasurable . . . like

The first volume of Löwisohn's history was also the last. Shortly after its appearance the author became mentally ill as a result of an unhappy love affair. His friends brought the sick author to his native city, and there he died[49] several months later at the age of thirty-two. It is difficult to estimate the loss which the new Hebrew literature sustained through his premature death.

Length of days was enjoyed by the other poet whom we mentioned earlier, Shalom ben Jacob Cohen, who was born in Mezhirech (in the region of Posen) in December, 1772.[50] Of his education, as of his youth in general, no details are known. Letteris and, after him, Klausner and other scholars indicate that Shalom Cohen left Poland at the age of seventeen and set out for Berlin. This, however, is not correct. In point of fact he came to Berlin ten years later, only in the summer of 1799. Cohen himself provides evidence of this. At the end of the introduction to his first work, *Mishlei Agur,* is the notation "Mezhirech, Tuesday, the 9th of Iyyar, 1799," and the letter he wrote three months later (17th of Menaḥem Av, 1799) to Isaac Euchel begins with the report, "From the land of my birth I came to this city of wisdom with the manuscript of a book written in elegant Hebrew, the first fruit of my thoughts." Thus we see that in 1799 he had just arrived in Berlin from his native country.

Apparently the young Shalom Cohen had already become a "heretic" in his native town, there obtained familiarity with the Berlin Haskalah, learned German, and become an ardent admirer of the Meassefim. As we learn from his letter to Euchel, Cohen came to Berlin with a completed manuscript of his first work. This was a collection of fables in verse entitled *Mishlei Agur,*[51] which he composed, as he writes in the introduction, "for Jewish children, so that they may be accustomed to a simple and clear language." But for those children who no longer understand Hebrew, he provides, next to the Hebrew

---

the pyramid at Sais . . . will in the latest ages still attract the glances of learned investagators, who will ponder with astonishment the nature of the people from whose midst such a structure came forth."

49. April, 1821.

50. It is clear that the Shalom of Mezhirech who is mentioned by Mendelssohn in *Or La-Netivah* as a participant in his edition of the Pentateuch is a completely different person. Shalom Cohen's biographer Meir Halevi Letteris, in his preface to *Amel Ve-Tirtzah,* also calls attention to this.

51. Only the first part, in which twenty fables are printed, was published (Berlin, 1799). The second part remained in manuscript. Cohen published only a few fables of this part many years later in *Bikkurei Ha-Ittim.*

text, a German prose translation. *Mishlei Agur* is hardly a successful work. The language is, indeed, "simple and clear," but also monotonous and colorless. The verses lack proper resonance, the moral is diffuse and petty in a householderly, respectable fashion.

It is worth dwelling on only one fable, built on the well-known theme of the frogs who decided they wanted a king. Cohen who, like many other patriotically-minded *maskilim*, celebrated kings and princes in special poems of praise relates in his fable the grievous punishment that came upon the frogs because of the fact that they trampled their happiness and freedom with their own feet. While living quietly and happily "without an officer and without a ruler," it suddenly occurred to them out of pride: "Let us make a king over ourselves." The king they chose was a true snake. The frogs mourned in their great distress, but no one could help them any longer. Then they deeply regretted what they had done and with pained hearts recited *mea culpa:* "How splendidly, how peacefully we lived when we were free, but we did not understand how well it was with us. We desired a king, and so we suffer for our folly."

Shalom Cohen's other work, *Matta'ei Kedem Al Admat Tzafon*, which appeared with a German translation in 1806 was more successful.

We have noted[52] the indirect influence of Rousseau's ideas that was strongly discernible in the early Haskalah literature. Back to nature, return to productive work on the soil—this was one of the most popular slogans, and village and pastoral idylls were among the favorite genres in the generation of the Measefim. This motif also resounds in the Bible drama *Meluchat Sha'ul* by Joseph Tropplowitz (Ha-Ephrati). The young David is afraid that later, when he achieves the highest stages of bliss,

> Perhaps I shall forget that the simple plowman
> Who cleaves the earth is a man like I am . . .
> Like I am? Ah, he is much better than I.

And he further expresses his strong conviction that only workers on the soil

> Will find joy, obtain rest,
> And call from the depths of their hearts to God their
> Creator.

52. See our *History*, Vol. VIII, beginning of Chapter V.

This tendency is carried through by Shalom Cohen in his Biblical poems published in *Matta'ei Kedem*. Especially characteristic is the first poem "Hatzalat Avram Be-Ur Kasdim." It is not the militant heretic and denier Abraham, full of tragic grandeur, who rises with axe in hand against the dead gods of the fathers, that impresses the poet. He is interested mainly in the idyllic aspect and portrays in lovely verses how the shepherd, the son of Terah, rests with his flocks on the bosom of magnificent nature. Idyllic motifs reverberate even more clearly in another poem "Mizmorim Ḥadashim," dedicated to the heroic King David. The much-tried king parts from his old fellow-villager Barzillai and assures him that he, with his little plot of ground and garden adorned with flowers, is far happier than the king in his palaces:

Happy are you, Barzillai, happier than princes,
Than the king in his magnificent palace; beautiful is your heritage.

The gardener and worker on the soil are also crowned with praises and paeans in the third part of *Matta'ei Kedem*, in the two-act drama *Maaseh Mi-Bet Ha-Yizre'eli.*

Matta'ei Kedem won Shalom Cohen a wide reputation. The aged Naftali Herz Wessely saw in him his heir. When Wessely was about to move from Berlin to Hamburg, his admirers expressed their regret that the pride of Hebrew literature was leaving Berlin. The aged poet consoled them: "You must not fret; Shalom Cohen remains with you and will restore the language of the Bible to its erstwhile glory and splendor."[53] But Shalom Cohen was not content with poetry. He also dreamed of creating a forum for the Hebrew word, of reviving *Ha-Meassef*, which for him represented the highest ideal. As soon as he came from his native land to Berlin he addressed a letter to the former editor of *Ha-Meassef*, Isaac Euchel, begging him to revive the journal that had succumbed, and he promised that he, Cohen, would exert all his powers to circulate *Ha-Meassef* as widely as possible and to gain for it the necessary numbers of subscribers. Euchel's despairing reply[54] convinced the enthusiastic poet that he must not rely on others but himself endeavor to revive the beloved journal. However, he lacked the material resources that were required, and only in 1808 was

53. See *Ketav Yosher*, 1820, pp. 95–96.
54. See our *History*, Vol. VIII, pp. 138–139.

he able to announce to the Jewish reading public that *Ha-Meassef* would resume publication in Berlin in 1809.

Shalom Cohen did not think of a new program or new tasks; he saw in the earlier *Ha-Meassef* the supreme degree of perfection. But the renewed magazine lacks, as a result of the placid and somewhat sentimental character of its editor, the sharply polemical and militant tone of the seventh volume of *Ha-Meassef.* As for the rest, everything is as before: commentaries on various verses of the Bible, translations of the idylls of Gessner, Kleist, and others, weak articles on general and Jewish history, and many diffuse poems. Like the earlier editors of *Ha-Meassef,* Shalom Cohen also sings wine songs.[55] Out of all the poems published in *Ha-Meassef,* signs of talent are noticeable only in the dramatic poem "Mosheh Ve-Tzipporah" by Gabriel Berger of Prague (*Ha-Meassef,* 1810–11) and in Dov Baer Ginzberg's poem "Shom Be-Eretz Ha-Galil" (*Ibid.*, Nissan 1810).[56] *Ha-Meassef* did not enjoy longevity. It appeared in Berlin only in its first year. Later, in 1810, it moved to Altona, and half a year later to Dessau, where in the course of a little more than a year and a half four numbers *(tekufot)* appeared, and then it lapsed into permanent silence. At the end of the last number, the decree of March 11, 1812 concerning the award of civic rights to the Jews in Prussia and the Rhenish provinces is printed in the original German. The fact that, along with the decree of equal rights, Hebrew literature lost its last platform in Germany seems definitely symbolic.

Shortly after the demise of *Ha-Meassef,* Shalom Cohen published his allegorical drama *Amel Ve-Tirtzah* (1812). The work is not only written according to the pattern of Moses Ḥayyim Luzzatto's *La-Yesharim Tehillah* but is also a continuation of Luzzatto's work in subject-matter. "It is to be considered a second part of this work," the author himself declares,[57] and he rightly notes in this connection that in *Amel Ve-Tirtzah* is carried through "another moral tendency: that virtue should not only be praised but rewarded as well."

As in *Matta'ei Kedem,* so in *Amel Ve-Tirtzah* a romantic affection for work on the soil is discernible. The first scene represents the farmer Amel striding with his basket of seeds over the field, scattering seeds generously into the plowed furrows, and

55. See his *Shir Ha-Gefen* (Iyyar, 5570).
56. Dov Baer Ginzberg was born in Brody in 1776 and died there in 1811 (on him, see *Bikkurei Ha-Ittim,* 5582, pp. 157–158.
57. *Ketav Yosher,* p. 86.

singing a paean to the earth, "the mother of all that lives." But *Amel Ve-Tirtzah* is not merely an idyll. The most interesting aspect of the work is the fact that social motifs are heard in it. The hero of the piece, Amel, works in the bitter sweat of his brow, but all his labor falls into the hands of the bloodsucking usurer who, with his deceit, lures the naive agriculturalist into his net. But the righteous intercessor *Sechel* (Reason) takes up the cause of the worker. He appeals to the supreme tribunal, and the judge and ruler of the land proudly declares that he is always concerned for the people and oppresses no one with heavy taxes. "I do not take the young men as soldiers, for there is peace at my borders; I do not carry on wars. I remember that I exist for the sake of my people, and not the people for my sake." The poet champions the cause of the farmer Amel and punishes the avaricious usurer. He is also concerned that Amel should obtain as his wife the lovely Tirtzah, and accompanies the happy bridegroom with the words: "Plow your field and be sustained by its fruits; happy is he who supports himself with the labor of his hands."

In 1813 Shalom Cohen left Germany, settled for a brief time in Amsterdam, and from there went to London where he attempted to establish a Jewish school and published a textbook *Shorashei Emunah* (1815). However, he was unsuccessful in England and returned to Germany, settling in Hamburg. In 1820 he was invited by the Viennese publisher Anton von Schmid to become chief proofreader in place of Solomon Löwisohn who had become ill. In the same year Cohen published at Schmid's press his Hebrew-German guide for writing letters in three parts, *Ketav Yosher*, which was highly popular for a long time and went through more than ten editions. The second part of this guide has a cultural-historical value, for in it letters and documents of Hebrew writers of the era of the Berlin Haskalah are collected.

In Vienna Cohen decided to make another attempt to realize the fond wish of which he had dreamed so many years—to create a forum for the Hebrew word. The Jewish community in Vienna was no less assimilated than that of Berlin. Nevertheless, Vienna was different from Berlin in one important respect: it was the capital city of many provinces where Jews lived in compact masses and where the movement of assimilation had had very slight influence. Cohen thought of again renewing the old platform and reviving the love of his youth, the erstwhile *Ha-Meassef.* And, indeed, he realized his dream. He managed to create the desired forum, but time was stronger than he. The journal which he founded was, contrary to his will, not merely a copy of the *Ha-Meassef* of Koenigsberg and Berlin; in it new tendencies are already discernible, and it belongs in fact to the later period which we shall discuss in the next volume.

Before we proceed to this period, we must dwell on the first shoots of Haskalah which appeared under the influence of the Berlin enlightenment in the eastern provinces (in Galicia and the Russian empire), as well as on the conflicts which occurred between the battlers for a new way of life and the orthodox circles. Of this in the next chapter.

CHAPTER EIGHT

Mendel Levin, Jacob Samuel Bick, and Chaim Ḥaykl Hurwitz

Mendel Levin-Satanow and his translation of the Bible into Yiddish—The style of Levin's translation of Proverbs—The rhetorician Tobias Gutman Feder—His tract *Kol Meḥatzetzim* against Levin's translation into the language of "concubines and servants"—Jacob Samuel Bick and his philosophy—*Riktzug der Frantzoysen*—Chaim Ḥaykl Hurwitz and his *Tzofnas Pane'akh*—The humanist-pedagogue and the enlightened merchant—The style of *Tzofnas Pane'akh*—The anonymous play *Di Genarte Velt*—Polemic on two fronts.

IN ONE of our earlier chapters[1] we noted that the "enlightener" Herz Homberg attempted to "educate" the Jews of Galicia by force and to make of them Europeans and useful citizens with the aid of normal schools and his own textbooks and catechisms. Hence, it is not surprising that the Jewish masses in Galicia regarded the enlightening work of the chief inspector, as well as the normal schools he supervised, as actually an attempt to push them into apostasy. However, not all the enlighteners were of Homberg's type. We spoke in a previous volume of our work[2] of the "truth seekers" who appeared at the end of the eighteenth century, men among whom the roots attaching them to the environment and the ancient culture of their people, to the heritage of their fathers, were still firm and strong. Their desire was not to tear themselves out of the familiar environment but to broaden and ventilate it, to open the closed windows so that

1. See our *History*, Vol. VIII, pp. 109ff.
2. *Ibid.*, pp. 213ff.

more light might penetrate and drive away the dark shadows.

One of the most important among these enlighteners or *maskilim* was Mendel Levin (Lefin) already known to us,[3] who spent his last years in Brody and in the neighboring city of Tarnopol and there soon became the focus around which all who aspired to knowledge and education grouped themselves. One must take into consideration in this connection that in the last decades of the eighteenth century Brody played a more significant role as a major center of trade than Shklov in Lithuania. After the great fire of 1742 the merchants of Brody obtained from the lord of the city, Count Potocki, a million Polish gulden as a loan, which enabled them to establish commercial relationships with the whole world. Ber Birkenthal of Bolechow relates in his memoirs,

When the merchants of Brody received this sum of money, they immediately dispersed over all the cities and lands of Europe, wherever there were good tradesmen and merchandise. They went to harbors and commercial centers, and for many years engaged in trade with the help of this large fund . . . In this way the merchants of Brody became great, multiplied, and were strengthened in all the commerce of the world.[4]

The fact that in 1778 Brody was declared a free city by decree of the emperor Joseph II contributed still further to the rise of the mercantile strata of its population.[5] The merchants had lively trade relationships with the European world, especially with the great German markets—Leipzig, Breslau, Frankfurt-am-Oder, and Berlin. Brody became an important shipping point for various commodities coming from western European countries not only to the interior of Russia but even further into the lands of the Near East.[6] This extensive commerce naturally strengthened interest in general education and secular culture in the commercial circles of Brody. We know from the memoirs of M. Letteris *(Zikkaron Ba-Sefer)* that many prominent merchants of Brody were frequent guests in the home of Moses Mendelssohn when they visited Berlin. Gradu-

3. Our *History*, Vol. VI, 274ff.
4. *Zichronot*, 64.
5. While, in 1764, the Jewish population attained a total of 7,191 persons, in 1779 it reached close to 9,000.
6. See Korobkov's work about the part of Jews in foreign trade in *Yevreyskaya Starina*, 1911, pp. 205–206, where the route which the European merchants followed from Brody through southern Russia until they reached Persia is indicated.

ally, at the end of the eighteenth century, Brody became the gathering point for a whole group of pioneers of Haskalah. There Israel Zamosc spent his last years. There also lived the cultured physician and communal leader, Dr. Abraham Uziel, who had studied in Germany. Brody was also the hometown of the well-known *maskilim* Dov Baer Ginzberg and Jacob Samuel Bick, and there in his old age came Mendel Levin-Satanow (or Mendel Lefin, as he was also called).[7]

Soon after his arrival in Galicia Levin-Satanow published his *Ḥeshbon Ha-Nefesh* (1808). There he also attempted to realize an enlightening work that he had long projected. We noted earlier[8] that Levin-Satanow planned a whole series of popular scientific editions, proceeding from the principle that every enlightener "must exert all his powers to disseminate among the masses the knowledge he has gathered, to familiarize the general public with it." In the preface to his *Refuot Ha-Am* he indicates that he took special pains to write in a clear, popular style so that his work "might be easy and quickly understandable." But Levin knew very well that the masses of the people did not understand Hebrew, and that if one wished to have some cultural influence on them he would have to address them in the only language comprehensible to them—plain Yiddish. He even wrote a special essay in German, "*Von der Wichtigkeit der Volksschriften in jüdischer Sprach zur Kultur und Aufklärung jüdischer Einwohner in Polen.*"[9]

While still living in Berlin in the 1780's, Levin, upon becoming familiar with Mendelssohn's translation of the Torah into literary German, decided to translate the Bible into plain Yiddish in simple, common language, so that it would be "easy and quickly understandable." Weinles is mistaken when he writes that Levin-Satanow first decided to produce a translation of the Bible in Yiddish in his old age.[10] In the *haskamah* or approbation of the rabbi of Satanow printed at the beginning of *Refuot Ha-Am*, which was written in May of 1789, Levin's translation of Ecclesiastes is already mentioned; but only many years later, when Levin settled in Galicia, did he, as a result apparently of

7. The youthful Solomon Rapoport writes enthusiastically about Brody: "The city of Brody is superior to all the cities of Israel in this country. The ways and thoughts of its people are higher than the ways and thoughts of people in the other cities of the country, just as the reason of a man of virtue is higher than the reason of a young child limited in the quality of understanding" (*Michtevei Venei Kedem*, 1862, p. 153).

8. Our *History*, Vol. VI, p. 278.

9. See Weinles' article in *YIVO-Bleter*, Vol. II, Nos. 4–5, 345.

10. *Op. cit.*, 344.

the financial aid of Joseph Perl, finally obtain the possibility of beginning to publish his translation. In 1814 his version of the Book of Proverbs in Yiddish appeared in Tarnopol.[11]

This translation is a truly important event in Yiddish literature. We noted in the previous chapter that Solomon Löwisohn attempted, in his *Melitzat Yeshurun*, to portray the books of the Bible not only as "holy writings," as religious books, but as superb examples of poetic power and beauty. Mendel Levin-Satanow ventures something quite different. He wishes to put an end to the standard style of the translations of the Bible that had been dominant for hundreds of years and according to which the children in the schools had had the Biblical text taught and translated to them. He wishes to give ordinary Jews, worn out with toil, the "holy books" without embroidered covers, but in the simple, weekday garment of the colloquial language, with its homely concepts and images, including its Slavisms, as it is spoken at home and in the marketplace. Like Aaron ben Samuel of Hergershausen[12] in his time, so Mendel Levin-Satanow did not print his translation of Proverbs in the special "women's type" customary for Judeo-German books, but in square Hebrew letters and with vowels. Levin's spelling is also characteristic of his translation; he writes the words mainly according to their phonetic sound. Thus, we find in his work *rufikh*, not *ruf ikh; nemtzakh*, instead of *nemt es aykh; lozim*, not *loz im; hobikh*, not *hob ikh; bemir*, instead of *bay mir; tsishen*, not *tsvishen; binikh*, not *bin ikh;* etc.

Levin, who was one of the finest stylists in neo-Hebrew literature, deliberately disregarded the great distinction between spoken and written language. He refused apparently to recognize that such classic works as Ecclesiastes and Proverbs ought to be translated in a completely different style—not in the language that the market-Jewess speaks to her customer in the street. Under different circumstances Levin's work might be branded as tasteless, but his translation of Proverbs must be considered a battle-slogan, a protest against the religious stamp that was placed on everything in the Jewish milieu. From this point of view, Levin, in his translation of the Bible, appears as an innovator, a fighter against the obsolete and outmoded forms of Hebrew translation and for a new, modern, secular style.

11. This edition is now extremely rare. We have employed the copy located in the Asiatic Museum in Leningrad.
12. See our *History*, Vol. VII, p. 224ff.

Levin, however, was not destined to publish his translation of the Bible in full, for his Proverbs in Yiddish evoked, immediately after its appearance, a literary scandal in which the chief role was played by Tobias Gutman ben Tzevi Feder, at that time a well-known *maskil* and "linguist."[13]

Tobias Feder was born in 1760 in Prezedborz (region of Cracow), received a traditional religious education, married in Petrokov, and was there imbued with the ideas of the Berlin Haskalah and came into contact with the Meassefim.[14] After 1788 he left Petrokov, whereupon his long years of wandering over Germany, Galicia, and the Ukraine began.[15] He lived in many cities, in Frankfurt-am-Oder where he became acquainted with Isaac Satanow, in Kempno, Chelmo, Wlodarka, Berdichev, Brody, and Tarnopol. He tried all kinds of occupations; he was a scribe and Torah reader, a cantor and teacher, a preacher and expositor, and with all these he and his family starved every day.[16] In Berdichev he had to live in winter with his family in an unheated stable. This had a deleterious effect on his character. He became an irascible person, constantly excited, and developed a weakness for alcohol.

Despite his poverty and distress, Feder devoted himself intensively to the study of philology. Like most of the *maskilim* of that day, he was in love with the language of the Bible, was renowned as a great rhetorician *(baal melitzah)*, and wrote in the typical Meassefim fashion that was filled to overflowing with Biblical verses and figures of speech. He also composed poems,[17] celebrated Czar Alexander I and his victory over Napoleon *(Hatzlahat Aleksander* and *Kol Simḥah)*, and wrote a Purim parody.[18] Above all, however, Feder occupied himself

13. For details of Feder's life and work, see introduction to *Kol Meḥatzetzim;* introduction to *Shem U-She'erit;* M. Tenenboim, in *Otzar Ha-Safrut*, III, Division "Satirah Ve-Humor," 1–4; S. Stanislavsky, *Yevreyskaya Starina*, 1912, 460–466; W. Zeitlin, *Kirjath Sepher;* J. Klausner, *op. cit.*, 213–219; M. Weissberg, *MGWJ*, 1927, 103–109.

14. See *Ha-Meassef*, 5548, p. 95.

15. See *Lahat Ha-Ḥerev*, 1866, p. 28.

16. In his letter to Bick, Feder complains: "For my time has consumed me, stunned me, given poison in my food and grapes of wrath for my thirst; smitten of God have I been since I came forth from the womb; there is nothing to give to [my] children crying for bread; I, too, have always been oppressed and deprived."

17. A.B. Gottlober published several of Feder's poems in a special collection called *Shem U-She'erit*, 1877.

18. *Zohar Ḥadash Le-Furim*, published by Moses Tenenboim in *Otzar Ha-Safrut*, III, Division "Satirah Ve-Humor." Tenenboim also had a bundle of Feder's letters. Moreover, we have found a large collection of Feder's letters and poems in Gottlober's archive, which is in our possession.

with philology and Biblical exegesis. In this area he produced some works which, with a few exceptions, have remained in manuscript.[19] For him the Bible was so revered and holy that when Aaron Wolfsohn and Isaac Satanow allowed themselves to depart from the recognized tradition in their commentaries, he issued forth against them in a polemic work entitled *Lahat Ha-Ḥerev* (1804). In point of fact, Feder does not here carry on a polemic but fights with the "gleaming sword," clamors and cries, bombards the reader with rhetorical flourishes and figures of speech from the Bible, and asserts that Wolfsohn is called Wolfsohn because "he consumes Jews with his corrupt studies"[20] and that "Satanow is the cause of sin for our contemporaries with his works that are so slight in knowledge and lacking in quality."[21]

Levin-Satanow's Proverbs in Yiddish was taken by Feder as literally a personal insult. Like most of the *maskilim* of that generation, Feder regarded the "despised jargon" with hostility and contempt. Mendelssohn and the contributors to his *Biur* set themselves the task of translating the Bible into pure German in order to displace the old Judeo-German translations and their "corrupt" language—and here comes "one of our own," a disciple and friend of Mendelssohn, one of the prominent representatives of Haskalah, and wishes to destroy the building that Mendelssohn and his followers had constructed! To be sure, Mendel Levin, with his plain and clear Hebrew style, could impress such a "master of rhetoric" as Feder very slightly, and the latter regarded Levin's earlier works, *Refuot Ha-Am* and *Ḥeshbon Ha-Nefesh*, with a certain scorn; everything in them was so clear, so simple, without flourishes, without quotations and fragments from the Bible.[22] And now Levin permits himself such unheard-of-impudence as to translate the holy books into the common language of the people, with its "vulgar" expressions and "gross" Slavisms. He

19. Of his philological works the only ones published were *Bet Ne'eman* (1894) and *Mevasser Tov* (1904).

20. *Lahat Ha-Ḥerev*, 1866, 3. In his letter to Bick mentioned before, Feder even asserts that with his attacks he drove Wolfsohn away from Germany to France ("He has left the land of Germany and gone to France and has still not returned").

21. *Ibid.*, 28.

22. See the introduction to *Kol Mehatzetzim*: "The man who hoped to produce grapes but obtained wild fruit . . . *Refuot Ha-Am*, and translations of Proverbs, and *Ḥeshbon* Ha-Nefesh—*all these the wind will carry* off and mud and mire sweep away, all who see them will know from whose belly they came forth; they were created not for help or benefit but for confusion."

ventures, for instance, to translate the sentence from Proverbs (14:1) "Every wise woman buildeth her house, but the foolish plucketh it down with her hands" in the following "vulgar" form: "A clever woman builds a house but a ne'er-do-well *spistoshit* [destroys, or lays waste] the house." Or the words "a man of understanding acquires skill" (1:5), he translates: "a clever man buys himself *spossibes* [means, or methods, or skills]." Feder was beside himself with rage, and immediately issued forth against Levin with a bitter tract called *Kol Me-ḥatzetzim O Siḥah Be-Olam Ha-Neshamot.* Even on the title-page he pours out his wrath against the translator:

Mockery and shame to the new translation of Proverbs, which is full of filth and ugliness. Its stench spreads all around. Whoever sees it shuns it. It ought to be torn to bits and burned, so that its name may no longer be mentioned. The stinking screed which the senile Mendel Satanow produced has no taste and no fragrance. It will find favor only in the eyes of concubines and maids, but they also shun it and declare: Have we so few madmen that this one also comes and plays mad?[23]

After a long introduction full of mighty rhetorical flourishes and ill-tempered attacks on Levin, who "covered the beautiful German language with mockery and associates with a corrupt tongue, who removed the silk shirt and clothed himself in rags," the "conversation in the land of life" *(siḥah be-eretz ha-ḥayyim)* is described. There, in the upper worlds, in the pure celestial heights, Mendelssohn sits on a chair engrossed in his philosophical reflections. The philosopher is surrounded by poets, writers and philologists: Moses Ḥayyim Luzzatto, Naftali Herz Wessely, Joel Brill, and others. All of them are happy and their hearts filled with joy as they recall the splendid memorials they left behind them in the realm of Jewish culture and literature. Only Isaac Euchel, the translator of Proverbs into High German, appears distressed and sad. Wessely inquires why he is so ill-disposed here where everyone ought to be happy and content. A conversation between them commences, and Euchel tells him of the revolution that took place in one of Mendelssohn's prominent fellow-battlers: "He despises the elegant writer; he spits in the face of those who orate beautifully. But the languages of the peasants—these find favor in his sight."

23. We quote according to the copy that we found in Gottlober's archive.

Wessely is beside himself. He refuses to believe Euchel, and declares this only gossip about Satanow. Euchel goes away insulted, with tears in his eyes. Soon, however, Jehudah Leib Ben-Ze'ev comes along with a book in his hand and a mocking smile on his lips. Mendelssohn asks what sort of book it is. Ben-Ze'ev tells him that it is ostensibly a German translation of Proverbs, but that in fact it is not in German and no scholar in the world can explain what this gibberish, which is a mixture of all kinds of languages, can mean. Ben-Ze'ev proceeds to read aloud several verses of the translation. All gape in amazement and cannot understand what language it is. Their distress increases when Ben-Ze'ev relates that the translation was made by none other than Levin-Satanow himself. Wessely begs pardon of Euchel. Mendelssohn is overwhelmed, and all conclude that such a "shameful translation must be burned and its filthy ashes thrown into a lavatory."

This tract was printed by Feder in Berdichev, but before *Kol Meḥatzetzim* came off the press Levin's friends in Brody learned of it.[24] The young Isaac Baer Levinsohn, who then lived seven versts from Brody in the town of Radziwill, came forth against Feder with an epigram in which he notes that the author of *Kol Meḥatzetzim* only becomes a courageous battler when "he fills his mouth with wine and beer:"

> Feder [meaning "pen"] is your name;
> Like a pen also is your tongue.
> The dry pen is dumb
> When it has no ink.
> So, in your case, without wine,
> Your tongue cleaves to your palate.[25]

Levinsohn indicates that he wrote this epigram at the request of his friend Jacob Samuel Bick of Brody. This *maskil*, who was Levin's best friend in Brody, is one of the most remarkable personalities among the "enlighteners" of that generation. Born into a wealthy and prestigious family in Brody (circa 1770), Bick was not only thoroughly proficient in Old-Hebrew literature[26] but also acquired a certain amount of

24. As may be seen from Bick's letter (see below), Levin's friends had a copy of Feder's *Kol Meḥatzetzim* sent to them.

25. *Eshkol Ha-Sofer*, 11.

26. Apparently Bick, in his youth, also devoted himself very little to arid *pilpul* and the legal codifiers. Samson Bloch notes this in his polemic letter to Bick of 1830: "Because you were not diligent from your youth [in] studying the books of the Talmud and the codifiers" (*Ha-Meassef*, I; in Letteris' edition, 1862, p. 181).

European culture and was familiar with modern German, French, and English literature. An excellent Hebrew stylist with a spark of the true poet, he translated French and English poems into Hebrew quite successfully.[27] The distinguished author with his ready wit was extremely popular in the circles of the *maskilim*. But these circles did not entirely satisfy Bick himself. A deeply sensitive, romantic nature, he found Haskalah rationalism uncongenial. In it he perceived at times a modernized form of the old, abstract, pilpulist world outlook. Also repugnant to him was the fanatical attitude of his fellow *maskilim* toward Hasidism, their refusal to recognize the great revolution in the spiritual life of the impoverished masses evoked by the creators and leaders of this movement, "who were able," as Bick puts it in one of his letters, "to become the guides of hundreds of thousands of Jews."[28]

It was precisely Bick, who belonged to the upper strata of the wealthy merchant class and whose family provided Brody with philanthropists for generations, who was the only true democrat among the *maskilim* of the city at that time. The romantic Bick saw among the contemporary Hasidic leaders not, as did the other *maskilim*, only avaricious *gute Yidn* who tried to extract more money from the common people. He observed among them also such "lovers of Israel" as Mosheh Leib of Sasov and Levi Yitzḥak of Berdichev who were prepared to sacrifice themselves for their poor brethren. He discovered that these uncultured, fanatical, and superstitious *tzaddikim* had more true love of mankind than the educated *maskilim* who were conversant with modern philosophy and wrote tracts on humanitarian ideas.[29] This finally brought him at the end of his days much closer to the Hasidim than to the *maskilim*.[30] Bick wrote memoirs in which he portrayed the condition of Jewish life in his time and also gave a critical estimate of both battling camps, the Hasidim and the *maskilim*, but decided not to publish these in his lifetime.[31] It is certainly a great loss for He-

27. See *Die hebräische Publizistik in Wien*, 1930, p. 26.
28. *Otzar Ha-Safrut*, III, Section "Orot Me-Ofel," 26.
29. Typical in this respect is Bick's statement to Solomon Jehudah Rapoport in one of his letters: "Since you read and translated much from the words of the gentle poet of the German people [Bick here means Schiller] whose ideas are so lofty, but you have not translated for yourself his cosmopolitan statement where he says: "A kiss for all the inhabitants of the world." And to change this quality to a Jewish quality, and with the power of this kiss to embrace and kiss all our brethren the children of Israel with all your heart and all your soul—even if this takes away reason and soul."
30. On the enormous impression that Bick's "betrayal" made at that time in the circles of the *maskilim*, we shall speak in the next volume.
31. See *Otzar Ha-Safrut*, III, 52.

brew literature that his valuable manuscripts disappeared after his death.[32]

On learning of Feder's tract, Bick wrote a long letter to him on the nineteenth of Tevet 1815. Because this letter, in which the writer presents his views on Yiddish, the tongue of the people, has a certain cultural-historical value, we present an extensive extract from it:

You compare the language in which he (Levin-Satanow) translated the book of Proverbs to the shrieking of birds and to the sound of beasts in the forest. But remember, my friend, that it is the language which our fathers and grandfathers spoke in Poland for four hundred years. In it spoke and thought and preached the great scholars, Rabbis Joel Sirkes, Moses Isserles, Joshua Falk, and Shabbetai Kohen. This language was also used by the Gaon of Vilna, may his memory be for a blessing. The scholar Fabro in his geographical work (Part I, p. 274, Halle, 1815), considers our language among the daughters of German. And if the parent tongue, German, is so precious to you, why do you not attack the translation of the Torah of *Ha-Maggid*, the translations of *Tze'enah U-Re'enah* and of *Naḥalat Tzevi?* In these books (which were useful for the reading public in their time) the language is highly corrupted and lacks many essential words, expressions, and terms. It is not capable of elevating the sentiments, of making an impression on a man of taste, as is the case with Satanow's translation. Satanow with his wisdom managed to go in the purest ways of the best translators, despite the fact that the language into which he translated has not even now been completely corrected. In the great city of Vienna a paper in this language, which the peasants and the common people in Austria speak, is issued weekly to the present day. If this is done for people who live in the vicinity of the capital, where all the laws and ordinances are written in pure German, the language which their emperor and their officials speak; if, for their benefit, the scholars endeavor to impart ethical instruction and wisdom in their vernacular, so that they may relate it in their homes and that it may remain inscribed in their memories—how much more so is this necessary in regard to Jews who are cast away in the Ukraine and can read no books written in any other language? Thus among all peoples do the sages and scholars behave who wish to be useful to people requiring their help. This is what it means to repay one's debt in an honorable way. The peasants labor in the bitter sweat of their brow to provide nourishment and sustenance for the wise and cultured. It is, therefore, a matter of simple justice that the learned, for their part,

32. Samuel Jacob Bick died in May 1831, at the time of the cholera epidemic. His memoirs were to have been published by the editor of *Kerem Ḥemed,* Samuel Goldenberg (see *Kerem Ḥemed,* I, 81) but he did not manage to accomplish this because, shortly thereafter, a great fire broke out in Brody and all of Bick's literary remains were lost.

should provide the common people with spiritual nourishment in such a language and such a form as the latter can comprehend. But if they refrain and do not consider it their duty to quicken their brethren who labor so hard for their sakes with the fruits of their wisdom, if they wish to write all their works in a language that the common people will not understand and these books are therefore of no use to them, then the scholars will also be obliged themselves to take up the scythe, the plow, the axe, and the saw, and not be sustained by the uncompensated work of others. The French and English languages are also a mixture of German, Gallic, Latin and Greek, but as a result of the effort put forth by the learned of every generation in the course of three hundred years, they were considerably refined; and now, despite the fact that they are a potpourri of various tongues, it is possible to produce the loveliest poems and to express the noblest thoughts and sentiments in them. Only a hundred years ago German was also at a rather low level. Eighty years ago Russian was a peasant language. The classical tongues, Greek and Latin, were also originally crude and clumsy, and only in the process of time did their sages and scholars purify and polish the words, perfect the forms, establish the principles and laws of grammar, until these languages attained a perfection that arouses astonishment in us. The people, the masses, are in every nation the creators of the language, and originally all of them are of one pedigree, none is finer or nobler than the other . . . All are at first halting, crude, unformed and unpolished, and it is the thinkers alone who make of the formless mass a marvelous instrument, a masterpiece. . . . So, my brother, you are mistaken. You will acquire no honor and no praise if you publish your tract. Better dispatch a letter to Mendel Satanow and beg his pardon for the fact that you have insulted him. . . . This is the counsel which your friend who always wishes you well, Jacob Bick, gives you.

Feder replied to Bick in a letter strongly seasoned with rhetorical flourishes and figures of speech, as was his fashion.[33] He declared that he agreed not to publish his composition if he would be reimbursed for the expenses he had paid out for this purpose (*Kol Meḥatzetzim* was already set in type). The *maskilim* of Brody promptly sent Feder a hundred rubles (considerably more than the printing cost) and *Kol Meḥatzetzim* was not published.[34] Feder's attack, however, so frightened the very peace-

33. Both letters are printed in *Kerem Ḥemed*, I, 96–102. Shortly after this Feder, who had moved to Tarnopol, died (Tammuz, 1817).

34. Only in 1853, when Mendel Levin and Feder were both long dead, did a Galician *maskil*, Abraham Mendel Mohr, publish Feder's lampoon with certain alterations. Mohr also weakened Feder's sharp polemic in places (see A. Habermann's notice in *YIVO-Bleter*, III, 472–475).

able and unaggressive Satanow that he lost the desire and the courage to publish his translation of the remaining books of the Bible. Only in 1873 did Jehudah Bari publish Satanow's translation of Ecclesiastes in Odessa.[35] The other translations were lost.[36]

While Mendel Levin-Satanow was attempting to give the books of the Bible to the Jewish reader in the common, spoken language, attempts were made within Russian Jewry to present works of purely secular content in the same language.

In 1813 a small book entitled *Riktzug der Frantzoysen* (The Retreat of the French) appeared in Vilna. On the title-page it is noted: "Here is described the invasion by the French of Russia up to nine miles beyond Moscow and the miserable retreat from there to Kovno; translated from the Polish language." The style of this work is not unitary. On the one side, the narrative manner of the eighteenth century is still noticeable in it, and on the other, the influence of the Berlin Haskalah. Hence one encounters in it such sentences as "It was plain to see that a very bloody war was waged against the enemy, a war in which nothing less than life or death was at stake," or "The Russian army was very large and full of high spirits, and on all sides of the country patriotism developed new forces for the army." The translator, however, allows himself to use certain Slavisms such as *rabunges, onitzes, kapeliushn, rogozis,* etc. In places the language already sounds quite Yiddish-like, for example, on page 4:

> Napoleon's predictions began to be fulfilled, and people began to believe that he would certainly keep his word. As soon as the French armies crossed the Niemen River, the Russians began to withdraw on all sides, and Poland began to give the enemy its forces, and the peoples of the same lands took up arms and united with the French to increase the tumult. Napoleon promised his soldiers that he would lead them to Moscow. There, said Napoleon, all your toil and trouble will have an end, and there a renowned peace and refreshment and rest will await you.

35. Mendel Levin's manuscript of his translation of the Book of Ecclesiastes was found by I. Weinles in Perl's library, and from it YIVO issued a facsimile edition. This version is different from the printed one.

36. According to a letter of Mendel Levin's that has been preserved (see *YIVO-Bleter,* II, Nos., 4–5, 345), his translations of the Books of Psalms, Job and Lamentations were already finished.

Incomparably more important in scope and significance is another work which appeared in 1817[37] in Berdichev. This is *Tzofnas Pane'akh* by Chaim Ḥaykl Hurwitz of Uman.

Chaim Ḥaykl Hurwitz came from a very prestigious family.[38] From his "pedigree" *(Yikhes-Brif)* only the year of his birth, 1749, has been established, but not the place. It is known merely that he lived with his family in Uman as a very wealthy timber merchant. In consequence of the extensive business affairs he carried on with Prussia, he had opportunity to become familiar with the Berlin Haskalah and with German literature. It would be erroneous, however, to believe that Hurwitz represents a typical *maskil* of the era of enlightenment. He was and remained, above all, a practical merchant of broad scope who became persuaded, as a result of his business travels, that for purposes of trade it was essential to have a more or less adequate notion of geography and of the way of life prevalent in other lands and countries.

To battle for enlightenment itself, for the study of languages, for spreading humanitarian ideas and against the "darkness of superstition" and the malevolence of the "rebels against light"—for this the wealthy merchant Hurwitz, who proudly traced his descent from the author of the *Shulḥan Aruch* and from Isaiah Horowitz, had little desire. This may be seen quite clearly from his comprehensive work in Yiddish. For a rather long time this work was virtually forgotten; not merely common readers but even historians of culture and literary scholars knew nothing of it. The first person who resurrected Hurwitz's life's-work in the memory of the Jewish reader was A. B. Gottlober in his well-known *Zikhroynes Vegn Yidishe Shraybers.*[39]

"Eighty or ninety years ago," Gottlober relates,

> there lived in the city of Uman a very cultured Jew, Reb Ḥaykl Hurwitz. This Reb Ḥaykl Hurwitz wrote jargon! He translated from the German Campe's *Die Entdeckung von Amerika* under the title *Columbus* with the approbation of the *maggid* of Zelva. At that time (it must certainly have been seventy years ago; I was still a child), this book was so widely circulated that almost all Jews read it, not to speak of the Jewish women, who gave up the *Tze'enah U-Re'enah* and the

37. It is beyond doubt, however, that the translation was already finished several years earlier, for Prince I.M. Dolgoruki, who visited Hurwitz's house in Uman in 1810, already knows of it and mentions it in his travel account (see p. 221).

38. See Ḥaykl Hurwitz's "genealogical letter," *Filologishe Shriftn*, III, pp. 83–88.

39. Published in Sholom Aleichem's *Yidishe Folks-Bibliotek.*

teḥinnot [in Yiddish, *tekhines*], even the *Bovo-Maaseh,* and read only *Columbus.* Until that time very few Jews even knew that there was an America in the world; in our day, America is as well known as a bad shilling. *Columbus* is written in such pure fashion that it can be read and understood everywhere, in Russia, Poland, Galicia, Romania—every place where there are Jews. Moreover, it is so beautifully printed that it is a delight to read. When I was still a young child, I derived great joy from it, and after my marriage, when I had already studied many books, even Hasidic and *Ḥabad* books, I obtained *Columbus* in Chernigov and found great pleasure in reading it again. My imagination carried me along with Columbus to America; I was with him in the ship at sea, I marvelled at the wild Indians, and even in my sleep they stood before my eyes.

As a result of this extraordinary popularity, Hurwitz's work was so thoroughly "read through" that already at the time Gottlober wrote his memoirs it was extremely rare, and since Gottlober was somewhat mistaken and did not report the title of the book quite correctly,[40] modern scholars confused Hurwitz's translation with another translation of Campe's *Entdeckung von Amerika* which was published in 1823 by Mordecai Aaron Günzburg. The author of these lines noted this confusion as early as 1912,[41] and N. Shtif was the first to call attention to the fact that Gottlober did not report the title of Hurwitz's work accurately and that its true name was *Tzofnas Pane'akh.*[42] Only in recent years were three copies of Hurwitz's book found, and Shtif[43] and Zalman Rejzen[44] obtained the opportunity to become directly acquainted with the extremely rare work and to provide more precise information about it.[45]

Like Mendel Levin's translation of Proverbs, so *Tzofnas Pane'akh* was printed not with customary "women's type" but in square letters, and like Levin also, Hurwitz wrote in clean, simple, popular language. Gottlober is quite right when he notes that Hurwitz's work "is written in such a pure fashion

40. *Columbus* is the name only of the first part of the work, not of the entire composition.

41. In the review of M. Pines' *History of Yiddish Literature, Razvet,* 1912, No. 7–9. (a Yiddish translation of Pines' work, originally written in French, appeared in Warsaw in 1911.)

42. *Pinkes,* 1913, 339.

43. *Oyfn Shprakhfront,* Nos. 2–3, 1932.

44. *YIVO-Bleter,* Vol. V, pp. 29–40.

45. We have employed the copy located in the YIVO library. We take this occasion to thank the administration of the library for the courtesy with which it gave us the opportunity to become familiar with this rare item.

that it can be read and understood everywhere." His remark that *Colombus* is merely a translation of Campe's *Entdeckung von Amerika*, however, is not altogether correct. *Tzofnas Pane'akh* is in fact not a translation but a *reworking;* since Hurwitz intended his Yiddish work for a very different audience, he completely altered the style and basic tendencies of Campe's book.

Joachim Heinrich Campe (1746–1818) acquired his reputation not merely as a prominent pedagogue and director of a model educational institution (the Philantropin) in Mendelssohn's native city of Dessau, but mainly as a talented writer for children and young people. Especially popular were his *Robinson Crusoe*, which went through hundreds of editions and was translated into numerous languages, and his *Entdeckung von Amerika*, consisting of three parts: *Columbus*, *Cortez*, and *Pizarro*. Both these works were written in the form of conversations. The head of a family, a skillful and humane educator of children, gathers young people around him and relates to them in the course of many evenings events in the life of Robinson Crusoe and the voyages of discovery made by Columbus and his colleagues. The father's narration is frequently interrupted by the children's comments or questions. The father responds to the cues of the young listeners and weaves into his narration various moral lessons and didactic maxims.

Quite in the spirit of that era, the basic tendencies of Campe's work are enlightenment and humanism: to give the youth moral instruction, to disseminate humanitarian ideas, to implant love for man and nature. As early as 1807 the twenty-five year old Moses ben Mendel (Mendelssohn) of Hamburg translated Campe's *Entdeckung von Amerika* into Hebrew.[46] In the review given in *Ha-Meassef*[47] it is noted that this successful translation is especially important for the "dear people of Poland" who do not read books in European languages. The "dear people of Poland," i.e., the Russian-Polish Jews, however, became familiar with Campe's *Entdeckung von Amerika* not through Mendelssohn's Hebrew translation but through Ḥaykl Hurwitz's *Tzofnas Pane'akh*.

46. "The discovery of the new land, containing all the great feats that were done at the time of its discovery . . . America in all its regions . . . Translated and gathered from the books of the nations in clear and easy language to teach the youth of the sons of Israel the beauty of this language and to make them know the mighty acts of the Lord and the marvels that He does in all the earth. By me Moses, the son of my lord and father, the renowned Torah scholar, our teacher our master, Rabbi Mendel, Altona, 5567." Mendelssohn published only the first part.
47. 5570, 97–101. Here also are given examples of the Hebrew translation.

The wealthy merchant and *maskil* of Uman, however, has completely different purposes than the "enlightener" and director of the Philanthropin, Joachim Campe. The factual material in Campe's work is, indeed, given by Hurwitz in its entirety. "From his [Campe's] description," he notes in the introduction, "I took out the essence and rewrote it in pure Yiddish, such as a man speaks to his neighbor." Any passage of *Tzofnas Pane'akh* will serve as an example. So we read, for instance, on page 47a:

Faras came to Columbus and stood before his bed where he lay ill and began to speak to him very defiantly. "Why," he asked, "do you refuse to lead us back to Spain?" Columbus answered him with a very mild mien: "I am not guilty of so doing. If anyone among you could find some means by which we could get to Spain, I would certainly follow it. I therefore wish to call all the officers together to take counsel on what to do, and how we can come to Spain." Even though Columbus answered him so well, Faras continued to be extremely impudent and to speak very sharply against Columbus: "This is no time for parades." He wished to go to Spain at once and began to cry: "Whoever wishes to follow me, let him come!"[48]

Hurwitz is not at all chary in using Slavisms. One encounters in him very frequently such words as *uchotnikes, pozvoliet, zich staren, derkutshen, verbovin, pokorne, nagrades, prezandnis, vigodi, ostrozne, regoliarne, laske, shliachetzki, pavoli, spossibes, ritzeris,* and many others. Most characteristic of Ḥaykl Hurwitz, however, is his pietistic style, his adaptation to the old-fashioned world outlook of his readers. This strongly impels him to alter the tendency of the original, to throw out the humanitarian and enlightening elements of Campe's work, to include only the factual narrative material, and to clothe it in a pious, Jewish vestment. Even in the introduction Hurwitz underscores the purely utilitarian aspect and indicates that "whoever reads this book will see the benefits which God has created for us through the discovery of the new world. We enjoy much good from America, and we must therefore render great praise and laudation to God." When in Campe, for instance, the father tells his young listeners that Columbus was sick and, because he could not leave the ship, was saved from a great danger, he concludes with this sentence: "See how what we shortsighted men consider a misfortune often proves to be

48. In this extract Hurwitz remains faithful to the German text (Campe, *Die Entdeckung von Amerika,* I, 249). We quote according to the fourth edition, 1796.

really a benefit from God."[49] In Hurwitz, however, this passage is rendered as follows: "The providence of God Blessed be He is very great. He did not wish such an unjust thing to happen; God therefore sent a lassitude on Columbus's limbs, so that he could not leave his ship." So on almost every page Hurwitz does not fail to mention "God Blessed be He."

Campe, for example, recalls the isthmus of Panama which separates the two oceans and notes in this connection that "nature covered the isthmus with a chain of very high mountains, so that it might withstand the storm waves of the two great oceans."[50] This passage is rendered by Hurwitz in an extremely Jewish, pietistic fashion: "God Blessed be He created the world and the isthmus, and on both sides of the isthmus He created the great sea that is called Ocean, and in order that the great sea should not tear through the isthmus and its waters become one, God created very large mountains on the isthmus."[51] Even of Cortez, whom the humane Campe cannot forgive for his bloody deeds and inhuman cruelty, Hurwitz speaks with the same pious mien: "God Blessed be He wished that Cortez should continue to live and conquer the Mexican lands."[52] This phrase is not to be found in Campe.

On the other hand, Hurwitz frequently abbreviates where Campe expatiates. In Campe, for instance, the father complains of Columbus because, knowing beforehand through his familiarity with astronomy that there would be an eclipse of the moon one night, Columbus exploited this fact to threaten the ignorant Indians and tell them that, in consequence of their refusal to sell him food, the gods would punish them and take away the moon at night. Campe's father explains to his young listeners that to do this was to spread superstition and strengthen obscurantism among ignorant men.[53] This entire passage was thrown out by Hurwitz. He also skips the whole passage in Campe in which the latter speaks indignantly of the fanaticism of the Spaniards who forced the Indians to convert to Catholicism. "Ah," the father exclaims emotively, "when will the happy time come when everything called superstition, fanaticism, and religious zealotry will be rooted out from all human hearts."[54] Also thrown out by Hurwitz is Campe's

49. Campe, *op. cit.*, I, 108.
50. *Op. cit.*, III, 15.
51. *Tzofnas Pane'akh*, folio 130b.
52. *Ibid.*, folio 114b.
53. Campe, *op. cit.*, I, 256.
54. *Ibid.*, II, 82.

lamentation over the injustice done to the poor Mexicans by the Spanish warriors and the destruction of their kingdom. When Campe stresses that Pizarro, like Cortez, was an extremely wicked and cruel man and, in this connection, offers the maxim that even brilliant capacities cannot "make an evil person worthy of love in the eyes of our fellow-men,"[55] this passage is also eliminated by Hurwitz because these great knights were, after all, God's agents in discovering a new world from which we enjoy "so much good."

The enlightened pedagogue and humanitarian Campe concludes his work with moral instruction. The father, in closing, wishes his young listeners that they may enter life as "superior, excellent, and brave men."[56] The *maskil* and merchant Ḥaykl Hurwitz, taking account of his readership, concludes his *Tzofnas Pane' akh* by listing "the benefits which the three parts of the world, Asia, Europe, and Africa, obtained from the fact that the knights discovered the new world and conquered it." He declares at the end: "An extensive trade is also carried on between our people and the people who dwell there. A great deal of business is done thereby. One also sees from this the providence of God Blessed be He who gave the knights the intelligence to risk their lives in going to such dangerous places for the general good."

Tzofnas Pane' akh is certainly an important phenomenon in neo-Yiddish literature from the point of view both of its content and its language. We have already noted that it would be erroneous to portray its author as a typical enlightener of that era. We see before us, above all, not the enlightener but the worldly merchant who understands that great changes are taking place in economic life, that one cannot live in isolation from the larger environment. If a man wishes to carry on business, to trade and travel, he must obtain the requisite practical knowledge and understand what is going on in the world. This must be explained to the old-fashioned and backward Jewish reading public, Hurwitz was firmly convinced, in the form and fashion that is congenial and accessible to it. So Hurwitz wrote a thick, worldly book which has to do with nothing but knights and bloody wars in such a style that even the pious *maggid* of Zelva, Meir Segal, gave his *haskamah* or approbation to it.

Another work that appeared at approximately the same

55. Campe, *op. cit.*, III, 44.
56. *Ibid.*, III, 264.

time[57] as Hurwitz's *Tzofnas Pane' akh* was written in Yiddish in a very different style. This is the anonymous play *Di Genarte Velt,* which was published in Zolkiew. This work, too, was eventually completely forgotten; only its name is mentioned by several bibliographers. However, not a single copy has been preserved. Only in recent times did the literary scholar M. Wiener find a copy of a much later, abbreviated, and apparently distorted edition (Lemberg, 1863) and become familiar with the content of the anonymous *Di Genarte Velt.*[58] The play is strongly under the influence of Wolfsohn's *Leichtsinn und Frömmelei* (Frivolity and Hypocrisy), but other tendencies than those of Wolfsohn are discernible in it. First of all, the anonymous author breaks with the tradition of Wolfsohn and Euchel; in him it is not only the old-fashioned personages but also the positive figures, who express the author's thoughts, who speak in mellifluous, pure Yiddish. Furthermore, the author leaves completely untouched the first half of Wolfsohn's theme, the frivolousness of the falsely enlightened, and places the entire emphasis on the second half, hypocrisy. In *Di Genarte Velt* the hypocrite is a *Ḥasid,* and the enlightened merchant, the positive figure, complains: "In times past one used to hear of *gute Yidn,* of *rebbes,* but of one in a whole country once a year. Now, however, the breed has cropped up, multiplied, spread, and infested the whole world; wherever there is a town, there are *rebbes.*"[59]

This motif, a *Kulturkampf* and polemic against Hasidism, is particularly noticeable precisely at that time, in the second decade of the nineteenth century. This battle broke out on two different fronts: on the one side, polemics and satirical attacks on the part of the Galician *maskilim* against the Hasidim and the *rebbes* and, on the other side, the battle in the Germanic territories centering around the question of religious reform. Of this in the next chapter.

57. According to M. Erik's conjecture, *Di Genarte Velt* was published in 1815–1816 (*Bibliografisher Zamlbukh,* I, 510).
58. *Bibliografisher Zamlbukh,* I, 142–147.
59. *Ibid.,* 147.

CHAPTER NINE

Anti-Hasidic Works;
THE STRUGGLE BETWEEN THE REFORMERS AND THE ORTHODOX

The Mitnagdim and Hasidim combine against the new enemy—Israel Zamosc opposes the Hasidim—The tract *Maaseh Ta'tu'im*—Jacob Calmanson against the "dangerous" sect—Mendel Levin's anti-Hasidic work *Der Ershter Khosid* and *Maḥkimat Peti*—The anti-Hasidic manuscript *Über das Wesen der Sekte Chassidim*—Joseph Perl as battler for culture—His satire *Megalleh Temirin*—Religious reform in Germany—The role of Israel Jacobson—The struggle of the Orthodox against the Reform party—*Nogah Ha-Tzedek* and the "legitimacy-verdicts"—Moses Kunitz and Aaron Chorin—Chorin's *Emek Ha-Shaveh* and *Kinat Ha-Emet*—Eliezer Liebermann and his *Or Nogah*—The significance of Liebermann's work—Naḥman Berlin's counter-argument—The *bet din* of Hamburg and *Eleh Divrei Ha-Berit*—The verdicts of the orthodox rabbis—David Caro and his *Berit Emet*—The rabbis of former days and of the present—Meir Bresselau's tract *Ḥerev Nokemet*—*Lahat Ha-Ḥerev Ha-Mithappechet*—Conclusion.

AT THE beginning of the nineteenth century, as we have noted, the struggle between the Mitnagdim and the Hasidim was allayed. The Hasidic movement at that time became so powerful that the Mitnagdim no longer had any hope of overcoming it. In a very considerable number of communities power was already in the hands of the Hasidim and their leaders, and to undertake a struggle against them smacked of martyrdom. The Mitnagdim in fact forfeited the battle. Only then, when the flame of war was diminished, did the Mitnagdim gradually arrive at the conviction that the Hasidic "sect" was by no means as dangerous to the survival of Judaism as they had imagined at first. The fear that the movement founded by the Baal Shem Tov would bring about a cessation of study of Torah also proved to be unfounded. This fear only contributed substantially to the fact that the disciples of the Gaon of Vilna, led by Rabbi Ḥayyim Volozhiner, established a new center of Torah, the famous *yeshivah* of Volozhin, which played a very significant role in Jewish cultural life in Lithuania for several generations. Both the Mitnagdim and the Hasidim, however, saw before themselves a new and more dangerous enemy: the movement of Haskalah.

We have dwelt previously[1] on the great inconsistency between the world outlook and cultural strivings of the proponents of Haskalah and the adepts of the Hasidic movement. It is quite understandable that when Rabbi Naḥman of Bratzlav returned from Lemberg, where he had opportunity to become acquainted with representatives of Haskalah, he at once told his disciples that this new heresy constituted the gravest peril for the survival of Judaism. The Hasidim regarded the "Berliners" with utmost hostility, and the Berliners, for their part, repaid their opponents in kind. Mendelssohn's teacher Israel Zamosc,[2] who spent his last years in Brody (he died in 1772), already presents in his *Nezed Ha-Dema* this portrait of the Hasidim of Galicia:

Woe to the people with the noise of wings, the proud crown of the drunkards in Ephraim, who in their arrogance ride in the heavens . . . and they speak new things about the God of the gods and know the knowledge of the Most High. . . . They know and understand how to gather the sparks of holiness. . . . And these also have been mistaken through wine and become confused through drinking beer—the priest, the prophet, and the "masters of the name." . . . Every day is a holiday for them, they eat and drink and carouse . . . and I have seen fine people seizing the cupboard and the *rebbe's* food-remnants *(shirayim)* and overturning the platter, and to fill his throat such a one takes a keg of whiskey, and when he is filled to the brim he expounds the lore of the Chariot-Throne. . . . He lifts his eyes to the Holy One

1. See above, pp. 191–192.
2. See our *History*, Vol. VI, pp. 244–45.

of Israel to relate what God does, and roars out from a heap of meat how ten times ten thousand worlds were created with truth and righteousness . . . and seeks the mysteries of the Torah and by brutish acts comprehends Him who is seated on high. . . . My son, go not with them.[3]

In 1790 there appeared in Frankfurt-am-Main an anonymous tract entitled *Maaseh Ta'tu'im*[4] and directed against the Kabbalist of Frankfurt, Nathan Adler, and his disciples, who believed that, as a result of their fervent prayers and fathoming of the mysteries of the *Zohar* and the Kabbalah of Rabbi Isaac Luria, the spirit of prophecy rested on them and they could predict what would happen to a person. These men terrorized people by predicting the day of their approaching death. We have unfortunately not had opportunity to become directly acquainted with this tract and know of it only from the quotations which are given in the review in *Ha-Meassef* (1790, pp. 28–30). Some notion of the style of the anonymous *Maaseh Ta'tu'im* is provided by the following verse in which the Talmudic dictum that since the Temple was destroyed "prophecy was taken away from the prophets and given to fools" is utilized:

From the time the holy Temple was destroyed
Visions ended, knowers of the future ceased,
For the wise of the city perished, the man of spirit
  disappeared;
O, from the time fools multiplied and combined,
Visionaries broke out and visions grew,
For the fool is a prophet, the madman is a man of spirit.[5]

Several years later in 1796 one of the first followers of the Berlin Haskalah in Warsaw, Jacob Calmanson, published a

3. *Nezed Ha-Dema*, 28–29. Graetz, *Geschichte der Juden*, Vol. XI, p. 548) and, after him, Dubnow, *op. cit.*, Vol. I, p. 120, note that Solomon Chelm already issued forth against the followers of the Baal Shem Tov in the introduction to his *Mirkevet Ha-Mishneh*. This, however, does not stand to reason. Since Chelm wrote his introduction in 1750, it is very difficult to believe that already at that time, when the Baal Shem Tov had only a small number of followers in the Ukraine, Rabbi Chelm, who then lived in Zamosc, already had precise knowledge of the movement.
4. The full title is: *Maaseh Ta'tu'im, Yazhir Me-Ḥevrat Anashim Tzevuim Po'alei Aven Maasei Ta'tu'im, Ha-Mitkadeshim Veha-Metaherim Be-Maasim Zarim Ve-Yasimu Eineihem Al Re'eihem Lifetoḥam Be-Imrei Shefer Ke-Chol Ha-Katuv Ba-Sefer.*
5. According to W. Zeitlin (*Kirjath Sepher*, p. 147) the author of *Maaseh Ta'tu'im* was the well-known Wolf Heidenheim (see our *History*, Vol. VIII, pp. 44, 180–81). Heidenheim's biographer Louis Levin denies this emphatically and conjectures that the lampoon was written by Moses Kerner, the author of *Rishfei Keshet* (*MGWJ*, 1932, p. 2).

little book in French, *Essai sur l'etat actuel des juifs de Pologne et leur perfectibilité.* Among the projects of reform which the author proposed to the government, he made a special point about destroying the Hasidic movement. The Hasidim, Calmanson declared, are a band of fanatics, and the dangerous sect must be rooted out.[6]

The Hasidim, on their side, however, were firmly persuaded that the *maskilim* with their "heretical" ideas were extremely pernicious and believed that "this dangerous sect must be deracinated." The greater the Hasidic movement grew in numbers and strength, the more frequently and sharply did its attacks on the enlightening circles become. Those who had formerly been the oppressed became the oppressors. "God preserve me from a persecuted person who has all at once become a persecutor," bitterly exclaims one of the most significant personalities for whom Jewish culture is indebted to for the Haskalah period, Naḥman Krochmal, in his well-known *Iggeret Hitnatzlut,*" on the excommunication with which the Hasidim of Lemberg, led by Rabbi Ornstein, issued forth against the *maskilim* of Galicia.[7]

At the same time the Hasidim also made their first energetic efforts to disseminate their ideas among the masses of the people through the printed word. Among them the question never arose whether one should use the popular language for cultural purposes, whether the "jargon" is contemptible and ugly or not. As an authentic movement of the people, Hasidim addressed the masses in plain Yiddish and employed it not only as a propaganda instrument but as a respected and highly important factor of culture, with the aid of which one can be hallowed and elevated to the loftiest states and degrees.

We have noted that *Sippurei Maasiyyot* by Rabbi Naḥman of Bratzlav and *Shivḥei Ha-Besht* were published in Yiddish in the same year (1815). Both editions enjoyed enormous success. This greatly enraged the small circles of *maskilim* which were formed at that time in Brody, Lemberg, and Tarnopol. Among them developed the determination to battle with the same weaponry, to utilize the popular language in their struggle against the dangerous enemy.

The first effort was made by the aged Mendel Levin who, in his French brochure (see our *History*, Volume VI, p. 276), had already issued forth with extreme hostility against the "new

6. We quote according to Dubnow's *Geshikhte Fun Khasidism,* I, p. 110; II, p. 74.

7. For a discussion of this ban, see the next volume.

sect [the Hasidim] that makes of fanaticism and superstition the chief foundation of religion." Already in that work Levin had indicated that "one must demand of the rabbis that they energetically attack the Hasidic movement with a deluge of writings, for if the Hasidim prevail, there can be no hope of enlightening the Jewish people." But Hasidism, he urged, must also be attacked in the enlightening writings and journals in ironic fashion, making the *tzaddikim* ridiculous and setting forth the comic aspects and clumsy explanations in their mystical writings.[8]

Now, with the rise of popular Hasidic literature, the elderly Levin himself made an attempt to realize his project, to produce a militant satirical Haskalah literature, and composed in Yiddish his *Der Ershter Khosid,* of which Gottlober tells in his memoirs. But the *maskilim* in Galicia were very few in number; hence, out of fear of repression on the part of the Hasidic fanatics, Levin did not publish his work and it was eventually lost. The tract against the Hasidim that Levin wrote in Hebrew, *Maḥkimat Peti,* was also not published, and only in recent years did Israel Weinles discover the manuscript in the Perl archives in the library at Tarnopol. This meritorious explorer of the Perl archives characterizes Levin's anti-Hasidic tract as follows:

The brochure is a tract against the Baal Shem Tov's Hasidim in the form of letters exchanged by a young Italian who came to Poland to a friend of his father's and to his father himself. A correspondence between the Hasidim, Asher Henoch and David Baer, and many others of the sect is also presented. On occasion quotations from *Shivḥei Ha-Besht* and *Likkutei Moharan* are introduced, and the ridiculous features and superstitions appearing in these compositions are disclosed. The great inconsistency between the Baal Shem Tov's new teaching, on the one hand, and the tradition and Talmudic literature, on the other, is especially explored. Naturally not these two works alone are quoted. The whole Hasidic literature, so far as it was known at that time, is arraigned and sharply criticized. The value and origin of the *Zohar* is also discussed. It is also demonstrated (?) that the author and publisher of *Shivḥei Ha-Besht* was a well-known "liar and swindler."[9]

Also unpublished was the tract written in German and entitled *Über das Wesen der Sekte Chassidim aus ihren eigenen Werken*

8. See M. Erik, *Etiudn Tsu Der Geshikhte Fun Der Haskole,* pp. 142–143.
9. *YIVO-Bleter,* Vol. II, p. 349.

gezogen, which was composed shortly after the excommunication directed against the *maskilim* in 1816. This work was circulated only in handwritten copies, and on the basis of such a copy the historian Simon Dubnow acquainted us with the content and character of this forgotten work.[10] The anonymous author notes that even if the Hasidic movement has not yet gained control of the entire Jewish population in Poland, it is, nevertheless, foreseeable that in the course of another fifty years it will spread with epidemic force and all the Polish Jews will be adherents of the "sect." This will certainly cause great injury to the entire people, for the new mystical teaching is completely alien to the spirit of authentic Judaism. The author cannot look on calmly as thousands of his brethren crawl ever more deeply into the swamp of superstition, despite the good intention of the government to "cultivate" and "educate" them. Thereby they arouse still greater hostility in the general populace toward the Jews. He considers himself obliged to disclose the danger inherent in the new mystical teaching, just as a man who sees that a fire has broken out in the night, and a conflagration has begun which may destroy the whole city, must raise the alarm.[11]

Dubnow notes that the material of this handwritten work was utilized by two older Jewish historians, Peter Beer and Marcus Jost,[12] in the chapters of their work in which they discuss Hasidism. Both historians indicate that they wrote on the basis of a manuscript sent to them by the Galician communal leader and writer Joseph Perl of Tarnopol.

It is beyond doubt that this anonymous work was produced in the small circle formed around the wealthy and cultivated Perl.[13] Indeed, Perl was among the first of the *maskilim* who had the courage to issue forth publicly, even if disguised under a pseudonym, with a caustic satire against the Hasidim and their leaders.

Joesph Perl was born into a wealthy merchant family in

10. *YIVO-Bleter*, Vol. I, pp. 4–8.

11. *YIVO-Bleter*, Vol. I, p. 5.

12. Jost indicates in his history of culture (*Kultur-Geschichte*, 1847, p. 80) that he received this manuscript, sent to him by Joseph Perl, in 1828.

13. In the journal *Sion* (1861, p. 301) it is noted that the work was ostensibly composed by a young man whose initials are B.S. of Tarnopol, a good friend of Perl's. Israel Weinles has conjectured (*YIVO-Bleter*, III, pp. 89–90) that under these initials is hidden Basilius Stern. However, this is difficult to believe, because Stern in 1816 was all of eighteen years old. Very likely Stern merely made a copy of the manuscript in Tarnopol and brought it with him to Odessa, but he was not the author.

Tarnopol in November, 1773. He speaks of his education and youth in a German letter of 1812:

Unfortunately there was here no place to obtain a purposeful education. There was no school and no suitable teachers. . . . A great obstacle also was the plan my parents had for my future. When still very young, I was set to work exclusively at Talmudic studies, for my parents desired to make a rabbi of me. And so I had to study German stealthily. In a hidden corner I began to read German books, and very frequently I had to have at hand a Hebrew book, which I would quickly open as soon as I heard my parents approaching and under which I hid the German book.[14]

At the age of fourteen Perl was married off. The young groom was provided with room and board by his in-laws, was an ardent Hasid, went around to *rebbes*, danced with the Hasidim, studied Kabbalah, and listened to miraculous stories about the *tzaddikim* of the time. But, in connection with his father's business affairs, the young Perl had occasion to visit large commercial cities in Austria and Germany and so began to gain familiarity with the broader European world and was infected with the Berlin Haskalah. With all the impetus of youth he undertook his own self-education, and eventually the erstwhile Hasid became an enlightener and battler for culture.

During the years Tarnopol was under Russian control (1809–1816) Perl established a modern model school for Jewish children in his own home. Under the leadership of its energetic and cultured director, the school became extremely popular.[15] Perl also made an interesting attempt to provide the children with a special periodical, and in the period 1814–1816 issued an annual almanac entitled *Tzir Ne'eman* which presented practical information, as well as popular scientific articles and shorter essays on ethics and morality.[16]

Upon the reversion of Tarnopol to Austria, Perl's school attained legal recognition as a middle school under the name "Deutsche-Israelitische Hauptschule." When in 1819 Perl

14. From Joseph Perl's archives in *Historishe Shriftn*, I, pp. 811–812.

15. It suffices to note that the school was opened with thirteen students, but in the year 1819 there were already 118 pupils studying there (*Historishe Shriftn*, I, p. 810), and in 1820 there were 160 students (*Bikkurei Ha-Ittim*, I, 143). Besides the Hebrew Bible, *Mishnah* and *Gemara*, the pupils studied European languages and elementary natural science (see Fuenn, *Safah Le-Ne'emanim*, p. 118: "The young people in this school study religion, the Bible, *Mishnah* and *Gemara*, various languages, and the elements of scientific studies").

16. See *Russian-Jewish Encyclopedia*, Vol. XII, p. 404.

handed the school over to the Jewish community, the government confirmed him as its director for life.[17] Near the school, which was already equipped with its own building, Perl established a Reform synagogue in which he would preach sermons in German on the holy days. The erstwhile Hasid was now the fierce enemy of Hasidism and perceived in it only obscurantist, gross superstition and the most serious threat to science and enlightenment. In Perl we already encounter something that is very characteristic of the *Kulturkampf* which the *maskilim* waged against the Hasidim. Weak and small in numbers, the *maskilim* in their bitter struggle against their most dangerous opponent considered all measures right and proper, not recoiling even from slandering it before the government.

Recently, a sharp denunciation by Perl to the praesidium of the *Kreisamt* or district office in Tarnopol was published (*MGWJ*, 1927, 303–311). Here Perl calls attention to the fact that the *tzaddik* of Zhidachov, Tzevi Hirsch Eichenstein, who at that time enjoyed great popularity, was planning to make a journey to Zbarazh for the Sabbath and that such a visit by this "chief of the pernicious sect of the Hasidim" might injure his school, for Jews from Tarnopol will also go there on the Sabbath and the *rebbe* will carry on his wild propaganda. Perl's denunciation was successful; the next day an order was dispatched to the magistracy of Zbarazh directing it to exercise strict supervision and, when this "false rabbi" *(Irrlehrer)* appears, to send him packing at once.

After the excommunication in Lemberg,[18] from which some of his friends suffered, Perl, aggressive and angry, was no longer content with the fact that, on his initiative, the above-mentioned anti-Hasidic document, *Über das Wesen der Sekte Chassidim*, had been produced. He wished to struggle against the "sect" he so despised with the sharpest weaponry, the lash of satire and mocking laughter. Hence, he wrote his well-known *Megalleh Temirin*, published in Hebrew in 1819 under the pseudonym Obadiah ben Petaḥiah.[19]

Until recent times only the Hebrew text of Perl's satire,

17. For a discussion of the history of Perl's school, see Baer Goldberg's *Ohel Yosef* (Lemberg, 1866).

18. On this, in the next volume.

19. Some scholars of literature have even expressed their doubts whether Joseph Perl was actually the author of *Megalleh Temirin*. Others, again, have conjectured that the renowned satire was composed by Isaac Baer Levinsohn. All of these conjectures, however, have proven groundless after Samson Bloch's and Solomon Rapoport's letters to Joseph Perl, in which it is explicitly noted that Perl is the author of *Megalleh Temirin*, were published in *Zehav Shebah* and in *Michtevei Venei Kedem*.

which was published in Vienna and thereafter twice reprinted, was known. Israel Weinles, however, some years ago made an exciting discovery. In the Perl archives, located in the library at Tarnopol, he found several manuscripts in pure, pithy Yiddish, including a romance in five parts entitled *Antigonos* and a Yiddish version of *Megalleh Temirin.*[20] Indubitably Perl employed as a model for his satire the famous *Epistolae obscurorum virorum* written three hundred years earlier (1515) at the height of the battle between the humanist Johannes von Reuchlin and the well-known apostate and Jew-hater Pfefferkorn, who was supported by the Dominicans and other reactionary elements in his attacks on the Talmud and Judaism. The anonymously published *Epistolae,* ostensibly written by various reactionaries and obscurantists to the chief opponent of the humanist movement Ortuinus Gratius, were produced in the humanist camp. These letters imitate very successfully the style of the contemporary scholastics and obscurantists; they are written in corrupted Latin, mixed with German words. The barbaric style, the outrageously foolish questions which are posed in the letters with such a serious, deeply learned mien, the petty intrigues and ideas of all the correspondents—everything is sharpened for a definite purpose: to cover the opposing side with mockery, to lay bare before the whole world the pettiness, lack of talent, and ignorance of those who battle against the humanists and the new world outlook.

Megalleh Temirin is also composed in the form of letters which some Jewish "obscure men" wrote to one another: the rebbe's *gabbai* Reb Zelig, the Hasid Reb Zanvil, and a pack of other Hasidim. The style of the letters in the Hebrew *Megalleh Temirin* is a parody of the style of *Shivḥei Ha-Besht,* a typical mixture of corrupted Hebrew filled with Yiddishisms and Slavisms. Perl, the bitter opponent of Hasidism and energetic battler for enlightenment, presents in his satire an extremely one-sided caricature of the Hasidim of Volhynia and Galicia, whom he so despised, and of their *rebbes.* All are portrayed in one color—pitch black. The *rebbes* are all avaricious swindlers, and the Baal Shem Tov himself is portrayed by Perl in the following way: "He was a common *baal shem* like others of his like and knew nothing, but he had great arrogance and was a terrible fraud, more than others of his ilk."[21] Nevertheless, the hand of an authentic master is discernible in this satire. Perl

20. This Yiddish text of *Megalleh Temirin* is now being printed for the first time in the library of YIVO, and we have used the galley sheets which YIVO has kindly sent us.
21. *Megalleh Temirin,* p. 122.

manages to create from the packet of letters (151 of them) a unitary, albeit very partial, portrait of the then backward and abnormal life of the Jews. Even the modern reader considers with interest the ludicrous gallery of crude and comical personages with their half-idolatrous world-view, their wild fear of everything transcending their petty understanding, and their profound hatred for the representatives of knowledge and enlightenment.

At the end of *Megalleh Temirin*, after the letters, there is a special biography of a Hasidic *rebbe:* "The Greatness of Rebbe Wolf of Czerny Ostrov" (pp. 221–242). Here Perl writes in his own language, and the language of this Galician *maskil* is vivid and substantive. We present here, as illustration, two quotations:

They have still not grasped the idea that God has nothing else in His world except that the *tzaddikim* should have joy of the spirit; hence, one must give them much money so that they may eat well, drink fine wines, go about in very expensive clothes, and dress their wives and daughters and grandchildren in pearls and diamonds. For whose sake did God create everything good in the world, if not for the sake of the *tzaddikim?* Can one imagine the joy that God together with the *Shechinah* have when the *rebbe* eats a great dinner and when people bring him money from all sides? Poor luckless souls scrape up the bottom of their little bit of poverty and present it as an offering to the *tzaddik* (p. 223).

There are pious souls who would like to approach the *rebbe* but, for lack of money, postpone doing so till later, on the chance that in the meantime God will grant them something. When they see the covered wagon in which the *rebbe* travels standing outside, then they hurry up. One runs to borrow money, a second pawns things, the wife of another steals from her husband. All rush—heavy hearts, those with delicate children, the miscarriage-prone, the sick—all make an effort with whatever power they can summon up, and push themselves in the crowd with their heads to be blessed, at last, wholesale (p. 240).

At the very time that the Galician *maskilim* fought against the Hasidic movement with their tracts written in Yiddish and Hebrew, the Hebrew tract served in Germany as a weapon in the battle which erupted over the question of religious reform.

In previous chapters we noted the powerful assimilationist tendencies in the intellectual circles of German and French Jewry. The slogan that "the Jews are by no means a people but are to be considered only a confession," i.e., that Jews are certainly not a nation but merely a religious group, was set forth. The logic of events, however, demanded a further step. Jews, it was maintained, are distinguished from their fellow-citizens only by their faith. But the faith is tied up with a cult, with various customs and traditions. Hence, the movement of assimilation had to penetrate into the religious realm, for the traditional Jewish cult was incompatible with the life of the contemporary Jew. If in daily life—at home, on the street, at gatherings—Jews behaved like all other citizens, wore the same clothing and spoke the same language, they wished to carry this over into the synagogue: let the Jewish house of prayer become similar to the Protestant church.

Moreover, it must be borne in mind that Judaism includes some highly prominent national elements which literally shocked the Germans "of the Mosaic persuasion." The romantic moods in German literature and society intensified interest in religious matters, and this further aroused in certain Jewish intellectual circles the desire to clothe their religion in forms that would be "best suited to the spirit of the modern world."

We noted[22] that in 1812, after the issuance of the edict granting civic equality to the Jews in Prussia, David Friedländer came forth with a brochure on religious reform among Jews. Even before Friedländer, the wealthy financier Israel Jacobson[23] made some practical attempts at religious reform. After 1801, when Jacobson established in Seesen a model school for children at his own expense, he constructed adjacent to it a chapel in which worship was conducted in a modern, reformed manner. At the dedication of this chapel, the bells in a nearby church were sounded in honor of the festivity.[24] Jacobson, dressed like a Protestant pastor, preached a sermon in German and, to the accompaniment of organ tones, the Protestant hymn "Wie gross ist des Allmächtigen Güte" and the Lutheran "Ein' feste Burg ist unser Gott" were chanted.

When Napoleon, after the peace of Tilsit (1807), established the kingdom of Westphalia and Jacobson was appointed head of the Jewish consistory, the financier at once endeavored to carry through a reform of the synagogues in all of Westphalia.

22. See our *History*, Vol. VIII, p. 117.

23. For precise details about Jacobson, see Graetz, *op. cit.*, Vol. XI; S. Bernfeld, *Toledot Ha-Reformatzyon Ha-Datit*, 1900, I.

24. In this school not only Jewish children but Christian children as well obtained instruction without tuition.

Westphalia, however, fell in 1813, shortly after Napoleon's defeat. Jacobson then left Cassel, the capital of Westphalia, and settled in Berlin, to which he transferred his plans for reform. Together with the banker Jacob Beer, the father of the famous composer Giacomo Meyerbeer, Jacobson opened in Berlin a Reform synagogue with organ, German sermons, and a modernized order of worship. Only part of the prayers were recited by the *ḥazzan*, or precentor, in Hebrew; the rest were in German. The silent *Shemoneh Esreh* was also abolished; to repeat it after the *ḥazzan* was considered sufficient. The Torah was read without cantillation and with the Sephardic pronounciation.

In this Reform synagogue the orthodox perceived a great threat to the preservation of Judaism, and so they sought assistance from the Prussian government. Under the auspices of the Holy Alliance, reaction spread over all of Europe after Napoleon's downfall; kings and princes were fearful of any innovation. The Prussian king Frederick William III was also an opponent of reform. The orthodox members of the Jewish community in Berlin understood how to exploit these moods, and the Reform synagogue was closed for a time. Eduard Kley, who had served as a preacher at the Reform services in Berlin, thereupon moved to Hamburg and propagandized there for a Reform synagogue modeled after that in Berlin. The energetic Israel Jacobson also aided the enterprise. In 1818 a "Reform Tempelverein," which assumed the task of effectuating this project as quickly as possible, was established in Hamburg; in the same year, on the anniversary of the battle of Leipzig (October 18), the Reform temple of Hamburg was opened with great pomp and ceremony. The reformers of Hamburg went further than their colleagues in Berlin. The order of worship was changed to an even greater extent, and the passages in which the hope for the "ingathering of the exiles" is expressed were simply eliminated.[25]

It would be historically unjustified, however, to explain all the changes which the Hamburg reformers introduced into Jewish ritual merely by assimilatory motives and to suggest that their entire undertaking was simply to imitate the Protestant church, to appear to be "like all other people." Some very different motives were also definitely involved here. We have already noted that, under the influence of the romantic cur-

25. The reformed prayerbook of the Hamburg Temple was put together and published by Meir Bresselau and Zekil Frankl. For a discussion of this prayerbook, see S. Bernfeld, *op. cit.*, 247–52.

rents as well as of the reactionary tendencies discernible even in the first years of the era of restoration, interest in religious matters and religious traditions grew in intellectual circles. The old-fashioned customs in the synagogue, the clamor and noise during worship, the arguments over the parcelling out of Torah honors, and the bargaining for the privilege of being summoned to the Torah—all these could hardly impress or attract the Jewish youth which already had a smattering of general culture and, moreover, understood very little of the language in which the prayers and hymns were written.

These young people looked with contempt on the "Asiatic" customs and on the "wild" order or, more correctly, lack of order prevalent in the synagogue. Furthermore, they had occasion to compare all these things with the exemplary order and the solemn, elevated mood prevalent in the Protestant churches during worship. Obviously, this was not the major cause of the fact that Jewish intellectual and pseudo-intellectual youths abandoned the religion of their fathers in droves and became brand new Christians.[26] The founders of the Reform temple—in any case, a considerable segment of them—believed, however, that the new temple would be a bulwark in the face of trouble, that when, as a result of religious reform, worship would be conducted in a modern fashion with organ music and lovely chanting, and gifted orators would present addresses in German setting forth the "light of Judaism," the pure morality of the Jewish religion, the young would desist from forsaking their origins and find it possible to quench their religious thirst in the Reform temple.

Israel Jacobson was delighted with the achievements of the reformers of Hamburg. He realized quite clearly, however, that the orthodox would attempt to represent the Reform synagogue before the Jewish community and before the government as a heretical, sectarian concoction. It was therefore extremely important to obtain betimes "authorization" for the new reforms from several more or less prominent rabbis. Jacobson found the right man to accomplish this in the person of Eliezer ben Ze'ev Wolf Liebermann who had just settled in Berlin.

Liebermann had had a remarkably zigzag career. Born into a rabbinic family in Alsace in the city of Hagenau, he obtained a strictly orthodox education and became quite proficient in Talmudic and rabbinic literature. Later he became familiar with the Berlin Haskalah, acquired a certain amount of Euro-

26. See our *History*, Vol. VIII, pp. 118ff.

pean education, and gained a reputation as a good Hebrew stylist and talented writer. With all this, however, he did not have a secure economic base, was a constant wanderer, had to obtain support from patrons and rich men, and lived in poverty. Eventually he changed his religion, adopted the Catholic faith,[27] became an associate of Pope Pius IX, and played a significant role in the Catholic world. His death was sincerely mourned by the pope and in modern times, in 1910, Liebermann was officially recognized as a "saint" by the Catholic church.* When he was still at the stage of being a wandering *maskil* and hardpressed financially, Liebermann was approached by Jacobson with the proposal that he become an agent of the Reform party. He eagerly agreed and took to his propagandist work with great energy.

Liebermann managed to obtain *haskamot* or approbations from four different rabbis stating that all the changes in worship instituted by the Reform party in Berlin and Hamburg were not at all contrary to Jewish law. To be sure, two of these rabbis, from Livorno (Leghorn) and Verona, were very little known. The other two were Moses ben Menaḥem Kunitz (Kunitzer) of Ofen and Aaron Chorin, chief rabbi of the Hungarian city of Arad. Moses Kunitz had a reputation as a great scholar. His work *Ben Yoḥai*, in which he attempted to show that the *Zohar* was actually composed by the Tanna Rabbi Simeon ben Yoḥai, evoked special interest.[28] Moses Kunitz's *haskamah* was written briefly, but his colleague Aaron Chorin replied to Liebermann's query with a brochure entitled *Kinat Ha-Emet*.

Chorin[29] belonged to the small number of rabbis who at that time agitated, as did Saul Berlin, for enlightenment and reforming the Jewish way of life. To be sure, he was more sincere than Berlin, but less gifted. His knowledge of general science was quite limited.[30] Moreover, he lacked character, being ag-

27. It must be noted in this connection that even after he left the Jewish faith, he did not turn away from his native brethren and would constantly intercede for the Jewish people as much as possible. Unfortunately, the Jewish sources lack further biographical details which might illuminate psychologically the remarkable life-stages of this highly interesting personality.

*I have not been able to discover any confirmation of this statement.—Trans.

28. For a discussion of Kunitz's life and work, see R. Fahn's article, "Le-Toledot Ha-Rav Mosheh Kunitz" in *Reshumot*, IV.

29. Born in Weiskirchen (Moravia) in 1766; died in Arad (Hungary) in 1844.

30. Chorin frequently likes to make use of arguments from the natural sciences, but how little competence he had in this realm can be seen in his *Emek Ha-Shaveh* where he notes (folio 11b) that glowing iron is heavier than cold, or where he speaks about the origin of comets (*ibid.*, folio 54) and of thunder (*ibid.*, folio 89a).

gressive but without the requisite courage.[31] It was also his fate to live in a backward, strictly orthodox environment in which every step of his provoked strong opposition and persecution for "heresy." As early as 1798 a controversy had broken out around him because of the fact that he had been lenient on the question whether eating sturgeon (in Russian, *asyotr*) is ritually permitted and had defended his point of view in two tractates entitled *Imrei Noam* and *Siryon Kashkeshet.*[32]

Chorin was persecuted even more intensely for his work *Emek Ha-Shaveh* which he composed in 1802 and published in Prague in 1803. In the first section, entitled *Rosh Amanah,* the author deals with the fundamental principles of the Mosaic Torah, following the order in which they had been formulated by Maimonides in his Thirteen Articles of Faith. Chorin is a weak stylist and even more deficient in structure. His thoughts are drowned in a sea of words and extraneous theories that have very slight relationship to the issue at hand. Moreover, the ideas that he expresses are not especially novel.[33] Chorin frequently repeats, for instance, the old, familiar idea that "the Torah and science are interwoven" (*ibid.*, p. 11), and also reiterates, in a diffuse and not altogether clear fashion, the thesis of Maimonides that only the man who has steeped himself both in the "revealed sciences," i.e., in the "nature of existence," and in the science of the Torah can attain the level of prophecy.[34] We also encounter in him the familiar thesis concerning the universal mission of the Jewish people, that God intended to create out of Israel a "kingdom of priests" which is destined to be a "light of the peoples," a tower of illumination and guide for all humanity, "to purify all . . . the whole human species."[35] Also interesting and not altogether new is Chorin's idea, discussed at length in the third part, *Dirat Aharon,* that the interpretations of the Torah were not codified and remained in oral form so that the sages and legislators of each generation might have opportunity to institute the ordinances which their time and circumstances require.[36]

31. A larger work about Chorin, written in a panegyric tone, was published by Leopold Loew in his journal *Ben Chananja* (1862–1863); reprinted in Loew's *Gesammelte Schriften,* II, pp. 251–420. See also M. Jost, *Kultur-Geschichte,* 1847, pp. 71–74.

32. On this, see Chorin's report in *Kerem Ḥemed,* II, pp. 97–98.

33. The influence of Schnaber's *Yesod Ha-Torah* (see our *History,* Vol. VIII, pp. 34–37) is felt especially strongly.

34. *Ibid.*, folio 30b.

35. *Ibid.*, 33–34.

36. *Ibid.*, folio 65: "For if the Torah and its interpretation had been given entirely in

Moses Kunitz provided a poem of praise for Chorin's *Emek Ha-Shaveh* in which he assures the author:

You will enlighten the eyes of the Hebrews, to deliver them from corruption;
Every mouth will praise you and every tongue tell your glory.

In fact *Emek Ha-Shaveh* was "praised" only by a few *maskilim*, such as Solomon Jehudah Rapoport and others.[37] In the orthodox camp, on the other hand, a great storm erupted over the work. *Emek Ha-Shaveh* (Vale of the Plain) was declared *Emek Ikkur* (Vale of Pollution), which ought to be destroyed by fire.[38] In Chorin's own community a controversy began. His opponents cast stones at him, and Chorin finally issued a written statement to the effect that he recanted the ideas expressed in *Emek Ha-Shaveh.*[39] The intimidated author was silenced for a rather long time, but the emissary of the Reform party, Eliezer Liebermann, aroused him from his silence. The enlightenment-minded rabbi again acquired a desire for battle and sent Liebermann his composition *Kinat Ha-Emet,* in which he attempts to show, with numerous quotations from the Talmud and rabbinic codes, that the new order of prayer which the reformers of Berlin had instituted is fully consonant with Jewish law and custom.

Liebermann published all four of the rabbinic responsa in a special work entitled *Nogah Ha-Tzedek* (Dessau, 1818). However, he was not content with this and, along with *Nogah Ha-Tzedek,* published his own work entitled *Or Nogah,* consisting of two parts. In the first he discusses the complaints of the orthodox against the innovations which the reformers had introduced in the synagogue. It is not difficult for him to show, through numerous citations from the old Hebrew literature, that "all the codes permit prayer in any language" and that many prominent authorities even noted that one who does not understand Hebrew is advised to pray in the language he does

---

writing, the sages in every generation would have been prevented from innovating anything . . . and there would not be place at any time for the sages of the generation to ordain fences according to the requirement of the generation and the age." Here also the influences of Schnaber's *Yesod Ha-Torah* is discernible.

37. *Ben Chananja,* 1863, p. 38.

38. *Kerem Ḥemed,* II, p. 98.

39. *Ibid.*, p. 104.

understand. In this connection, the following point is interesting. Liebermann, who was not at all chary of quotations, never refers to the old Judeo-German, or Yiddish, literature in which the question of prayer in the vernacular is so frequently discussed.[40] Aside from the contempt with which the *maskilim* generally regarded this literature, another motive was at work here.

Like Aaron Wolfsohn-Halle in his day,[41] Liebermann intended to show not merely that one ought to pray in a comprehensible language; the chief thing for him is that the comprehensible language must absolutely be an honored language, grammatically pure and elegant in literary form. Indeed, he explicitly notes that everything he says about "the subject of prayer" and his proof of the permissibility of prayer in *Lashon Ashkenazit* (German) is in regard to the majority of the German Jews, who are accustomed from childhood on to speak clean, elegant German. The situation is different, however, among the Jews in other lands, for instance, the "people of Poland and their like." They also speak *Lashon Ashkenazit*, but among them the German language is corrupted and full of errors; they cannot speak pure German. On the other hand, they are far more proficient in Hebrew than the German Jews. Hence, it is preferable that these Polish Jews retain the custom of their ancestors and pray in the pure and seven times refined Hebrew language, not in their ignorant and corrupted German speech.[42]

Liebermann's love for the language of the Bible, however, impels him also to admonish German Jewry that some prayers ought to be recited in the synagogue in Hebrew even among the reformers and modern Jews, and this for the following reason:

First of all, there are in our liturgy such sacred and noble prayers as, for example, the *Shema* and others, which it is more fitting to recite in the language we have inherited from our ancestors. And if someone raises the question, How can I require of my son that he recite any prayer in Hebrew when he has no understanding whatever of this language?, I answer such a person with astonishment: Why do you not teach your children Hebrew, the oldest of all tongues? After all, you spend a large fortune in giving your children an education; you teach them all kinds of sciences and various languages. Why,

40. See our *History*, Vol. VII, pp. 23ff., 33ff., 218ff.
41. See our *History*, Vol. VIII, pp. 80ff., 93ff., 100ff.
42. *Or Nogah*, I, 9.

then, do you neglect our precious language, the legacy of our fathers?"[43]

Of significantly broader scope is the second part of *Or Nogah.* Here Liebermann is no longer content to deal merely with the matter of synagogue reform. He poses the question of altering the whole abnormal way of life among Jews. In this respect he may be considered a predecessor of Isaac Baer Levinsohn and other battlers for *Haskalah.* During his years of wandering among various Jewish centers,[44] Liebermann had opportunity to become well acquainted with the abnormal life of the Jewish community, especially in those places where they lived in compact masses. It is with this painful problem that he attempts to deal in the second part of his work.

With genuine publicistic talent he portrays in clear and incisive language the spiritual and intellectual decay he observed in Jewish life: on the one side, those who "grope in the darkness," cling stubbornly and without criticism and understanding to the old and obsolete, decline to recognize any of the new demands of life, refuse to understand that life cannot remain static and congealed in one place; and on the other side, the "seductive luminaries" and enlighteners who reject everything, speak disparagingly and contemptuously of the Talmud and the ancient sages, and adopt an attitude of hostility and scorn toward, and uncritically despise, everything that belongs to the past, that bears the stamp of the fathers' legacy, that smacks of faith and tradition.[45]

Like all the *maskilim,* Liebermann attacks the old-fashioned method of education. What, he asks, does the ordinary man among us know of the Jewish religion, of Jewish morality? He was brought up like a wild man, without knowledge, without faith, without moral instruction. Whence should he have obtained such knowledge, and from whom learned it? From the rabbi with his hairsplitting lectures, which the common man cannot even begin to grasp? When he comes into the synagogue this man's lips move, but he does not understand what he is saying.[46] Like a typical *maskil,* Liebermann confuses historical events with their effects and asserts that the fearful persecutions which Jews suffered in the Middle Ages derived from the

43. *Ibid.,* 23–24.
44. Liebermann himself notes that he spent a rather long time in such centers as Prague and Lemberg (*Or Nogah,* I, 17, 21).
45. *Ibid.,* II, 7–8, 13–15.
46. *Ibid.,* II, 25.

fact that they were unenlightened and superstitious. Can we, he exclaims emotively, forget the blood of our people that was shed like water in former generations? But who and what caused this misfortune? Only our own foolishness, our barbaric behavior, our bizarre customs which were so alien and conspicuous among the neighboring peoples. These are what brought us to all these troubles. If our sages and leaders had been genuine guardians of the people and preserved them from all the stumbling blocks and snares, if they had led the Jewish community with understanding according to the demands of the time and taught them how one must fulfill his service of the Creator—to love the king, to seek the welfare and happiness of their neighbors, to serve the fatherland loyally, to study "every wisdom and science, language and morality"—, would we have come to these misfortunes?[47]

Later, in the 1860's, the poets J. L. Gordon and Mikhel Gordon feelingly aroused their people: "Awake, my people, arise from your slumber, be not led astray in follies!" But more than forty years earlier Liebermann expostulated with his people in virtually the same terms:

> My brethren, my heart can find no consolation when I see how low our people has fallen! Open your eyes and look about. Observe how all the peoples strive toward the wells of knowledge, are highly successful and attain their goal, but we remain veiled in darkness, steeped in foolish fantasies, in heavy clouds of madness . . . While in the world about us culture blooms and the obscurantism and superstition of former times is dispersed and driven away, the flower of knowledge and science has still not blossomed among our people. The dark clouds in which we wander lost are still not chased away. How long, my people, shall we not understand that until now we have dwelt in darkness, been cradled in the sleep of indolence, dreamed in the lap of impracticality, void of all knowledge and science, understanding and proper conduct of life? Everything associated with common sense is repugnant to us. Every artisanry is despised by us. Darkness among us is declared light, and light darkness.[48]

As Isaac Baer Levinsohn did several years later in his *Te'udah Be-Yisrael,* Liebermann also endeavors to demonstrate with numerous quotations from Talmudic literature that every Israelite is obliged "to know and understand and search as far as the

47. *Ibid.*, 30.
48. *Ibid.*, 30–31.

power of the mind reaches," and that in ancient times, in the age of the Talmud and also in later generations, the scholars of Israel were rich in knowledge, proficient in the "external wisdoms," i.e., the natural sciences, and familiar with the languages of the neighboring peoples and cultures, for such knowledge is essential both for the requirements of practical life and for the elucidation of religious problems and the fulfillment of the commandments concerning service of the Creator.[49]

Or Nogah, with its beautiful, emotive style and numerous quotations from the Talmud and rabbinic codes, made a definite impression. The Reform party gained adherents, and the number of worshippers in the Reform temple grew. Naturally, the orthodox could not look on calmly at this development. As soon as Liebermann's double work appeared, a certain Naḥman ben Simḥah Berlin of Lissa ventured to issue forth with a thick counter-document entitled *Et Le-Dabber*. Since, however, he deemed it necessary to warn the public as quickly as possible "of the poison hidden in Liebermann's work" he issued in the meantime, on the spur of the moment (in 1818), a pamphlet entitled *Kaddur Katan*, which was supposed to serve as an introduction to his *Et Le-Dabber*. To provide some notion of the tone in which the pamphlet is written, it suffices to quote the following passage:

> What will the nations of the world say when they learn that among us there are persons who summon us to revolution and preach that we ought to rebel against the religious commandments and precepts? They will certainly think: Now you revolt against your own religion; soon you will also rebel against the orders of the government... Now you have the presumption to cast off the customs of your ancestors; soon your arrogance will grow to the point that you will also persuade people of other religions to cast off the yoke of their religion. In this, as is known, lies a great threat to civilized mankind.[50]

The author of *Kaddur Katan* is certain that as soon as the rabbis and scholars become familiar with *Or Nogah*, they will realize that the work deserves to be burned and that the author ought to be excommunicated "wherever he is" (*ibid.*, p. 5).

Et Le-Dabber, which appeared in 1819, is written in such boring and talentless fashion that it is not worth dwelling on. A certain interest pertains only to those pages in which Naḥ-

49. *Ibid.*, 30–31.
50. *Kaddur Katan*, 6–7.

man ben Simhah, himself from Berlin, describes the conduct of the wealthy Berlin Jews of the previous generation and the changes that later took place in these circles through the guilt of the "seducers and enticers to sin" who appeared in the Jewish quarter.[51]

Naḥman Berlin deplores the fact that the rabbis are silent and do not issue forth against the "seducers." The rabbis, however, were on guard. Shortly after the appearance of Liebermann's work, the *bet din*, or rabbinic court, of Hamburg issued a proclamation to the leaders of the day, the eminent rabbis of various European countries, summoning them to come forward against the "new sect," the "seducers and enticers" who had built a special "temple" with an organ, make alterations in the order of the prayers, sing German hymns during the service, turn about customs insituted from ancient times, etc. In this connection they also noted the four rabbis who, with their responsa, support the new sect, and also pointed to Liebermann's *Or Nogah.*

The contemporary leaders were astonished at this phenomenon. Their wrath at the heretical Rabbi Aaron Chorin was intense. It appears that severe measures were once more taken against him, as was the case after the appearance of his *Emek Ha-Shaveh*, and Chorin, for his part, demonstrated again how little suited he was for the battler's role. He, who was not content with the responsum *Kinat Ha-Emet* but also supplied two poems of praise for Liebermann's *Or Nogah* in which he celebrates "the light of knowledge" which "his beloved friend Eliezer" spreads, promptly changed his mind and declared that all his words in *Kinat Ha-Emet* are "null and void."[52] This, however, did not prevent him a year later, as soon as circumstances had changed and the fear of new persecutions diminished, from coming forth with a brochure entitled *Davar Be-Itto* in which he again defends the very premises which he had just recanted and declared null and void.[53]

More than thirty-five rabbis from Germany, Poland, Bohemia, Moravia, Hungary, Italy, Alsace, and Holland responded to the summons of the rabbis of Hamburg and sent in their responsa, which were promptly published in a special

51. *Et Le-Dabber*, 64–66.
52. *Eleh Divrei Ha-Berit*, 98, 131.
53. See also his attack against the "rabbis in this generation" who are "in error and make others to err" and "degrade the honor of the religion" (*Kerem Ḥemed*, II, pp. 105–108).

collection entitled *Eleh Divrei Ha-Berit.*[54] At the end of the volume the essence of the responsa is given in German translation.[55]

Several of these responsa are signed by truly great scholars, the foremost rabbis of that era, such as Akiva Eger, his son-in-law Moses Sofer, Mordecai Banet, and others. On reading *Eleh Divrei Ha-Berit* with its clumsy, stammering style,[56] its arid *pilpul* and clever subtleties, one is forcibly reminded of Heine's bitter complaint concerning the Jewish guardians: "How badly defended Israel is!" When Jacobson attempted to institute Reform synagogues with organs and worship in the German language in Westphalia, there was an orthodox rabbi named Samuel Eger who had the understanding to put forward a national reason for his opposition to Reform, namely, that Hebrew is the bond of union which holds the scattered members of the exiled people together[57] and that the reformers wish to destroy this bond. But among the rabbis who appear

54. The full title (in translation): "These are the words of the covenant for Jacob, an ordinance for Israel, an eternal covenant. God spoke one thing, and He will never change His religion. According to the Torah and the verdict which proceeded from the mouth of the righteous rabbinic court of the holy community of Hamburg, may the Lord protect it. And their hands were strengthened by the great scholars in the lands of Germany, Poland, France, Italy, Bohemia, Moravia and Hungary. All of them answer as one and say: With a decree of guardian angels was it decided and with a statement of the saints was it requested to annul the new religion (which some ignorant individuals who are not men of Torah have fabricated) to establish customs that are not according to Moses and Israel. Therefore the pious and holy scholars and distinguished rabbis arose to 'fix a tent-pin in a secure place.' They found a wide-open valley and erected a fence around it to proclaim a prohibition against the three transgressions which were sinned mortally. And these are the following: (1) it is forbidden to change the order of worship that is customary in Israel from the Morning Benediction *(Birkhat Ha-Shaḥar)* until after "Aleinu Le-Shabe'aḥ" and even more so to diminish from it; (2) it is forbidden to pray the [statutory] order of worship in any language save the holy tongue, and every prayerbook that is printed improperly and not according to our custom is invalid and it is forbidden to pray from it; (3) it is prohibited to play any musical instrument in the synagogue on the Sabbath and on the festivals even through non-Jews. Altona, 1819."

55. The German translation was provided by the poet Shalom Cohen (see *Berit Emet*, p. 43; Graetz, *op. cit.*, p. 386).

56. Some of the verdicts, e.g., the long letter sent by the rabbis of Padua (*Eleh Divrei Ha-Berit*, pp. 46–51) are written in such a confused language that in places it is difficult to grasp the meaning.

57. Eger's letter to Jacobson: "My master asks his servant why people complain in our city about the singing and praying in the German language in the boys' school the consistory established . . . Behold, all Israel are brethren, comrades everywhere their foot treads, through a single language and identical words, and these fashion bonds of love which bind them together" (we quote according to W. Auerbach's *Geschichte der israelitischen Gemeinde Halberstadt*, pp. 219–221.

with such great wrath and clamor in *Eleh Divrei Ha-Berit* the most important and persuasive reason is: This has been the custom; it is forbidden to change it! "The custom of Israel is Torah," declare the rabbinic court of Hamburg on the one hand, and the president of the rabbinic court of Hanau, on the other.[58] Rabbis from various lands and countries all argue unanimously: "It is forbidden to change any fixed custom;" "It is completely forbidden to alter anything of the customs of our fathers;" "God forbid that we change anything;" "It is a tradition of the fathers and there is no power to alter it." The substance of their argument is always the same: We may not change, we may not diminish even "by a hair's breadth."[59]

The great scholar of the age, Akiva Eger, notes that it is a firmly established principle "not to alter any of the customs instituted and ordained for us by our ancestors throughout the generations, from Moses our teacher, peace be upon him."[60] Akiva Eger's son-in-law Moses Sofer asserts, for his part, "It is not permitted for us to fabricate and permit what our fathers and our father's fathers prohibited."[61] In this connection, he embarks on a long, pilpulistic discussion to show, through ingenious subtleties, that in our generation no rabbinic court is conceivable that would be "greater than earlier rabbinic authorities in wisdom and number" and thereby be competent to nullify a custom which a court of a previous generation had instituted.[62] Who does not know, ask the rabbis of Livorno in astonishment, that the author of *Bayyit Ḥadash* tells of two great scholars who were punished "because they abolished the recitation of *piyyutim* (supplementary liturgical poems) in their community?"[63] How can it occur to anyone, the president of the rabbinic court of Triesch, Rabbi Eliezer, exclaims in amazement, to change even one letter of the order of worship that our prophets, elders, and sages established?[64]

No less artificial and ingenious is the verdict which the rabbis and scholars issue on the question whether it is permissible to pray not in Hebrew alone but in another language. The rabbis naturally know quite well that the Mishnah explicitly teaches that the recitation of the *Shema*, the *Tefillah*, and *Birchat*

58. *Eleh Divrei Ha-Berit*, I, p. 70.
59. *Ibid.*, pp. 3, 23, 25, 47, 48, 76ff.
60. *Ibid.*, p. 27.
61. *Ibid.*, p. 32.
62. *Ibid.*, p. 8.
63. *Ibid.*, p. 66.
64. *Ibid.*, p. 89.

Ha-Mazon (grace after meals) may be recited in any language. They are also aware that many medieval authorities ruled that those who do not understand Hebrew ought to pray in the language which they do understand.

Nevertheless, Rabbis Akiva Eger, Moses Sofer, Abraham Tiktin, and others[65] endeavor to prove that congregational prayer "in a language not the holy language" is "impossible under any circumstances," and for this reason: in every word, in every letter of the prayers, countless tremendous mysteries, "great and fearful things," are hidden; and how can these mysteries and *kavvanot* or intentions be transferred to another language, when we do not know what hidden intentions there are in them? If, however, we recite the prayers exactly as the Men of the Great Synagogue ordained them, even though we do not know their hidden intentions, "our prayer is accepted—which is not the case when we pray in another language." Even prayers, for the rabbis of *Eleh Divrei Ha-Berit,* are included not among the "duties of the heart" but among the "duties that are commanded" which must be fulfilled simply because it has been so ordained.[66]

The question of playing the organ in the synagogue is resolved by the scholars in no less ingenious fashion. Mordecai Banet puts forth many keen subtleties to prove that in playing the organ on the Sabbath day there is a suspicion of *shevut de-shevut* and arrives at the conclusion that "in any case, we see that it is utterly forbidden even for a non-Jew to play the organ on the Sabbath." The rabbi of Amsterdam, for his part, shows that since the Temple was destroyed, no instrument may be played, "since you may not rejoice jubilantly like the nations."[67] Other scholars raise the question: How shall we come before the King of the universe with instruments and rejoicing when we know how sinful we are? "Let the sinner not glory, let the sinner not glory."[68]

All these proofs and arguments are spiced by the rabbis, in order to give them greater effect, with outrageous insults and epithets. The reformers are described in such terms as "the criminals of the generation": "they are neither Jews nor Christians"; "they are deniers of the root principles of the faith"; "the house of the wicked will be destroyed and the arms of the

65. *Ibid.*, pp. 10, 11, 25, 27, 49, 66.
66. *Ibid.*, p. 15–16.
67. *Ibid.*, p. 61.
68. *Ibid.*, p. 78–79.

wicked will be broken"; "vile men have gone forth"; "the fool hath said in his heart, 'There is no God' "; "sinful men"; "let the lips of falsehood be made dumb"; "a congregation of evildoers"; "the brutish among the people"; "these are fools"; "a mixed multitude"; "a staff of wickedness"; "the sinners and rebels"; "an assembly of deceivers"; "a breed of wicked men"; "a seed of evil-doers, children who deal corruptly"; "rash and foolish persons"; "impudent fellows"; "misleaders and seducers"; "abominable persons who spoil the vineyard of the Lord of Hosts"; "men of wickedness"; "doers of abomination"; "fools void of the fear of sin"; "the little foxes that spoil the vineyard of the Lord"; "tricksters"; "an evil band"; "fools"; etc.[69] *Nogah Tzedek* is for them a "blemished book," an "evil darkness" that was produced "to entice and seduce."

Some of the rabbis, however, are not satisfied with this. They believe that it is a duty to denounce such wicked men to the *nachalstvo*, or government authorities, just as the Mitnagdim in their battle against the Hasidim had wished to exploit the fear of "new sects" on the part of the czar Paul I.[70] Now twenty years later the rabbis wished to exploit the reactionary tendencies which the Holy Alliance, led by Alexander I, spread over Europe. The rabbi of Triesch, Rabbi Eliezer, counsels the *bet din* of Hamburg:

> Go to the court of the nobles, and request them to strengthen weakened hands and not support the perpetrators of wickedness. Let not the house of Israel be split by a new sect, for all the kings of the earth are now extremely punctilious about this. We have heard that the officials of the city of Hamburg are men of right and justice. Therefore let understanding and God-fearing persons be selected and let them come to the officials with weeping, and the house of the wicked will be destroyed and their arms will be broken.[71]

The president of the rabbinic court of Trieste, Abraham Eliezer Halevi, also notes that the rabbis and scholars who occupy the rabbinic chair and have occasion "to stand in the court of the government" must not allow any schism and must pursue and persecute these wicked men "to destruction."[72]

Especially characteristic in this respect is the rabbi of Lissa. He develops further the idea expressed by his townsman, the

69. *Ibid.*, pp. 17, 22, 24, 26, 30, 48, 52, 53, 58, 59, 61, 64, 83, 85.
70. See above, pp. 104ff.
71. *Eleh Divrei Ha-Berit*, pp. 23–24.
72. *Ibid.*, 80.

author of *Et Le-Dabber*,[73] and endeavors to show that those who adhere to the Reform party are not only utterly heretical and wicked but also rebels against the government. He, the pious rabbi, assumes the role of the ardent patriot and declares that just as we believe with perfect faith that the Holy One Blessed be He is the ruler of the world, so we also believe "that the king and the government are chosen by God to act for Him." After all, we know, he points out in his responsum, that the rulers of every land are very solicitous that all men "*be bound up in the chains of their religion and faith and not be divided into separate sects,* so that everyone does what he pleases. King Solomon wrote: 'Fear thou the Lord and the king, my son, and do not meddle with those who are given to change.' This means: *You must not associate with those who wish to make changes and to turn away from our fathers, for thereby you will lose reverence both for God and for the king.*" From this we see very clearly, the pious rabbi concludes, that "*the changing of the order of of prayers is a bitter poison and, like a serpent, attempts to destroy religion, the order of the state, and the existence of the world*" (underscoring by the rabbi of Lissa).[74]

Eleh Divrei Ha-Berit did not enrage the Reform party alone; in certain orthodox circles the bitterly hostile tone in which the pietistic, traditionalist rabbis issued forth against the Reform synagogues provoked definite displeasure. Even before *Eleh Divrei Ha-Berit* appeared, the orthodox and very distinguished scholar of Hamburg, Eliezer Riesser,[75] came forth (in December, 1818) with his *Sendschreiben an meine Glaubensgenossen in Hamburg, oder eine Abhandlung über den israelitischen Kultus,* in which he castigates the Hamburg *bet din* and its associates because they wish to provoke a schism in the Jewish community and portray the Reform party as sinners in Israel and heretics denying the root principles of Judaism.

Eleh Divrei Ha-Berit, which appeared shortly afterwards, was promptly attacked by the Reform faction in two counter documents, *Berit Emet* and *Ḥerev Nokemet Nekam Berit. Berit Emet* appeared under the pseudonym *Emet Avida Aḥizedek,* and the place of publication was also deliberately given incorrectly.[76] The author of the work was a teacher from Posen, David Caro,

73. See above, pp. 252–53.

74. Shortly after *Eleh Divrei Ha-Berit* there appeared against the Reform party Abraham bar Aryeh Leib Loewenstamm's *Tzeror Ha-Ḥayyim* (1820), in which the complaints that were already expressed in *Eleh Divrei Ha-Berit* are merely rehearsed.

75. Eliezer was the son-in-law of the well-known Rabbi of Hamburg, Raphael Kohen.

76. On the title-page is noted Constantine. However, the work was printed in Dessau.

who made his literary debut with a long article in *Ha-Meassef* (1810–1811) on the education of children, entitled "Giddul Banim."

Berit Emet consists of two parts: *Berit Elohim* and *Berit Ha-Kehunah* (or *Techunat Ha-Rabbanim*).[77] The first part is of slight interest. The author carries on a polemic against the rabbis of *Eleh Divrei Ha-Berit* and their responsa and discloses the errors and incorrect premises stated in each responsum. Caro himself notes in the introduction that the second part is the more important. This section has, indeed, a definite cultural-historical interest. It is the first harbinger, after Wolfsohn's *Siḥah Be-Eretz Ha-Ḥayyim*, of the *Kulturkampf* which the *maskilim* undertook in neo-Hebrew literature against the rabbis. *Techunat Ha-Rabbanim* (The Traits of the Rabbis) is the title of this second part, which discusses what the rabbis once were, what they are now, and what they ought to be.

To be a leader and educator of the community, the rabbi, in Caro's view, must fulfill seven conditions, of which the most important are the following: (1) He must be a morally clean person. (2) He must penetrate thoroughly into the spirit of Judaism, not considering something of secondary importance as a major principle and regarding a major principle as secondary. (3) He must be proficient in the sciences and have command of the language of the nation in which he lives. (4) He must preach to the people, educate them, familiarize them in clear and simple language with the basic moral principles of the Torah, explain to them how children should be raised, and call attention to the fact that every father ought to take care that, if his son be not suited for the sciences, he teach him a trade or accustom him to agriculture, which is the most important and useful of all occupations.[78] The rabbi is obliged to preach to his congregation love of mankind in general (tolerance and humanitarianism, the author explains), the idea that every man ought to love all others without distinction of nationality or religion. He must further seek to implant patrio-

77. The historian Heinrich Graetz and the bibliographer William Zeitlin indicate that the second part was composed not by David Caro but by Jehudah Miesis. This, however, is in complete contradiction with David Caro's own statement in *Allgemeine Zeitung des Judenthums*, 1837, p. 370, where he notes that he is also the author of *Techunat Ha-Rabbanim*. Testimony to this is also provided by several thoughts and opinions from *Giddul Banim* that are repeated in *Techunat Rabbanim*. The wealthy Jehudah Leib Miesis merely printed Caro's work at his expense and added a whole series of notes whose purpose it was to sharpen the attacks against the rabbis.

78. The author further speaks especially of the importance of agriculture, pp. 126–128.

tism and love of the fatherland. Finally, (5) he must take account of the requirements of the time and circumstances and adapt the conduct of his people to the cultural situation of the land. He must understand that the stale atmosphere which presses over the heads of his community must be ventilated and cleansed of accumulated spider webs.

In former generations, the author asserts, the leaders of the community fulfilled all these conditions. In our time, however, foolishness and barbarism are so widespread that people elect a rabbi before making inquiries whether he is suited, in knowledge and moral qualities, for this responsible position. Nowadays a man comes forward and, as long as he can chirp in Talmud and halachic codes, he is at once handed the rabbinic staff. Are such rabbis, who have no notion either of science or of culture and proper conduct, the leaders of the house of Israel? The guides of former generations, the sages of the Talmud, were at the pinnacle of contemporary culture and science, but we in our times have as leaders men who are devoid of all knowledge and despise science. Every book in a foreign language is, for them, a *sefer pasul*, a forbidden book, and everything written in it is pure heresy. Their own language is a bastard language, without mother or father, a mixture of the languages spoken in the lands where our grandfathers sojourned, a corrupted, poverty-stricken, mutilated language.[79]

The sages of the Talmud, Caro asserts, took account of the requirements of the time; they instituted new ordinances according to the needs of the day and, in this connection, would even occasionally nullify "what is written in the Torah." And now? Now there is no people or language that is so overladen with customs, laws, and rules as we presently are. From the moment a man opens his eyes in the morning to the time he lies down to sleep at night he has to fulfill heaps upon heaps of customs and laws. Every movement of the most insignificant limb is bound up with all kinds of prohibitions and restrictions, and all these are based on the dictum that "blessing will come on the strict constructionist of the law."

Typical is the reply which the enlightened David Caro gives at the end to the question: What shall we do? The author believes that, aside from radically reforming the education of

79. The author speaks with no less contempt about the Old-Yiddish morality literature with "which the rational soul is disgusted," meaning such works as *Tze'enah U-Re'enah* and *Kav Ha-Yashar*.

children, the following must first of all be done. The understanding and cultured persons of every country must convene and come to the king with this request: We are your servants, along with the other inhabitants of the land. We participate equally in the economy of the kingdom. We pay taxes willingly and are wholeheartedly devoted to the land. Grant, then, that we also be equal to all other citizens in the following respect: Let an assembly of persons who are recognized for their knowledge of Judaism and for their love of righteousness and justice be appointed, and let them be authorized to supervise all Jewish affairs, to decide what must be corrected and what nullified. Let them also have the right to appoint a rabbi in every community. Let the Jewish congregation no longer be like sheep without a shepherd. Then the fetters of barbarism and ignorance will fall away from us and we also, your people Israel, will become competent, useful citizens, like all the other inhabitants of your land.[80]

In a word, all power over the community should be given to the enlightened and educated and these, the enlightened men, shall be the "shepherds of Israel," the watchers and guardians of the people, instead of the rabbis.

David Caro lived far from the seat of battle, but even before his *Berit Emet* appeared in print, in Hamburg itself one of the chief leaders of the Reform party issued forth against the orthodox contributors to *Eleh Divrei Ha-Berit.* This was Meir Israel Bresselau, whose *Ḥerev Nokemet Nekam Berit*[81] is one of the sharpest as well as most brilliant tracts in neo-Hebrew literature.[82]

It was not only the aggressive tone of the orthodox rabbis, their malicious, undeserved attacks, and crude invective, that offended and enraged Meir Bresselau. The "shepherds of Israel" aroused his wrath with their clumsy arguments, their arid hair-splitting, their childish ideas. Unconsciously and instinctively there cried out from him woe for the wretched,

80. *Berit Emet,* 142.

81. The tract appeared anonymously and the place of printing is also not indicated. Only the date 5579 is noted. We have employed the first edition. S. Bernfeld reprinted the work in the supplements to his *Toledot Ha-Reformatzyon.*

82. On the basis of a certain passage in the counter-document *Lahat Ha-Ḥerev Ha-Mithappechet* one may perhaps conjecture that the reformers also issued illustrated caricatures of the orthodox rabbis. For there (p. 5) it is noted: "Did you consider this, too, has wisdom: to produce seal engravings with a pen of iron and lead for the purpose of strife and contention, shaming and degrading the great luminaries, men of renown and models of our generation, the chief shepherds, the chariot of Israel and its riders?"

defenseless situation of the people which at such an important moment, in such a historic crisis, had leaders and representatives like these. He considers it superfluous to carry on debates with them, to demonstrate how unjustified and backward they are. No, in Bresselau's view they must be set forth naked and bare in their whole outmodedness and isolation from the world. Not with logical arguments but with the whip of satire, the sharp arrows of ridicule and laughter, must one issue forth and do battle against them. And Bresselau is not only a fighter by nature but also a remarkable stylist, a master of the language of the Bible. Every phrase in *Ḥerev Nokemet* is filled with venom, every line a sharply pointed arrow hurled with hatred and indignation at the "worthless shepherds," at the "dry bones," whose "love and enmity and zeal are already lost, and who have no more share in the world."

The members of the *bet din* of Hamburg had announced at the end of *Eleh Divrei Ha-Berit* that, if "private persons" will arise who "write something against this book," they declare beforehand that they "believe it beneath their dignity" to "enter into a battle of pens" and that "no documentary attack will be answered." But the arrows of *Ḥerev Nokemet* were too painful and the tract itself made too strong an impression; hence there was no alternative, and a reply had to be made. As response to *Ḥerev Nokemet*, M. L. Reinitz's *Lahat Ha-Ḥerev Ha-Mithappechet* soon appeared (1820). The author attempts to imitate, but without success, Bresselau's brilliant Biblical style, and repeats tediously and at length the arguments of the rabbis of *Eleh Divrei Ha-Berit*. Every page is ornamented with such literary flowers as: scoundrels, fornicators, assembly of traitors, fools and idiots, a band of madmen, dog, wretch, wicked men, etc.

Such refutations could be of little avail. But the champions of orthodoxy obtained help from another side—indeed, from that side to which the rabbis of Triesch and Lissa had pointed, namely the monarchs and officials of the land. The orthodox dispatched one complaint after another to the king of Prussia against the deniers and "heretics" who had appeared in their community. And the king, "the man of righteousness and justice," listened to their petition. The Prussian monarch was not free of missionary tendencies. Indeed, at the beginning of 1822 a missionary society with the special task of propagandizing among the Jews, enlightening their eyes with the eternal truths of the Christian church, was founded in Prussia. The reformers had indicated that the purpose of their innovations and reforms was that the Jewish youth might not abandon the religion of their fathers. Hence, the royal government deliberately fulfilled the request of the orthodox and forbade the institution of any changes in the Jewish cult; even sermons in the German language in the synagogue were proscribed.[83]

The orthodox prevailed. This victory, however, was worse than the severest defeat. The process of discrediting congealed *Shulḥan Aruch* rabbinism, the process so strongly advanced during the seven-year "battle of amulets" between Jacob Emden and Jonathan Eybeschütz, reached its peak two generations later in the battle against the Reform party in the first years of the period of reaction.

But the zigzag path of national Jewish culture, which is so closely interwoven with the varied cultural, social, and political conditions of the environment, is strangely tortuous. Precisely in the 1820's some highly important events pertaining to Jewish national culture and literature occurred. In Germany, Jewish scholars, led by the young Leopold Zunz, undertook, with purely apologetic purposes, to establish a memorial for the Judaism of the past, to draw up the balance of everything that the Jewish community had produced in the realm of spirit and thought in the course of its millennial peregrinations. From this venture grew a unique structure—*Ḥochmat Ha-Yahadut* or *die Wissenschaft des Judentums.*

In Austria the poet Shalom ben Jacob Cohen founded the journal *Bikkurei Ha-Ittim.* His purpose was, indeed, quite restricted—merely to renew the traditions of *Ha-Meassef,* to follow its paths, to warm himself in its rays. The results, however, transcended the editor's limited conceptions. The erstwhile admirer of *Ha-Meassef* was pushed aside and, while he was engrossed in creating a pallid copy of Wessely's *Shirei Tiferet,* his thick-bellied *Nir David,* the foreground was occupied by thinkers and scholars such as Naḥman Krochmal, Solomon Jehudah Rapoport, and Samuel David Luzzatto, and satirists such as Isaac Erter. At the same time Isaac Baer Levinsohn came forth with his *Te'udah Be-Yisrael* and Manasseh of Ilya with his *Alfei Menasheh,* and laid the foundation-stones of Haskalah literature in Russia. The indefatigable Israel Aksenfeld endeavored to accomplish the same, even though with different methods, in the realm of the folk language, and in Poland the young Solomon Ettinger made the bold attempt to utilize the popular language not only as a means of struggle and enlightenment but also as a polished instrument for genuine artistry.

Of this in the subsequent volumes.

83. See S. Bernfeld, *op. cit.*, p. 92.

BIBLIOGRAPHICAL NOTES

The Berlin Haskalah

CHAPTER ONE

JACOB FRANK AND THE FRANKIST MOVEMENT

On the after-effects of the Sabbatian movement, see M. Balaban, "Sabataizm w Polsce," in *Ksiega Jubileuszowa ku czci profesora Dr. M. Schorr* (1935), 47–90; A. Elmaleh, *Shabbetai Tzevi, His Sects and the Remnants of his Messianic Movement in Our Days* (Hebrew, 1927); I.M. Jost, *Geschichte der Israeliten . . .*, 8ter Theil (1828), 100–34; David Kahana, *Toledot Ha-Mekubbalim Ha-Shabbeta'im Veha-Ḥasidim*, two volumes (1913–1914); Gershom Scholem, *Major Trends in Jewish Mysticism*, 3rd rev. ed. (1954); idem, *Sabbatai Sevi: The Mystical Messiah* (1973); idem, *The Messianic Idea in Judaism and Other Essays* (1971); I. Tishby, *Netivei Emunah U-Minut* (1964); and idem, "Bein Shabbeta'ut Le-Ḥasidut," *Keneset*, IX (1945), 238–268.

On Jacob Frank and the Frankist movement, see Jacob Emden, *Sefer Shimmush* (1762); idem, *Megillat Sefer* (1896); E. Fleckeles, *Ahavat David* (1800); P. Arnsberg, *Von Podolien nach Offenbach* (1965); S. Back, in *MGWJ*, XXVI (1877); M. Balaban, *Le-Toledot Ha-Tenuah Ha-Frankit*, two parts (1934–35); idem, in *Livre d'hommage à . . . S. Poznánski* (1927), 25–75; Peter Beer, *Geschichte, Lehren, und Meinungen religiösen Sekten der Juden*, Vol. II (1823); A.G. Duker, in *Jewish Social Studies*, XXV (1963), 287–333; A.J. Brawer, *Galitzyah Ve-Yehudeha* (1966), 197–275; idem, in *Joshua Starr Memorial Volume* (1963), 191–201; N.M. Gelber, "Di Zikhroynes Fun Moyshe Porges," *YIVO Historishe Shriftn*, I (1929), cols. 253–296; idem, in *Zion*, II (1937), 326–32; Heinrich Graetz, *Frank und die Frankisten* (1868); idem, in *MGWJ*, XXII (1873); T. Jeske-Choínski, *Neofici polscy* (1904), 46–107; R. Kestenberg-Gladstein, *Neuere Geschichte der Juden in den böhmischen Ländern*, Vol. I (1969), 123–91; J. Kleinmann, "Moral i poezya Frankisma," *Yevreyski Almanakh* (1923), 195–227; A. Kraushar, *Frank i frankísci polscy*, two volumes (1895); F. Mauthner, *Lebenserinnerungen* (1918), 295–307; O. Rabinowicz, in *JQR*, *75th Anniversary Volume* (1967), 429–45; A.G. Schenk-Rink, *Die Polen in Offenbach* (1866–69); Gershom Scholem, *Major Trends in Jewish Mysticism*, 3rd rev. ed. (1954); ibid., "Mitzvah Ha-Ba'ah Be-Averah," *Keneset*, II (1937), 347–92; idem, in *Revue d'histoire des religions*, CXLIV (1953–54), 42–77; ibid., in *Sefer Yovel Le-Yitzḥak Baer* (1960), 409–30; idem, article "Frank, Jacob, and the Frankists," *Encyclopedia Judaica*, VII (1971), cols. 55–71; idem, *The Messianic Idea in Judaism and Other Essays* (1971), 78–141; ibid., in *Zeugnisse T. W. Adorno zum Geburtstag* (1963), 20–32; idem, in *Max Brod Gedenkbuch* (1969), 77–92; idem, in *Commentary*, LI (January, 1971), 41–70; C. Seligmann, in *Frankfurter Israelitisches Gemeindeblatt*, X (1932), 121–3, 150–2; M. Wishnitzer, in: *Memoires de l'Académie . . . de St. Petersbourg*, series 8. Hist-Phil. Section, XII, No. 3 (1914); A. Yaari, in *Sinai*, XXXV (1954), 120–82; XLII (1958), 294–306; and V. Zacek, "Zwei Beiträge zur Geschichte des Frankismus in den böhmischen Ländern," *Jahrbuch für Geschichte der Juden in der Čechoslovakishen Republik*, IX (1938), 343–410.

CHAPTER TWO

ISRAEL BAAL SHEM TOV

The literature on the Hasidic movement, its major personalities, and its teachings is vast. Among the most important works are the following: J. Abelson, *Jewish Mysticism* (1913); A.Z. Aescoly-Weintraub, *Le Hassidisme, Essai Critique* (1928); idem, in *Beit Yisrael Be-Polin*, Vol. II (1954), 86–141; Y. Alfasi, *Toledot Ha-Ḥasidut* (1959); M. Ben-Yeḥezkel (Halpern), *Sefer Ha-Ma'asiyyot*, six volumes, 3rd ed. (1968); I. Berger, *Zechut Yisrael*, four volumes, (1902–10); C. Bloch, *Die Gemeinde der Chassidism: ihr Werden und ihre Lehre* (1920); M. Bodek, *Seder Ha-Dorot Ha-Ḥadash* (1865); Martin Buber, *Hasidism*, translated by Greta Hort and others (1948); idem, *Hasidism and Modern Man*, edited and translated by M. Friedman (1958); idem, *The Origin and Meaning of Hasidism*, edited and translated by M. Friedman (1960); B. Dinur (Dinaburg), *Be-Mifneh Ha-Dorot* (1955), 83–227; S.H. Dresner, *The Zaddik* (1960); S.M. Dubnow, *Toledot Ha-Ḥasidut*, three parts (1930–

32; second edition, 1960; German translation, *Die Geschichte des Chassidismus,* translated by A. Steinberg, two volumes (1931–32); idem, *A History of the Jews in Russia and Poland from the Earliest Times Until the Present Day,* three volumes, translated by I. Friedlaender (1916–20); S. Ettinger, *Toledot Yisrael Ba-Et Ha-Ḥadashah,* edited by H.H. Ben-Sasson (1969), Index, s.v. *Ḥasidism* and *Ḥasidut;* Y.Y. Grunwald, *Toyzent Yor Yidish Lebn in Ungarn* (1945); L. Gulkowitsch, *Das Kulturhistorische Bild des Chassidismus* (1938); idem, *Der Hassidismus, Religionswissenschaftlich Untersucht* (1927); idem, *Die Grundgedanken des Chassidismus als Quelle seines Schicksals* (1938); I. Halpern, *Ha-Aliyyot Ha-Rishonot Shel Ha-Ḥasidim Le-Eretz Yisrael* (1946); idem, in *Zion,* XXII (1957), 194–213; S.A. Horodetzky, *Ha-Hasidut Veha-Ḥasidim,* four volumes, (1923; second edition, 1928; third edition, 1951); idem, *Leaders of Hasidism* (1928); A. Kahana, *Sefer Ha-Ḥasidut* (1922); Y.A. Kamelhaar, *Dor De'ah* (1933); M.A. Lipschitz, *Faith of a Hasid* (1967); J.L. Maimon (Fishman), editor, *Sefer Ha-Besht* (1960); A. Markus ("Verus"), *Der Chassidismus* (1901); J.S. Minkin, *The Romance of Hasidism,* second edition (1955); Mordecai Ben-Yeḥezkel, "Le-Mahut Ha-Ḥasidut," in *Ha-Shiloaḥ,* XVII (1907), 219–30; XX (1909), 38–46, 161–71; XXII (1910), 251–61, 339–50; XXV (1912), 434–52; H.M. Rabinowicz, *A Guide to Hasidism* (1960); idem, *The World of Hasidism* (1970); W.Z. Rabinowitsch, *Der Karliner Chassidismus, seine Geschichte und Lehre* (1935); idem, *Lithuanian Hasidism* (1970); Y. Raphael, *Sefer Ha-Ḥasidut,* second edition (1955); A. Rubenstein, in *Areshet,* III (1961), 193–230; idem, in *Kiryat Sefer,* XXXVIII (1962–63), 263–72, 415–24; XIL (1963–64), 117–36; idem, in *Tarbiz,* XXXV (1965–66), 174–91; idem, *Sefer Ha-Shanah Shel Bar-Ilan,* IV-V (1967), 324–39; Rivka Schatz (Schatz-Uffenheimer), "Contemplative Prayer in Hasidism," in *Studies in Religion Presented to Gershom G. Scholem on His Seventieth Birthday* (1967), 209–226; idem, article "Ḥasidism," *Encyclopedia Judaica,* VII (1971), cols. 1390–1420; idem, *Ha-Ḥasidut Ke-Mistikah* (1968), with English summary; Solomon Schechter, "The Chassidim," *Studies in Judaism,* First Series (1896), 1–45; Gershom G. Scholem, *Major Trends in Jewish Mysticism,* third revised edition (1954); idem, in *Zion,* VI (1941), 89–93; XX (1955), 73–81; idem, in *Hagut . . . S.H. Bergman* (1944), 145–51; idem, "Devekuth, Communion with God in Early Hasidic Doctrine," *The Review of Religion,* XV (1950), 115–39; idem, in *Molad,* XVIII (1960), 335–56; A. Shochat, in *Zion,* XVI (1951), 30–43; E. Steinman, *Be'er Ha-Ḥasidut,* ten volumes (1951–62); idem, *Garden of Hasidism* (1961); I. Tishby, "Bein Shabbeta'ut Le-Ḥasidut," *Keneset,* IX (1945), 238–68; M. Unger, *Khasides Un Lebn* (1946); idem, *Di Khasidishe Velt*

(1955); J.G. Weiss, "Contemplative Mysticism and 'Faith' in Hasidic Piety," *Journal of Jewish Studies*, IV (1953), 19–29; idem, "A Circle of Pre-Ḥasidic Pneumatics," *Journal of Jewish Studies*, VIII (1957), 199–213; idem, "The *Kavvanoth* of Prayer in Early Hasidism," *Journal of Jewish Studies*, IX (1958), 163–92; idem, "Via Passiva in Early Hasidism," *Journal of Jewish Studies*, XI (1960), 137–55; idem, in *Erchei Ha-Yahadut* (1953), 81–90; idem, in *Alei Ayin* (1952), 245–91; idem, in *Zion*, XVI (1951), 46–105 (second pagination); idem, in *Tarbiz*, XXVII (1957–58), 358–71; idem, "Beginnings of Hassidism," (Hebrew) *Zion*, XVI (1951), 46–105; idem, "The Great Maggid's Theory of Contemplative Magic," *Hebrew Union College Annual*, XXI (1960), 137–48; idem, in *Meḥkarim . . . Gershom Scholem* (1968), 101–13; S. Werses, in *Molad*, XVIII (1960), 379–91; A. Wertheim, *Halachot Ve-Halichot Be-Ḥasidut* (1960); A. Yaari, in *Kiryat Sefer*, XIL (1963–64), 249–72, 394–407, 552–62; T. Ysander, *Studien zum Best'schen Hasidismus in seiner Religionsgeschichtlichen Sonderart*, translated by Ilse Meyer-Lune (1933); Hillel Zeitlin, *Ha-Ḥasidut* (1912); idem, *Beha-Pardes Ha-Ḥasidut Veha-Kabbalah*, (1965); and A.Z. Zweifel, *Shalom Al Yisrael*, four volumes, (1868–73).

Many of the books and articles noted above contain material on Israel ben Eliezer, the Baal Shem Tov. The literature especially devoted to the founder of Hasidism, or throwing particular light on him, is very extensive. Among the most important works are the following: Jacob Joseph of Polonnoye, *Toledot Ya'akov Yosef* (1780); idem, *Ben Porat Yosef* (1781); idem *Tzafenat Pa'ane'aḥ* (1782); idem, *Ketonet Passim* (1866); Moses Ḥayyim Ephraim, *Degel Maḥaneh Efrayim* (1811); Aaron Ha-Kohen of Apta, *Keter Shem Tov* (1794–95); Isaiah of Yanov, *Seder Tzavva'ot Me-Rabbi Yisrael Baal Shem Tov Ve-Hanhagot Yesharot* (1794); idem, *Likkutei Yekarim* (1792); Ch. Bloch, *Kovetz Michtavim Mekoriyyim Meha-Besht Ve-Talmidav* (1920); M. Bodek, *Sefer Ha-Dorot Mi-Talmidei Ha-Besht* (1865); E. Eindelman, *Rabbi Yisrael Baal Shem Tov* (1961); D. Fraenkel, *Michtavim Meha-Besht Ve-Talmidav* (1923); J. Günzig, *Rabbi Israel Baal-Shem der Stifter des Chassidismus, Sein Leben und Seine Lehre* (1908); M.J. Gutmann, *Rabbi Yisrael Baal Shem Tov* (1922); S.A. Horodetzky, *Leaders of Hassidism* (1928); A. Kahana, *Rabbi Yisrael Baal Shem Tov* (1901); B. Landa, *Ha-Besht U-Venei Heichalo* (1961); J.L. Maimon (Fishman), editor, *Sefer Ha-Besht* (1960); M. Mark, *Rabbi Yisrael Baal Shem Tov* (1960); Y. Raphael in *Aresheth*, II (1960), 358–77, III (1961), 440–1; M.L. Rodkinson, *Toledot Baal Shem Tov* (1876); A. Rubenstein, in *Tarbiz*, XXXV (1965–66), 174–91; J.I.

Schochet, *Rabbi Israel Baal Shem Tov: A Monograph on the Life and Teachings of the Founder of Chassidism* (1961); G. Scholem, in *Review of Religion*, XV (1950), 115–39; idem, "The Historical Image of Rabbi Israel Baal Shem Tov," (Hebrew), *Molad*, XVIII (1960), 335–56; S.Z. Setzer, *Rabbi Yisrael Baal Shem Tov, sein Leben und Wirken*, two volumes (1919); Ch. Shmeruk, in *Zion*, XXVIII (1963); E. Steinman, *Rabbi Yisrael Baal Shem Tov* (1960); Y. Twersky, *Ha-Baal Shem Tov* (1959); M. Unger, *Reb Yisroel Baal-Shem-Tov* (Yiddish, 1963); S.M.M. Wodnik, *Sefer Baal Shem Tov* (1938); T. Ysander, *Studien zum Best'schen Hasidismus* (1933); and H. Zeitlin, *Rabbi Yisrael Baal Shem Tov* (1910).

CHAPTER THREE

THE DISCIPLES OF THE BAAL SHEM TOV

On Rabbi Dov Baer, the Maggid of Mezhirech, see M. Buber, *Der Grosse Maggid und seine Nachfolger* (1922); idem, *Tales of the Hasidim*, second edition, Vol. I (1968), 98–112; S. Dubnow, *Toledot Ha-Ḥasidut*, second edition (1960), 76–99; A.J. Heschel, in *Sefer Ha-Yovel Shel Hadoar* (1952), 279–85; S.A. Horodetzky, *Ha-Ḥasidut Veha-Ḥasidim*, Vol. I (1923), 75–102; R. Schatz-Uffenheimer, *Ha-Ḥasidut Ke-Mistikah* (1968); G. Scholem, in M. Buber and N. Rotenstreich (eds.), *Hagut* (1944), 147–51; idem, in *Review of Religion*, XIV (1950), 115–39; J.G. Weiss, "The Great Maggid's Theory of Contemplative Magic," *Hebrew Union College Annual*, XXI (1960), 137–48; and idem, in *Erchei Ha-Yahadut* (1953), 81–90.

On the Hasidic *tzaddik* and the origins of tzaddikism, see S.H. Dresner, *The Zaddik: The Doctrine of the Zaddik According to the Writings of Rabbi Yaakov Yosef of Polnoy* (1960; second edition, 1974).

Many of the works on Hasidism in general listed under Chapter Two contain material on the beginnings of the controversy between the Hasidim and the Mitnagdim. On the controversy, see also M. Wilensky, *Ḥasidim U-Mitnaggedim* (1970); and idem, "Remarks Concerning the Controversy between the Ḥasidim and the Mitnaggedim" (Hebrew), *Tarbiz*, XXX (1961), 396–404.

On Jacob Joseph Ha-Kohen of Polonnoye, see B. Dinur, *Be-Mifneh Ha-Dorot* (1955), 147–55; S.H. Dresner, *The Zaddik* (1960, second edition, 1974); S. Dubnow, *Toledot Ha-Ḥasidut*, second edition (1960), 93–101; S. Ettinger, *Toledot Am Yisrael Ba-Et Ha-Ḥadashah*, Vol. III (1969), 57, 59; idem, in *Journal of World History*, XVII (1968), Nos. 1–2; S.A. Horodetzky, *Ha-Ḥasidut Ve-Ḥasidim*, third edition, Vol. I (1951), 105–32; G. Nigal, *Leader and Community: Theories and Parables in the Beginning of Hasidism According to the Writings of Rabbi Jacob Joseph of Polonnoye* (Hebrew: *Manhig Ve-Edah*, 1962); A. Rubenstein, in *Aresheth*, III (1961), 193–230; and M. Wilensky, in *Joshua Starr Memorial Volume* (1953), 183–89.

CHAPTER FOUR

TZADDIKISM AND ḤABAD

On the Hasidic *tzaddik* and the origins of tzaddikism, see S.H. Dresner, *The Zaddik: The Doctrine of the Zaddik According to the Writings of Rabbi Yaakov Yosef of Polnoy* (1960; second edition, 1974).

On Elimelech of Lyzhansk, see Y. Berger, *Eser Tzaḥtzaḥot* (1900), 17–41; M. Buber, *Tales of the Hasidim*, second edition, Vol. I (1968), 243–64; S. Dubnow, *Toledot Ha-Ḥasidut*, second edition (1960), 178–188; S.A. Horodetzky, *Ha-Ḥasidut Veha-Ḥasidim*, third edition, Vol. II (1953), 149–273; J.A. Kleiman, *Nifla'ot Elimelech* (1916); B. Landau, *Rabbi Elimelech Mi-Lyzhansk* (1963); A.H.S.B. Michaelson, *Ohel Elimelech* (1914); R. Schatz, in *Molad*, XVIII (1960), 365–78.

On Shneur Zalman and Ḥabad Hasidism, see M. Buber, *Tales of the Hasidim*, second edition, Vol. I (1968), 265–71; H.I. Bunin, "Ha-Ḥasidut Ha-Ḥabadit," in *Ha-Shiloaḥ*, XXVIII (1913), 250–58, 348–59, XXIX (1913), 217–27; XXXI (1914–15), 44–52, 242–52; idem, *Mishneh Ḥabad* (1936); B. Chavel, "Shnuer Zalman of Liady" in Leo Jung, editor, *Jewish Leaders* (1953), 51–75; A.H. Glicenstein, *Ha-Admor Ha-Emtzai* (1950); idem, *Rabbenu Ha-Tzemaḥ Tzedek* (1967); idem, *Sefer Ha-Toledot* (1967); A.M. Habermann, in *Alei Ayin* (1953), 293–370; H.M. Heilman, *Bet Rabbi* (1965); N. Mindel, *Rabbi Joseph Isaac Schneersohn* (1947); idem, *Rabbi Schneur Zalman* (1964); W.Z. Rabinowitsch, *Lithuanian Hasidism* (1970); M.L. Rodkinson, *Toledot Ammudei Ḥabad* (1876); Rivkah Schatz-Uffenheimer, in *Molad* (1963), 171–72; J.I. Schneersohn, *The Lubavitcher Rabbi's Memoirs* (1966); idem, *On the Teaching of Chassides* (1959); idem, *Some Aspects of Chabad Chasidism* (1957); idem, *The Tzemach Tzedek and the Haskalah Movement* (1962); M.M. Schneersohn,

Mafte'aḥ (1968); idem, *Sefer Ha-Toledot* (1947): E. Steinman, *Sefer Mishnat Ḥabad*, two volumes (1957); M. Teitelbaum, *Ha-Rav Mi-Ladi U-Mifleget Ḥabad*, Part I (1910), Part II, (1913); J. Unna, "Rabbi Senior Salman aus Ladi, der Begründer der Chabad," *Festschrift zum 70ten Geburtstag David Hoffmans* (1914); Herbert Weiner, "The Lubavitcher Movement I," *Commentary*, XXIII (1957), 231–41; and idem, "The Lubavitcher Movement II," *Commentary*, XXIII (1957), 316–27.

Shneur Zalman's *Likkutei Amarim* or *Tanya* was translated into English by Nissan Mindel and others (1962, 1965). D.Z. Hillman's *Iggerot Baal Ha-Tanya U-Venei Doro* (1953) contains many of Shneur Zalman's letters.

CHAPTER FIVE

LOVERS OF ISRAEL: LEVI YITZḤAK OF BERDICHEV AND NAḤMAN OF BRATZLAV

Many of the works listed in the first paragraph of bibliographical notes under Chapter Two above contain material on the outstanding Hasidic leaders discussed in this chapter. See also A.I. Bromberg, *Mi-Gedolei Ha-Ḥasidut*, 24 volumes (1949–69), and M. Gutman, *Mi-Gibborei Ha-Ḥasidut*, second edition (1953).

On Levi Yitzḥak of Berdichev, see A.Z. Aescoly, *Introduction à l'étude des hérésies religieuses parmi les juifs. La Kabbale. Le Hassidisme* (1928); M. Buber, *Tales of the Hasidim: The Early Masters* (1947), 203–34; S. Dubnow, *Toledot Ha-Ḥasidut*, second edition (1960), 151–57, 193–201, 479–81; *ibid.*, *Chassidiana* (Hebrew), supplement to *He-Avar*, II (1918); S.A. Horodetzky, *Ha-Ḥasidut Veha-Ḥasidim*, second edition, Vol. II (1951), 71–96; M.E. Gutman, *Mi-Gedolei Ha-Ḥasidut*, second edition (1953); S. Gutmann, *Tiferet Bet Levi* (1909); I. Halpern, in *Tarbiz*, XXVIII (1959), 90–98; L. Jung (ed.), *Men of the Spirit* (1964), 403–13; Ch. Liebermann, in *Sefer Ha-Yovel Le-Chevod Alexander Marx* (1943), 15–17; and J. Twersky, *Ḥayyei Rabbi Levi Yitzḥak Mi-Berdichev* (1960). An important recent work is S. H. Dresner, *Levi Yitzhak of Berditchev: Portrait of a Hasidic Master* (1974).

Naḥman of Bratzlav's *Likkutei Moharan* (comments on the Bible, Talmud, and Midrash) was edited by Nathan ben Naftali Herz Sternhartz of Nemirov and first published in Ostrog in 1806. A second volume, *Likkutei Moharan Tinyana*, appeared posthumously in Moghilev in 1811. A new edition of *Likkutei*

Moharan was published in Israel in 1969. Nathan of Nemirov's *Shivḥei Ha-Ran* and *Siḥot Ha-Ran* were translated and annotated by Aryeh Kaplan under the title *Rabbi Nachman's Wisdom* (1973).

The tales which Naḥman of Bratzlav began to tell his disciples in his last years were published in a bilingual edition—the original Yiddish and a Hebrew translation by Nathan Sternhartz—in Berdichev in 1815 under the title *Sippurei Maasiyot.* S.A. Horodetzky published the Hebrew version alone in Berlin in 1922. Martin Buber's German version was translated into English by Maurice Friedman under the title *The Tales of Rabbi Nachman* in 1956. A new Hebrew edition of *Sippurei Maasiyyot* was published in 1972.

Nathan ben Naftali Herz Sternhartz's *Likkutei Tefillot (Selected Prayers;* based upon Naḥman of Bratzlav's *Likkutei Halachot)* was published originally in Bratzlav in 1821–27 and reprinted in Jerusalem in 1905.

A collection of the writings of Rabbi Naḥman of Bratzlav, *Kitvei Rabbi Naḥman,* was edited by Eliezer Steinman (1956). Naḥman of Bratzlav's various journeys are described in his biography *Ḥayyei Moharan* (1875), and in *Yemei Moharan* (two volumes, 1904), both by his disciple Nathan Sternhartz. Another important source for his life is *Shivḥei Ha-Ran,* Lemberg (1901). A translation of *Shivhei Ha-Ran* is included in Aryeh Kaplan, trans., *Rabbi Nachman's Wisdom* (1973).

On Rabbi Naḥman, see Y. Alfasi, *Rabbi Naḥman Mi-Bratzlav* (1953); S.A. Horodetzky, *Torat Rabbi Naḥman Mi-Bratzlav* (1923); idem, introduction to *Sippurei Maasiyyot Le-Rabbi Naḥman Mi-Bratzlav,* second edition (1923); N.Z. Koenig, *Neveh Tzaddikim* (1969); Ch. Liebermann, "Reb Nakhmen Bratslaver Un Di Umaner Maskilim" in *YIVO-Bleter,* XXXIX (1947), 201–19; J.K. Miklishinsky, in *Ha-Ḥasidut Ve-Tziyyon* (1963), 246–56; G. Scholem, *Elleh Shemot Sifrei Moharan Mi-Bratzlav* (1928); J. Weiss, in *Kiryat Sefer,* XLI (1965–66), 557–63; XLIV (1968–69), 279–97; idem, *Gershom Scholem Jubilee Volume* (Hebrew and English, 1968), 101–13; idem, Introduction to *Ma'gelei Si'aḥ* (1947); idem, in *Erchei Ha-Yahadut* (1953), 81–90; idem, in: *Tarbiz,* XXVII (1957–58), 358–71 (*Gershom Scholem Jubilee Volume,* Hebrew, 1958, 232–45); idem, in *Alei Ayin* (1952), 245–91; Hillel Zeitlin, *Rabbi Naḥman Mi-Bratzlav, Ḥayyav Ve-Torato* (1910): idem, *Rabbi Nakhman Braslaver, Der Ze'er Fun Podolye* (1952); S. H. Setzer, *Di Nesie Fun Rabbi Nakhman Braslaver Kayn Eretz Yisrael* (1928); Mendel Piekarz, *Hasidut Braslav* (1972); Yehudit Kuk, *Rabbi Naḥman Mi-Braslav: lyyunim Be-Sippurav* (1973); David Hardan, ed., *From the*

World of Rabbi Nahman of Bratzlav, translated by Miriam Arad, with an introduction by Aharon Applefield (1973).

CHAPTER SIX

HASIDIC TALES; ATTACKS ON THE MOVEMENT

The best easily available edition of Dov Baer ben Samuel's *Shivḥei Ha-Besht* is that published, with introduction and notes, by S.A. Horodetzky in Berlin in 1922 (second edition, Tel Aviv, 1960).

A bibliography of all editions of *Shivḥei Ha-Besht* will be found in Y. Raphael (Isaac Werfel), "Shivḥei Ha-Besht," *Aresheth*, II (1960), 358–77, 440–441.

On *Shivḥei Ha-Besht*, see Ch. Shmeruk, "Tales about Rabbi Adam Baal Shem in the Versions of *Shivḥei Ha-Besht*," Hebrew, *Zion*, XXVIII (1963), 86–105; Menashe Unger, "Yiddish Words in the *Shivḥei Ha-Besht*," *Yidishe Shprakh*, XXI (1961), 65–73; Abraham Yaari, "Two Basic Recensions of *Shivḥei Ha-Besht*," Hebrew, *Kiryat Sefer*, XXXIX (1964), 249–72, 394–407, 552–62; and idem, "Miscellaneous Bibliographical Notes, 10. Three Yiddish Translations of *Shivḥei Ha-Besht*," Hebrew, *Kiryat Sefer*, XII (1935), 129–31.

Shivḥei Ha-Besht was edited and translated into English under the title *In Praise of the Baal Shem Tov: The Earliest Collection of Legends About the Founder of Hasidism* by D. Ben-Amos and J.R. Mintz (1970).

On collections of Hasidic Tales see Martin Buber, *Die chassidischen Bücher* (1928); idem, *Tales of the Hasidim, the Early Masters*, translated by Olga Marx (1947); idem, *Tales of the Hasidim, the Later Masters*, translated by Olga Marx (1948); idem, *Jewish Mysticism and the Legends of the Baalshem*, translated by Lucy Cohen (1931); idem, *The Legend of the Baal-Shem*, translated by Maurice Friedman (1955); Joseph Dan, *The Hasidic Novella*, Hebrew, (1966); idem, "Research Techniques for Hasidic Tales," Hebrew, *Fourth World Congress of Jewish Studies: Papers*, Vol. II (1968), 53–57; J.R. Mintz, *Legends of the Hasidim: An Introduction to Hasidic Culture and Oral Tradition in the New World* (1968); L.I. Newman and S. Spitz, editors, *The Hasidic Anthology; Tales and Teachings of the Hasidim* (1934); and idem, editors, *Maggidim and Hasidim: Their Wisdom* (1962).

On Israel Loebl and his anti-Hasidic writings, see S. Dubnow, *Toledot Ha-Ḥasidut,* second edition (1960), 278–86 and Index; I. Bacon, in *Zion,* XXXII (1967), 116–22; H. Liberman, in *Kiryat Sefer,* XXVI (1950), 106, 216; M. Mahler, *Ha-Ḥasidut Veha-Haskalah* (1961), Index; G. Scholem, "New Material on Israel Loebl and His Anti-Hasidic Polemics," Hebrew, *Zion,* XX (1955), 153–162; and M. Wilensky, *Ḥasidim U-Mitnaggedim* (1970).

On David of Makow, see S. Dubnow, *Toledot Ha-Ḥasidut,* second edition (1960), Index; E.R. Malachi, in *Sefer Ha-Yovel Shel Hadoar* (1952), 286–300; M. Wilensky, "The Polemic of Rabbi David of Makow Against Hasidism," *American Academy for Jewish Research: Proceedings,* XXV (1956), 137–56; idem, in *Tarbiz,* XXVII (1957–58), 550–55; idem, in *Divrei Ha-Congress Ha-Olami Ha-Revii Le-Madda'ei Ha-Yahadut,* II (1968), 237–51; idem, *Ḥasidim U-Mitnaggedim* (1970), Index; A. Rubenstein, in *Kiryat Sefer,* XXV (1959–60), 240–49; and idem, in *Kovetz Bar-Ilan,* VIII (1970), 225–43.

CHAPTER SEVEN

ELIE HALÉVY, SOLOMON LÖWISOHN, AND SHALOM COHEN

On *Sulamith,* the first German-language periodical for Jews, see S. Stein, in *Zeitschrift für die Geschichte der Juden in Deutschland,* VII (1937), 193–226.

On Napoleon Bonaparte and the Jews and Judaism, see R. Anchel, *Napoléon et les Juifs* (1928); E.A. Halphen, *Recueil des lois, décrets et ordonnances concernant les Israélites* (1851); Sagnac, in *Revue de l'histoire moderne et contemporaine,* II–III (1901–02); Gelber, in *REJ,* LXXXIII (1927), 1–21, 113–45; F. Kobler, *The Vision Was There* (1956), 42–47; F. Pietri, *Napoléon et les Israélites* (1965); and B. Mevorakh, *Napoleon U-Tekufato* (1968).

On Elie Halfon Halévy, see J. Klausner, *Historyah Shel Ha-Safrut Ha-Ivrit Ha-Ḥadashah,* second edition, Vol. I (1952), 322–25.

On Solomon Löwisohn, see S. Klein, *Toledot Ḥakirat Eretz Yisrael Ba-Safrut Ha-Ivrit Veha-Kelalit* (1937), 74–80; J. Fichmann, *Anshei Vesorah* (1938), 50–56; H.N. Schapira, *Toledot Ha-Safrut Ha-Ivrit Ha-Ḥadashah* (1939), 454–78; Schwartz, in *Moznayim* (1963), 373–83; and J.L. Landau, *Short Lectures on Hebrew Literature* (1939), Index.

On Shalom Cohen, see J.L. Landau, *Short Lectures on Modern Hebrew Literature* (1939), 121–34; R. Mahler, *Divrei Yemei Yisrael,* I, Part Two (1954), 275–79; and J. Klausner, *Historyah Shel Ha-*

Safrut Ha-Ivrit Ha-Ḥadashah, second edition, Vol. I (1952), 275–90.

CHAPTER EIGHT

MENDEL LEVIN, JACOB SAMUEL BICK, AND CHAIM ḤAYKL HURWITZ

On Menaḥem Mendel Levin (Lefin) see J. Klausner, *Historyah Shel Ha-Safrut Ha-Ivrit Ha-Ḥadashah,* second edition (1952), Vol. I, 224–53 (includes bibliography); W. Zeitlin, *Bibliotheca Hebraica Post-Mendelssohniana* (1891–95), 202–04; J.S. Raisin, *The Haskalah Movement in Russia* (1913), 99–101; N.M. Gelber, in *Abraham Weiss Jubilee Volume* (1964), 271–305, Hebrew part; idem, in *Aus Zwei Jahrhunderten* (1924), 39–57; J. Weinles, in *Ha-Olam,* XIII (1952), issues 39–42; idem, "Mendel Lefin-Satanover," *YIVO-Bleter,* III (1931), 334–57; J.L. Landau, *Short Lectures on Modern Hebrew Literature,* second edition (1939), 187–92; M. Wiener, *Tsu Der Geshikhte Fun Der Yidisher Literatur In 19ten Yohrhundert* (1945), 38–44; S. Katz, "Targumei Tanach Me-Et Menaḥem Mendel Mi-Satanov," *Kiryat Sefer,* XVI (1939–40), 114–33; M. Erik, *Etiudn Tsu Der Geshikhte Fun Der Haskole,* 1934, 135–51; and Ch. Shmeruk, in *Yidishe Shprakh,* XXIV (1964), 33–52.

On Tobias Gutman Feder, see the bibliography for Mendel Levin above. See also Klausner's *Historyah Shel Ha-Safrut Ha-Ivrit Ha-Ḥadashah,* second edition (1952), Vol. I, 239ff.

Most of the literary works written by Jacob Samuel Bick were destroyed by a fire. However, shortly before World War II, Professor Dov Sadan discovered in the Joseph Perl library in Tarnopol the manuscripts of three anti-Hasidic plays written by Bick in Hebrew and belonging probably to his early period before his disillusionment with, and renunciation of, the ideology of Haskalah.

On Bick see S. Werses, in *YIVO-Bleter,* XIII (1938), 505–36; G. Bader, *Medinah Ve-Ḥachameha* (1934), 36–37; and D. Sadan, *Mazkeret Levi* (1953), 96–108.

On Chaim Ḥaykl Hurwitz, see M. Weinreich, *Bilder Fun Der Yidisher Literatur-Geshikhte* (1928); S. Niger, *Dertseyler Un Romanistn* (1946), 25–27; and Schlosberg, in *YIVO-Bleter,* XII, (1937), 546–58.

CHAPTER NINE

ANTI-HASIDIC WORKS; THE STRUGGLE BETWEEN THE REFORMERS AND THE ORTHODOX

On the polemics in the early nineteenth century of the protagonists of Haskalah against Hasidism and the Hasidim, see R. Mahler, "The Austrian Government and the Hasidim during the Period of Reaction 1818–1848" in *Jewish Social Studies,* I (1939), pp. 195–240; idem, *Ha-Ḥasidut Veha-Haskalah* (1961); D. Patterson, "The Portrait of Ḥasidism in the Nineteenth Century Hebrew Novel," *Journal of Semitic Studies,* V (1960), 359–77; S. Werses, "The Image of Hasidism in the Haskalah Literature" (Hebrew), *Molad,* XVIII (1960), 379–91; and S.J. Horowitz, *Ha-Ḥasidut Veha-Haskalah* (1909).

On Israel Zamosc, see Ch. Liebermann, in *Bitzaron,* XXXII (1955), 113–20; G. Scholem, "The Polemic against Hasidism and Its Leaders in the Book *Nezed Ha-Dema*" (Hebrew), *Zion,* XX (1955), 73–81; R. Mahler, *Divrei Yemei Yisrael Be-Dorot Aḥaronim,* 4 (1956), 26–30, 260–63; and G. Kressel, *Leksikon Ha-Safrut Ha-Ivrit Ba-Dorot Ha-Aḥaronim,* Vol. I (1965), 755–56.

On Jacob Calmanson, see S. Dubnow, *Divrei Yemei Am Olam,* Vol. VIII (1933), 168–69; J. Shatzky, *Geshikhte Fun Yidn In Varshe,* Vol. I (1947), Index; and R. Mahler, *Ha-Ḥasidut Veha-Haskalah* (1961), 391, n. 26.

On Joseph Perl, see Israel Davidson, *Parody in Hebrew Literature* (1907), 61–74; J. Klausner, *Historyah Shel Ha-Safrut Ha-Ivrit Ha-Ḥadashah,* Vol. II (1937), 278–314; I. Weinles, in *Yosef Perls Yidishe Ksovim* (1937), 7–70; Raphael Mahler, *Ha-Ḥasidut Veha-Haskalah* (1961), 155–208; Ch. Shmeruk, in *Zion,* XXI (1957), 94–99; S. Werses, in *Tarbiz,* XXXII (1962–63), 396–401; idem, in *Ha-Sifrut,* I (1968–69), 206–27; idem and Ch. Shmeruk, editors, *Yosef Perl: Maasiyyot Ve-Iggerot* (1969), 11–86, English summary; A. Rubenstein, in *Kiryat Sefer,* XXXVII (1961–62) and XXXVIII (1962–63).

On Israel Jacobson, the pioneer spirit of Reform Judaism in Germany, see S. Bernfeld, *Toledot Ha-Reformatzyon Ha-Datit Be-Yisrael,* second edition (1923), index; Lazarus, in MGWJ, LVIII (1914), 81–96; Jacob Marcus, in *Yearbook of the Central Conference of American Rabbis,* XXXVIII (1928), 386–498; idem, *Israel Jacobson, The Founder of the Reform Movement in Judaism* (1972); David Philipson, *The Reform Movement in Judaism,* revised edition (1967), index; G. Ruelf, *Einiges aus der ersten Zeit und über den Stifter der Jacobson-Schule in Seesen* (1890); C. Seligmann, *Die Geschichte der jüdischen Reformbewegung* (1922), 170ff.; Silberstein, in *Jahrbuch für jüdische Geschichte und Literatur* (1927), 100–09; P. Zimmerman, in *Brunsvicensia Judaica*, XXXV (1966), 23–42; H. Schnee, *Die Hoffinanz und der Moderne Staat*, Vol. II (1954), 109–54, Vol. V (1965), 210–18; M. Eliav, *Ha-Ḥinnuch Ha-Yehudi Bi-Germanyah . . .* (1961), 96–100, 119–26; Jacob J. Petuchowski, *Prayerbook Reform in Europe* (1968), index.

On the beginnings of the Reform movement in Germany see J.L. Blau, *Modern Varieties of Judaism* (1966); D. Rudavsky, *Emancipation and Adjustment* (1967); D.J. Silver and B. Martin, *A History of Judaism*, Vol. II (1974); D. Philipson, *The Reform Movement in Judaism*, revised edition (1967); M. Wiener, *Jüdische Religion im Zeitalter der Emanzipation;* idem, *Abraham Geiger and Liberal Judaism* (1962); J.J. Petuchowski, *Prayerbook Reform in Europe* (1968); W.G. Plaut, *The Rise of Reform Judaism* (1963); C. Seligmann, *Die Geschichte der jüdischen Reformbewegung* (1922); S.B. Freehof, *Reform Responsa* (1960); S. Dubnow, *Die neueste Geschichte des jüdischen Volkes*, Vols. I–II (1920); H. Graetz, *Die Geschichte der Juden*, edited by M. Brann, Vol. XI, second edition (1900); I.M. Jost, *Die neuere Geschichte des jüdischen Volkes*, Vol. I, second edition (1922).

On Aaron Chorin, see J.J. Greenwald, *Ha-Yehudim Be-Hungaryah* (1913), 59–63; idem, *Korot Ha-Torah Veha-Emunah Be-Hungaryah* (1921), 41–44; idem, *Li-Felagot Yisrael Be-Hungaryah* (1929), 7, 9–11, 14–23; R. Fahn, *Pirkei Haskalah* (1936), 192–96; M. Peli, "Milḥamato Ha-Ra'ayonit Veha-Halachit Shel Ha-Rav Aharon Ḥorin Be-Ad Reformah Datit Be-Yahadut," *Hebrew Union College Annual*, XXXIX, 1968, 63–79, Hebrew section; J.J. Petuchowski, *Prayerbook Reform in Judaism* (1968), index; L. Loew, *Aron Chorin*, originally appeared in *Ben Chananja*, IV (1861), separately printed in 1863, and reprinted in his *Gesammelte Schriften*, Vol. II (1890), 251–420; S. Bernfeld, in *Keneset Yisrael*, III (1888), 91ff.; and idem, *Toledot Ha-Reformatzyon Ha-Datit Be-Yisrael* (1900), index.

On David Caro, see J. Klausner, *Historyah Shel Ha-Safrut Ha-Ivrit Ha-Ḥadashah*, second edition (1952), Vol. II, 275–77, 279–82; Robert Katz, in *CCAR Journal*, XIII, No. 4 (1967), 4–46; and N. Lippmann, *Leben und Wirken des jüdischen Literaten David Caro* (1840).

Glossary of Hebrew and Other Terms

Glossary of Hebrew and Other Terms

Aggadah (or Haggadah): The non-legal part of the post-Biblical Oral Torah, consisting of narratives, legends, parables, allegories, poems, prayers, theological and philosophical reflections, etc. Much of the Talmud is aggadic, and the Midrash (see below) literature, developed over a period of more than a millennium, consists almost entirely of Aggadah. The term *aggadah*, in a singular and restricted sense, refers to a Talmudic story or legend.

Amora (plural, Amoraim): The title given to the Jewish scholars of Palestine and especially Babylonia in the third to the sixth centuries whose work and thought is recorded in the Gemara of the Talmud.

Baal Shem (in Hebrew, "master of the Name"): A title given to persons believed capable of working miracles through employing the divine Name. The title was not uncommon in Eastern Europe in the seventeenth and eighteenth centuries, where it frequently implied a quack or impostor who produced magical amulets, pronounced incantations, etc.

Bar Mitzvah: The Hebrew words mean "one obliged to fulfill the commandment," but the term is generally employed to denote the ceremony marking the induction of a boy, when he has reached the age of thirteen, into the Jewish community and into adult observance of the commandments of the Torah.

Bet Ha-Midrash: In the Talmudic age, a school for higher rabbinic learning where students assembled for study and discussion, as well as prayer. In the post-Talmudic age most synagogues had a Bet Ha-Midrash or were themselves called by the term, insofar as they were places of study.

Ein Sof: A Kabbalist term, meaning literally "without end" or "infinite." In the Spanish and later Kabbalah it was used to denote the impersonal aspect of the Godhead, the *deus absconditus*, about whom nothing can be thought or said and with whom men cannot enter into personal relationships.

Gabbai: Originally, in Talmudic times, the term meant a "collector" or "tax-gatherer." The *gabbai tzedakah* was the charity collector or overseer of the poor. The use of the term was later extended to designate the treasurer of the synagogue or other community institutions and sometimes its general officers, even those without financial functions.

Gaon (plural, Geonim): The spiritual and intellectual leaders of Babylonian Jewry in the post-Talmudic period, from the sixth through the eleventh centuries C.E. The head of the two major academies of Babylonia, at Sura and Pumbeditha, held the title Gaon. The Geonim had considerable secular power as well as religious authority, and their influence extended over virtually all of world Jewry during the larger part of the Geonic age. The title Gaon is occasionally applied, in a general honorific sense, to a very eminent Judaic scholar.

Gemara: The second basic strand of the Talmud (see below), consisting of a commentary on, and supplement to, the Mishnah (see Mishnah).

Gematria: A system of exegesis based on the interpretation of a word or words according to the numerical value of the constituent letters in the Hebrew alphabet.

Ḥacham: Hebrew for "wise man." Originally, an officer of the rabbinic courts in Palestine and Babylonia. Later the term was applied to an officiating rabbi in Sephardic communities.

Haggadah: The ritual recounting the exodus of the Israelites from Egypt, recited in the home on the first evening of

Passover (in the Diaspora, the first two evenings) and employing various symbols to represent major elements in the exodus narrative.

Havdalah: The Hebrew word means "distinction" or "division" and refers to the ceremony marking the end of the Sabbath, consisting of benedictions over wine, spices, and flame.

Haskalah: The movement for disseminating modern European culture among Jews from about 1750 to 1880. It advocated the modernization of Judaism, the westernization of traditional Jewish education, and the revival of the Hebrew language.

Hoshanna Rabbah: The popular name for the seventh day of Sukkot, or the Festival of Tabernacles. During the morning service worshippers make seven circuits around the synagogue carrying the palm branch and citron and beating willow branches against the pews.

Kabbalah: The mystical religious movement in Judaism and/or its literature. The term Kabbalah, which means "tradition," came to be used by the mystics beginning in the twelfth century to signify the alleged continuity of their doctrine from ancient times.

Kahal: A term applied in eastern Europe to the autonomous Jewish community vested with disciplinary power over its members and responsible for taxation. The kahal was officially abolished in the nineteenth century.

Kiddush: The Hebrew term means "sanctification" and refers to the ceremonial blessing recited on the Sabbath and the Holy Days over wine and bread, and a blessing proclaiming the sacredness of the occasion.

Kol Nidrei: In Aramaic, meaning "all vows." A formula recited on the evening of the Day of Atonement for the annulment of vows. The custom probably originated in the early Geonic period and was the object of repeated protests by rabbinic authorities. However, it became popular among the Jewish masses and rooted in tradition especially by reason of its haunting melody.

Maggid: The Hebrew term means "preacher" and was the name given by Jews in eastern Europe to the popular preacher, frequently an itinerant, who wandered from city to city and preached both on Sabbaths and weekdays.

Maskil (plural, Maskilim): An adherent of Haskalah (see above).

Matzah (plural, Matzot): The unleavened bread prescribed by Jewish tradition for consumption during the Passover season as a memorial of the bread baked in haste by the Israelites departing from Egypt.

Midrash (plural, Midrashim): The discovery of new meanings besides literal ones in the Bible. The term is also used to designate collections of such Scriptural exposition. The best-known of the Midrashim are the *Midrash Rabbah, Tanḥuma, Pesikta De-Rav Kahana, Pesikta Rabbati,* and *Yalkut Shimeoni.* In a singular and restricted sense, *Midrash* refers to an item of rabbinic exegesis.

Mishnah: The legal codification containing the core of the post-Biblical Oral Torah, compiled and edited by Rabbi Judah Ha-Nasi at the beginning of the third century C.E.

Mitnagdim: The opponents of Hasidism. They obtained this title after the issuance of an excommunication against the adherents of the Hasidic movement by Elijah, the Gaon of Vilna, in 1772.

Mitvah (plural, Mitzvot): A Hebrew term meaning "commandment," and referring to any precept of the Torah, positive or negative. According to the Talmud, there are 613 mitzvot in the Pentateuch, apart from other commandments ordained by the rabbis.

Musaf: A supplementary service recited in the synagogue on those days when an additional sacrifice was offered in the Temple. The Musaf is recited on Sabbaths, New Moons, the three Pilgrimage Festivals, the New Year Day, and the Day of Atonement.

Musar: Traditional Jewish ethical literature, intended to heighten moral sensitivity and increase religious devotion and inward piety.

Neilah: The Hebrew term means "closing" and refers to the prayer recited at the time of the closing of the gates of the Temple. At present, this prayer service is recited only on the Day of Atonement and is understood as referring to the sealing of each man's judgment as the heavenly gates are supposedly closed.

Notrikon: A method of abbreviating Hebrew words and phrases by writing only single letters, usually the initials.

Pilpul: In Talmudic and rabbinic literature, a clarification of a difficult point. Later the term came to denote a sharp dialectical distinction or, more generally, a certain type of Talmudic study emphasizing dialectical distinctions.

Rebbe: Yiddish form of the term rabbi, applied generally to a teacher but also, and especially, to a Hasidic rabbi.

Rosh Ha-Shanah: Hebrew, literally "head of the year." The Jewish New Year, a holiday which inaugurates the Ten Days of Penitence culminating in the Day of Atonement or Yom Kippur. It is regarded as a day of judgment for the entire world and for individuals when the fate of each man for the coming year is inscribed in the Book of Life.

Rosh Yeshivah: The principal or rector of a *yeshivah* (see below).

Seder: In Hebrew, "order." The ritual dinner conducted in the Jewish home on the first night (and outside Israel, the first two nights) of Passover. The story of the exodus from Egypt is recounted and a number of symbols related to it are included in the ritual.

Sefirah (plural, Sefirot): A technical term in Kabbalah, employed from the twelfth century on, to denote the ten potencies or emanations through which the Divine manifests itself.

Shechinah: A term used to imply the presence of God in the world, in the midst of Israel, or with individuals. In contrast to the principle of divine transcendence, Shechinah represents the principle of divine immanence.

Shema: The Hebrew term for "hear" and referring to "Hear O Israel, the Lord our God, the Lord is One" (Deuteronomy 6:4)—Judaism's supreme confession of faith.

Shemoneh Esreh: The chief prayer, consisting of eighteen benedictions, in the Jewish liturgy.

Shofar: A horn of a ram, the sounding of which is prescribed by Biblical law for the New Year as well as to proclaim the year of release. At various times the *shofar* was also sounded on fast days, on the occasion of proclaiming a rabbinic edict, at times of famine or plague, and as a part of the ceremony of excommunication.

Siddur: Hebrew, "order." Among Ashkenazic Jews, the volume that contains the statutory daily prayers.

Tallit: The prayer shawl worn by adult (generally married) males during the morning prayers.

Talmud: The title applied to the two great compilations, distinguished as the Babylonian Talmud and the Palestinian Talmud, in which the records of academic discussion and of judicial administration of post-Biblical law are assembled. Both Talmuds also contain Aggadah (see above), or non-legal material.

Tanna (plural, Tannaim): A teacher mentioned in the Mishnah, or in literature contemporaneous with the Mishnah, and living during the first two centuries C.E.

Tefillah: The Hebrew word means prayer. It is sometimes used to denote specifically the *Shemoneh Esreh* (see above).

Tefillin: Two black leather boxes, fastened to leather straps, worn on the arm and head by an adult male Jew, especially during the weekday morning prayer. The boxes contain portions of the Pentateuch written on parchment.

Teḥinnah (plural, Teḥinnot): Private devotions recited by the individual as a supplement to the standard congregational liturgy. Devotional books in Yiddish, intended for women, also came to be known as *teḥinnot.*

Torah: In its narrowest meaning, the Pentateuch. Torah is also known in Judaism as the Written Law. In its broader meaning, Torah comprises as well the Oral Law, the traditional exposition of the Pentateuch and its commandments developed in the late Biblical and post-Biblical ages. In its widest meaning Torah signifies every exposition of both the Written and the Oral Law, including all of Talmudic literature and its commentaries. The term is sometimes used also to designate the scroll of the Pentateuch read in the synagogue service.

Tosafot: Hebrew, "addenda." Critical and explanatory notes on the Talmud by Jewish scholars in France and Germany during the twelfth to fourteenth centuries. Among the most famous of the Tosafists are Rabbenu Tam, Rabbi Samuel ben Meir, and Rabbi Isaac of Dampierre.

Yeshivah (plural, Yeshivot): A traditional Jewish school devoted primarily to the study of the Talmud (see above) and rabbinic literature.

Zohar: The chief work of the Spanish Kabbalah (see above) traditionally ascribed to the *Tanna* Simeon ben Yoḥai (second century) but probably written by the Spanish Kabbalist Moses de Leon at the end of the thirteenth century.

Index

Index

Börne, Ludwig, 195.
Bovo-Maaseh, 226.
Brawer, A.J., 10n, 15n, 18n.
Brawer, A.W., 107n.
Bresselau, Meir Israel, 244n, 261, 262.
Brill (Loewe), Joel, 200, 219.

Calmanson, Jacob, 235, 236.
Campe, Joachim Heinrich, 225, 227ff.
Caro, David, 258–261.
Casanova, 9, 22.
Chelm, Solomon, 235n.
Chmielnitzki, Bogdan, 144.
Chorin, Aaron, 246, 248, 253.
Cicero, 202.
Cohen, Shalom ben Jacob, 200, 206ff, 254n, 263.
Columbus (Joachim Campe), 227.
Columbus (Chaim Ḥaykl Hurwitz), 225, 226, 227.
Columbus, Christopher, 227, 228, 229.
Cortez (Joachim Campe), 227.
Cortez, Hernán, 229, 230.
Crescas, Ḥasdai, 134.

Dante, Alighieri, 61.
Davar Be-Itto (Aaron Chorin), 253.
David (King), 21, 60n, 67, 205, 207, 208.
David of Makow, 35, 131n, 184, 186–188.
Deborah (Biblical), 10n, 203.
Degel Maḥaneh Efrayim (Moses Ḥayyim Ephraim of Sudylkow), 36, 37n, 39n, 140.
Delmedigo, Joseph Solomon, 100, 123.
Dembowski, Andreas, 14, 15, 21.
Dirat Aharon (Aaron Chorin), 247.
Divrei Tzaddikim, 40n, 171.
Dolgoruki, I.M., 225n.
Dominicans, 241.
Dönmeh, 8.
Dov Baer (son of the rabbi of Lyady), 108.
Dubnow, Simon, 10n, 28, 34, 52n, 67n, 80n, 83n, 84, 85n, 91n, 107n, 130n, 131n, 164, 183, 183n, 184, 235n, 236n, 238.

Ecclesiastes, Book of, 69, 121, 215, 216, 224.
Eger, Akiva, 254, 255.
Eger, Samuel, 254.
Eichenstein, Tzevi Hirsch, 240.
Ein Yaakov, 29, 141.
Eleh Divrei Ha-Berit, 253n, 254, 255n, 256, 257n, 258, 259, 261, 262.
Eliezer (Baal Shem Tov's father), 28.
Elijah ben Solomon Zalman (Gaon of Vilna), 83, 91, 100, 102, 103, 104, 105, 159, 180, 181, 182, 185n, 189, 222, 234.
Elim (Joseph Solomon Delmedigo), 100, 123.
Elimelech of Lyzhansk, 94, 95, 99, 100, 107, 158, 172, 178, 187.
Emden, Jacob, 5, 9n, 14n, 15n, 82, 89, 263.
Emek Ha-Shaveh (Aaron Chorin), 246n, 247, 248, 253.
Emet Avida Aḥizedek (pseudonymous title of *Berit Emet* by David Caro), 258.
Entdeckung von Amerika, Die (Joachim Campe), 225, 226, 227.
Ephraim of Kutow, 30.
Epistolae obscurorum virorum, 241.
Eretz Kedumim (Solomon Löwisohn; reprint by Jacob ben Solomon Kaplan of *Meḥkerei Aretz*), 205.
Erik, Max (pseudonym of S. Merkin), 231n, 237n.
Ershter Khosid, Der (Mendel Levin), 237.
Erter, Isaac, 263.
Esau (Biblical), 22, 25.
Eshkol Ha-Sofer (Isaac Baer Levinsohn), 220n.
Essai sur l'état actuel des juifs de Pologne et leur perfectibilité (Jacob Calmanson), 236.
Et Le-Dabber (Naḥman ben Simḥah Berlin), 252, 253n.
Etiudn Tsu Der Geshikhte Fun Der Haskole (Max Erik), 237n.
Ettinger, Solomon, 263.
Etz Ḥayyim (Ḥayyim Vital), 110, 146.
Euchel, Isaac, 206, 208, 219, 220, 231.
Even Boḥan (Israel Loebl), 188.
Exodus, Book of, 76.
Eybeschütz, Jonathan, 6, 71, 89, 263.

Fabro (author of German geographical work), 222.
Fahn, R., 246n.
Falk, Joshua, 222.
Feder, Tobias Gutman ben Tzevi, 217ff.
Feiga (grand-daughter of Israel Baal Shem Tov), 140.
Feivish of Balshvetz, 176.
Fleckeles, Eliezer, 11n, 20n.
Frank, Eve (Jacob Frank's daughter), 12, 16.
Frank i frankiści polscy (A. Kraushaar), 10n.
Frank, Jacob ben Leib; Frankist movement, Frankists, Chapter One, 50, 52n, 82, 83, 103.
Frank und die Frankisten (H. Graetz), 10n, 51n.
Frank Ve-Adato (A. Kraushaar), 8n, 15n, 16n, 20n, 21n, 26n, 28n.
Fränkel, David, 192, 195.
Frankl, Zekil, 244n.
Franz Joseph (emperor of Austria), 178, 179.